Great Men of the Bible

Volume I

CHRISTIAN
CLASSICS

Great Men of the Bible

Volume
I

F. B. Meyer

ZONDERVAN/MARSHALL MORGAN & SCOTT

GREAT MEN OF THE BIBLE, VOL. 1

Copyright © 1981, The Zondervan Corporation
Grand Rapids, Michigan and
Marshall Morgan & Scott
1 Bath Street, London ECIV 9LB

First printing November 1981

Library of Congress Cataloging in Publication Data

Meyer, F. B. (Frederick Brotherton), 1847–1929.
    Great men of the Bible.

    1. Bible—Biography. I. Cumbers, Frank Henry. II. Title.

BS571.M49   1981   220.9'2 [B]   81-12940
ISBN 0-310-44271-0   AACR2

ISBN 0-551-00905-5

Printed in the United States of America

CONTENTS

ABRAHAM

1

The Hole of the Pit
Acts 7:2–3 and Isaiah 51:1–2

In the gray dawn of history the first great character that arrests our attention at any length is that of Abraham, if for nothing else than that he is spoken of as the "Friend of God." Surely it must be well worthy of our devout consideration to study the inner life and outward carriage of such a man.

Abraham's portrait is drawn with such detail that it lives before us with the same hopes and fears, golden hours and hours of depression, that are familiar factors in our own lives. Then, also, his life is so constantly referred to in the Old Testament and in the New that it would seem as if the right understanding of it is necessary to give us the clue to many a difficult passage in the succeeding pages of the Bible.

Our story takes us back two thousand years before the birth of Christ, and to the ancient city of Ur. We must look for Ur, not in Upper Mesopotamia, where a mistaken tradition has fixed it, but in the ruins of Mugheir, in the near vicinity of the Persian Gulf. Forty centuries, slowly silting up the shore, have driven the sea back about a hundred miles. But at the time of which we speak it is probable that Abraham's natal city stood on the coast near the spot where the Euphrates poured the volume of its waters into the ocean waves.

In olden days it was a large and flourishing city, standing on the sea, and possessed of fleets of vessels which coasted along the shores of the Indian Ocean, freighted with the products of the rich and fertile soil.

The corn crop was of marvelous abundance, and the date-palm attained to an extraordinary growth, repaying richly the scanty labors of the people; pomegranates and apples, grapes and tamarisks grew wild. Chaldaea was a long green strip of garden land, sufficient to attract and maintain vast populations of men, and specially suitable for the settlement of those shepherd tribes that required extensive pasture lands for their herds and flocks.

These sons of Ham were grossly *idolatrous.* In that clear transparent atmosphere, the heavenly bodies blazed with extraordinary effulgence, beguiling the early Chaldaeans into a system of nature-worship, which speedily became identified with rites of gross indulgence and impurity, and it was evident that some expedient must be speedily adopted to arrest the progress of moral defilement and to save mankind. This enterprise was undertaken by Him, who later could say, with majestic emphasis, "Before Abraham was, I AM." And He accomplished His purpose then, as so often since, by *separating* to Himself one man, so that through him and his descendants, when they had been thoroughly purified and prepared, He might operate on the fallen race of man, recalling it to Himself and elevating it by a moral lever, working on a pivot outside itself.

Four centuries had passed since the Flood, and they must have been centuries abounding in emigrations. The sons of Japheth pushed northward, to colonize Europe and Asia, and to lay the foundations of the great Indo-European family. The sons of Ham pushed southward, over the fertile plains of Chaldaea, where, under the lead of the mighty Nimrod, they built towns of baked clay; reared temples, of which the ruins remain to this day; and cultivated the arts of civilized life to an extent unknown elsewhere. They are said to have been proficient in mathmatics and astronomy; in weaving, metal-working, and gem-engraving; and to have preserved their thoughts by writing on clay tablets.

Now, it so happened, that into the midst of this Hamite colonization had come a family of the sons of Shem. This clan, under the lead of Terah, had settled down on the rich pasture lands outside Ur. The walled cities, civilized arts, and merchant traffic, had little attraction for them; for they were a race of shepherds, living in tents, or in villages of slightly-constructed huts. And if Noah's prediction were verified (Gen. 9:26), we may believe that their religious life was sweeter and purer than that of the people among whom we find them.

But, alas! the moral virus soon began its work. The close association of this Shemite family with the idolatrous and abominable practices of the children of Ham, tainted the purity and simplicity of its early faith; and it is certain that a leveling-down process was subtly at work, lowering its standard to that of its neighbors.

Amid such scenes Abraham was born, and in them he grew from youth to manhood. But, from the first, if we may credit the traditions that have lingered in the common talk of the unchanging East, he offered an uncompromising opposition to the evil practices that were rife, not only in the land, but in his father's house. He refused to bow at the bidding of the monarch before the subtle element of fire and under the penalty of martyrdom. Thus early was he being detached from the quarry of heathendom, preparatory to being shaped as a pillar in the house of the Lord.

There is nothing of all this in Scripture, but there is nothing inconsistent with it. The mature character, the faith, and the ready obedience of this man, when he first comes under our notice, convince us that there must have been a long previous period of severe trial and testing.

At last, the God of glory appeared to him. In what form of glory Jehovah revealed Himself we cannot guess, but we must believe that there was some outward manifestation that dated an epoch in Abraham's life, and gave him unmistakable basis of belief for all his future. The celestial vision was accompanied by a call, like that which in all ages of the world has come to loyal hearts, summoning them to awake to their true destiny, and take their place in the regeneration of the world: "Get thee out of thy country, and from thy kindred, and from thy father's house, unto the land that I will show thee" (Gen. 12:1).

It is impossible to tell into whose hands these words may fall. Young men amid the godless tea planters of India, or in the wild bush-life of Australia. Sailors aboard ship and soldiers in camp. Lonely confessors of Christ in worldly and vicious societies; where there is everything to weaken, and nothing to reinforce the resistance of the brave but faltering spirit. Let all such take heart! They are treading a well-worn path, on which the noblest of mankind have preceded them.

One symptom of being on that path is *loneliness*. It was a loneliness that pressed hard on the heart of Jesus, but it is a loneliness that is assured of divine companionship (see John 8:16, 29; 16:32).

Despair not for the future of the world. Out of its heart will yet come those who shall lift it up to a new level. Sauls are being trained in the bosom of the Sanhedrin;

Luthers in the cloisters of the church; Abrahams under the shadows of great heathen temples. God knows where to find them. And, when the times are darkest, they shall lead forth a host of pilgrim spirits, numberless as the sand on the seashore; or as the stardust, lying thick through the illimitable expanse of space.

2

The Divine Summons
Genesis 12:1–2

While Abraham was living quietly in Ur, protesting against the idolatry of his times, with all its attendant evils, and according to tradition, suffering bitter persecution for conscience sake, "The God of glory appeared unto him, and said, Get thee out of thy country, and from thy kindred, and come into the land which I shall show thee" (Acts 7:2–3).

When this divine appearance came we do not know; but suddenly there shone from heaven a great light round about Abraham, and a visible form appeared in the heart of the glory, and a voice spoke the message of heaven in his ear. God doesn't speak to us in that way now, and yet it is certain that He still speaks in the silence of the waiting spirit, impressing His will, and saying, "Get thee out." Listen for that voice in the inner shrine of your heart.

This same voice has often spoken since. "Come out from among them, and be ye separate, saith the LORD, and touch not the unclean thing." Has it not come to you? Strange, if it has not. Yet, if it has, let nothing hinder your obedience; strike your tents, and follow where the God of glory beckons; and in that word come, understand that He is moving on in front and that if you would have His companionship, you must follow.

1. THIS CALL INVOLVED HARDSHIP. It was no small matter for Abraham to break up his camp, to tear himself from his nearest and dearest, and to start for a land which, as yet, he did not know.

And so must it always be. We must be prepared to take up our cross daily if we would follow where He points the way. Each step of real advance in the divine life will involve an altar on which some dear fragment of the self-life has been offered.

It is true that the blessedness that awaits us will more than compensate us for the sacrifices that we may have to make. And this is God's winnowing fan, which clearly separates chaff and wheat. Many cannot endure a test so severe and searching in its demands. Like Pliable, they get out of the slough by the side nearest to their home. Like the young man, they go away sorrowful from the One to whom they had come with haste. Shall this be the case with you?

Nothing is more clear than that, in these critical days, God is summoning the whole church to a great advance.

2. BUT THIS CALL WAS EMINENTLY WISE. It was wise for *Abraham himself*. Nothing strengthens us so much as isolation and transplantation. Let a young man emigrate, or be put into a responsible position; let him be thrown on his own resources, and he will develop powers of which there would have been no trace, if he had always lived at

home, dependent on others. Under the wholesome demand his soul will put fourth all her native vigor.

But what is true of the natural qualities of the soul is preeminently true of faith. So long as we are quietly at rest amid favorable and undisturbed surroundings, faith sleeps as an undeveloped sinew within us. But when we are pushed out from all these surroundings, with nothing but God to look to, then faith grows suddenly into a cable, a monarch oak, a master-principle of the life.

As long as the bird lingers by the nest, it will not know the luxury of flight. As long as the trembling boy holds to the bank, or toes the bottom, he will not learn the ecstasy of battling with the ocean wave. Abram could never have become Abraham, the father of the faithful, the mighty exemplar of faith, if he had always lived in Ur. No; he had to journey forth into the untried and unknown, so that faith could rise up to all its glorious proportions in his soul.

It may not be necessary for us to withdraw from home and friends; but we shall have to withdraw our heart's deepest dependence from all earthly props and supports, if we are ever to learn what it is to trust simply and absolutely on the eternal God.

It was wise *for the world's sake*. On this one man rested the hope for the future of the world. Had he remained in Ur, it is impossible to say whether he would have continued true; or whether he might not have been seriously infected by the idolatry around. Was it not, therefore, wise that he should be taken right away from his home and early associations, to find a fresh religious starting point for the race?

It is impossible to move our times, so long as we live beneath their spell; but when once we have risen up, and gone, at the call of God, outside their bounds, we are able to react on them with an irresistible power. Archimedes vaunted that he could lift the world, if only he could obtain, outside of it, a pivot on which to rest his lever. Do not be surprised then, if God calls you out to be a people to Himself, that by you He may react with blessed power on the great world of men.

3. THIS CALL WAS ACCOMPANIED BY A PROMISE. God's commands are not always accompanied by reasons, but always by promises, expressed or understood. As a shell encloses a kernel, so the divine commands hide promises in their heart. If this is the command: "Believe on the Lord Jesus Christ"; this is the promise: "And thou shalt be saved." If this is the command: "Leave father and mother, houses and lands"; this is the promise: "Thou shalt have a hundredfold here, and everlasting life beyond." If this is the command: "Be ye separate"; this is the promise: "I will receive you and be a Father to you." So in this case: Though you are childless, I will make of you a great nation: though you are to be torn from your own family, in you shall all the families of the earth be blessed. And each of those promises has been literally fulfilled.

It may seem that the hardships involved in the summons to exile are too great to be borne; yet study well the promise that is attached. And as the "City which hath foundations" looms on the view, it will dwarf the proportions of the Ur in which you have been content to spend your days; and you will rise to be done.

St. Francis de Sales used to say, "When the house is on fire, men are ready to throw everything out of the window; and when the heart is full of God's true love, men are sure to count all else but worthless."

4. THIS CALL TEACHES US THE MEANING OF ELECTION. Everywhere we find beings and

things more loftily endowed than others of the same kind. There is at first a jarring wonder at the apparent inequality of the divine arrangements; until we understand that the superior endowment of the few is intended to enable them the better to help and bless the rest. "I will bless thee, and thou shalt be a blessing."

Is this not a glimpse into the intention of God, in selecting Abraham, and in him the whole family of Israel? It was not so much with a view to their personal salvation, though that was included; but that they might pass on the holy teachings and oracles with which they were entrusted. It was needful that definitions and methods of expression should be first well learned by the people, who, when they had learned them, might become the teachers of mankind. There is no need to envy God's elect ones.

They are the exiles, the cross-bearers, the martyrs among men; but careless of themselves, they are all the while learning God's deepest lessons, away from the ordinary haunts of men; and they return to them presently with discoveries that pass all human thought, and are invaluable for human life.

5. THIS CALL GIVES THE KEY TO ABRAHAM'S LIFE. It rang a clarion note at the very outset, which continued to vibrate through all his history. The key to Abraham's life is the word "separation." He was from first to last a separated man. Separated from his fatherland and kinsfolk; separated from Lot; separated, as a pilgrim and stranger, from the people of the land; separated from the rest of mankind by special sorrows, which brought him into closer fellowship with God than has ever been reached by man; separated to high and lofty fellowship in thoughts and plans, which God could not hide from him.

May such separation be ours! May we catch the divine call, irradiated by the divine promise! And as we hear of that fair land, of that glorious city, of those divine delights that await us, may we leave and relinquish those lesser and injurious things that have held us too long, spoiling our peace, and sapping our power; and, striking our tents, obey our God's call, though it may lead us we know not where!

3

"He Obeyed"
Hebrews 11:8

Ah, how much there is in those two words! If Abraham had permanently refused obedience to the voice that summoned him to sally forth on his long and lonely pilgrimage, he would have sunk back into the obscurity of an unknown grave in the land of Ur, like many an Eastern sheikh before and since. But, thank God, Abraham obeyed, and in that act laid the foundation stone of the noble structure of his life.

It may be that some will read these words whose lives have been a disappointment, and a sad surprise. You have failed to realize the early promise of your life. And may not the reason lie in this, that back in your life there rang out a command that summoned you to an act of self-sacrifice from which you shrank? And *that* has been your one fatal mistake.

Would it not be well to ascertain if this is so, and to hasten back to fulfill even now the long-delayed obedience, supposing it to be possible? "He is merciful and gracious, slow to anger, and plenteous in goodness and truth." Do not use your long delay as an argument for longer delay, but as a reason for immediate action. "Why tarriest thou?"

Abraham, as the story shows, at first met the call of God with a mingled and partial obedience, and then for long years neglected it entirely. But the door stood open for him to enter, and that gracious hand still beckoned him, until he struck his tents and started to cross the mighty desert with all that owned his sway. It was a partial failure, which is pregnant with invaluable lessons for ourselves.

1. AT FIRST, THEN, ABRAHAM'S OBEDIENCE WAS ONLY PARTIAL. *He took Terah with him;* indeed, it is said that "Terah took Abram his son, and Lot the son of Haran, and Sarai his daughter-in-law; and they went forth with them from Ur of the Chaldees" (Gen. 11:31). How Terah was induced to leave the land of his choice, and the graves of his dead, where his son Haran slept, we cannot tell. He was not whole hearted, nor were his motives unmixed; and his presence in the march had the disastrous effect of slackening Abraham's pace, and of interposing a parenthesis of years in an obedience which, at first, promised so well.

The clan marched leisurely along the valley of the Euphrates, finding abundance of pasture in its broad alluvial plains, until at last they reached Haran—the point from which caravans for Canaan leave the Euphrates to strike off across the desert. There they halted, and there they stayed until Terah died. Was it that the old man was too weary for future journeyings? Did he like Haran too well to leave it? Whatever the reason, he would go no farther on the pilgrimage, and probably for as many as fifteen years, Abraham's obedience was stayed; and for that period there were no further commands, no additional promises, no hallowed communings between God and His child.

"When his father was dead, he removed him into this land" (Acts 7:4). Terah must die before Abraham would resume the forsaken path. Here we may get a solution for mysteries in God's dealings with us, which have long puzzled us; and we may understand why our hopes have withered, our schemes have miscarried, our income has dwindled, our children have turned against us. All these things were hindering our true development; and, out of mercy to our best interests, God has been compelled to take the knife in hand, and set us at liberty.

2. ABRAHAM'S OBEDIENCE WAS RENDERED POSSIBLE BY HIS FAITH. "So Abram departed, as the LORD had spoken unto him. And he took Sarai his wife, and Lot, his brother's son, and all their substance that they had gathered, and the souls that they had gotten in Haran, and they went forth" (Gen. 12:5). No easy matter that! At night, as Abraham walked to and fro beneath the stars, he may have sometimes been inclined to give up in despair; but then that sure promise came back again on his memory, and he braced himself to obey. "BY FAITH Abraham, when he was called to go out into a place which he should after receive for an inheritance, *obeyed*" (Heb. 11:8). When he would go, he didn't know; it was enough for him to know that he went with God. He leaned not so much on the promise as on the Promiser: he looked not on the difficulties of his lot, but on the King eternal, immortal, invisible, the only wise God; who had appointed his course, and would certainly vindicate Himself.

And so the caravan started out—the camels, heavily laden, attended by their drivers; the vast flocks mingling their bleatings with their drovers' cries; the demonstrative sorrow of Eastern women mingling with the grave farewells of the men; the forebodings in many hearts of imminent danger and prospective disaster. Sarah may even have been broken down with bitter regrets. But Abraham did not falter. He did not stagger through unbelief. "He was fully persuaded that what God had promised, he was able to perform."

Ah, glorious faith! this is your work, these are your possibilities—contentment to sail with sealed orders, because of unwavering confidence in the love and wisdom of the Lord High Admiral: willingness to arise up, leave all, and follow Christ, because of the glad assurance that earth's best cannot bear comparison with heaven's least.

3. ABRAHAM'S OBEDIENCE WAS FINALLY VERY COMPLETE. "They went forth to go into the land of Canaan, *and into the land of Canaan they came*" (Gen. 12:5). For many days after leaving Haran, the eye would sweep a vast monotonous waste, broken by the scantiest vegetation. The camels would tread the soft sand beneath their spreading, spongy feet, and the flocks would find but scanty nutriment on the course, sparse grass.

At one point only would the travelers arrest their course. In the oasis, where Damascus stands today, it stood then, furnishing a welcome resting place to weary travelers over the waste. A village near Damascus is still called by the patriarch's name. And there is surely a trace of his slight sojourn there in the name of his favorite and most trusted servant, Eliezer of Damascus, of whom we shall read later.

But Abraham would not stay here. He could not feel that it was God's choice for him. Therefore, before long he was again on the southern track, to reach Canaan as soon as he could. Our one aim in life must ever be to follow the will of God, and to walk in those ways in which He has preordained us to walk. And it is well when the pilgrim of eternity gives perfect obedience to the extreme demands of God. When you journey to the land of Canaan, do not rest until you reach it. Anything short of complete obedience nullifies all that has been done. The Lord Jesus must have all or none; and His demands must be fulfilled up to the hilt. But they are not grevous.

Let us therefore give to Christ our prompt and unlimited obedience; sure that, even if He bids us ride into the valley of death, it is through no blunder or mistake, but out of some sheer necessity, which forbids Him to treat us otherwise, and which He will before long satisfactorily explain.

4

The First of the Pilgrim Fathers
Genesis 12:4–9

All through the history of mankind there has been a little band of men, in a sacred and unbroken succession, who have confessed that they were pilgrims and strangers upon earth. Sometimes they are found afar from the haunts of men, wandering in deserts and in mountains, dwelling in the dens and caves of the earth. But often they are to be found in the market places and homes of the men, distinguished only by their simpler dress, their girded loins, their restrained and abstemious appetite, their loose hold on gold, their independence of the maxims and opinions and applause of the world around, and the faraway look that now and again gleams in their eyes, the certain evidence of affections centered, not on the transitory things of time and earth, but on those eternal realities which, lying beneath the veil of the visible, are revealed only to faith.

These are the pilgrims. For them the annoyances and trials of life are not so crushing or so difficult to bear, because such things as these cannot touch their true treasure, or affect their real interest. They are children of a sublimer realm. The pilgrim has no other desire than to pass quickly over the appointed route to his home, fulfilling the duties, meeting the claims, and discharging faithfully the responsibilities devolving on him, but ever remembering that here he has no continuing city, and seeks one which is to come.

The Apostle Peter wrote to scattered strangers (1 Peter 1:1), and reminded them *as strangers and pilgrims,* to abstain from fleshly lusts. And long before that day, in the sunniest period of Jewish prosperity, David, in the name of his people, confessed that they were *strangers and sojourners as were all their fathers.*

We left the patriarch moving leisurely southward, and thus he continued to journey through the land of promise, making no permanent halt, until he reached the place of Sichem, or Schechem, in the very heart of the land where our Lord years later sat and rested by the well. There was no city or settlement there then. The country was sparsely populated. The only thing that marked the site was a venerable oak. Beneath this oak on the plain of Sichem, the camp was pitched; and there, at last, the long silence was broken, the silence which had lasted since the first summons was spoken in Chaldaea, "And the LORD appeared unto Abram, and said, Unto thy seed will I give this land: and there builded he an altar unto the LORD, who appeared unto him" (Gen. 12:7).

He did not stay there permanently, however, but moved a little to the south, to a place between Bethel and Ai, where there is now a high and beautiful plain, presenting one of the finest tracts of pasturage in the whole country.

Three things can engage our thought here: the Tent, the Altar, and the Promise.

1. THE TENTS. When Abraham left Haran his age was seventy-five. When he died he was one hundred and seventy-five years old. And he spent that intervening century moving to and fro, dwelling in a frail and flimsy tent, probably of dark camel's hair. And that tent was only a befitting symbol of the spirit of his life.

He held himself aloof from the people of the land. He did not stay in any permanent location, but was ever on the move. The tent which had no foundations, which could be erected and struck in half-an-hour, was the apt symbol of his life.

To the end he dwelt in a tent. It was from a tent that he was carried to lie beside Sarah in Machpelah's rocky cave. "Abraham dwelt in tents, because he looked for the city which hath the foundations" (Heb. 11:9–10 ASV). The tent life is the natural one for those who feel that their fatherland lies beyond the stars.

It is of the utmost importance that the children of God should live this detached life as a testimony to the world. How will people believe us, when we talk about our hope, if our hope does not pull us from excessive devotion to the things around us?

We must not go on as we are. Professing Christians are too much taken up in business cares, in pleasure seeking, in luxury, and self-indulgence. There is little difference between the children of the kingdom and the children of this generation.

Yet how is it to be altered? Shall we denounce the present practice? Shall we inveigh against the reckless worldliness of the times? This will not affect a permanent cure. Let us rather paint with glowing colors that city that John saw. Let us unfold the glories of that world to which we are bound, and surely there will come into many a life a separateness of heart and walk that will impress men with the reality of the unseen, as no sermon could do, however learned or eloquent.

2. THE ALTAR. Wherever Abraham pitched his tent, he built an altar. And long after the tent was shifted, the altar stood to show where the man of God had been.

Let us also remember that the altar means sacrifice, whole burnt offering, self-denial, and self-surrender. In this sense the altar and the tent must ever go together. We cannot live the detached tent-life without some amount of pain and suffering, such as the altar bespeaks. But it is out of such a life that there spring the most intense devotion, the deepest fellowship, the happiest communion.

If your private prayer has been lately hindered, it may be that you have not been living enough in the tent. Confess that you are a stranger and a pilgrim on the earth; and you will find it pleasant and natural to call on the name of the Lord. We do not read of Abraham building an altar so long as he dwelt in Charran; he could not have fellowship with God while living in open disobedience to Him.

But Abraham's altar was not for himself alone. At certain periods the whole clan gathered there for common worship. "I know Abraham," said God, "that he will command his children and his household after him" (Gen. 18:19). He, in whom all families of the earth were to be blessed, practiced family religion; and in this he sets a striking example to many Christians whose homes are altarless.

3. THE PROMISE. "Unto thy seed will I give this land" (Gen. 12:7). As soon as Abraham had fully obeyed, this new promise broke upon his ear. And it is ever thus. Disobey—and you tread a path unlit by a single star. Obey, live up to the claims of God—and successive promises beam out from heaven to light your steps, each one richer and fuller than the one before. The separated pilgrim life always acquires promises.

There was no natural probability of that promise being fulfilled because "the Canaanite was then in the land." Powerful chieftains like Mamre and Eshcol; flourishing towns like Sodom, Salem, and Hebron; the elements of civilization—all were there. The Canaanites were not wandering tribes. They had settled and taken root. Every day built up their power, and made it more unlikely that they could ever be dispossessed by the descendants of a childless shepherd.

But God had said it; and so it came to pass. I do not know what promise may be overarching your life with its bow of hope; but this is certain, that if you fulfill its conditions, and live up to its demands, it will be literally and gloriously fulfilled. Do not look at the difficulties and improbabilities of the Promiser. Promise after promise will light your life.

5

Gone Down Into Egypt
Genesis 12:10

The path of the separated man can never be an easy one. It is a life, therefore, which is possible only to faith. When faith is strong, we dare cut ourselves adrift from the moorings that coupled us to the shore, and launch out into the deep, depending only on the character and word of Him at whose command we go. But when faith is weak, we dare not do it; and, leaving the upland path, we herd with the men of the world, who have their portion in this life, and who are content with that alone.

1. "AND THERE WAS A FAMINE IN THE LAND." A famine? A famine in the Land of Promise? A stranger in a strange land, surrounded by suspicious and hostile peoples, weighted with the responsibility of vast flocks and herds—it was no trivial matter to stand face to face with the sudden devastation of famine.

Did it prove that Abraham had made a mistake in coming to Canaan? Happily the promise that had lately come to him forbade his entertaining the thought. And this may have been one principal reason why it was given. It came, not only as a reward for the past, but as a preparation for the future; so that the man of God might not be tempted beyond what he was able to bear. Do not be surprised if a famine meets you. This does not mean your Father is angry, but the trial is permitted to come to test you—or to root you deeper—as the whirlwind makes the tree grapple its roots deeper into the soil.

2. "AND ABRAM WENT DOWN INTO EGYPT TO SOJOURN THERE." In the figurative language of Scripture, Egypt stands for alliance with the world and dependence on an arm of flesh. "Woe to them that go down to Egypt for help; and stay on horses, and trust in chariots, because they are many; and in horsemen, because they are very strong; but they look not unto the Holy One of Israel, neither seek the LORD!" (Isa. 31:1).

There were occasions in Jewish story when God Himself bade His servants seek a temporary asylum in Egypt. While Jacob was halting in indecision on the confines of Canaan, longing to go to Joseph, and yet reluctant to repeat the mistakes of the past, Jehovah said, "I am God, the God of thy father: fear not to go down into Egypt; for I will there make of thee a great nation: I will go down with thee into Egypt" (Gen. 46:3–4). And, in later days, the angel of the Lord appeared to Joseph in a dream, saying, "Arise, and take the young child and his mother, and flee into Egypt" (Matt. 2:13).

But it does not appear that Abraham received any such divine direction. He acted simply on his own judgment. He looked at his difficulties. He grasped at the first means of deliverance that suggested itself, much as a drowning man will catch at a straw. And thus, without taking counsel of his heavenly Protector, he went down into Egypt.

Ah, fatal mistake! But how many make it still. They may be true children of God: and yet, in a moment of panic, they will adopt methods of delivering themselves which, to say the least, are questionable. Christian women plunge into the marriage bond with those who are the enemies of God, in order that they may be carried through some financial difficulty. Christian merchants take ungodly partners into business for the sake of the capital they introduce. What is all this, but going down to Egypt for help?

How much better would it have been for Abraham to have thrown the responsibility back on God, and to have said, "Thou hast brought me here; and Thou must now bear the whole weight of providing for me and mine: here will I stay until I clearly know what Thou wilt have me to do." If any should read these lines who have come into positions of extreme difficulty, put God between yourself and the disasters that threaten you. Cast the whole responsibility on Him. Has He not thus brought you into difficulties, that He may have an opportunity of strengthening your faith, by giving some unexampled proof of His power? Wait only on the Lord, trust also in Him: His name is Jehovah-jireh; He will provide.

3. SEE HOW ONE SIN LEADS TO ANOTHER. When Abraham lost his faith and went down into Egypt, he also lost his courage, and persuaded his wife to call herself his sister. He had heard of the licentiousness of the Egyptians and feared that they might take his life to get possession of Sarah, who, even at the age she had reached, must have been possessed of very considerable charms.

There was an element of truth in the statement that Sarah was his half-sister, but it was meant as a lie, and it certainly misled the Egyptians, for she "was taken into Pharaoh's house." It was a mean and cowardly act on Abraham's part, which was utterly indefensible. And it endangered the promised seed. Yet so it happens; when we lose our faith, and are filled with panic for ourselves, we are prepared to sacrifice our nearest and dearest, if only we may escape.

The world may treat us well (Gen. 12:16), but that will be a poor compensation for our losses. There is no altar in Egypt, no fellowship with God, no new promises; but a desolated home, and a wretched sense of wrong. When the prodigal leaves his Father's house, though he may win a brief spell of forbidden pleasure, he loses all that makes life worth living, and brings himself down to the level of the swine. In such a case there is no resource, save to retrace the way that we have come, to "do the first works," and like Abraham to go up out of Egypt to the place of the altar where we were "at the first" (Gen. 13:4). Abraham's failure in Egypt gives us an insight into the original nature of the patriarch, which was by no means heroic, and betrays a vein of duplicity and deceit, similar to that which has so often reappeared in his posterity.

How thankful we should be that the Bible does not shrink from recording the story of the sins of its noblest saints! What a proof of its veracity is here, and what encouragement there is for us! For if God was able to make His friend out of such material as this, may we not aspire to a like privilege, though we, too, have grievously violated the high calling of faith? The one thing that God requires of His saints is implicit obedience— entire surrender. Where these are present, He can still make Abrahams out of us, though, by nature, the soil of our being is prone to barrenness and weeds.

6

Separated From Lot
Genesis 13:9

"Abram went up out of Egypt, he, and his wife, and all that he had, and Lot with him, into the south."

1. WHO WAS LOT? He was the son of Abraham's dead brother, Haran. He had probably succeeded to his father's inheritance. He seems to have been one of those men who take right steps, not because they are prompted by obedience to God, but because their friends are taking them. Around him was the inspiration of an heroic faith, the fascination of the untried and unknown, the stir of a great religious movement; and Lot was swept into the current, and resolved to go too. He was the Pliable of the earliest Pilgrim's Progress. He may have thought that he was as much in earnest as Abraham but it was a great mistake. He was simply an echo.

In every great religious movement there always has been, and always will be a number of individuals who cast in their lot with it, without knowing the power that inspires it. Beware of them! They cannot stand the stress of the life of separation to God. The mere excitement will soon die away from them, and, having no principle to take its place, they will become hindrances and disturbers of the peace. As certainly as they are harbored in the camp, or their principles are allowed within the heart, they will lower the spiritual tone. They will allure to worldly policy, suggest methods which would not otherwise occur to us, and draw us toward the Egypt-world.

Nothing but supreme principle can carry any one through the real, separated, and surrendered life of the child of God. If you are prompted by anything less, you will first be a hindrance, and end by being a failure. Examine yourselves, whether you are in the faith. Prove your own selves. And, if you are consciously acting from a low and selfish motive, ask God to breathe into you His own pure love. Better act from an inferior motive, if only it be in the right direction, but covet earnestly the best.

2. THE NECESSITY OF SEPARATION. Had Abraham been left to himself, he might never have thought of going down to Egypt: and, in that case, there would have been another paragraph or passage in the Bible describing the exploits of faith that dared to stand to God's promise, though threatened by disaster, and hemmed in by famine; waiting until God should bid it move, or make it possible to stay. There is something about that visit to Egypt that savors of the spirit of Lot's afterlife.

The outward separation of the body from the world of the ungodly is incomplete, unless accompanied and supplemented by the inner separation of the spirit. It is not enough to leave Ur, Haran, and Egypt. We must be rid of Lot also. Though we lived in a monastery, yet so long as there was an alien principle in our breast, a Lot in our heart-life, there could not be that separation to God which is the condition of the growth of faith, and of all those higher forms of the true life which make earth most like heaven. Lot must go. "Know that the LORD hath set apart him that is godly for himself" (Ps. 4:3). No other foot then must intrude within the enclosure of the divine proprietorship.

O souls that sigh for saintliness as harts pant for waterbrooks, have you counted the cost? Can you bear the fiery ordeal? The manufacture of saints is no child's play. The block has to be entirely separated from the mountain bed before the divine chisel can begin to fashion it. The gold must be plunged into the cleansing fire before it can be molded or hammered into an ornament of beauty for the King.

We must be prepared to die to the world with its censure or praise; to the flesh, with its ambitions and schemes; to the delights of a friendship that is insidiously lowering the temperature of the spirit; to the self-life, in all its myriad subtle and overt manifestations; and even, if it be God's will, to the joys and consolations of religion.

All this is impossible of ourselves. But if we will surrender ourselves to God, we shall find that He will gradually and effectually, and as tenderly as possible, disentwine the clinging tendrils of the poisoning weed, and bring us into heart-union with Himself.

It may be that Abraham had already felt for himself the ill effect of association with Lot, and may have longed to be free from him, without knowing how the emancipation could be effected. In any case, somewhat akin to this may be the condition of some who will read these words. Entangled in an alliance which you seem powerless to break off, your only hope is to bear it quietly until God sets you at liberty. That time will come at length; for God has a destiny in store for you, so great that neither He nor you can allow it to be forfeited for any light or trivial obstacle.

3. HOW THE SEPARATION WAS BROUGHT ABOUT. The valleys around Bethel, which had been quite adequate for their needs when first they came to Canaan, were now altogether insufficient. The herdsmen were always wrangling for the first use of the wells, and the first crop of the pastures. The cattle were continually getting mixed. "The land was not able to bear them, that they might dwell together."

Abraham saw at once that such a state of things must not be allowed to go on: especially as "the Canaanite and the Perizzite dwelled then in the land." For if those war-like neighbors heard of the dissensions in the camp, they would take an early opportunity of falling on it. United they stood; divided, they must fall. Would that the near presence of the world might have the same wholesome effect of checking dissension and dispute among the children of the same Father!

And so Abraham called Lot to him, and said, "Let there be no strife . . . between me and thee, and between my herdmen and thy herdmen; for we be brethren. Is not the whole land before thee? separate thyself, I pray thee, from me: if thou wilt take the left hand, then I will go to the right; or if thou depart to the right hand, then I will go to the left" (Gen. 13:8-9).

The proposal was very *wise*. Abraham saw that there was a cause for the disturbance, which could lead to similar troubles continually. So he went to the root of the matter, and proposed their separation.

His line of action was very *magnanimous*. He had undoubted right to the first choice, but he waived his right in the interests of reconciliation.

But, above all, it was *based on faith*. Had not God pledged Himself to take care of him, and to give him an inheritance?

The man who is sure of God can afford to hold very lightly the things of this world. God Himself is his inalienable heritage, and, in having God, he has all. The man who "hedges" for himself does not do as well in the long run as the man who, having the right of choice, hands it back to God, saying: "Let others choose for themselves, if they please; but as for myself, you shall choose my inheritance for me."

7

The Two Paths
Genesis 13:9

Abraham and Lot stood together on the heights of Bethel. The Land of Promise spread out before them as a map. On three sides at least there was not much to attract a shepherd's gaze. The eye wandered over the outlines of the hills which hid from view the fertile valleys nestling within their embrace. There was, however, an exception in this monotony of hill, toward the southeast, where the waters of the Jordan spread out in a broad valley, before they entered the Sea of the Plain.

Even from the distance the two men could discern the rich luxuriance. This specially struck the eye of Lot; he was eager to do the best for himself, and determined to make the fullest use of the opportunity which the unexpected magnanimity of his uncle had thrown in his way.

But the time would come when he would bitterly rue his choice, and owe everything to the man of whom he was now prepared to take advantage.

Lot chose all the plain. He did not ask what God had chosen for him. His choice was entirely determined by the lust of the flesh, the lust of the eyes, and the pride of life.

Let us not condemn Lot too much because he chose without reference to the moral and religious conditions of the case, lest, in judging him, we pronounce sentence on ourselves. Lot did nothing more than is done by scores of professing Christians every day.

A Christian asks you to go over and see the place he is about to take in the country. It is certainly a charming place: the house is spacious and well-situated, the air balmy, the garden and pasture large; the views enchanting. When you have gone over it, you ask how he will fare on Sunday. "Well," he says, "I really have never thought of it." Or perhaps he answers, "I believe there is nothing here like we have been accustomed to; but one cannot have everything: and they say that the society here is extremely good." Is not this the spirit of Lot, who bartered the altar of Abraham's camp for the plains of Sodom, because the grass looked green and plentiful? So many persist in lifting up their eyes to choose for themselves, and with sole reference to the most sordid considerations.

If Abraham had remonstrated with Lot, do you not suppose that he would have answered petulantly: "Do you not think that we are as eager as you are to serve the Lord? Sodom needs just that witness we will be able to give. Is it not befitting that the light should shine in the darkness; and that the salt should be scattered where there is rot." Abraham might not be able to contest these assertions, and yet he would have an inner conviction that these were not the considerations that were determining his nephew's choice. Of course, if God sends a man to Sodom, He will keep him there, as Daniel was kept in Babylon, and nothing shall by any means hurt him. But if God does not clearly send him to Sodom, it is a blunder, a crime, a peril to go.

Mark how Lot was swiftly swept into the center, first he saw, then he chose, then he separated himself from Abraham, then he journeyed east, then he pitched his tent toward Sodom, then he dwelt there, then he became an alderman of the place, and sat in the gate. But his power of witness-bearing was gone. Or if he lifted up his voice in protest against deeds of shameless vice, he was laughed at for his pains, or threatened with violence. He was carried captive by Chedorlaomer. His property was destroyed in the overthrow of the cities. His wife was turned into a pillar of salt. And the blight of Sodom left but too evident a brand on his daughters. Wretched, indeed, must have been the last days of that hapless man, cowering in a cave, stripped of everything, face to face with the results of his own shameful sin.

Now, let us turn to a more inviting theme, and further consider the dealings of the Almighty God with Abraham, the one man who was being educated to hold fellowship with Jehovah as a friend.

1. GOD ALWAYS COMES NEAR TO HIS SEPARATED ONES. "And the LORD said unto Abram, *after that Lot was separated from him.*" It may be that Abraham was feeling very lonely. We all dread being separated from companions and friends. It is hard to see them drop away one by one; and to be compelled to take a course alone. And yet, if we really wish to be only for God, it is inevitable that there should be many a link snapped, many a companionship forsaken, many a habit and conventionalism dropped.

But let us not stand looking on this aspect of it—the dark side of the cloud. Let us rather catch a glimpse of the other side, illuminated by the rainbow promise of God. And let this be understood that, when once the spirit has dared to take up that life of consecration to the will of God to which we are called, there break upon it visions, voices, comfortable words, of which the heart could have formed no previous idea.

2. GOD WILL DO BETTER FOR THOSE WHO TRUST HIM THAN THEY COULD DO FOR THEM-SELVES. Twice here in the context we meet the phrase—"lifted up his eyes." But how great the contrast! Lot lifted up his eyes, at the dictate of worldly prudence, to spy out his own advantage. Abraham lifted up his eyes, not to discern what would best make for his material interests, but to behold what God had prepared for him. How much better it is to keep the eye steadfastly fastened on God until He says to us, "Lift up now thine eyes, and look from the place where thou art northward, and southward, and eastward, and westward: For all the land which thou seest, to thee will I give it, and to thy seed for ever" (Gen. 13:14–15).

God honors those who honor Him. He withholds "no good thing from them that walk uprightly." If only we will go on doing what is right, giving up the best to our neighbor to avoid dispute, considering God's interests first, and our own last, expending ourselves for the coming and glory of the kingdom of heaven, we shall find that God will charge Himself with our interests. And He will do infinitely better for us than we could.

It is difficult to read these glowing words, *northward, and southward, and eastward, and westward,* without being reminded of "the length, and breadth, and depth, and height, of the love of Christ, that passeth knowledge." God's promises are ever on the ascending scale. One leads up to another, fuller and more blessed than itself. It is thus that God allures us to saintliness. Not giving anything until we have dared to act—that He may test us. Not giving everything at first—that He may not overwhelm us. And always keeping in hand an infinite reserve of blessing.

3. GOD BIDS US APPROPRIATE HIS GIFTS. "Arise, walk through the land in the length of it and in the breadth of it." This surely means that God wished Abraham to feel as free in the land as if the title-deeds were actually in his hands. He was to enjoy it; to travel through it; to look on it as his. By faith Abraham was about to act toward it as if he were already in absolute possession.

There is a deep lesson here, as to the appropriation of faith. "Be strong and very courageous" was addressed six separate times to Joshua. "Be strong" refers to the strength of the wrists to grasp. "Be very courageous" refers to the tenacity of the ankle joints to hold their ground. May our faith be strong in each of these particulars. Strong to lay hold, and strong to keep.

We need not be surprised to learn that Abraham moved to Hebron (which signifies fellowship), and built there an altar to the Lord. New mercies call us to deeper fellowship with our Almighty Friend, who never leaves or forsakes His own.

8

Refreshment Between the Battles
Genesis 14:9

The strife recorded in Genesis 14 was no mere border. It was an expedition for chastisement and conquest. Chedorlaomer was the Attila, the Napolean of his age. His capital city, Susa, lay across the desert, beyond the Tigris, in Elam. Years before Abraham had entered Canaan as a peaceful emigrant, this dreaded conqueror had swept southward subduing the towns that lay in the Jordan Valley, and thus possessing himself of the master key to the road between Damascus and Memphis. When Lot took up his residence toward Sodom, the cities of the plain were paying tribute to this mighty monarch.

At last the men of Sodom and Gomorrah, of Admah and Zeboiim, became weary of the Elamite yoke and rebelled, and Chedorlaomer was compelled to undertake a second expedition to chastise their revolt and regain his power. His plan was evidently to ravage the whole country bordering those Jordan towns before actually settling in them.

At last the allied forces concentrated in the neighborhood of Sodom, where they encountered fierce resistance. Encouraged by the pitchy nature of the soil, in which horsemen and chariots would move with difficulty, the townsfolk risked an engagement in the open. However, in spite of the bitumen pits, the day went against the effeminate and dissolute men of the plain. The defeat of the troops was followed by the capture and sack of those wealthy towns, and all who could not escape were manacled as slaves and carried off in the train of the victorious army.

"And they took Lot, Abram's brother's son, who dwelt in Sodom, and his goods, and departed" (Gen. 14:12). Then one of the survivors of that fatal day made for Abraham's encampment; "And when Abram heard that his brother was taken captive, he armed his trained servants . . . and divided himself against them" (Gen. 14: 14–15).

1. HERE IS THE UNSELFISH AND SUCCESSFUL INTERPOSITION OF A SEPARATED MAN, ON THE BEHALF OF OTHERS. Hidden in the configuration of the country, Abraham had watched the movements of the devastators from afar.

But true separation never argues this way. Granted that the separated one is set apart for God, yet he is set apart that he may react more efficiently on the great world over which God yearns, and toward which He has entertained great purposes of mercy, in the election of the few. Genuine separation is the result of faith, which always works by love; and this love tenderly yearns for those who are entangled in the meshes of worldliness and sin. Faith makes us independent, but not indifferent. It is enough for it to hear that its brother is taken captive, and it will arm instantly to go in pursuit.

But Abraham's interposition was as *successful* as it was unselfish and prompt. The force with which he set out was a very slender one, but his raw recruits moved quickly, and thus in four or five days they overtook the self-reliant and encumbered host amid the hills where the Jordan takes its rise. Adopting the tactics of a night attack, he fell suddenly on the unsuspecting host, and chased them in headlong panic, as far as the ancient city of Damascus. "And he brought back all the goods, and also brought again his brother Lot, and his goods, and the women also, and the people" (Gen. 14:16).

The men who live the life of separation and devotion towards God, are they who act with most promptness and success when the time for action comes.

2. THE TIME OF A GREAT SUCCESS IS OFTEN THE SIGNAL FOR A GREAT TEMPTATION. The king

of Sodom had not been amongst the prisoners. He had probably saved himself, by a timely flight to the hills, from the field of battle. When therefore he received tidings of the patriarch's gallant and successful expedition, he set out to meet and welcome him.

The two met at the King's Dale, a place to become memorable as the years went on, and situated near the city of Salem, a title that was destined to develop into the word "Jerusalem."

Grateful for Abraham's succour and deliverance, the king of Sodom proposed to him to surrender only the persons of the captives, while he kept all the spoils to himself and his allies.

It must have been a very tempting offer. It was no slight matter for a shepherd to have the chance of appropriating all the spoils of settled townships, so large and opulent, especially when he seemed to have some claim on them.

But Abraham would not hear of it for a moment. Indeed, he seems to have already undergone some exercise of soul on the matter, for speaking as of a past transaction, he said, "I have lifted up mine hand unto the LORD, the most high God, the possessor of heaven and earth, that I will take from a thread even to a shoelatchet, and that I will not take any thing that is thine, lest thou shouldst say, I have made Abram rich." What glorious outburst of the independence of a living faith!

There is a close parallel between this suggestion of the king of Sodom and the temptation of our Lord in the wilderness, when Satan offered Him all the kingdoms of the world for one act of obeisance. And does not this temptation assail us all? Are we not all tempted to take the gilded wage of the world? The world is aware that, if we will only accept its subsidies, we shall have surrendered our position of independence and have stepped down to its level, no longer able to witness against it, shorn of the locks of our strength, and become weak as other men.

Besides, what right have we to depend on revenues of the world, we, who are heirs to the possessor of heaven and earth, the children of the great king: to whom, in giving us His Son, He has also pledged to give us all things? Happy are they who prefer to be pensioners on the daily providence of God to being dependent on the gold of Sodom—the wages of iniquity.

3. THE PREVENIENT GRACE OF GOD. It may be that Abraham would not have come off so grandly in the second conflict if he had not been prepared for it by the wondrous encounter with a greater king than either we have named. After his deafet of Chedorlaomer, the Hebrew had met Melchizedek, the priest-king of Salem. He brought bread and wine, and blessed the weary conqueror. Is not this the work of the Lord Jesus still? He comes to us when we wearily return from the fight. He comes to us when He knows we are on the eve of a great temptation. He not only prays for us, as for Peter; but He prepares us for the conflict. Some new revelation, some fresh glimpse into His character, some holy thought—these are given to fill the memory and heart against the advent of the foe. Oh, matchless mercy! He forewarns and forearms us. He prevents us with the blessings of His goodness.

O King of loyal hearts, may we meet Thee more often on life's highway, especially when some tempter is preparing to weave around us the meshes of evil; and bending beneath. Thy blessing, may we be prepared by the communications of Thy grace for all that may await us in the unknown future!

9

Melchizedec
Hebrews 7:1

There is a sense in which Christ was made *after the order of Melchizedec;* but there is a deeper sense in which Melchizedec was made *after the order of the Son of God.* The writer to the Hebrews tells us that Melchizedec was "made like unto the Son of God" (Heb. 7:3) that there might be given among men some premonition, some anticipation, of that glorious life that was already being lived in heaven on man's behalf, and which, in due course, would be manifested on our world, and at that very spot where Melchizedec lived his Christlike life.

1. MELCHIZEDEC WAS A PRIEST. He seems to have had that quick sympathy with the needs of his times which is the true mark of the priestly heart (Heb. 4:15). And he had acquired thereby so great an influence over his neighbors that they spontaneously acknowledged the claims of his special and unique position. Man must have a priest. And in all ages, men have selected from among their fellows one who should represent them to God, and God to them. It is a natural instinct. And it has been met in our glorious Lord, who, while He stands for us in the presence of God, face to face, ever making intercessions, at the same time is touched with the feeling of our infirmities, succors us in our temptations, and has compassion on our ignorance. Why need we travel farther afield?

2. THIS PRIESTHOOD WAS ALSO CATHOLIC. Abraham was not yet circumcised. He was not a Jew, but a Gentile still. It was as the father of many nations that he stood and worshiped and received the benediction from Melchizedec's saintly hands. It was not this way with the priesthood of Aaron's line. To share its benefit a man had to become a Jew, submitting to the initial rite of Judaism. None but Jewish names shone in his breastplate. Only Jewish wants or sins were borne on his consecrated lips. But Christ is the priest of man. He draws *all men* to Himself. The one sufficient claim upon Him is that we bear the nature that He has taken into irreversible union with His own—that we are sinners and penitents pressed by conscious need. Then have we a right to Him, which cannot be disallowed. He is our Priest—our own; as if none other had claim on Him. All kindreds, and people, and nations, and tongues, converge in Him, and are welcome; and all their myriad needs are satisfactorily met.

3. THIS PRIESTHOOD WAS SUPERIOR TO ALL HUMAN ORDERS OF PRIESTS. If there ever was a priesthood that held undisputed supremacy among the priesthoods of the world, it was that of Aaron's line. Yet even the Aaronic must yield obeisance to the Melchizedec priesthood. And it did. For Levi was yet in the loins of Abraham when Melchizedec met him; and he paid tithes in Abraham, and knelt in token of submission, in the person of the patriarch, beneath the blessing of this greater than himself (Heb. 7:4–10).

4. THIS PRIESTHOOD PARTOOK OF THE MYSTERY OF ETERNITY. We need not suppose that this mystic being had literally no father or mother, beginning of days, or end of life. No information is afforded us on any of these points. And these details were doubtless

shrouded in obscurity, that there might be a still clearer approximation of the type to the glory of the Antitype, who abides continually. He is the Ancient of Days; the King of the Ages; the I AM. "He is made after the power of an endless life." "He ever liveth to make intercession." If, in the vision of Patmos, the hair of His head was white as snow, it was not the white of decay, but of incandescent fire. "He continueth ever, and hath an unchangeable priesthood." "He is the same yesterday, today, and for ever." He does for us now what He did for the world's gray fathers, and what He will do for the last sinner who shall claim his aid.

5. THIS PRIESTHOOD WAS ROYAL. "Melchizedec, king of Salem, priest." Here again there is no analogy in the Levitical priesthood.

The royal and priestly offices were carefully kept apart. Uzziah was struck with the white brand of leprosy when he tried to unite them. But how marvelously they blended in the earthly life of Jesus! As Priest, He pitied, and helped, and fed men: as King, He ruled the waves. As Priest, He uttered His sublime intercessory prayer: as King, He spoke the "I will" of royal prerogative. As Priest, He touched the ear of Malchus; as the disowned King, to whom even Caesar was preferred, He was hounded to the death. As Priest, He pleaded for His murderers, and spoke of Paradise to the dying thief, while His kingship was attested by the proclamation affixed to his cross. As Priest, He breathed peace on His disciples; as King, He ascended to sit on His throne.

Ah, souls, what is your attitude toward Him? There are plenty who are willing enough to have Him as Priest, who refuse to accept Him as King. But it will not do. He must be King, or He will not be Priest. And He must be King in this order, first making you right, then giving you His peace that passes all understanding. Waste not your precious time in paltering, or arguing with Him; accept the situation as it is, and let your heart be the Salem, the city of peace, where He, the Priest-King, shall reign forever.

6. THIS PRIESTHOOD RECEIVES TITHES OF ALL. "The patriarch Abraham gave the tenth of the spoils" (Heb. 7:4). This ancient custom shames us Christians. The patriarch gave more to the representative of Christ than many of us give to Christ Himself. Come, if you have never done so before, resolve to give your Lord a tithe of your time, your income, your all. "Bring all the tithes into his storehouse." Nay, glorious One, we will not rest content with this; take all, for all is Yours.

10

The Firmness of Abraham's Faith
Genesis 15

In this chapter, for the first time in Scripture, four striking phrases occur, but each of them is destined to be frequently repeated with many charming variations. First, we meet the phrase, "the word of the LORD came." Here, first, we are told that "the Lord God is a shield." For the first time there rings out the silver chime of that divine assurance, "Fear not!" And now we first meet in human history that great, that mighty word, "believed."

The "word of the LORD" came to Abraham about two distinct matters.

Abraham

1. GOD SPOKE TO ABRAHAM ABOUT HIS FEAR. Abraham had just returned from the rout of Chedorlaomer and there was a natural reaction from the long and unwonted strain as he settled down again into the placid and uneventful course of a shepherd's life. In this state of mind he was most susceptible to fear; and there was good reason for fear. He had defeated Chedorlaomer, it is true; but in doing so he had made him his bitter foe. The arm of the warrior-king had been long enough to reach to Sodom; why should it not be long enough and strong enough to avenge his defeat on that one lonely man?

Besides all this, as a night wind in a desert land, there swept now and again over the heart of Abraham a feeling of lonely desolation, of disappointment, of hope deferred. More than ten years had passed since he had entered Canaan. Three successive promises had kindled his hopes, but they seemed as far from realization as ever. Not one inch of territory! Not a sign of a child! Nothing of all that God had foretold!

It was under such circumstances that the word of the Lord came unto him, saying, "Fear not, Abram: I am thy shield, and thy exceeding great reward." But God does not content Himself with vague assurances. He gives us solid ground for comfort in some fresh revelation of Himself. What could have been more reassuring at this moment to the defenseless pilgrim, with no stockade or walled city in which to shelter, but whose flocks were scattered far and wide, than to hear that God Himself was around him and his, as a vast, impenetrable, though invisible shield. "I am thy shield."

Mankind, when once that thought was given, eagerly reached for it, and it has never been allowed to die. It is a very helpful thought for some of us! We go every day into the midst of danger; men and devils strike at us; now it is the overt attack, and now the stab of the assassin; unkind insinuations, evil suggestions, taunts, gibes, threats; all these things are against us. But if we are doing God's will and trusting in God's care, ours is a charmed life. The divine environment pours around us, rendering us impervious to attack. Happy are they who have learned the art of abiding within the inviolable protection of the eternal God, on which all arrows are blunted, all swords turned aside, all sparks of malice extinguished with the hissing sound of a torch in the briny waters of the sea.

Nor does God only defend us from without. He is the *reward* and satisfaction of the lonely heart. It was as if He asked Abraham to consider how much he had in having Himself. "Come now, my child, and think; even if you were never to have one foot of soil, and your tent were to stand silent, amid the merry laughter of childish voices all around—yet you would not have left your land in vain, for you have Me. Am I not enough? I fill heaven and earth; cannot I fill one lonely soul? Am not I 'thy exceeding great reward'; about to compensate you by My friendship, to which you art called, for any sacrifice that you may have made?"

2. GOD SPOKE TO ABRAHAM ABOUT HIS CHILDLESSNESS. The patriarch was sleeping in his tent, when God came near him in a vision; and it was under the shadow of that vision that Abraham was able to tell God all that was in his heart. And in that quiet watch of the night, Abraham poured out into the ear of God the bitter agony of his heart's life. "Behold, to me thou hast given no seed: and, lo, one born in my house is mine heir." It was as if he said, "I promised for myself something more than this; I have conned Thy promises, and felt that they surely prognosticated a child of my own flesh and blood; but the slowly moving years have brought me no fulfillment of my hopes; and I suppose that I mistook Thee. Thou never intendest more than that my steward should inherit my

name and goods. Ah, me! it is a bitter disappointment; but Thou hast done it, and it is well."

So we often mistake God, and interpret His delays as denials. But such delays are not God's final answer to the soul that trusts Him. They are but the winter before the burst of spring. "And, behold, the word of the LORD came unto him, saying, This shall not be thine heir; but he that shall come forth out of thine own bowels shall be thine heir. Look now toward heaven, and tell the stars, if thou be able to number them. . . . So shall thy seed be" (Gen. 15:4–5). And from that moment the stars shone with new meaning for him, as the sacraments of divine promise.

3. "AND HE BELIEVED IN THE LORD." What wonder that those words are so often quoted by inspired men in after ages.

a. *He believed before he underwent the Jewish rite of circumcision.* The apostle Paul lays special emphasis on this, as showing that they who were not Jews might equally have faith, and be numbered among the spiritual children of the great father of the faithful (Rom. 4:9–21; Gal. 3:7–29). The promise that he should be the heir of the world was made to Abraham, when as yet he was only the far-traveled pilgrim; and so it is sure to all the seed, not to that only which is of the law, but to that also which is of the faith of Abraham, who is the father of us all.

b. *He believed in face of strong natural improbabilities.* Appearances were dead against such a thing as the birth of a child to that aged pair. The experience of many years said, "It cannot be." The nature and reason of the case said, "It cannot be." Any council of human friends and advisers would have instantly said, "It cannot be!" And Abraham quietly considered and weighed them all "without being weakened in faith" (Rom. 4:19 asv). Then he as carefully looked into the promise of God. He reckoned on the faithfulness of God. He relied implicitly on the utter trustworthiness of the divine veracity. He was "fully assured that what he had promised He was able also to perform." Ah, child of God, for every look at the unlikelihood of the promise, take ten looks at the promise: this is the way in which faith waxes strong. "Looking unto the promise of God, he wavered not through unbelief, but waxed strong" (Rom. 4:20 asv).

c. *His faith was destined to be severely tried.* If you take to the lapidary the stones you have collected during the summer, he will probably send the bulk of them home to you in a few days. But some one or two of the number may be kept back, and when you inquire for them, he will reply: "Those stones that I returned are not worth much: there was nothing in them to warrant the expenditure of my time and skill; but with the others, the case is far otherwise; they are capable of taking a polish and of bearing a discipline which it may take months and even years to give; but their beauty, when the process is complete, will be all the compensation that can be wished."

Some men pass through life without much trial, because their natures are light and trivial, and incapable of bearing much, or of profiting by the severe discipline which, in the case of others, is all needed, and will yield a rich recompense, after it has had its perfect work. God will not let any one of us be tried beyond what we are able to bear. But when He has in hand a nature like Abraham's, which is capable of the loftiest results, we must not be surprised if the trial is long continued, almost to the last limit of endurance. The patriarch had to wait fifteen years more, making twenty-five years in all, between the first promise and its fulfillment in the birth of Isaac.

d. *His faith was counted to him for righteousness.* The righteousness of Abraham resulted not from his works, but from his faith. "He believed God; and it was reckoned unto him for righteousness" (Gal. 3:6 ASV). Oh, miracle of grace! if we trust ever so simply in Jesus Christ our Lord, we shall be reckoned as righteous in the eye of the eternal God. We cannot realize all that is included in those marvelous words. This only is evident, that faith unites with Him so absolutely to the Son of God that we are *one* with Him forevermore.

Some teach imputed righteousness as if it were something apart from Christ, flung over the rags of the sinner. But it is truer and better to consider it as a matter of blessed identification with Him through faith; so that as He was one with us in being made sin, we are one with Him in being made the righteousness of God. Jesus Christ is made unto us righteousness, and we are accepted in the Beloved. There is nothing in faith, considered in itself, which can account for this marvelous fact of imputation. Faith is only the link of union, but inasmuch as it unites us to the Son of God, it brings us into the enjoyment of all that He is as the Alpha and Omega, the Beginning and the End, the First and the Last.

11

Watching With God
Genesis 15:7

It is not easy to watch with God, or to wait for Him. He holds on His way through the ages; we tire in a few short hours. And when His dealings with us are perplexing and mysterious, the heart that had boasted its unwavering loyalty begins to grow faint with misgivings, and to question, When shall we be able to trust absolutely, and not be afraid?

In human relationships, when once the heart has found its rest in another, it can bear the test of distance and delay. Years may pass without a word or sigh to break the sad monotony. Strange contradictions may baffle the understanding and confuse the mind. But the trust never varies or abates. It knows that all is well. It is content to exist without a token, and to be quiet without attempting to explain or defend. Ah, when shall we treat God so? Surely that were heaven, when the heart of man could afford to wait for a millennium, unstaggered by delay, untinged by doubt.

At this stage of his education, Abraham had not learned this lesson. He answered the divine assurance that he should inherit the land of which he as yet did not own a foot, by the sad complaint: "Lord GOD, whereby shall I know that I shall inherit it?"

How human this is! It was not that he was absolutely incredulous: but he yearned for some tangible token that it was to be as God had said, something he could see, something that should be an ever-present sacrament of the coming heritage.

1. WATCHING BY THE SACRIFICE. In those early days, when a written agreement was very rare, if not quite unknown, men sought to bind one another to their word with the most solemn religious sanctions. The contracting party was required to bring certain animals, which were slaughtered and divided into pieces. These were laid on the ground in such a manner as to leave a narrow lane between; up and down which the covenanting party passed to ratify and confirm his solemn pledge.

It was to this ancient and solemn rite that Jehovah referred, when he said, "Take me an heifer of three years old, and a she goat of three years old, and a ram of three years old, and a turtledove, and a young pigeon. And he took unto him all these and divided them in the midst, and laid each piece one against another" (Gen. 15:9–10).

It was still the early morning. The day was young. And Abraham sat down to watch. Hour after hour passed by; but there was neither voice, nor any to answer.

Higher and ever higher the sun drove its chariot up the sky, and shone with torrid heat on those pieces of flesh lying there exposed upon the sand; but still no voice or vision came. The unclean vultures, attracted by the scent of carrion, drew together as to a feast, and demanded incessant attention if they were to be kept away. Did Abraham ever permit himself to imagine that he was sitting there on a fool's mission? Did he shrink from the curious gaze of his servants, and of Sarah his wife, because he was half-conscious of having taken up a position he could not justify?

This is in a line with the discipline through which we all have to pass. Hours of waiting for God! Days of watching! Let us see to it that we never relax our attitude of patience, and let us give the unclean birds no quarter. We cannot help them sailing slowly through the air, or uttering dismal screams, or circling around us as if to pounce. But we *can* help them settling down. And this we must do, in the name and by the help of God. "If the vision tarry, wait for it."

2. THE HORROR OF A GREAT DARKNESS. The sun at last went down, and the swift Eastern night casts its heavy veil over the scene. Worn out with the mental conflict, the watchings, and the exertions of the day, Abraham fell into a deep sleep. And in that sleep his soul was oppressed with a dense and dreadful darkness; such as almost stifled him, and lay like a nightmare upon his heart. "Lo, an horror of great darkness fell upon him."

It was a long and dark prospect which unfolded itself before Abraham. He beheld the history of his people through coming centuries, strangers in a foreign land, enslaved and afflicted. Did he not see the anguish of their soul, and their cruel bondage beneath the taskmaster's whips? Did he not hear their groans, and see mothers weeping over their babes, doomed to the insatiable Nile? Did he not witness the building of Pyramid and Treasure-city, cemented by blood and suffering? It was, indeed, enough to fill him with darkness that could be felt.

And yet the sombre woof was crossed by the warp of silver threads. The enslaved were to come out, and to come out with great substance, their oppressors being overwhelmed with crushing judgment. They were to come into that land again. While, as for himself, he should go to his fathers in peace, and be buried in a good old age.

It is thus that human life is made up: brightness and gloom; shadow and sun; long tracks of cloud, succeeded by brilliant glints of light. And amid all, divine justice is working out its own schemes.

Oh, ye who are filled with the horror of great darkness because of God's dealings with mankind, learn to trust that infallible wisdom which is co-assessor with immutable justice; and know that He who passed through the horror of the darkness of Calvary, with the cry of forsakenness, is ready to bear you company through the valley of the shadow of death, till you see the sun shining upon its further side.

3. THE RATIFICATION OF THE COVENANT. When Abraham awoke, the sun was down. Darkness reigned supreme. "It was dark." A solemn stillness brooded over the world.

Then came the awful act of ratification. For the first time since man left the gates of Eden there appeared the symbol of the glory of God; that awful light which was afterward to shine in the pillar of cloud, and the Shekinah gleam.

In the thick darkness, that mysterious light—a lamp of fire—passed slowly and majestically between the divided pieces; and, as it did so, a voice said: "Unto thy seed have I given this land, from the river of Egypt unto the great river, the river Euphrates" (Gen. 15:18).

Remember that promise made with the most solemn sanctions, never repealed since, and never perfectly fulfilled. For a few years during the reign of Solomon the dominions of Israel almost touched these limits, but only for a very brief period. The perfect fulfillment is yet in the future.

By two immutable things, His word and oath, God has given strong assurance to us who are menaced by the storm, drawing us on to a rock-bound shore. Let us, by our Forerunner, send forward our anchor, Hope, within the veil that parts us from the unseen: where it will grapple in ground that will not yield, but hold until the day dawn, and we follow it into the heaven guaranteed to us by God's immutable counsel (Heb. 6:19–20).

12

Hagar, the Slave Girl
Genesis 16:1

None of us knows all that is involved when we tear ourselves from the familiar scenes of our Harans to follow God into the lands of separation that lie beyond the river.

There is here a very startling manifestation of the tenacity with which Abraham's self-life still survived. The long waiting of ten slow-moving years, the repeated promises of God, the habit of contact with God Himself—all this had surely been enough to eradicate and burn out all desire to help himself to the realization of the promises of God. Surely, now, this much-tried man will wait until, in His own time and way, God shall do as He has said. We might have expected that he would have strenuously resisted every endeavor to induce him to realize for himself God's promise about his seed. Surely he will wait meekly and quietly for God to fulfill His own word, by means best known to Himself.

Instead of this he listened to *the reasoning of expediency*. Simple-hearted faith waits for God to unfold His purpose, sure that He will not fail. But mistrust, reacting on the self-life, leads us to take matters into our own hands.

1. THE QUARTER FROM WHERE THESE REASONINGS CAME. "Sarai said unto Abram." Poor Sarah! She had not had her husband's advantages. When he had been standing in fellowship with God, she had been quietly pursuing the routine of household duty, pondering many things.

It was clear that Abraham should have a son; but it was not definitely said by God that the child would be hers. Abraham was a strict monogamist; but the more lax notions of those days warranted the filling of the harem with others, who occupied an inferior rank to that of the principal wife, and whose children, according to common practice, were reckoned as if they were her own. Why should not her husband fall in with those notions of the marriage vow? Why should he now marry the slave girl? It was a heroic sacrifice for her to make. But her love to Abraham, her despair of having a child of her own, and her inability to conceive of God fulfilling His word by other than natural means—all these things combined to make the proposal.

No one else could have approached Abraham with such a proposition, with the slightest hope of success. But when Sarah made it, the case was altered. It seemed to be a likely expedient for realizing God's promise, and "Abram hearkened to the voice of Sarai."

2. THE SORROWS TO WHICH THEY LED. As soon as the end was obtained, the results, like a crop of nettles, began to appear in that home, which had been the abode of purity and bliss; but which was now destined to be the scene of discord. Raised into a position of rivalry with Sarah, and expectant of giving the long-desired son to Abraham, and a young master to the camp, Hagar despised her childless mistress, and took no pains to conceal her contempt.

This was more than Sarah could endure. It was easier to make one heroic act of self-sacrifice, than to bear each day the insolent carriage of the maid whom she had herself exalted to this position. Nor was she reasonable in her irritation; instead of assuming the responsibility of having brought about the untoward event, so fraught with misery to herself, she passionately upbraided her husband, saying: "My wrong be upon thee: the LORD judge between me and thee" (Gen. 16:5).

Out of this fleshly expedient sprang many sorrows. Sorrow to Sarah, who on this occasion, as afterward must have drunk to the dregs the cup of bitter gall, of jealousy and wounded pride, of hate and malice. Sorrow to Hagar, driven forth as an exile from the home of which she had dreamed to become the mistress, and to which she had thought herself essential. Sorrow to Abraham, loath to part with one who, to all human appearance, would now become the mother of the child who should bless his life: stung, moreover, as he was, by the unwonted bitterness of his wife's reproaches.

3. THE VICTIM WHOSE LIFE COURSE WAS SO LARGELY INVOLVED. Abraham, for the sake of the peace of his home, dared not interpose between his wife and her slave. "Behold," he said, "thy maid is in thy hand; do to her as it pleaseth thee." Not slow to act upon this implied consent, the irate mistress dealt so bitterly with the girl that she fled from her face, and took the road, trodden by the caravans, toward her native land.

"The angel of the LORD" (and here, for the first time, that significant expression is used, which is held by many to express some evident manifestation of the Son of God in angel form) "found her by a fountain of water" which was familiarly known in the days of Moses. There, worn and weary and lonely, she sat down to rest. How often does the angel of the Lord still find us in our extremity! And what questions could be more pertinent, whether to Hagar or to us: "Whence camest thou? and whither wilt thou go?" Reader, answer those two questions, before you read further. What is your origin and destiny?

Then there followed the distinct command, which applies to us evermore, "Return . . . and submit." The day would come when God Himself would open the door, and send Hagar out of that house (21:12–14). But until that moment should come, after thirteen years had rolled away, she must return to the place she had left, bearing her burden and fulfilling her duty as best she might. "Return . . . and submit."

We are all prone to act as Hagar did. If our lot is hard, and our cross is heavy, we start off in a fit of impatience and wounded pride. We make our own way out of the difficulty. But we shall never get right this way. Never! We must retrace our steps; we must meekly bend our necks under the yoke. We must accept the lot that God has ordained for us, even though it be the result of the cruelty and sin of others. We shall conquer by yielding. We shall escape by returning. By and by, when the lesson is perfectly learned, the prison door will open of its own accord.

Meanwhile the heart of the prodigal is cheered by promise (Gen. 16:10). The angel of the Lord unfolds all the blessed results of obedience. And as the spirit considers these, it finds the homeward way no longer lined by flints, but soft with flowers.

13

"Be Thou Perfect!"
Genesis 17:1

Thirteen long years passed slowly after the return of Hagar to Abraham's camp. The child Ishmael was born and grew up in the patriarch's house—the acknowledged heir of the camp, and yet showing symptoms of the wild nature of which the angel had spoken (16:12). Abraham must have been perplexed with those strange manifestations, and yet the heart of the old man warmed to the lad, and clung to him, often asking that Ishmael might live before God.

And throughout that long period there was no fresh appearance, no new announcement. Not since God had spoken to him in Charran had there been so long a pause. And it must have been a terrible ordeal, driving him back on the promise that had been given, and searching his heart to ascertain if the cause lay within himself.

At last, "when Abram was ninety years old and nine," the Lord appeared to him again, and gave him a new revelation of Himself. He unfolded the terms of His covenant, and addressed to him that memorable charge that rings its summons in the ear and heart of every believer still: "Walk before me, and be thou perfect."

1. THE DIVINE SUMMONS. "Walk before me, and be thou perfect." Men have sadly stumbled over that word "perfect." They have not erred when they have taught that there is an experience, denoted by the phrase, which is possible to men. But they have sadly erred in pressing their own significance into the word, and in then asserting that men are expected to fulfill it, or that they have themselves attained it.

"Perfection" is often supposed to denote sinlessness of moral character, which at the best is only a negative conception, and fails to bring out the positive force of this mighty word. Surely perfection means more than sinlessness. And if this is admitted, and the further admission is made that it contains the thought of moral completeness, then it becomes yet more absurd for any mortal to assert it of himself. The very assertion shows the lack of any perfection, and reveals little knowledge of the inner life and of the nature of sin. *Absolute sinlessness* is surely impossible for us so long as we do not have perfect knowledge; for as our light is growing constantly, so are we constantly discovering evil in things which we once allowed without uneasiness. Surely the language of the apostle Paul should be on our lips as he cried, "Not as though I had already attained, or were already perfect; but I follow after."

Besides all this, the word "perfect" bears different renderings from those often given to it. For instance, when we are told that the man of God must be *perfect* (2 Tim. 3:17), the underlying thought is that of a workman being "thoroughly equipped for his work." Again, when we join the prayer that the God of peace would make us *perfect* in every good work to do His will, we are, in fact, asking that we may be "put in joint" with the blessed Lord; so that the glorious Head may freely secure through us the doing of His will (Heb. 13:20–21).

What, then, is the true force and significance of this word, "Walk before me, and be thou perfect"? A comparison of the various passages where it occurs establishes its meaning beyond a doubt, and compels us to think the conception of "wholehearted-ness." It denotes the entire surrender of the being.

This quality of wholehearted devotion has always been dear to God. It is for this that He pleads with Abraham; and it was because He met with it to so large an extent in his character and obedience that He entered into eternal covenant bond with him and his.

Here let each reader ask, Is my heart perfect with God? Am I wholehearted toward Him? Is He first in my plans, pleasures, friendships, thoughts, and actions? Is His will my law, His love my light, His business my aim, His "well-done!" my exceeding great reward? Do others share me with Him?

And such an attitude can be *maintained* only by a very careful walk. "Walk before me, and be thou perfect." We must seek to realize constantly the presence of God, becoming instantly aware when the fleeciest cloud draws its vail for a moment over His face, and asking whether the cause may not lie in some scarcely-noticed sin. We must cultivate the habit of feeling Him near, as the Friend from whom we would never be separated, in work, in prayer, in recreation, in rest. And yet we shall not live forced or unnatural lives. None so blithe or light-hearted as we. Would you walk before God? Then let there be nothing in heart or life that you would not open to the inspection of His holy and pitiful eye.

2. THE REVELATION ON WHICH THIS SUMMONS WAS BASED. "I am the Almighty God" (*El-shaddai*). What a name is this! And what emotions it must have excited in the rapt heart of the listener! God had been known to him by other names, but not by this. And this was the first of a series of revelations of those depths of meaning that lay in the fathomless abyss of the divine name, each disclosure marking an epoch in the history of the race.

In God's dealings with men you will invariably find that some transcendent revela-tion precedes the divine summons to new and difficult duty; promise opens the door to precept: He gives what He commands, therefore He commands what He wills. And on this principle God acted here. It was no child's play to which He called His servant. To walk always before Him—when heart is weak, and strength is frail, and the temptation strong to swerve to right or left. To be perfect in devotion and obedience, when so many crosslights distract, and perplex, and fascinate the soul. To forego all methods of self-help, however tempting. To be separated from all alliances that others permit or follow. This is possible only through the might of the Almighty. And, therefore, there broke on him the assurance: "I am the Almighty God."

All this is as true today as ever. And if you will dare venture forth on the path of separation, cutting yourself aloof from all creature aid, and from all self-originated effort; content to walk alone with God, with no help from any but Him—you will find that all the resources of the divine almightiness will be placed at your disposal, and that the resources of Omnipotence must be exhausted before their cause can fail for want of help.

3. THE COVENANT THAT WAS DIVINELY PROPOSED. "I will make my covenant between me and thee." A covenant is a promise made under the most solemn sanctions, and binding the consenting parties in a definite and impressive way. We can't help but consent to the fact that the Almighty God proposed to enter into an everlasting covenant with His creature, a covenant that was ordered in all things and sure, and more stable than the everlasting hills!

a. *It referred to the seed.* And there was a marked advance. In Haran it was, "I will make of thee a great nation." At Bethel, "Thy seed shall be as the dust of the earth." At Mamre, "Tell the stars; so shall thy seed be." But now, three times over, the patriarch is told that he would be the father of many nations, a phrase explained by the apostle as including all, of every land, who share Abraham's faith, though not sprung from him in the line of natural descent (Gal. 3:7–29). In memory of that promise his name was slightly altered, so that it signified the "father of a great multitude."

b. *It referred to the land.* "I will give unto thee, and to thy seed after thee, the land wherein thou art a stranger, all the land of Canaan, for an everlasting possession." This promise waits for fulfillment. The word "everlasting" must mean something more than those few centuries of broken fitful rule. But there will be a time, when our covenant-keeping God will build again the tabernacle of David, which is fallen down, and will repair its ruins, and the land will be again inhabited by the seed of Abraham His friend.

c. *It referred to the coming child.* Until then Abraham had no other thought than that Ishmael should be his heir. God said, Sarah thy wife shall bear thee a son indeed; and thou shalt call his name Isaac" (v. 19).

God pledges Himself to be the God of our seed. And it is for us to claim the fulfillment of His pledge—not in heart-rending cries, but in quiet, determined faith, let us ask Him to do as He has said.

14

The Sign of the Covenant
Genesis 17:2

Three times in Scripture Abraham is called "the friend of God." In that moment of agony, when tidings came to King Jehoshaphat of the great heathen alliance that had been formed against him, he stood in the temple, and said, "Art not thou our God, who didst drive out the inhabitants of this land . . . and gavest it to the seed of Abraham, thy friend, for ever?" (2 Chron. 20:7).

And the apostle James, at the close of his argument about faith and works, tells us that when Abraham believed God, "it was imputed unto him for righteousness, and he was called the Friend of God" (James 2:23).

But, better than all, Jehovah Himself uses the title of friendship, and acknowledges the sacred tie between this much tried spirit and Himself: "Thou Israel art my servant, Jacob whom I have chosen, the seed of Abraham my friend" (Isa. 41:8).

And it would almost appear as if these two chapters, Genesis 17 and 18, had been written to show the familiarity and intimacy that existed between the eternal God and the man who was honored to be called His "friend." However, we must not suppose that there was something unique in this marvelous story. It is surely intended as an example of the way in which the eternal God is willing to deal with truehearted saints in all ages. To hundreds, and perhaps thousands, of His saints, God has been all that He was to Abraham; and He is willing to be all that to us still.

Let us peruse these ancient lines beneath the flood of light shed on them by our Savior, when He said: "Henceforth I call you not servants; for the servant knoweth not what his lord doeth: but I have called you friends" (John 15:15).

The friendship of God is freely offered to us in Jesus Christ our Lord. We cannot merit or deserve it. We are simply His bankrupt debtors forever, wondering at the heights and depths, the lengths and breadths, of the unsearchable riches of His grace. Let us not say that one ultimate cause of this friendship is in the yearning of the heart of the eternal for fellowship? But it must remain forever a mystery why He should seek it among us, the fallen children of Adam.

What a wondrous destiny there is within our reach! One to which the firstborn sons of light might aspire in vain! At the best they can only be ministers, flames of fire, hearts of love, excelling in strength, hearkening to His word. But we may be the *friends* of God; sons and daughters of the great King; members of the body of Christ. The brain almost reels under the conception that flashes before it of the blessedness that awaits us, both in this world, and in those ages that rear their heads in the far distance.

Oh, *friends of God!* why do you not make more of your transcendent privileges? Why do you not talk to Him about all that wearies and worries you, as freely as Abraham did? Life should be one long talk between God and us. No day at least should close without our talking over its history with our patient and loving Lord; entering into His confessional; relieving our hearts of half their sorrow, and all their bitterness, in the act of telling Him all. And if only we get low enough, and be still enough, we will hear His accents sweet and thrilling, soft and low, opening depths which eye hath not seen, nor ear heard; but which He has prepared for those who love and wait for Him.

There are, however, three conditions to be fulfilled if we would enjoy this blessed friendship: *separation, purity,* and *obedience,* each of which was set forth in the rite of circumcision, which was given to Abraham for himself and his descendants at this time.

"It is only in proportion as we know the spiritual meaning of circumcision that we can enter into the joyous appropriation of the friendship of God. But if we are willing, our Lord and Savior is both able and ready to effect in us this blessed spiritual result.

1. SEPARATION. Abraham and his seed were marked out by this rite as a separated people. And so it may be that any of us can be admitted into the friendship of God. Blood shedding and death—the cross and the grave—must lie between us and our own past life; yes, between us and all complicity with evil.

There are times when we may be expressly bidden to abide where we were originally called of God, but this will be for special purposes of ministry, and because the darkness needs light. For the most part the clarion note rings out to all who wish to know the sweets of divine fellowship: "Come out from among them, and be ye separate, saith the Lord, and touch not the unclean things; and I will receive you, and will be a Father unto you" (2 Cor. 6:17–18).

This was the key to Abraham's life; and is the inner meaning of the rite of circumcision.

2. PURITY. "Putting off the body of the sins of the flesh by the circumcision of Christ" (Col. 2:11). There is hardly a single grace dearer to God than this—to keep pure amid the defiling atmosphere; to walk with unspotted garments even in Sardis; to be as sensitive to the taint of impurity as the most delicate nostril to an evil odor. Ah, this is a condition of great price in the sight of God, and one to which He unveils Himself.

Purity can be attained only by the special grace of the Holy Spirit, and by doing two things: first, by our turning instantly from anything that excites impure imaginations; second, by our seeking immediate forgiveness, when we are conscious of having yielded, even for a moment, to the deadly and insidious fascinations of the flesh.

Let us trust Him to keep His own property in the perfect loveliness of that purity and chastity that are so dear to God; this is the circumcision of Christ.

3. OBEDIENCE. For Abraham this rite might have seemed less necessary than for some in his camp. But no sooner was it commanded than it was done. "In the selfsame day was Abraham circumcised, and Ishmael his son." Does it not remind us of Him who said, "Ye are my friends, if ye do whatsoever I command you"? Instant obedience to known duty is an indispensable condition of all intimacy with God; and if the duty is irksome and difficult, then remember to claim all the more of the divine grace; for there is no duty to which we are called that is too difficult for us to fulfill if we but stretch forth our hands to receive the strength God offers.

We do not obey in order to become friends; but having become friends we hasten to obey. Love is more inexorable than law, and for the love of Him who calls us by so dear a title, we are glad to undertake and accomplish what Sinai with all its thunders would fail to nerve us to attempt.

15

The Divine Guest
Genesis 18:1

When, in the course of some royal progress, a sovereign decides to stay in the home of one of the subjects of his realm, the event becomes at once the theme of chroniclers, and the family selected for so high an honor is held in deepened respect. But what shall we say in the presence of such an episode as this—in which the God of heaven became the guest of His servant Abraham!

There is no doubt as to the august character of one of the three who visited the tent of the patriarch. In verse 1 we are expressly told that Jehovah appeared to him in the plains of Mamre, as he sat in the tent door in the heat of the day. And in verse 10 there is the accent of Deity, in the words of promise that tell how certainly Sarah would have a son. Besides that, we are told that two angels came to Sodom in the evening. Evidently they were two of the three who had sat as Abraham's guests beneath the tree that sheltered his tent in the blazing noon. But as for the other, who throughout the wondrous hours had been the only spokesman, His dignity is disclosed in the amazing discussion that took place on the heights of Mamre, when Abraham stood yet before the Lord, and pleaded with Him as the Judge of all the earth.

Abraham, at the outset, evidently did not realize the full meaning of the episode in which he was taking part. So too we often fail to value aright characters with whom we come in contact. It is only as they pass away from us forever, and we look on them, that we realize that we have been entertaining angels unawares. Let us so act always and everywhere, that as we review the past we may have nothing to regret; and may not have to reproach ourselves because we omitted to do something or other, which we would have done had we only realized our opportunities.

1. ABRAHAM TREATED HIS VISITORS WITH TRUE EASTERN HOSPITALITY. He *ran* to meet them, and bowed himself toward the ground. He proposed water for their feet, and rest for their tired frames, beneath the spreading shadow of the tent. He started his wife kneading the meal for baking the bread on the scorching stones. He ran to choose his tenderest calf, refusing to delegate the work to another's hand. He served his visitors himself, and stood as a servant by their side, under the tree, while they ate. Christians do not have much to boast of—and a good deal to learn—as they consider the action of this old-time saint, and his dealings with the three strangers who came to his tent.

2. MAY IT NOT BE THAT CHRIST COMES TO US OFTEN IN THE GUISE OF A STRANGER? Does He not test us this way? Of course if He were to come in His manifested splendor as the Son of the highest, every one would receive Him, and provide Him with sumptuous hospitality. But this would not reveal our true character. So He comes to us as a wayfaring man, hungry and thirsty; or as a stranger, naked and sick. Those who are His will show Him mercy, in whatsoever disguise He comes, though they do not recognize Him, and will be surprised to learn that they ministered to Him. Those, on the other hand, who are not really His, will fail to discern Him, will let Him go away unhelped, and will wake up to find that "inasmuch as ye did it not to one of the least of these, ye did it not to me" (Matt. 25:45).

3. BUT GOD NEVER LEAVES US IN HIS DEBT. He is careful to pay for His entertainment, royally and divinely. He uses Peter's fishing vessel, and gives it back, nearly submerged by the weight of the fish He had driven into the nets. He sits down with His friends to a country marriage feast, and pays for their simple fare by jars brimming with water turned to wine. He uses the five barley loaves and two small fishes; but the lad has an ample meal. He sends His prophet to lodge with a widow, and provides meal and oil for him and her for many days. And Abraham was no loser by his ready hospitality, for as they sat at meat the Lord foretold the birth of Sarah's child: "I will certainly return unto thee . . . and, lo, Sarah thy wife shall have a son."

Sarah was sitting behind the flimsy curtain of camel's hair, and as she heard the words, she laughed the laugh of incredulity. That laugh was at once noticed by Him from whom nothing can be hid, and whose eyes are as a flame of fire. "And the LORD said unto Abraham, Wherefore did Sarah laugh, saying, Shall I of a surety bear a child, which am old? Is anything too hard for the LORD?" (Gen. 18:13–14).

With strange simplicity she answered through the curtain, denying that she had laughed, for she was afraid. But her reply was met by the stern and uncompromising affirmation, "Nay; but thou didst laugh." These were the only audible words that we know to have passed between God and Abraham's wife. However, she seems to have been led by these words into a true faith; for it is said, "Through faith also Sarah herself received strength to conceive seed, and was delivered of a child when she was past age, because she judged him faithful who had promised" (Heb. 11:11).

4. THIS IS THE TRUE LAW OF FAITH. Do not look at your faith or at your feelings, but look away to the word of promise, and, above all, to the Promiser. His power is omnipotent and would He ever have pledged Himself to do what He could not effect? "He is faithful who promised." Look from faith to the promise, and from the promise to the Promiser.

5. "IS ANYTHING TOO HARD FOR THE LORD?" That is one of God's unanswered questions. It may seem to you hard, almost impossible, that God should keep his word, in the conversion of that friend for whom you have prayed, according to 1 John 5:16. It may seem hard to vindicate your character from the aspersions with which it is being befouled; hard to keep your evil nature under control, and to cast down your evil thoughts, bringing every thought into captivity to the obedience of Christ; hard to make you sweet and gentle, forgiving and loving, hard to produce from you the fruits of a lovely and holy nature. It may be hard, but it is not too hard for the Lord. "With God all things are possible." And, as Sarah found, all things are possible to those who believe.

The one thing that hinders God is our unbelief. Sarah and Abraham had to believe before the child of promise could be born. And so must it be with us. As soon as we believe, then, according to our faith it is done to us; yes, exceedingly abundantly beyond all we had asked or thought.

You ask how to obtain this faith. Remember that faith is the receptive attitude of the soul, begotten and maintained by the grace of God. Christ is the Author and Finisher of faith; not only in the abstract, but also in the personal experience of the soul. Faith is the gift of God. If, then, you would receive it, put your will on the side of Christ. May it not be a passing wish, but the whole will of your being: will to believe patiently, persistently, yearningly; let your eyes be ever toward the Lord; study the promises of God; consider the nature of God; be prepared to be rid of everything that grieves His Holy Spirit; and it is as certain as the truth of Christ, that you will have begotten and maintained in you the faith that can move mountains and laugh at impossibilities.

16

Pleading for Sodom
Genesis 18:22–23

As the day wore on, Abraham's mysterious guests went off across the hills toward Sodom, and Abraham went with them to bring them on their way. But all three did not reach the guilty city over which the thunder clouds had already begun to gather. That evening two angels entered it alone. And where was their companion? He had stayed behind to talk yet further with His friend. Tradition still points out the spot on the hills at the head of a long steep ravine leading down to the sullen waters of the Dead Sea where the Lord tarried behind to tell Abraham all that was in His heart.

Abraham was the "friend of God," and friendship constitutes a claim to be entrusted with secrets hidden from everyone else. The Septuagint version has well brought out the spirit of the divine discussion, when it puts the question this way: "Shall I hide from Abraham, *my servant*, that thing which I do?" The Lord does nothing that He does not first reveal to His holy servants and prophets.

But the words that follow point to a further reason for the full disclosures that were made: "For I know him, that he will command his children and his household after him, and they shall keep the way of the LORD to do justice and judgment" (Gen. 18:19). Was there a fear lest Abraham and his children might doubt the justice of the judgment of God if the righteous were summarily cut off with the wicked; and if the cities of the plain were destroyed without a revelation of their sin on the one hand, and the display of the divine mercy on the other?

1. THE BURDEN OF THE DIVINE ANNOUNCEMENT. "The cry of Sodom and Gomorrah is great." No sound travelled to the patriarch's ear. Quiet though Sodom seemed, yet to God there was a cry—the cry of the earth compelled to carry such a scar; the cry of inanimate creation, groaning and travailing in pain; the cry of the oppressed, the downtrodden, the victims of human violence and lust. These were the cries that had entered into the ears of the Lord God of Sabaoth.

"I will go down now, and see." God always carefully investigates the true condition of the case before He executes His sentences. He is prepared, no, eager to give us the benefit of any excuse. But flagrant sin, like that which broke out in Sodom that night, is enough to settle forever the fate of a godless community when standing at the bar of Him who is Judge and Witness both.

"And if not, I will know." There was something very ominous in these words that Abraham clearly understood to indicate the approaching destruction of the place; for in his prayer he again and again alludes to the imminence of its doom. But what is there that God does not know? Yes, ungodly soul, who may read this page: remember that no secrets can be hid from God. He will search out the most hidden ramifications of your sins, bringing them out before the gaze of the universe, and justifying His righteous judgments which He will not spare.

2. THE IMPRESSION THAT THIS ANNOUNCEMENT MADE ON ABRAHAM'S MIND. As soon as the angels had left, leaving Abraham alone with the Lord, his mind was filled with a tumult of emotion. He hardly dared reason with God: what was he, but "dust and ashes"? And yet he was impelled to make some attempt to avert the doom that threatened the cities of the plain.

The motives that prompted him were twofold: There was a natural anxiety about his kinsman, Lot. Twenty years had passed since Lot had left him; but he had never ceased to follow him with the most tender affection. The strong impulse of natural affection stirred him to make one strenuous effort to save Sodom, lest his nephew might be overwhelmed in its overthrow. Real religion tends not to destroy, but to fulfill all the impulses of true natural love.

There was also a fear lest the total destruction of the cities of the plain might prejudice the character of God in the minds of the neighboring peoples. Abraham did not deny that the fate which was about to overtake the cities was deserved by many of the people of that enervating and luxuriant valley: but he could not bring his mind to suppose that the whole of the population was equally debased. He feared that if all were summarily swept away, the surrounding nations would have a handle of reproach against the justice of his God, and would accuse Him of unrighteousness, inasmuch as He destroyed the righteous with the wicked.

This passion for the glory of God burned with a clear, strong flame in Abraham's heart, and it was out of this that there arose his wondrous intercession. And when he became as closely identified with the interests of God as he was, we shall come to feel as he did. We will be eager that the divine character should be vindicated among the children of men; content, if need be, to lie dying in the ditch, so long as we can hear the shouts of triumph amid which our King rides over us to victory.

3. The elements in Abraham's intercession.

a. *It was lonely prayer.* He waited until there was no living man to overhear this marvelous outpouring of a soul: "He stood before the Lord." It is fatal to all the strongest devotion to pray always in the presence of another, even the dearest. Every saint must have a closet of which he can shut the door, and in which he can pray to the Father who is in secret.

b. *It was prolonged prayer.* "Abraham stood yet before the Lord." The story takes but a few moments to read, but the scene may have lasted for the space of hours. We cannot climb the more elevated pinnacles of prayer in a hasty rush. Of course, our God is ever on the alert to hear and answer those prayers which we fire through the day, but we cannot maintain this posture of ejaculatory prayer unless we cultivate the prolonged occasions. How much we miss because we do not wait before God!

c. *It was very humble prayer.* "Behold now, I have taken upon me to speak unto the Lord, which am but dust and ashes." "Oh, let not the Lord be angry, and I will speak." "Behold now, I have taken upon me to speak unto the Lord." "Oh, let not the Lord be angry, and I will speak yet but this once." The nearer we get to God, the more conscious are we of our own unworthiness; before Him angels veil their faces, and the heavens are not clean in His sight.

d. *This prayer was based on a belief that God possessed the same moral institutions as himself.* "Wilt thou also destroy the righteous with the wicked . . . that be far from thee. Shall not the Judge of all the earth do right?" There is an infinite interest in this. It was as if Abraham had said: "Almighty God, I could not think it right to destroy the righteous with the wicked; and I am sure that any number or righteous men would shrink from doing so. And if this is binding on man, of course it must be much more binding on Thee, because Thou art the Judge of the earth." And God was not angry; indeed, He assented to Abraham's plea. And, therefore, we may say that though God may act in ways above our reason, yet He will not contradict those instincts of the moral sense which He has placed within our hearts.

e. *This prayer was persevering.* Six times Abraham returned to the charge, and as each petition was granted his faith and courage grew; and, finding he had struck a right vein, he worked it again, and yet again. It looks at first sight as if he forced God back from point to point and wrung his petitions from an unwilling hand. But this is a mistake. In point of fact, *God was drawing him on;* and if he had dared to ask at first what he asked at the last, he would have got more than all that he asked or thought at the beginning of his intercession. What a pity that he stopped at ten! There is no knowing what he might have reached, had he gone on. As it was, the Almighty was obliged, by the demands of His own nature, to exceed the limits placed by Abraham, in bringing out of Sodom the only persons that could, by any possibility, be accounted "righteous."

There were not ten righteous men in Sodom; but Lot, and his wife, and his two daughters were saved, though three of them were deeply infected with the moral contagion of the place. And God's righteousness was clearly established and vindicated in the eyes of the surrounding peoples.

We note one of the great principles in the divine government of the world. A whole city would have been spared, if ten righteous men could have been found within its walls. Ungodly men little realize how much they owe to the presence of the children of God in their midst. How little the world realizes the debt it owes to its saints, the salt to stay its corruption, the light to arrest the reinstitution of the reign of chaos and night! We cannot but yearn over the world as it rolls on its way toward its sad, dark doom. Let us plead for it from the heights above Mamre. And may we and our beloved ones be led out from it into safety, before the last plagues break full upon it in inevitable destruction!

17

Angel Work in a Bad Town
Genesis 19

The waters of the Dead Sea ripple over a part of the site where the cities of the plain once stood, with their busy stir of life, and thought, and trade. But all the sounds of human joy, sorrow, or industry, the tread of the soldier, the call of the herdsman, the murmur of the market, the voices of little children playing in the open spaces—*all* are hushed in that awful solitude, the aspect of which is a striking testimony to the truth of the inspired Word.

Embosomed in gaunt mountains, the Dead Sea lies 1300 feet below the level of the Mediterranean Sea. And as the traveler wanders around the spot, he is irresistibly reminded of the time when "the LORD rained upon Sodom and upon Gomorrah brimstone and fire from the LORD out of heaven; and he overthrew those cities, and all the plain, and all the inhabitants of the cities and that which grew upon the ground."

1. THE REASONS THAT JUSTIFIED THIS SUPREME ACT OF DESTRUCTION.

a. *It was a merciful warning to the rest of mankind.* The lesson of the Flood had almost faded from the memory of man; and, heedless of all restraint, the human family had made terrible advances in the course of open shameless vice. It was surely, therefore, wise and merciful to set up a warning which reminded transgressors that there were limits beyond which the Judge of all the earth would not permit them to go.

God's warnings have a merciful intention, even where they are unheeded; and this Sodom catastrophe has been well said to belong to that class of terrors in which a wise man will trace "the lovingkindness of the Lord."

b. *Moreover, in this terrible act the Almighty simply hastened the result of their own actions.* Nations are not destroyed until they are rotten at the core. It would have been clear to any thoughtful observer who had ventured out arter dark in Sodom that the city must inevitably fall. Unnatural crime had already eaten out the national heart and, in the ordinary course of events, utter collapse could not be delayed long.

Go into the tents of Abraham, and you find simplicity, hospitality, the graces of a truly noble character, which guarantee the perpetuity of his name and the glorious future of his children. Now go to Sodom, and in that sultry climate you find a population enervated with luxury, cankered to the core with vice, not ten righteous men among them all, while the purity and sanctity of home are idle words.

This suggests a solemn lesson for ourselves. The tide of empire has ever set westward. India, Babylon, Egypt, Greece, and Rome have successively wielded supreme power and have later sunk into oblivion. Shall it depart from us, as it has departed from the rest? It need not do so. Yet, as we observe the increase of extravagance and luxury, the reckless expenditure on pleasure, the shameless vice that flaunts itself in our streets, the adulation of wealth, the devotion to gambling, the growing laxness of the marriage tie—we may well entertain the darkest fears about the future of our country. The only hope for us is based on the important part that we called to play in facilitating the evangelization of the world. Should we fail in this, nothing can avert our fall.

c. *Besides, this overthrow only happened after careful investigation.* "I will go down now and see." Beneath these simple words we catch a glimpse of one of the most sacred principles of divine action. God does not act hastily, nor upon hearsay evidence; He must see for Himself if there may not be some mitigating or extenuating circumstances. This deliberation is characteristic of God. He is unwilling that any should perish. He is slow to anger. Judgment is His strange work. He has not done *without cause* all that He has done (Ezek. 14:23).

d. *There is this consideration also–that, during the delay, many a warning was sent.* First, there was the conquest by Chedorlaomer, some twenty years before the time of which we write. Then there was the presence of Lot which was enfeebled by his inconsistencies, but was yet a protest on the behalf of righteousness (2 Peter 2:7–8). Finally, there was the deliverance and restoration by the energetic interposition of Abraham. Again and again had God warned the men of these cities of their inevitable doom, if they did not repent.

Nor is His usage different in the case of individuals. The course of every sin is against a succession of menacing red lights and exploding fog signals, warning of danger if that course is pursued. God arranged that no downward step can be taken without setting off vast numbers of shrill bells that tell of danger ahead. Transgressor! the signals are all against you.

To regard these alarm tokens is to be saved. To disregard them, persevering in spite of all, is to deaden the soul and harden the heart, and run the risk of blasphemy against the Holy Ghost. For that unpardonable sin is not an act, but a state—the condition of the soul that does not, and cannot, feel; that it is utterly insensible and careless of its state; and is not forgiven, simply because it does not admit or feel its need of forgiveness, and, therefore, does not ask for it.

e. *It is worthy of notice that God saved all whom He could.* Lot was a sorry wreck of a noble beginning. When he started forth, as Abraham's companion from Ur, he gave promise of a life of quite unusual power and fruit. But he was one of those characters that cannot stand success.

When Lot first went down to Sodom, attracted by the sole consideration of its pastures, it was no doubt his intention to keep aloof from its people, and to live outside its walls. But the moth cannot with impunity flutter about the flame. He was with difficulty dragged out of Sodom, as a brand plucked from the burning, and over the closing scenes of his life it is decent to draw a veil. And yet such a wreck was saved!

Nor was he alone saved, but his wife also, who did not take many steps outside the city before, by looking back, with a mixture of disobedience and regret, showed herself utterly hopeless; and her two daughters, whose names are branded with eternal infamy. If God was so careful to secure their safety, how bad must those have been whom He left to their fate! Is it not clear that He saved all who came within the range of mercy's possibilities? There will not be one soul among the lost who had the faintest claim to be among the saved; and there will be a great many among the saved whose presence there will be a very great surprise to us. "They shall come from the east and west . . . but the children of the kingdom shall be cast out."

2. THE MOTIVE OF THE ANGEL'S VISIT. These were three:

a. *The proximate, or nearest cause was their own love to man.* The angels love us. Though they know that we are destined to a dignity before which that of the loftiest seraphs must pale, no envy eats out the pure benevolence that throbs within their holy spirits. It is enough that God has willed it so, and that we are dear to their sweet Master, Christ.

b. *The efficient cause was Abraham's prayer.* "And it came to pass, when God destroyed the cities of the plain, that God remembered Abraham, and sent Lot out of the midst of the overthrow" (Gen. 19:29). Pray on, beloved reader. Pray on for that dear one far away in the midst of a very Sodom of iniquity. It may seem impossible for you to go down into it for his rescue, or to help him in any other way; but, in answer to your prayer, God will send His angels wherever your loved one may be. God's angels go everywhere. A Sodom cannot hold its victims back from their touch, any more than their bright presences can be soiled by the polluting atmosphere through which they pass. While you are praying, God's angels are on their way to perform your desire, albeit that their progress may be hindered by causes hidden from our sight or knowledge (see Dan. 10:12).

c. *But the ultimate cause was God's mercy.* "The Lord being merciful to him." Mercy: that is the last link in the chain. Is it not the staple in the wall? There is nothing beyond it. And this shall be our theme also through that eternity whose daystar has already arisen in our hearts.

The world is full of Sodoms still; and Lots, whom we have known and loved or who have a claim on us, are sitting at their gates. Oh, why are we behind the angels in eagerness to pluck them as brands from the burning?

3. THE ANGELS WENT TO WHERE LOT WAS. "There came two angels to Sodom at even." What! did angels go to Sodom? Yes, to Sodom—and yet angels. And as a ray of light may pass through the foetid atmosphere of some squalid court, and emerge without a stain on its pure texture, so may angels spend a night in Sodom, surrounded by crowds of sinners, and yet be untainted angels still.

This is the spirit of Christ's gospel. "He goeth after that which is lost till he find it."

We must not wait for sinners to come to us; we must go to them—wherever men are found we must go to them, to preach the gospel. The most unlikely places will yield Lots, who would have died in their sins if they had not been sought out.

4. THEY WERE CONTENT TO WORK FOR VERY FEW. Special value is attached to hand-picked fruit. All our Lord's choicest followers were the result of His personal ministry. To one and another He said, "Follow me!" His life was full of personal interviews. He sought out individual souls (Matt. 4:19, 21; 9:9; Luke 14:5). He would spend much time and thought to win one solitary woman, her character none too good (John 4). He believed in going after one sheep that was lost. The apostle Paul says that he warned every man, and taught every man, that he might "present every man perfect in Christ Jesus" (Col. 1:28).

It is a question whether more men are not saved by individual appeal than by all our preaching. It is not the sermon that wins them, but the quiet talk with a Christian worker, or the letter of a parent, or the words of a friend.

We never know what we do when we win one soul for God. Is not the following instance, culled from the biography of James Brainerd Taylor—called home to God too early, and yet not before he had won hundreds of souls by his personal appeals—a fair example of many more?

On one occasion he reined up his horse to drink at a roadside well. Another horseman at the same moment did the same. The servant of God, as the horses were eagerly quenching their thirst, turned to the stranger, and spoke some burning words concerning the duty and honor of Christian discipleship. In a moment more they had parted, and were riding in different directions. But the word of God remained as incorruptible seed, and led to the conversion of that wayside hearer. He became a Christian and a missionary. He often wondered who had been the instrument of his conversion, and sought for him in vain. But he did not succeed in identifying him till years after, when in a packet of books sent him from his native land, he opened the story of that devoted life, and in the frontispiece beheld the face that had haunted him, in sleeping and waking hours, even since that slight but memorable interview.

It has been said that the true method of soul winning is to set the heart on some one soul, and to pursue it until it has either definitely accepted or finally rejected the gospel of the grace of God. Christ found work enough in a village to keep Him there for thirty years. Philip was torn from the great revival in Samaria to go into the desert to win one seeker after God.

Have you ever spoken to your postman, your fellow worker, your neighbor? It would not take long to evangelize the world if every man would teach his neighbor, and every man his brother, saying, "Know the Lord!"

5. THEY TOLD LOT PLAINLY OF HIS DANGER. "Hast thou here any besides? . . . bring them out of this place: for we will destroy this place, because the cry of them is waxen great before the face of the LORD; and the LORD hath sent us to destroy it" (Gen. 19: 12–13). We are rather squeamish today of talking to men in this manner. We have lined our lips with velvet. We aim to be gentler than Christ. He did not hesitate to speak of an undying worm and a quenchless flame. The gnashing of teeth; the wail of despair; the knock to which no door would open—were arguments that came more than once from His lips. (See Matt. 8:12; 13:42, 50; 22:13; 24:51; 25:10–12, 30; Mark 9:43–48; Luke

13:25–28.) He evidently taught as if men might make a mistake which they could not possibly repair.

It may be that the day of grace is nearer to its close than we think. Escape, my reader, for your life; look not behind you, neither stay anywhere short of the cleft side of Jesus, where only we may hide from the just judgment of sin. Rest not till you have put the Lord Jesus between yourself and the footsteps of pursuing justice.

6. THEY HURRIED HIM. "When the morning arose, then the angels hastened Lot" (19:15). They had been reluctant to stay in his house, unlike the alacrity with which they accepted Abraham's hospitality; and they spent the short sultry night in urging on Lot the certainty and terror of the approaching destruction. So much so that they actually got him to go to arouse his sons-in-law. But an inconsistent life cannot arrest the wanderer, or startle the sleeper into awakening about his soul. People say that we must conform a little to the manners of our time if we would exert a saving influence over men. It is a fatal mistake. If we live in Sodom, we will have no power to save the people of Sodom. You must stand outside of them, if you would save them from the gurgling rapids. "He seemed as one that mocked unto his sons-in-law."

When he came back from his ineffectual mission, Lot seemed infected by the scepticism that had ridiculed his warnings. "He lingered." How could he leave his children, and household goods, and property, on what seemed to be a fool's errand? "And while he lingered, the men laid hold upon his hand."

It was hand help. It was the urgency of love that would take no denial. The two angels had four hands, but each hand was full, and each clasped the hand of a procrastinating sinner. Would that we knew more fully this divine enthusiasm that pulls men out of the fire! (Jude 23).

Let us hasten sinners. Let us say to each one: "Escape for your life; better lose all than lose your soul. Linger nowhere outside the City of Refuge, which is Jesus Christ Himself. Make haste!" "Behold, now is the accepted time: behold, now is the day of salvation."

18

A Bit of the Old Nature
Genesis 20:9

For many years an evil may lurk in our hearts, permitted and unjudged, breed failure and sorrow in our lives. But that which escapes our knowledge is patent in all its naked deformity to the eye of God. When He has laid bare the cancerous growth, He may bring us to long for and invite the knife that shall set us free from it forever.

These words have been suggested by the thirteenth verse of this chapter, which indicates an evil compact, into which Abraham had entered with Sarah some thirty years earlier. Addressing the king of the Philistines, the patriarch let fall a hint that sheds a startling light on his failure, when he first entered the Land of Promise and, under stress of famine, went down into Egypt; and upon that repetition of his failure which we must now consider. Here is what he said: "And it came to pass, when God caused me to wander from my father's house, that I said unto [my wife], This is thy kindness which thou shalt shew unto me; at every place whither we shall come, say of me, He is my brother."

This secret compact between Abraham and his wife, in the earliest days of his exodus, was due to his weak faith in God's power to take care of them, which again sprang from his limited experience of his Almighty Friend.

But the existence of this hidden understanding was inconsistent with the relation into which he had now entered with God. It was a secret flaw in his faith that would destroy its effectiveness in the dark trials that were approaching. God could afford to pass it over in those early days, when faith itself was yet young, but it could not be permitted when that faith was reaching to a maturity in which any flaw would be instantly detected.

The judgment and eradication of this lurking evil were brought about in this way. The day before Sodom's fall, the Almighty told Abraham that, at a set time in the following year, he would have a son and heir. And we would expect that he would have spent the slow-moving months beneath the oak of Mamre, already hallowed by so many associations. But he "journeyed from thence toward the south country, and dwelled between Kadesh and Shur, and sojourned in Gerar" (Gen. 20:1).

Gerar was the capital of a race of men who had dispossessed the original inhabitants of the land, and were gradually passing from the condition of wandering shepherd life into that of a settled and warlike nation. Their chieftain bore the official title of Abimelech, "My Father the King."

Here, the almost forgotten agreement between Sarah and himself offered itself as a ready expedient, behind which Abraham's unbelief took shelter. He knew the ungoverned license of his time. He dreaded, lest the heathen monarch, enamored with Sarah's beauty, might slay him for his wife's sake. So he again resorted to lying by calling her his sister. He acted as if God could not have defended him and her, screening them from all evil; as He had done so often in days gone by.

1. HIS CONDUCT WAS VERY DISHONORING TO GOD. Among those untutored tribes Abraham was well known as the servant of Jehovah, and they could judge the character of Him whom they could not see only by the traits they discerned in His servant. How sad that Abraham's standard was lower than their own! So much so that Abimelech was able to rebuke him.

It is heartbreaking when the heathen rebukes a professor of superior godliness for speaking lies. And it is lamentable to confess that such men often have higher standards of morality than those who profess godliness. The temperate Hindu is scandalized by the drunkenness of the American whose religion he is invited to embrace. The employee abhors a creed that is professed by his employer for one day of the week, but is disowned on the other six. Let us walk circumspectly toward those who are without.

2. IT ALSO STOOD OUT IN POOR RELIEF AGAINST THE BEHAVIOR OF ABIMELECH. Abimelech commends himself to us as the nobler of the two. He rises early in the morning, prompt to set the great wrong right. He warns his people. He restores Sarah with munificent presents. His reproach and rebuke are spoken in the gentlest, kindest tones. He simply tells Sarah that her position as the wife of a prophet would be a sufficient security and veil (v. 16). There is the air of high-minded nobility in his behavior that is exceedingly winsome.

Let us ponder, as we close, some practical lessons:

a. *We are never safe as long as we are in this world.* Abraham was an old man. Thirty years had passed since that sin had last shown itself. Never boast against once-cherished sins: only by God's grace are they kept in check; and if you cease to abide in Christ, they will revive and revisit you.

b. *We have no right to throw ourselves into the way of the temptation that has often mastered us.* Those who daily cry, "Lead us not into temptation," should see to it that they do not court the temptation against which they pray. We must not expect angels to catch us every time we choose to cast ourselves from the mountian brow.

c. *We may be encouraged by God's treatment of Abraham's sin.* Although God had a secret controversy with His child, He did not put him away. He told Abimelech that he was a dead man; He stopped him by the ministry of an ominous disease; and bade him apply to the intercession of the very man by whom he had been so grievously misled, and who, in spite of all his failures, was a prophet still, having power with God.

Have you sinned, bringing disrepute on the name of God? Do not despair. Go alone, as Abraham must have done, and confess your sin with tears and childlike trust. Trust then in the patience and forgiveness of God, and let His love, as consuming fire, rid you of concealed and hidden sin.

19

Hagar and Ishmael Cast Out
Genesis 21:10

The Almighty lover of souls knew the trial that awaited His child, and He set Himself to prepare him for it by ridding him of certain clinging inconsistencies that would have paralyzed the action of his faith in the hour of trial. We have already seen how one of these—the secret compact between Abraham and Sarah—was exposed to the light and judged. We have now to see how another matter, the patriarch's connection with Hagar and her child, was also dealt with by Him.

In what way the presence of Hagar and Ishmael hindered the development of Abraham's noblest life of faith, we cannot entirely understand. Did his heart still cling to the girl who had given him his firstborn son? Was there any secret satisfaction in the arrangement, which had at least achieved one cherished purpose, though it had been unblessed by God? Was there any fear that if he were summoned to surrender Isaac, he would find it easier to do so, because he could fall back on Ishmael, as both son and heir? One darling idol after another was rent away that he himself might be cast naked and helpless on the omnipotence of the Eternal God. "The thing was very grievous in Abraham's sight" (v. 11).

The final separation from Abraham of ingredients that would have been prejudicial to the exercise of a supreme faith was brought about by the birth of the long-promised child, which is alluded to at the beginning of this chapter (Gen. 21), and which led up to the crisis with which we are now dealing.

"The LORD visited Sarah as he had said, and the LORD did unto Sarah as he had spoken" (Gen. 21:1). It is impossible to trust God too absolutely. God's least word is a spar of imperishable wood driven into the Rock of Ages, which will never give, and on which you may hang your entire weight forever.

1. But we must be prepared to wait God's time. "Sarah bare Abraham a son in his old age, *at the set time* of which God had spoken to him." The set time came at last; and then the laughter that filled the patriarch's home made the aged pair forget the long and weary vigil. "And Abraham called the name of his son that was born unto him, whom Sarah bare unto him, Isaac" (that is "Laughter"). Take heart, waiting one, who waits for One who cannot disappoint you; and who will not be five minutes behind the appointed moment: before long "your sorrow shall be turned into joy."

The laughter of incredulity, with which Sarah received the first intimation of her approaching motherhood (18:12), was now exchanged for the laughter of fulfilled hope.

Ah, happy soul, when God makes you laugh! Then sorrow and crying shall flee away forever, as darkness before the dawn.

The peace of Abraham's house remained at first unbroken, though there may have been some slight symptoms of the rupture that was at hand. The dislike that Sarah had manifested to Hagar, long years before, had never been extinguished: it had only smoldered in her heart, waiting for some slight incident to stir it again into a blaze. Nor had the warm passionate nature of Hagar ever forgotten those hard dealings that had driven her away, to fare as best she might in the inhospitable desert. Abraham must often have been sorely put to it to keep the peace between them. At last the women's quarters could conceal the quarrel no longer, and the scandal broke out into the open.

2. The immediate occasion of this open rupture was the weaning of the young Isaac. "The child grew, and was weaned : and Abraham made a great feast the same day that Isaac was weaned." But amid all the bright joy of that happy occasion, one shadow suddenly stole over the scene, and brooded on the mother's soul. Sarah's jealous eye saw Ishmael mocking. And that should be no surprise. This awoke all Sarah's slumbering jealousy, which may often have been severely tested during the last few years by Ishmael's assumption and independent bearing. She would stand it no longer. Why should she, the chieftain's wife, and mother of his heir, brook the insolence of a slave? And so she said to Abraham with a sneer and the sting of the old jealousy, "Cast out this bondwoman and her son: for the son of this bondwoman shall not be heir with my son, even with Isaac."

3. We cannot but recall the use that the Apostle Paul makes of this incident. In his days the Jews, priding themselves on being the lineal descendents of Abraham, refused to consider it possible that any but themselves could be children of God, and the heirs of promise. They arrogated to themselves exclusive privileges and position. And when large numbers of Gentiles were born into the Christian church under the first preaching of the gospel, and claimed to be the spiritual seed with all the rights pertaining thereto; they who, like Ishmael, were simply born after the flesh, persecuted them who, like Isaac, were born after the Spirit. The Jews everywhere set themselves to resist the preaching of the gospel, which denied to them their exclusive privileges; and to harry those who would not enter the church through the rites of Judaism. And before long the Jewish nation was rejected, put aside, cast out. Succeeding ages have seen the

building up of the church from among the once-persecuted ones, while the children of Abraham have wandered in the wilderness fainting for the true water of life (Gal. 4:29).

4. BUT THERE IS STILL DEEPER REFERENCE. Hagar, the slave, who may even have been born in the Sinaitic Desert, with which she seems to have been so familiar, is a fitting representative of the spirit of legalism and bondage, seeking to win life by the observance of the law, which was given from those hoary cliffs. Hagar is the covenant of Mount Sinai in Arabia, "which gendereth to bondage," and "is in bondage with her children" (Gal. 4:24–25). Sarah, the free woman, on the other hand, represents the covenant of free grace. Her children are love, and faith, and hope; they are not bound by the spirit of "must," but by the promptings of spontaneous gratitude; their home is not in the frowning clefts of Sinai, but in Jerusalem above, which is free, and is the mother of us all. Now, argues the apostle, there was no room for Hagar and Sarah, with their respective children, in Abraham's tent. If Ishmael was there, it was because Isaac was not born. But as soon as Isaac came in, Ishmael must go out. So the two principles—of legalism, which insists on the performance of the outward rite of circumcision; and of faith, which accepts the finished work of the Savior—cannot coexist in one heart. It is a moral impossibility. So, addressing the Galatian converts, who were being tempted by Judaizing teachers mix legalism and faith, the apostle bade them follow the example of Abraham, and cast out the spirit of bondage that keeps the soul in one perpetual agony of unrest.

5. THE REMAINING HISTORY IS BRIEFLY TOLD. With many a pang Abraham sent Hagar and her child from his home, bidding them a last, sad farewell. In the dim twilight they left, before the camp was astir. Abraham must have suffered keenly as he put the bread into her hand, and with his own fingers bound the bottle of water on her shoulder, and kissed Ishmael once more.

It was better so. And God provided for them both. When the mother's hopes were on the point of expiring, and her son lay dying of thirst in the scorching noon, under the slender shade of a desert shrub, the Angel of God stayed her sobs, pointed out the well of water to which her tears had made her blind, and promised that her child would become a great nation. "And God said unto Abraham, Let it not be grievous in thy sight . . . in all that Sarah hath said unto thee, hearken unto her voice" (21:12).

One more weight was laid aside, and one more step taken in the preparation of God's "friend" for the supreme victory of his faith; for which his whole life had been a preparation, and which was now at hand.

20

A Quiet Resting Place
Genesis 21:33–34

We have already seen how wisely and tenderly Abraham's Almighty Friend had been preparing him for his approaching trial; first, in searching out his hidden compact with Sarah; and then in ridding him of the presence of Hagar and her son. And now some further preparation was to be wrought in his spirit, through this period of peaceful rest beside the well of the oath. Leaving Gerar, the patriarch traveled with his slow-moving flocks along the fertile valley, which extends from the sea into the country. Having reached a suitable camping ground, Abraham dug a well, which is probably one of those that remain to this day; and of which the water lying some forty feet below the surface is pure and sweet. Drinking troughs for the use of cattle are scattered around in close proximity to the mouth of the well, the curbstones of which are deeply worn by the friction of the ropes used in drawing up the water by hand. It is not improbable that these very stones were originally hewn under the patriarch's direction, even though their position may have been somewhat altered by the Arab workmen of a later date.

Shortly after Abraham had settled there, Abimelech the king, accompanied by Phichol, the chief captain of his host, came to his encampment, intent on entering into a treaty that would be binding, not only on themselves, but on their children: "Swear unto me here by God, that thou wilt not deal falsely with me, nor with my son, nor with my son's son" (v. 23). Before formally binding himself under these solemn sanctions, Abraham brought up a matter that is still a subject of dispute in Eastern lands. The herdsman of Abimelech had violently taken away the well of water that the servants of Abraham had dug. But the king immediately repudiated all knowledge of their action. It had been done without his knowledge and sanction. And in the treaty into which the two chieftains entered, there was, so to speak, a special clause inserted with reference to this well, destined later to be so famous. It was called "Beer-sheba," the well of the oath, or "the well of the seven," with reference to the seven gifts, or victims, on which the oath was taken.

In further commemoration of this treaty, Abraham planted a tamarisk tree which, as a hardy evergreen, would long perpetuate the memory of the transaction in those lands where the mind of man eagerly catches at anything that will break the monotony of the landscape. There also he erected an altar, or shrine, and called on the name of the Lord, the Everlasting God. "And Abraham sojourned in the land of the Philistines many days." Ah! those long, happy days! Who could have foretold that the greatest trial of all his life was yet to come, and that from a clear sky a thunderbolt was about to fall, threatening to destroy all his happiness at a single stroke?

1. LET US LIVE BY THE WELL. There is a great tendency among Christians today to magnify special places and scenes that have been associated with times of blessing; but so many of these, and of others, are in danger of forgetting that instead of making an annual pilgrimage to the well, they should take up their abode beside it, and live there.

The water of that well speaks of the life of God, which is in Jesus Christ our Lord, and is stored up for us in the fathomless depths of the Word of God. The well is deep; yet faith's bucket can reach its precious contents and bring them to thirsty lip and yearning heart. Oh for a practical realization of what Jesus meant when He said, "The water that I shall give him shall be in him a well of water, springing up into everlasting life."

Open your hearts to the teaching of the Holy Ghost. Rest content with nothing short of a deep and loving knowledge of the Bible.

2. LET US TAKE SHELTER BENEATH THE COVENANT. Abraham was quiet from the fear of evil, because of Abimelech's oath. How much more sure and restful should be the believing soul, which shelters beneath that everlasting covenant that is "ordered in all

things and sure." There are some Christians doubtful of their eternal salvation, and fearful lest they should ultimately fall away from grace and be lost, to whom this advice is peculiarly appropriate: "Live by the well of the oath."

The one question is, Do you believe in Jesus Christ? Or, to put it still more simply, Are you willing that the Holy Ghost should create in you a living faith in the Savior of people? If so, you may appropriate to yourself the blessings of the covenant confirmed by the counsel and oath of God.

This, then, becomes true of us, if we believe. We are forgiven; our name is inscribed on the roll of the saved; we are adopted into the family of God; we have within us the beginning of a life that is eternal as the life of God. And shall this not comfort us amid many heartbreaking sorrows? Nothing can break the bonds by which our souls are knit with the eternal God.

Rejoice in all the good things that the Lord your God gives you. Plant your trees; be comforted by their shade, and fed by their fruit. Listen to the ringing laughter of your Isaac. Dread not the future; but trust the great love of God. Live by the well, and take shelter beneath the covenant. So, if trial approaches you will be the better able to meet it with a calm strong heart.

21

The Greatest Trial of All
Genesis 22:2

As long as men live in the world, they will turn to this story with unwaning interest.

1. "GOD DID TEMPT ABRAHAM." A better rendering might be "God did put Abraham to the test." Satan tempts us that he may bring out the evil that is in our hearts; God tries or tests us that He may bring out all the good.

The common incidents of daily life, as well as the rare incessant opportunities of exercising, and so strengthening, and exceptional crises, are so contrived as to give us the graces of Christian living.

2. GOD SENDS US NO TRIAL, WHETHER GREAT OR SMALL, WITHOUT FIRST PREPARING US. He "will with the temptation also make a way to escape, that ye may be able to bear it" (1 Cor. 10:13). Trials are therefore God's vote of confidence in us. Many a trifling event is sent to test us before a greater trial is permitted to break on our heads. "It came to pass *after these things,* that God did tempt Abraham."

3. GOD OFTEN PREPARES US FOR COMING TRIAL BY GIVING US SOME NEW AND BLESSED REVE-LATION OF HIMSELF. I notice that at the close of the preceding chapter we are told that "Abraham called on the name of the LORD, the everlasting God." We do not learn that he had ever looked on God in this light before. He had known Him as God, the Almighty (17:1), but not as God, the Everlasting. The unchangeableness, the eternity, the independence of change, and time, and tense, which mark the being of Jehovah— all these broke suddenly on his soul about that time in a fresh and more vivid manner. The new name was to enable him to better withstand the shock of coming sorrow.

4. THE TRIAL TOUCHED ABRAHAM AT HIS TENDEREST POINT. It concerned his Isaac. Nothing else in the circumference of his life could have been such a test as something connected with their heir of promise, the child of his old age, the laughter of his life. *His love was tested.* For love of God, he had done much. But at whatever cost, he had always put God first, glad to sacrifice all, for very love of Him. For this he had torn himself from Charran; for this he had been willing to become a homeless wanderer; for this he had renounced the hopes he had built on Ishmael, driving him, as a scapegoat, into the wilderness to return no more. But if he had been asked if he felt that he loved God most of all, he perhaps would not have dared to say that he did. We can never gauge our love by feeling. The only true test of love is how much we are prepared to do for the one to whom we profess it. But God knew how true and strong His child's love was, and that he loved Him best. So He put him to a supreme test, that all men might hereafter know that a mortal man can love God so much as to put Him first, though his dearest lay in the opposite scale of the balance of the heart. Would you not like to love God like this? Then tell Him you are willing to pay the cost, if only He will create that love within you.

5. IT WAS ALSO A GREAT TEST OF HIS FAITH. Isaac was the child of promise. "In Isaac shall thy seed be called." With reiterated emphasis this boy had been indicated as the one essential link between the aged pair and the vast posterity that was promised them. And now the father was asked to sacrifice his son's life. It was a tremendous test to his faith. How could God keep His word, and let Isaac die? It was utterly inexplicable to human thought. If Isaac had been old enough to have a son who could perpetuate the seed to future generations, the difficulty would have been removed. But how could the child-less Isaac die, and still the promise stand of a posterity through him, innumerable as stars and sand? As the Epistle to the Hebrews tells us, one thought filled the old man's mind, *God is able.* He "accounted that God was able to raise him up, even from the dead" (Heb. 11:19). He felt sure that somehow God would keep His word. It was not for him to reason how, but simply to obey. He had already seen divine power giving life where all was as good as dead; why should it not do it again? In any case he must go on, doing as he was told, and calculating on the unexhaustable stores in the secret hand of God. Oh, for faith like this! To simply believe what God says; to be assured that God will do just what He has promised; looking without alarm, from circumstances that threaten to make the fulfillment impossible, to the bare word of God's unswerving truthfulness.

6. IT WAS A TEST OF ABRAHAM'S OBEDIENCE. It was in the visions of the night that the word of the Lord must have come to him, and early the next morning the patriarch was on his way. The night before, as he lay down, he did not have the least idea of the mission on which he would be started at the early beams of dawn. But he acted immediately. "And Abraham rose up early in the morning" (v. 3). No other hand was permitted to saddle the ass, or cleave the wood, or interfere with the promptness of his action. He "saddled his ass . . . and clave the wood for the burnt offering, and rose up, and went unto the place of which God had told him."

7. THIS TEST DID NOT OUTRAGE ANY OF THE NATURAL INSTINCTS OF HIS SOUL. First of all, he was too familiar with God's voice to mistake it. Too often had he listened to it to make a mistake in this solemn crisis. And he was sure that God had some way of deliverance,

which, though he might not be able to forecast it, would secure the sparing of Isaac's life. Besides, he lived at a time when such sacrifices as that to which he was called were very common; and he had never been taught decisively that they were abhorrent to the mind of his almighty Friend. One of the first principles of that old Canaanitish religion demanded that men should give their firstborn for their transgression, the fruit of their body for the sin of their soul. It was not that fathers were less tender than now, but because they had a keener sense of the terror of unforgiven sin that they cowered before gods whom they knew not, and to whom they imputed a thirst for blood and suffering. They counted no cost too great to appease the awful demands that ignorance, and superstition, and a consciousness of sin made on them.

Perhaps Abraham had lately witnessed these rites; and as he did so, he had thought of Isaac. He may have wondered if he could do the same with him, and marveled why such a sacrifice had never been demanded at his hands. So it did not startle him when God said, "Take now thy son . . . and offer him up." He was to learn that while God demanded as much love as the heathen gave their cruel and imaginary deities, yet heaven would not permit human sacrifices or the offering of sons. A greater Sacrifice was to be made to put away sin. Abraham's obedience was therefore allowed to go up to a certain point, and then peremptorily stayed—that in all future time we might know that God would not demand, or permit, or accept human blood at our hands, much less the blood of a bright and noble boy; and that in such things He could have no delight.

What those three days of quiet traveling must have been to Abraham, we can never know. And yet, despite the patriarch's preoccupation with his own special sorrow, the necessity was laid on him to hide it under an appearance of resignation, and even happiness; so that neither his son nor his servants might guess the agony that was gnawing at his heart.

At last, on the third day, he saw from afar the goal of his journey. God had informed him that He would tell him which of the mountains was the appointed spot of the sacrifice. Tradition, which seems well authenticated, has always associated that "mountain in the land of Moriah" with the place on which, years later, stood the threshing floor of Araunah the Jebusite, and the site of Solomon's Temple; and there is a wonderful appropriateness in the fact that this great act of obedience took place on the very spot where hecatombs of victims and rivers of blood were to point to that supreme Sacrifice that this prefigured.

As soon as the mountain came into view, Abraham said unto his young men: "Abide ye here with the ass; and I and the lad will go yonder and worship, and come again to you." What a significant expression, in this connection, is that word *worship!* It reflects the mood of the patriarch's mind. He was preoccupied with that Being, at whose command he had gone forth on this sorrowful errand. He looked on his God, at the moment when He was asking so great a gift, as only deserving adoration and worship. It seemed to him as if his costliest and dearest treasure was not too great to give to that great and glorious God who was the one object of his life.

It is of the utmost importance that we should emphasize the words of *assured confidence* that Abraham addressed to his young men before he left them. "I and the lad will go yonder and worship, and come again to you." This was something more than unconscious prophecy: it was the assurance of an unwavering faith that somehow or other God would interpose to spare his son; or at least, if necessary, to raise him from the dead. In any case Abraham was sure that Isaac and he would before long come again.

8. THE INFLUENCE OF ABRAHAM'S BEHAVIOR WAS FELT BY HIS SON. He caught his father's spirit. We do not know how old he was; he was at least old enough to sustain the toil of a long march on foot, and strong enough to carry uphill the wood, laid on his shoulders by his father. But he gladly bent his youthful strength under the weight of the wood, just as through the *Via Dolorosa* a greater than he carried His cross. It is beautiful to see the evident interest the boy took in the proceedings as they went "both of them together."

At all previous sacrifices Abraham had taken a lamb with him, but on this occasion Isaac's wondering attention was drawn to the fact there was no lamb to offer, and with a simplicity that must have touched Abraham to the quick, he said, "My father . . . behold the fire and the wood: but where is the lamb for a burnt offering?" What a stab this was to Abraham's sorely tried heart. With a gleam of prophetic insight, mingled with unwavering faith in Him for whose sake he was suffering, the father answered, "My son, God will provide himself a lamb for a burnt offering; so they went both of them together."

9. AT LAST THE DISCOVERY COULD NO LONGER BE WITHHELD. "They came to the place which God had told him of; and Abraham built an altar there, and laid the wood in order." Can you not see the old man slowly gathering the stones, bringing them from the furthest distance possible, placing them with a reverent and judicious precision, and binding the wood with as much deliberation as possible? But at last everything is complete, and Abraham turns to break the fatal secret to his young son who has stood wonderingly by. Inspiration draws a veil over that last tender scene—the father's announcement of his mission, the broken sobs, the kisses wet with tears, the instant submission of the son who was old enough and strong enough to rebel if he had had the mind. Then the binding of that tender frame which, indeed, needed no compulsion because the young heart had learned the secret of obedience and resignation. Finally, the lifting him to lie upon the altar, on the wood. Here was a spectacle that must have arrested the attention of heaven. Here was a proof of how much mortal man will do for the love of God. Here was an evidence of childlike faith that must have thrilled the heart of the eternal God, and moved Him in the very depths of His being. Do you and I love God like this? Is He more to us than our nearest and dearest? Suppose they stood on this side, and He on that side: would we go with Him, though it cost us the loss of all? You think you would. It is a great thing to say.

The blade was raised high, flashing in the rays of the morning sun, but it was not permitted to fall. With the temptation God also made a way of escape. "And the angel of the LORD called upon him out of heaven, and said, Abraham!" Abraham would surely seize at anything that offered the chance of respite or of pause! and he said, his uplifted hand returning gladly to his side, "Here am I!" Then followed words that spoke release and deliverance: "Lay not thine hand upon the lad, neither do thou any thing upon him: for now I know that thou fearest God, seeing thou hast not withheld thy son, thine only son, from me" (v. 12).

"Abraham called the name of that place Jehovah-jireh" (The Lord will provide). So it passed into a proverb, and men said one to another, "In the mount of the Lord deliverance shall be seen." It is a true word. Deliverance is not seen till we come to the mount of sacrifice. God does not provide deliverance until we have reached the point of our extremest need. It is when our Isaac is on the altar, and the knife is about to descend on him, that God's angel interposes to deliver.

Near the altar was a thicket, and, as Abraham lifted up his eyes and looked around, he beheld a ram caught there by its horns. Nothing could be more opportune. He had wanted to show his gratitude and the fullness of his heart's devotion, and he gladly went and took the ram, and offered him up for a burnt offering in place of his son. Here, surely, is the great doctrine of substitution; and we are taught how life can be preserved only at the cost of life given.

Abraham's act enables us better to understand the sacrifice that God made to save us. The gentle submission of Isaac, laid on the altar with throat bare to the knife, gives us a better insight into Christ's obedience to death. Isaac's restoration to life, as from the dead, and after having been three days dead in his father's purpose, suggests the resurrection from Joseph's tomb.

Before they left the mountain brow, God said: "By myself have I sworn . . . because thou hast done this thing, and hast not withheld thy son, thine only son: that in blessing I will bless thee; and in multiplying I will multiply thy seed as the stars of heaven, and as the sand which is upon the sea shore; and thy seed shall possess the gate of his enemies; and in thy seed shall all the nations of the earth be blessed; because thou hast obeyed my voice" (vv. 16–17). Do not think, O soul of man, that this is a unique and solitary experience. There is nothing that God will not do for a man who dares to step out upon what seems to be the mist; who then finds rock beneath him as he puts his foot down.

10. ALL WHO BELIEVE ARE THE CHILDREN OF FAITHFUL ABRAHAM. We then, Gentiles though we are, divided from Abraham by the lapse of centuries, may inherit the blessing that he won; and the more so as we follow closely in his steps. That blessing is for us if we will claim it. With a new light in his heart, with a new composure on his face, Abraham returned to his young men. "And they rose up and went together to Beersheba; and Abraham dwelt at Beersheba," but the halo of the vision lit up the common places of his life, as it shall do for us, when from the mounts of sacrifice we turn back to the lowlands of daily duty.

22

Machpelah, and its First Tenant
Genesis 23:4, 19

When Abraham came down the slopes of Mount Moriah, hand in hand with Isaac, fifty years of his long life still lay before him. Of those fifty years, twenty-five passed away before the event recorded in this chapter. In all likelihood one year was as much as possible like another. Few events broke their monotony.

Perhaps we can never realize how much the members of such a household as Abraham's would be to one another. Through long, unbroken periods they lived together, finding all their society in one another. Thus it must have happened that the loss through death of one loved and familiar face would leave a blank never to be filled, and scarcely ever to be forgotten. We need not wonder, therefore, that so much stress is laid on the death of Sarah, the chief event of those fifty years of Abraham's life.

Abraham

1. WE ARE FIRST ARRESTED BY ABRAHAM'S TEARS. "And Sarah died in Kirjath-arba; the same is Hebron in the land of Canaan." Abraham seems to have been away from home, perhaps at Beersheba, when Sarah breathed her last; but he came at once "to mourn for Sarah, and to weep for her." This is the first time we read of Abraham weeping. But now that Sarah is lying dead before him, the fountains of his grief are broken up.

Sarah had been the partner of his life for seventy or eighty years. She was the only link to the home of his childhood. She alone could sympathize with him when he talked of Terah and Nahor, or of Haran and Ur of the Chaldees. She alone was left of all who thirty years before had shared the hardships of his pilgrimage. As he knelt by her side, what a tide of memories must have rushed over him of their common plans, and hopes, and fears, and joys! He remembered her as the bright young wife, as his pilgrim, as the childless persecutor of Hagar, as the prisoner of Pharoah and Abimelech, as the loving mother of Isaac, and every memory would bring a fresh rush of tears.

There are some who chide tears as unmanly, unsubmissive, unchristian. They would comfort us with a chill and pious stoicism, bidding us meet the most agitating passages of our history with rigid and tearless countenance. With such the spirit of the gospel and of the Bible, has little sympathy. Religion does not come to make us un- natural and inhuman, but to purify and ennoble all those natural emotions with which our complex nature is endowed. Jesus wept. Peter wept. The Ephesian converts wept on the neck of the apostle whose face they thought they were never to see again. Christ still stands by each mourner, saying, "Weep, my child; weep, for I have wept."

2. NOTICE ABRAHAM'S CONFESSION. "Abraham stood up from before his dead, and spake unto the sons of Heth, saying, I am a stranger and a sojourner with you: give me a possession of a buryingplace with you" (vv. 3–4). See how sorrow reveals the heart. To look at Abraham as the great and wealthy patriarch, the emir, the chieftain of a mighty clan, we cannot guess his secret thoughts. He has been in the land for sixty-two years; and he is probably as settled and naturalized as any of the princes round. So you might think, until he is widowed of his beloved Sarah! Then, admist his grief, you hear the real man speaking his most secret thought: "I am a stranger and a sojourner with you."

These are remarkable words, and they were never forgotten by his children. So deeply had those words of Abraham sunk in the national mind, that the apostle inscribes them over the cemetery where the great and the good of the Jewish nation lie en- tombed: "These all died in faith, not having received the promises, but having seen them afar off, and were persuaded of them, and embraced them, and confessed that they were strangers and pilgrims on the earth" (Heb. 11:13).

We may ask what it was that maintained this spirit in Abraham for so many years. There is but one answer: "They that say such things declare plainly that they seek a country" (Heb. 11:14). Uprooted from the land of his birth, the patriarch could never take root again in any earthly country, and his spirit was always on the alert, eagerly reaching out toward the city of God. He refused to be contented with anything short of this, and therefore God was not ashamed to be called his God, because He had prepared for him a city. How this elevation of soul shames some of us! We profess to look for a city, but we take good care to make for ourselves an assured position among the citizens of this world. We profess to count all things as dross, but the eagerness with which, muckrake in hand, we strive to heap together the treasures of earth is a startling commentary on our words.

3. Notice Abraham's faith. Men are wont to bury their dead alongside their ancestors. The graves of past generations are the heritage of their posterity. The American loves to visit the quiet English churchyard where his fathers lie. The Jew elects in old age to journey to Palestine, that dying he may be buried in soil consecrated by the remains of his race. And it may be that Abraham first thought of that far distant grave in Charran, where Terah and Haran lay buried. Should he take Sarah there? He decided against it, saying, "that country, has no claim on me now. The only land on which I have a claim is this wherein I have been a stranger. Here in years to come shall my children live. Here the generations that bear my name shall spread themselves out as the sands on the seashore, and as the stars in the midnight sky. It is therefore necessary that I should place our grave, in which Sarah their mother, and I their father, shall lie, in the heart of the land—to be a nucleus around which our descendants shall gather in years to come."

When the chieftains to whom he made his appeal heard it, they instantly offered him the choice of their sepulcher affirming that none of them could withhold his sepulcher from so mighty a prince. And afterward, when he sought their intercession with Ephron the son of Zohar, for the obtaining of the cave of Machpelah, which was at the end of his field, and Ephron proposed to give it him in the presence of the sons of his people, Abraham steadfastly refused. So, after many courteous speeches, in the dignified manner that still prevails amongst Orientals, "the field, and the cave . . . and all the trees . . . were made sure unto Abraham for a possession in their presence of the children of Heth, before all that went in at the gate of his city" (vv. 17–18). Their witness had the same binding effect in those rude days as legal documents have in our own.

There Abraham buried Sarah; there Isaac and Ishmael buried Abraham; there Isaac was buried, and Rebecca his wife; there Jacob buried Leah; and there Joseph buried Jacob his father; and there in all likelihood, guarded by the jealous Moslem, untouched by the changes and storms that have swept around their quiet resting place, those remains are sleeping still, holding that land in fee, and anticipating the time when on a larger and more prominent scale the promise of God to Abraham will be accomplished.

23

The Soul's Answer to the Divine Summons
Genesis 24:58

Think back thirty-seven centuries. The soft light of an Oriental sunset falls gently on the fertile grazing grounds watered by the broad Euphrates, and as its gloom lights up all the landscapes dotted by flocks, and huts, and villages, it irradiates with an especial wealth of color the little town of Haran, founded one hundred years before by Terah, who, traveling northward from Ur, resolved to go no further. The old man was hurting deeply at the recent loss of his youngest son, and after him the infant settlement was named. There Terah died, and from there the caravan had started at the command of God across the terrible desert for the unknown Land of Promise. One branch of the family, however—that of Nahor—lived there still. His son, Bethuel, was the head; and in that family, at the time of which I speak, there was at least a mother, a brother named Laban, and a young daughter, Rebekah.

It is Rebekah who occupies the central place in the pastoral scene before us. All her young life had been spent in that old town. She knew by name all the people who dwelt in that little town, and she had heard of those of her kindred who before her birth had gone beyond the great desert, and of whom hardly a word had traveled back for so many years. She little guessed the greatness of the world, and in her wildest dreams she never thought of doing more than living and dying within the narrow limits of her native place. Elastic in step, modest in manner, pure in heart, amiable and generous, with a very fair face, as the sacred story tells us—how little did she imagine that the wheel of God's providence was soon to catch her out of her quiet home, and whirl her into the mighty outer world that lay beyond the horizon of desert sand.

One special evening a stranger halted at the well outside the little town. He had with him a stately caravan of ten camels, each richly laden, and all bearing traces of long travel. There the little band waited, as if not knowing what to do next. Its leader was probably the good Eliezer, the steward of Abraham's house. Abraham was now advanced in years. Isaac his son was forty years of age, and the old man longed to see him suitably married. Though his faith never doubted that God would fulfill His promise of the seed, yet he was desirous of clasping in his aged arms the second link between him and his posterity. He had therefore bound his trusty servant by a double oath: first, that he would not take a wife for Isaac from the daughters of the Canaanites around them, but from his own kin at Haran; and second, that he would never be an accomplice to Isaac's return to the land he had left.

Having arrived at the city well toward nightfall—"even, the time that women go out to draw water"—the devout leader asked that God would send him "good speed," addressing the Almighty as the Lord God of his master Abraham, and pleading that in prospering his way He would show kindness to his master. The simplicity and trustfulness of his prayer are beautiful, and are surely the reflection of the piety that reigned in that vast encampment gathered around the wells of Beersheba, and which was the result of Abraham's own close walk with God.

It is our privilege to talk with God about everything in life. The minutest things are not too small for Him who numbers the hairs of our heads. It was a holy and a happy inspiration that led the godly servant to ask that the damsel who responded with courteous promptness to his request for water should be she whom God had appointed as a bride for his master's son; and it happened to him as it will always happen to those who have learned to trust like little children, that "before he had done speaking," his answer was waiting by his side.

We need not tell in detail all that followed: the gifts of heavy jewelry; the reverent recognition of God's goodness in answering prayer, as the man bowed his head and worshiped the Lord; the swift run home; the admiration of mother and brother at the splendid gifts; the breathless telling of the unexpected meeting; the proffered hospitality of Laban, whose notions of hospitality were quickened by his keen eye for gain, and who spoke the words of welcome with extra heat because he saw the rich lading of the camels; the provision of straw and provender for the camels, of water for the feet of the weary drivers, and of food for their leader, and the refusal to eat until his errand was unraveled and its purpose accomplished; the story, told in glowing words, of Abraham's greatness; the narrative of the wonderful way in which the speaker had been led, and Rebekah indicated; the final request that her relatives would deal kindly and truly in the matter; and their unhesitating and swift consent in words that drew the old servant prostrate to the ground in holy ecstasy as he worshiped the Lord. "Behold," they said, "Rebekah is before thee; take her and go, and let her be thy master's son's wife, as the LORD hath spoken."

Then from his treasures he brought forth jewels of silver and jewels of gold, and raiment with which to deck Rebekah's fair form; her mother and Laban also received precious things to their heart's desire. "And they did eat and drink, he and the men that were with him, and tarried all night." In the early dawn, refusing all invitation to stay longer, Abraham's steward started back again, taking with him Rebekah and her nurse; and through the fragrant morning air she caught the last voice from her home. They addressed Rebekah and said to her, "Thou art our sister, be thou the mother of thousands of millions; and let thy seed possess the gate of those which hate them."

We must thus pass over the details of this story, but let us elicit two or three lessons to illustrate by it the divine summons, and the answer of the soul.

1. A LESSON TO THOSE WHO CARRY THE SUMMONS OF GOD.

a. *Let us saturate our work with prayer.* Like his master, the servant would not take a single step without prayer. He had a most difficult thing to do. Was it likely that a young girl would leave her home to cross the vast expanse of sand in company with a complete stranger, and become the wife of one whom she had never seen? "Peradventure the woman will not follow me!" and even if she was willing, her relatives might not be. But Eliezer prayed, and prayed again, and God's good speed crowned his errand with complete success.

We too are sometimes sent on very unlikely errands, Humanly speaking, our mission seems likely to prove a failure, but those who trust in God do not have the word "failure" in their vocabulary. They succeed where they seem menaced with certain disappointment. Christian worker! never start on any mission for God, whether to an individual soul or to a congregation, without the prayer, "Send me good speed this day."

b. *Let us say much in praise of our Master.* It is beautiful to notice how eloquent the old man is about his master. He does not say one word about himself, or extol himself in any way, so absorbed was he in the story of his absent, distant lord. Was not this also characteristic of the apostles, who preached not themselves, but Christ Jesus the Lord; and whose narratives are like colorless glass, only letting His glory through? Let us also lose ourselves in our theme. And when success attends our words, we must be sure to give all the glory to Him from whom it has come.

2. THE SUMMONS ITSELF was a call to a simple, penniless girl to ally herself in marriage to one of the wealthiest and noblest of earth's aristocracy. It was not sent because of her worth, or wealth, or beauty; but because it was so willed in the heart and counsel of Abraham. Such a call is sent to every soul that hears the gospel. He has one Son, His only-begotten and well-beloved. He has resolved to choose from among men those who as one church shall constitute His bride forever. He sends this call to you, not because you are worthy, or wealthy, or beautiful; but because He has so willed it in the counsel of His own heart.

And if that call is obeyed, you will lose your own name, sinner, in His name; you will be arrayed in His fair jewels; you will share His wealth; you will sit down with Him on His throne; all things will be yours. Will you go with this Man? Will you leave all to be Christ's? Come and put yourself under the convoy of the blessed Holy Spirit, who pleads the cause of Jesus, as did Abraham's servant that Isaac; and let Him lead you to where Jesus is.

3. How to deal with this summons.

a. *We must find room for it.* The Master says, "Where is the guest-chamber?" There was no room for Christ in the inn; but we must make room for Him in the heart.

b. *We must bear witness.* "The damsel ran, and told them of her mother's house." As soon as you have heard the call, and received the jewels of promise, which are the earnest of your inheritance, you must go home to your friends and tell them what great things the Lord has done for you.

c. *We must not procrastinate, or confer with flesh and blood.* Men, and circumstances, would rather defer our starting on pilgrimage. There must be no dallying or delay, but when the inquiry, "Wilt thou go with this man?" is put to us, we must promptly and swiftly answer, "I will go."

The journey was long and toilsome, but all the way the heart of the young girl was sustained by the tidings told her by the faithful servant, who filled the weary miles with stories of the home to which she was journeying, and the man with whom her life was to be united. She already loved him, and ardently longed to see him.

One evening the meeting came. Isaac had gone to meditate at eventide, sadly lamenting the loss of his mother, eagerly anticipating the coming of his bride, and interweaving all with holy thought. And when he lifted up his eyes across the pastures, lo, he saw camels coming, and the two young souls leaped to each other. Happy meeting! Rebekah oblivious to all the trials and hardships of her journey, and the loss of her friends.

And after awhile in that silent home there was again the prattle of children's voices; and for several years the patriarch rejoiced in the presence of his grandchildren to whom he would tell the history of the past, on which his aged soul loved to dwell. And of one narrative those children would never tire; that which told how their father had once climbed the summit of Moriah, to be, as it were, raised from the dead.

24

Gathered to His People
Genesis 25:8

No human name can vie with Abraham's for the widespread reverence it has evoked among all races throughout all time. What was the secret of this widespread renown? It is not because he headed one of the greatest movements of the human family; nor yet because he evinced manly and intellectual vigor; nor because he possessed vast wealth. It was rather the remarkable nobility and grandeur of his religious life that has made him the object of veneration to all generations of mankind.

1. At the basis of his character was a mighty faith. "Abraham believed God." In that faith he left his native land and traveled to one that was promised, but not clearly indicated. In that faith he waited through long years, sure that God would give him the promised child. In that faith he lived a nomad life, dwelling in tents, and making no

attempt to return to the settled country from which he had come out. In that faith he was prepared to offer Isaac, and buried Sarah.

2. To FAITH HE ADDED VIRTUE, OR MANLY COURAGE. What could have been more manly than the speed with which he armed his trained servants; or than the heroism with which he, with a train of undisciplined shepherds, attacked the disciplined bands of Assyria, returning victorious down the long valley of the Jordan?

3. AND TO MANLY COURAGE HE ADDED KNOWLEDGE. All his life he was a student in God's college of divinity. He grew in the knowledge of God and the divine nature, which at the first had been to him a *terra incognita*. An unknown country grew beneath his gaze.

4. AND TO KNOWLEDGE HE ADDED TEMPERANCE, OR SELF-CONTROL. That he was master of himself is evident from the way in which he repelled the offer of the king of Sodom; and curbed his spirit amid the irritations caused by Lot's herdsmen. There is no type of character more attractive than that of the man who is master of himself, because he is the servant of God; and who can rule others rightly because he can rule himself well.

5. AND TO TEMPERANCE, PATIENCE. Speaking of him, the voice of New Testament inspiration affirms that he "patiently endured" (Heb. 6:15). It was no ordinary patience that waited through the long years, not murmuring or complaining, but prepared to abide God's time (Ps. 131:2–3).

6. AND TO HIS PATIENCE HE ADDED GODLINESS. One of Abraham's chief characteristics was his piety—a constant sense of the presence of God in his life, and a love and devotion to Him. Wherever he pitched his tent, there his first care was to erect an altar. Shechem, Hebron, Beersheba—alike saw these tokens of his reverence and love. In every time of trouble he turned as naturally to God as a child to its father; and there was such holy intercourse between his spirit and that of God that the name by which he is now best known throughout the East is *The Friend*.

7. AND TO GODLINESS HE ADDED BROTHERLY KINDNESS. Some men who are devoted toward God are lacking in the more tender qualities toward those most closely knit with them in family bonds. It was not so with Abraham. He was full of affection. Beneath the calm exterior and the erect bearing of the mighty chieftain there beat a warm and affectionate heart. Listen to that passionate cry, "Oh that Ishmael might live before thee!"

8. AND TO BROTHERLY KINDNESS HE ADDED CHARITY, OR LOVE. In his dealings with men he could afford to be generous, openhearted, openhanded; willing to pay the large price demanded for Machpelah's cave without haggling or complaint; destitute of petty pride; right with God, and therefore able to shed on men the rays of a genial, restful noble heart.

9. ALL THESE THINGS WERE IN HIM AND ABOUNDED, and they made him neither barren nor unfruitful; they made his calling and election sure; they prepared for him an abundant entrance into the everlasting kingdom of God our Savior.

10. "ABRAHAM GAVE UP THE GHOST." There was no reluctance in his death; he did not cling to life—he was glad to be gone; and when the angel-messenger summoned him, without a struggle, and with the readiness of glad consent his spirit returned to God who gave it.

11. HE WAS GATHERED TO HIS PEOPLE. This cannot refer to his body, for that did not sleep beside his ancestors, but side by side with Sarah's. Surely then it must refer to his spirit.

What a lovely synonym for death! To die is to rejoin our people; to pass into a world where the great clan is gathering, welcoming with shouts each newcomer through the shadows. Where are your people? I trust they are God's people; and if so, those who bear your name, standing on the other shore, are more numerous than the handful gathered around you here; many whom you have never known, but who know you; many whom you have loved and lost awhile; many who without you cannot be made perfect in their happiness. There they are, rank on rank, company on company, regiment on regiment, watching for your coming. Be sure you do not disappoint them!

12. "AND HIS SONS, ISAAC AND ISHMAEL, BURIED HIM IN THE CAVE OF MACHPELAH." There were great differences between these two. Ishmael, the child of his slave: Isaac, of the wedded wife. Ishmael, the offspring of expediency: Isaac, of promise. Ishmael, wild and masterful, "the wild ass"; strongly marked in his individuality; proud, independent, swift to take an insult, swift to avenge it: Isaac, quiet and retiring, submissive and meek, willing to carry wood, to be kept in the dark, to be bound, to yield up his wells, and to let his wife govern his house. And yet all differences were wiped out in that moment of supreme sorrow; and coming from his desert fastnesses, surrounded by his wild and ruffian freebooters, Ishmael united with the other son of their common father, who had displaced him in his inheritance, and who was so great a contrast to himself; but all differences were smoothed out in that hour.

The remains of the man who had dared to trust God at all costs, and who with pilgrim steps had traversed so many weary miles, were solemnly laid beside the dust of Sarah, his faithful wife. There, in all probability, they rest even to this day, and thence they will be raised at the coming of the King.

Out of materials which were by no means extraordinary, God built up a character with which He could hold fellowship as friend with friend; and a life that has exerted a profound influence on all people since.

JACOB

1

First Impressions
Genesis 25

There are many reasons why the story of Jacob is such an interesting account of a Bible "great."

1. JACOB WAS THE FATHER OF THE JEWISH RACE, AND A TYPICAL JEW. The Jews called themselves by the name of Jacob; and surnamed themselves by the name of Israel (Isa. 44:5). We speak of Jacob, rather than Abraham, as the founder of the people to which he gave his name because, though Abraham was their ancestor, he was not so exclusively. The wild son of the desert claims him as Father as does the industrious Jew. Nor is that all. We Gentiles have reason to be proud that we can trace back our lineage to the first great Hebrew, the man who *crossed over*, and whom God designated as His friend.

No thoughtful person can ignore this wonderful people. Their history is, without doubt, the key to the complications of modern politics; and it may be that their redemption is to be the fruit of that mighty travail, that is beginning to convulse all peoples, announced as it is, by all the national calamities we are seeing today.

If we can understand the life of Jacob, we can understand the history of his people. The extremes which startle us in them are all in him. Like them, he is the most successful schemer of his times; and, like them, he has that deep spirituality, that far-seeing faith, which are the grandest of all qualities, and make a man capable of the highest culture that a human spirit can receive. Like them, he spends the greatest part of his life in exile, and amid trying conditions of toil and sorrow; and, like them, he is inalienably attached to that dear land, his only hold on which was by the promise of God and the graves of the heroic dead.

But Jacob's character was purified by tremendous discipline. Through such discipline his people have been passing for centuries; and surely, before its searching fires, the baser elements of their natures will be expelled, until they recognize the true Joseph of their seed.

2. JACOB ALSO HAS SO MANY POINTS OF CONTACT WITH OURSELVES. His *failings* speak to us. He takes advantage of his brother when hard pressed with hunger. He deceives his father. He meets Laban's guile with guile. He thinks to buy himself out of his trouble with Esau. Mean, crafty and weak, are terms we can apply to him, but who is there who does not feel the germs of this harvest to be within his own breast. "There, but for the grace of God, go I."

His *aspirations* speak to us. We too have our angel-haunted dreams and make our vows when we leave home. We too count hard work a trifle, when inspired by all-mastering love. We too cling in a paroxysm of yearning to the departing angels, that they should bless us before they go. We too get back to our Bethels and bury our idols. We too confess ourselves pilgrims and strangers on the earth. We too recognize the shepherd care of God (Gen. 48:15). We too wait for God's salvation (Gen. 49:18).

His *sorrows* speak to us. In every life there is a leaving home to go forth alone, and a weary struggle for existence, and a limp that reminds us of some awful crisis, and the gray hairs of sorrow. And we have mourned over hopes that have mocked us with their nonfulfillment: "I have not attained" (Gen. 47:9).

What a comfort it is to find that the Bible saints, who now shine as stars in the firmament of heaven, were men of like passion with ourselves! Take heart; for if God was able to take up such men as Jacob and Simon Bar-Jona, and make of them princes and kings, surely He can do as much for you. The discipline may be keen as fire, but the result will be glorious.

3. IN JACOB WE CAN TRACE THE WORKINGS OF DIVINE LOVE. "Jacob have I loved" (Mal. 1:2). It was *prenatal* love. Before Jacob was born, he was the object of God's love (Rom. 9:11). It did not begin because of what we were; and it will continue in spite of what we are.

It was *fervent* love. It was so strong that, in comparison, the love that shone around Esau might almost be termed hatred (Rom. 9:13), for God loved Esau as he loves all men. He hates nothing that He has made. But there were as many degrees of temperature between His love to Jacob and that to Esau, as there are in human hearts between love and hate.

It was a *disciplinary* love. We have low thoughts of love. We can only count that as love that which caresses, and soothes, and says sweet things. We have little notion of a love that can say, "No"; that can use the rod, and scourge, and fire; but such is the love of God.

If we had been asked to tell which of these two men was heaven's favorite, we would, in all likelihood, have selected the wrong one.

Here stands Esau, the shaggy, broad-shouldered, red-haired huntsman, full of generous impulse, affectionate to his aged father, forgiving to the brother who had done him such grievous wrong. He became a chieftain of renown, and the ancestor of a princely line (Gen. 34). And, as we consider him, we are inclined to imitate the words of Samuel, when Jesse's eldest son entered his presence, and say: "Surely, the LORD'S anointed is before him!"

There, on the other hand, is Jacob. He is in his young manhood, an exile from his father's house; in his mature manhood, a hireling, in the employ of a kinsman; in his declining years, worn by anxiety and trouble; in his old age, a stranger in a strange land. Yet *he* was the beloved of God; and it was because of that special love that he was exposed to such searching discipline.

4. JACOB'S LIFE GIVES A CLUE TO THE DOCTRINE OF ELECTION. There is election here. Jacob was the younger son; and his life is as much a gospel for younger sons as is that matchless parable of the prodigal. The children were not born when God foretold and fixed their destiny.

It is impossible to ignore election; it has been truly said to be the key to the order of all nature and history. Some men are evidently born to be the leaders, teachers, masters of mankind. But to what are these elect? To comfort, ease, success? No, for these things fall to the lot rather of the Esaus than the Jacobs. The elect of God seem chosen to bear the brunt of the storms of sorrow, pain, and care.

May we not hold that election refers largely, if not primarily, to the *service* that the elect are qualified to render to others throughout all time? They are elect, not for themselves, or for the sake of their own future, but rather for the sake of the work that their position of privilege may enable them to do for mankind.

This, certainly, has been one result of the election of Jacob and his people. They were elect to be the spiritual leaders and teachers of mankind. Not for the sake of their own comfort, but for the sake of the dark and dying world, God gave them light and life, and sustained them in existence against overwhelming odds, and stored in them streams of spiritual force as in some mighty battery.

This, then, will explain also the terrific discipline through which they passed. It was needed, not for their sakes alone, but for the race they were destined to serve; that they might be set free from deteriorating influences and stand forth as God's chosen vessels, brimming with blessing for the world.

2

The Sale of the Birthright
Genesis 25

These two men were brothers, yes, twin brothers; but brothers could not differ more widely. Before their birth their difference was foretold. At their birth it was evident. From their birth it began to broaden and increase.

They differed in appearance. Esau was rough-skinned and hairy. He would give the impression of great bodily strength, a capacity for vast physical fatigue, and a temperament that would incline him to exciting and hazardous pursuits. Jacob was the reverse: smooth in skin, dark in feature, slight in build, no match for his burly brother in physical force, but more than his match in guile.

They differed in pursuits. Esau was a cunning hunter, a man of the field and chase. Jacob, on the other hand, loved the home life. The violent exercise and hazards for which Esau pined, had no fascination for him. And while Esau was away, he was content with the peaceful occupations of an uneventful pastoral life. Each man to his taste!

They differed most in character. There is much in Esau that makes us like him; and we would certainly have been more quickly attracted to him than to his brother. If he was impetuous, he was generous. If he was rash, he was frank. If he was singularly wanting in religious fervor, he was a good son. If his heart doted on the pleasures of the chase, he was good company, and every inch a man. But, for all this, he was decidedly sensual—Scripture calls him *profane*—i.e., he was a slave to his senses; he hailed anything and everything that would thrill him with pleasant though transient excitement.

Jacob was a "plain" man (a "quiet" man) but under that calm exterior there were depths and depths. Amid all the craft and duplicity of his nature, there was immense capacity for religious fervor and religious faith. He could understand, as Esau never could, the meaning of the birthright, with all its spiritual glow and glory. And while Esau was occupied with pleasure, Jacob could feel within him the strange stirrings of a nature that could not be satisfied with anything within the narrow limits of his tents, but which yearned for that spiritual heritage that was summed up in the word "birthright."

Let us consider the Birthright, the Barter, and the Bitter Cry.

Jacob

1. THE BIRTHRIGHT. What was it? It was not worldly prosperity, for of this, Esau, who lost it, probably had more than Jacob, who won it.

It was not immunity from sorrow. When Jacob received it every human ill was let free into his life. Staff in hand, he tore himself from home, and sought a distant country. He spent the best years of manhood's prime as a hireling in a kinsman's house. Halting on his thigh, he bowed before Esau; buried his favorite Rachel; chafed over the open sores of his home life; was bereaved of his children; and moaned that the days of the years of his pilgrimage had been evil and few. It was a sad and weary life that breathed itself out in that hieroglyphed chamber in the land of the Pharoahs. Whatever the birthright was, it evidently was not freedom from pain and grief; for these, Jacob, who won it, had infinitely more than Esau, who lost it.

The birthright was a spiritual heritage. It gave the right to become the priest of the family or clan. It constituted a link in the line of descent by which the Messiah was to be born into the world.

2. THE BARTER. One day Jacob was standing over a caldron of savory pottage, made of those red lentils which to the present day form a dish highly relished in Syria and in Egypt. At that moment, who should come in but Esau, faint with hunger. "Give me some of that," he cried impatiently.

Now Jacob was not wholly a selfish man, but it suddenly occurred to him that this would be a good opportunity to win the right to be the spiritual leader of the clan. So knowing well how little his brother counted on his rights, he made the extraordinary proposal to exchange the mess of pottage for the birthright.

Esau closed with the proposal. "Behold," said the bluff hunter, "I am on the point to die; and what profit shall this birthright do to me?" So he turned over his birthright to Jacob. And Jacob gave him bread and pottage of lentils; and he ate and drank, and went his way.

We cannot exonerate either of these men from blame. Jacob was not only a traitor to his brother, but he was faithless toward God. Had it not been distinctly whispered in his mother's ear that the elder of the brothers should serve the younger?

And as for Esau, we can never forget the beacon words of Scripture: "Look diligently . . . lest there be any fornicator, or profane person, as Esau, who for one morsal of meat sold his birthright" (Heb. 12:16). How many are there among us, born into the world with wonderful talents, who yet fling away all these possibilities of blessing and blessedness, for one brief plunge into the Stygian pool of selfish and sensual indulgence!

Had we been at Esau's side, how eagerly we would have laid our hand on his shoulder, entreating him to pause and consider before he bartered the spiritual for the physical, the eternal for the temporal, the unseen for the seen. The devil's pottage steams; it smells savory; it promises to do more good to us than all the Bible put together.

3. THE BITTER CRY. When Esau saw that God had taken him at his word, and had taken away from him the birthright, "he cried with a great and exceeding bitter cry" (Gen. 27:34). But that cry came too late. "He found no place of repentance, though he sought it carefully with tears" (Heb. 12:17).

"No place of repentance!" On many hearts those words have run the death knell of hope. As the heartbroken sinner has reviewed a blighted past with bitter tears and cries, the adversary of souls has whispered that he has sinned too deeply for repentance, and wandered too far to return; and he had backed the insinuation with these terrible words—"*no place of repentance.*"

And is it so? Is it possible for a soul, on this side of death, to reach a position where tears and prayers will strike against the brazen heavens, and rebound, only an echo? It cannot be. It is possible that a man should become too callous and hard to desire salvation: *this* is the sin to death; *this* is the sin that never has forgiveness; and it has no forgiveness because the sinner does not desire or seek it. But it is impossible for a man to desire to repent and not find a ready help in the grace of the Holy Ghost.

The "repentance" mentioned here is not repentance to salvation, but the power of reversing the past. Esau could not undo what he had done. He had long despised his birthright, and that act of surrender was not a solitary one, but the outcome of a state of heart. The sinful past is irrevocable. We all know this. We would give worlds to blot out the record, and to make them as if they had never been. But it is impossible. There is no place of repentance, though we seek it carefully and with tears. We cannot undo.

But though the past is irrevocable, it is not irreparable. God Himself cannot undo the past, but He can and will forgive. He will even "restore the years that the canker-worm has eaten" (Joel 2:25). He will give us new opportunities to show how truly we repent the decisions of the past and how loyally we desire to serve Him in the decisions of the future. He will not even mention the thrice denial; but He will give us three opportunities of saying how much we love Him.

3

The Stolen Blessing
Genesis 27

We need not be astonished to learn that temptation was allowed to come to Jacob from an unexpected source, taking him unawares.

1. THE TEMPTATION ORIGINATED IN A SENSUOUS REQUEST OF ISAAC. We sometimes find it hard to think that the Isaac of this chapter is the same person as the submissive boy who carried the altar wood on his stalwart young shoulders, and wondered about the lamb, and meekly submitted to being bound as a sacrifice. That was a radiant dawn for a human life, which for some reason became quickly overcast.

What was that reason? Was it the prosperity of which we read in the previous chapter? Was it an inordinate love for the pleasures of the table? There seems to have been too much of this in his constitution. He said to Esau, "Make me savoury meat, such as I love." Rebekah was keenly aware of her husband's weakness in this respect: "I will make them savoury meat for thy father, such as he loveth." There is a sad suggestiveness in all this, and enough to account for everything. The man who, on the supposed point of death, thinks most of all of a good dish of delicious venison, is not likely to shine as a specially brilliant star in the heavenly firmament.

Many years had passed since that memorable day on Mount Moriah, and many signs told Isaac that his sun was setting. Chief among these was dimming sight. God has mercifully arranged that such reminders, like warning bells, should ring out to show us how far we have traveled, and how near we are to the terminus of life. Many people, who otherwise would have dropped carelessly into the grave, have awakened by such things to say to themselves, "Behold, now I am old; I know not the day of my death. I must prepare for the final act."

There are glimpses of the better things in Isaac's character in the threefold preparation he made for his end.

He made his last testamentary disposition. If you have not done this, do it at once—no time so good as this. Leave nothing uncertain; nothing to chance; no loophole for heartburning or heartbreak among your heirs. *He laid aside his earthly cares.* He lived for several years after this, but he was a man set apart. It was the gloaming of his life, the fittest time for meditation and prayer. *He handed on the blessing.* Even though he proposed to counterwork the purposes of God, yet there is a significant beauty in the desire of the old man to bless before he died.

2. THIS TEMPTATION WAS PRESENTED TO JACOB THROUGH THE UNSCRUPULOUS LOVE OF RE-BEKAH. Jacob was her favorite son. There was a closer relationship between them than there could be between her and the more random Esau. As soon as she overheard Isaac's request to Esau, she resolved at once to win his blessing for her younger son.

We cannot but admire her love. She threw herself away on this son, whom she was never to see again. She was reckless of personal consequences. She didn't care what might come to herself, so that he might win. "Upon me be thy curse, my son." For him she sacrificed husband, elder son, principle—*all.* It is with such prodigality of affection that women constantly give themselves for their beloved.

But Rebekah's love was not based on principle. And such love is as terrible as the fire that has burst from the restraints of iron bars, and leaves behind it a scorched and blackened trail. Love is either the bliss or bane of life: its bliss, if rooted and grounded in an all-mastering and all-penetrating devotion to purity, truth, principle—or in a word, to God; but its curse, if it steers the ship of life according to its own wild whim. Let us keep our hearts above all that we guard, since out of them are the issues of life.

3. THIS TEMPTATION WAS GREEDILY RESPONDED TO BY THE WEAK AND CRAFTY NATURE OF JACOB. Jacob was not a thoroughly vicious man; but he was deplorably weak. He would not have concocted this plot or laid the train himself, but he did not have the courage to say no to the strong will and wish of his mother, especially when she was ready to take all risks. And so, when his mother put strong pressure on him, summoning him by the obedience he owed her as her son (v. 8), he weakly did not refuse on the ground that it was unlawful; but suggested it was inexpedient, lest they should be found out. "Behold, Esau my brother is a hairy man, and I am a smooth man; my father peradventure will feel me, and I shall seem to him as a deceiver, and I shall bring a curse upon me, and not a blessing." When a man retreats from the position of what is right, to the urging of what is likely to be expedient and to pay—that man is near a fall.

Such a fall was Jacob's. So long as we take our stand on what is lawful we are impregnable. But when once we argue with the tempter on the lower grounds of possible discovery and failure, we shall find ourselves outmatched by his arithmetic, and led as garlanded oxen to the slaughter house. Into this fault, to which all weak men are so liable, Jacob fell; and so, when his mother commanded him a second time to obey her voice (v. 13), and go to the flock for two good kids of the goats, "he went, and fetched, and brought them to this mother."

When once the first step had been taken, it was quickly followed by others which it seemed to render needful.

He simulated his brother's dress and skin. While the meat was cooking, Rebekah was engaged in turning over Esau's wardrobe, to find some suitable garments, highly perfumed. This done, she prepared the delicate skins of the kids for his hands and neck. All was done with haste; lest Esau might come in. And when all was ready, Jacob arrayed himself to play his part.

He deceived his father with a direct falsehood. "I am Esau thy firstborn; I have done according as thou badest me . . . eat of my venison, that thy soul may bless me."

He made an impious use of the name of God. In answer to Isaac's question as to how he had found it so quickly, he dared to say, "The LORD thy God brought it to me."

Yet what horror must have thrilled him as he found himself forced to take step after step, aware that he was being carried out by a rushing stream, yet not daring to stop. How his heart must have stood still when the old man became suspicious, and doubted his voice, and insisted on feeling, smelling, and having him near! What if God should strike him dead! What a relief when he came out again into the fresh air!—though the words of the coveted blessing hardly repaid him for the agony he had passed through. How he must have loathed himself. The sun itself seemed shorn of half its light.

Yet this is the man who became the prince of God. And if he became so, is there not hope for us, who can trace in Jacob many resemblances to ourselves? If the almighty Workman could fashion such clay into so fair a vessel, what may He not do for us?

But remember, God must implant the nature that He educates into Israel the Prince. When we speak of God's education we must be very careful what we mean, and how we express it, lest we should countenance error. Amidst all his sin, there must have been in Jacob a better self, which was capable of receiving the education of God and of being developed into Israel. And it was the possession of this better nature that made Jacob capable of rising to a spiritual level, for which Esau had neither the aptitude nor the taste.

No doubt the God of love had thoughts of love toward Esau, but there was not, in his worldly nature, the faith or the elements of nobility, which, through faith, had been implanted in his brother's heart. Put a stone into a flowerpot, cover it with mold, give it water and sunshine, and light and air—it will always be a stone: so if Esau had passed through the discipline of Jacob, he would always have been an Esau. So the discipline of God's grace in a human life can do nothing, unless there is the germ of that new and divine nature of which our Lord spoke to Nicodemus: "That which is born of the flesh is flesh; that which is born of the Spirit is spirit. Ye must be born again."

4

The Angel-Ladder
Genesis 28

When Esau found that Jacob had stolen his blessing, he hated him, and vowed to kill him. This was nothing less than might have been expected from his headstrong and impetuous nature. These threats came to Rebekah's ears and filled her with fear, lest she should be deprived of them both in one day—Jacob, the jewel of her eye, by the hand of his brother; and Esau, by being compelled, like a second Cain, to become an outlaw for his brother's murder.

But Rebekah understood Esau's temperament perfectly. If only Jacob absented himself for a short time, all would be forgotten. So Rebekah made up her mind that he should go across the desert to Haran; to abide for a time with her brother Laban. She did not tell her husband all her reasons why Jacob should go to Haran but she adduced very good and obvious ones, in the necessity of preserving from defilement the holy seed, and of procuring for Jacob a suitable wife.

Isaac fell in with the proposal; and "called Jacob, and blessed him, and charged him, and said unto him, Thou shalt not take a wife of the daughters of Canaan. Arise, go to Padan-aram; and take thee a wife from thence of the daughters of Laban thy mother's brother. And God Almighty bless thee!" And Jacob, not without many a tear, went out from Beersheba, and went toward Haran. And it was on his way that this revelation by means of his dream of the angels and ladder was made to him.

1. THE CIRCUMSTANCES IN WHICH THIS REVELATION WAS MADE TO HIM. Jacob was lonely. He was not what we should call a young man for he reached mature years: but it is almost certain that this was the first time he left the shelter of his home. In the early morning light, as he started forth, there may have been an exhilarating sense of independence, freshness, and novelty; but as night drew its curtains over the world there stole over his mind a sense of loneliness and melancholy. This was God's chosen time, when He drew near to his spirit. And so it has often been with men. Recall, for a moment, your first night away from home—as a schoolboy, or apprentice, or servant, or student, and tell me if that was not a sacred epoch in your history, when God took up the trailing tendrils of your love and twined them around Himself, and you realized His presence and clung to Him as never before.

Jacob was also standing on the threshold of independence. It is a solemn moment when a man enters on independence. But it is at such a moment that the Almighty, as a wayfaring man, offers His company for the untrodden path. Happy is he who accepts the proffered help, and transfers the feeling of dependence from the early to the heavenly Friend. When you are willing to be taken up by Him, there need be no further anxiety or care, for as soon as your spirit yields itself to the God of love, that moment He takes it, and assumes all responsibility, and makes Himself answerable for all its needs. Would that all the children of God might know what it is to hand over, moment by moment, as they occur, all worries, anxieties, and cares, to the compassionate Lord, sure that He takes them straight from their hands! There is actually no real independence for the believer. To be independent of Christ is to be cast forth as a branch to wither. The secret of rest, and fruit, and power is an abiding union with Him, a union that time cannot impair and death cannot dissolve.

Jacob was also in fear. What would hinder Esau, when he heard of his flight, from pursuing him? He was well acquainted with those parts; he was fleet of foot, or might use dogs, so as to track him and run him down. Besides, the country was full of robbers and wild beasts. And it was then that God calmed his fears by showing him that that lone spot was teeming with angel-hosts, willing and eager to encamp about him, with celestial watch and ward. The most lonely spot is as safe for us as the most crowded, since God is there. There comes assurance of One who cannot lie: "Fear not!" so that we may boldly say, "The Lord is my helper, and I will not fear what man shall do unto me" (Heb. 13:6).

2. THE ELEMENTS OF WHICH THIS REVELATION CONSISTED. The Spirit of God always conveyed His teachings to His servants in language borrowed from their surroundings. Bethel was a bleak moorland that lay in the heart of Palestine. There was nothing remarkable about it. The hillsides and upland slopes were strewn with large sheets of bare rock.

Fleeing northward, the wanderer suddenly found himself overtaken by the swift Eastern night. There was nothing else to do but to lie down on the hard ground, taking the stones as a pillow for his head. Thus he slept, and as he slept he dreamed; and in his dream his mind wove together many of his waking thoughts in fantastic medley. The striking appearance of those huge boulders, the memory that Abraham had built one of his earliest altars there, his last look upward at that wondrous heaven, studded with the brilliant constellations of an Eastern night—all these wove themselves into his dreams. It seemed as if the huge slabs of limestone came near together, and built themselves up into a gigantic staircase, reaching from the spot where he lay to the starry depths above him, and on that staircase angels came and went, peopling by their multitudes that most desolate region, and evidently deeply concerned with the sleeper that lay beneath. Nor was this all; for, from the summit, the voice of God fell like music.

There are here three points of interest:

a. *The ladder.* Jacob may have been oppressed by a sense of his insignificance, and sin, and distance from home. And it was very pleasant to know that there was a link between him and God.

The weakest and most sinful may climb through Jesus from the verge of the pit of hell to the foot of the eternal throne.

Thank God, we are not cut adrift to the mercy of every current; this dark coal ship is moored alongside the bright ship of heavenly grace. Yes, and there is a plank from the one to the other.

b. *The angels.* The angels ascended: there is the ascent of our prayers. The angels descended: there is the descent of God's answers. We are reminded of the afferent and efferent nerves of the body—up which flash the sharp stings of pain from the extremities to the head; and down which come the directions how to act. It would do as well to ponder more frequently the ministering care of the angels. God gives His angels charge concerning us, to keep us in *all* our ways; they bear us up in their hands. They are "sent forth to minister [to the] heirs of salvation" (Heb. 1:14).

What comfort Jacob must have realized! He found, to his great surprise, that that lone spot was *the gate of heaven,* for it seemed as if the populations of heaven were teeming around him, thronging to and fro. We need never yield to feelings of loneliness again, if we remember that, in our most retired hours, we are living in the very heart of a vast throng of angels; and we should hear their songs, and see their forms, if only our senses were not clogged with sin.

c. *The voice of God.* God answered his thoughts. He felt lonesome, but God said, "I will be with thee." He feared Esau; but God said, "I will keep thee." He knew not what hardships he might meet with; and God promised to bring him safely back again. Appearances seemed to contradict the divine promise; but God said, "I will do that which I have spoken to thee of."

Is it not remarkable that Jacob did not see these glorious realities until he slept? God was as much brooding in the wilderness before he slept as afterward; only he *knew it not*. It was only when he slept that he came to know it.

There is a lesson for us in this old story of how the Lord waited until His servant slept before He revealed to him the secret of His presence. May we not be rather too wide awake—too wakeful to the passing things of earth? And would it not be better if we were more oblivious to these things, that our spiritual vision might behold the things that are unseen and eternal?

It is impossible to walk with God unless we have these seasons of quiet vision. We need to escape from ourselves, our cares and gains, our personal individualities, in order that we may be at leisure to receive the revelations of God. And if we are to have this blessed sleep, it must be the gift of God in answer to our childlike trust.

Jesus Christ finds you out, and comes just where you are. The one pole of this ladder is the gold of His deity; the other is the silver of His manhood; the rungs are the series of events from the cradle of Bethlehem to the right hand of power, where He sits. Oh, that you would send away your burdens of sin and care and fear, by the hands of the ascending angels of prayer and faith—so as to be able to receive into your heart the trooping angels of peace, and joy, and love, and glory.

5

The Noble Resolve
Genesis 28

We are studying the education of a human spirit in the story of Jacob, who became Israel the Prince, in whose original constitution there was little to admire. There were *three steps* in God's dealings with this mean and crafty spirit.

To begin with, God revealed Jacob to himself. He might have gone on for years in dreamy self-content, ignorant of the evils that lurked within his breast. So a strong temptation was permitted to cross his pathway. There was no necessity for him to yield; but he did yield. And in yielding, he stood face to face with the unutterable baseness of his own heart. The first and indispensable work of the Holy Ghost, in the human spirit, is to convict of sin.

In the next place, God permitted Jacob to suffer the loss of all earthly friends and goods. We saw in our last chapter that he was lonely, destitute, and in fear. He had little or no property, but a cruse of oil (5:18) and his staff (32:10). He dreaded his brother's wrath. He was compelled to content himself with a stone for his pillow on the moorland waste. But he was not the last man who has had reason to bless God, to all eternity, for having swept his life clear of much which he had accounted absolutely needful to his existence. The "still small voice" can only be heard when all other voices are hushed.

Finally, God thrust into Jacob's life a revelation of His love. "Behold, a ladder set up on the earth, and the top of it reached to heaven." That ladder symbolized the love of God. Can you not remember the moment when the love of God in Jesus Christ first broke on you? There stole into your heart the conviction that it was all for you—a conviction that forced tears to your eyes, and these words from your lips: "He loved *me*, and gave himself for *me*."

The revelation of God's love will have five results on the receptive spirit.

1. IT WILL MAKE US QUICK TO DISCOVER GOD. Jacob had been inclined to localize God in his father's tents: as many localize Him now in chapel, church, or minster; supposing that prayer and worship are more acceptable there than anywhere beside. *Now* he learned that God was equally in every place—on the moorland waste as well as by Isaac's altar, though his eye had been too blind to perceive Him. If your spirit is reverent, it will discern God on a moorland waste. If your spirit is thoughtless and careless, it will fail to find Him even in the face of Jesus Christ. If only we were full of God, we would find that every spot was sacred, every moment hallowed, every act a sacrament; from every incident we would see a ladder stretching up to heaven; and our happy spirits would be constantly availing themselves of the opportunity to run up the shining way and embrace our dearest Lord.

Up to this moment the Lord has been in many of the moorland wastes of your life; *but you have not known it.* He has been beside you in that lonely chamber of pain; in that irksome situation; on that rugged pathway; but your eyes have been holden. What wonder that your path has been so drear! But if you will only take home to yourself the message of the cross of Jesus, "God loves me," then you will never feel lonely or outcast again. You will discover that a desolate moor is one of the mansions of your Father's house. You will be able to commune with Him equally on the hillside as amid the congregation. And you will often be compelled to exclaim, as you meet with fresh revelations of Himself, in the most unlikely places, *"This* is none other but the house of God; and *this* is the gate of heaven."

2. IT WILL INSPIRE US WITH GODLY FEAR. "He was afraid, and said, How dreadful is this place!" "Perfect love casteth out fear"—the fear that has torment; but it begets in us another fear, the fear that reveres God, and shudders to grieve Him; and dreads to lose the tiniest chance of doing His holy will. True love is always fearless and fearful. It is fearless with the freedom of undoubting trust; but it is fearful lest it should miss a single grain of tender affection, or should bring a moment's shadow over the face of the beloved.

3. IT WILL CONSTRAIN US TO GIVE OURSELVES TO GOD. The ordinary reading might lead us to suppose that, true to his worst self, Jacob tried to make a bargain with God; and promised to take Him as his, on certain conditions. *"If* God will be with me, and keep me in my way, and give me bread to eat and raiment to put on: *then*—." But a better reading relieves him of this sad imputation; and tones the words down to mean that if the Lord would be his God, then the stone should be God's house. But, however the words may run, this was evidently the moment of his consecration.

Have you done thus? It is the sole condition of soul-health, and peace, and power. Give yourself to Him now. And, as soon as you will to do so, He takes that which you give. Or, if you cannot give yourself, then lie low at His feet, and ask Him to take all you are and have. He will answer your prayer, and make you His forever.

4. IT WILL PROMPT US TO DEVOTE OUR PROPERTY TO HIM. "Of all that thou shalt give me, I will surely give the tenth unto thee." There is no reason to doubt that this became the principle of Jacob's life: and if so, he shames the majority of Christian people—most of whom do not give on principle; and give a very uncertain and meager percentage of their income. The church would have no lack if every one of its members acted on this principle.

Let each Christian resolve to give systematically to the Lord's cause; and to put aside, as firstfruits from all profits and receipts, a certain part, which shall be considered as distinctly and exclusively the Lord's, to be applied as He may direct.

It is failure in this that so often brings barrenness and joylessness into Christian lives. This is the reason that so many of the ascending angels never come down again, or return with empty hands. This is why we sow much, and bring in little; eat, and have not enough; drink, and are not satisfied; and put our wages into a bag with holes. We have robbed God in tithes and offerings. But if we would resolve to give Him tithes of all, and to bring them into His storehouse, we should find that He would open the windows of heaven, and pour us out such a blessing that there would not be room to receive it.

5. IT WILL FILL US WITH JOY. "Then Jacob lifted up his feet" (29:1, *marg.*). Does that not denote the lighthearted alacrity with which he sped on his way? His feet were winged with joy, and seemed scarcely to tread the earth. And this will be our happy lot, if only we will believe the love that God has for us. "Our soul shall make her boast in the Lord; the humble shall hear thereof, and be glad."

6

The Education of Home
Genesis 29

Next to the love of God comes the love of man or woman, as a factor in the education of a human spirit. Jacob's encounter with Rachel at the first well he came to, reminds us that though there is nothing more important than the union of heart with heart, there is nothing into which people drift more heedlessly.

Of course we do not deny that Jacob may find his other self in the beautiful girl at the well, under the Eastern noon; and that she may prove to be the one without whom his life would be incomplete. Nevertheless, it is the highest folly to leave so momentous a matter to be decided by a transient passion, or by the charms of a fascinating manner and a pretty face. Gird up the loins of your mind; test the spirits whether they be of God. Do not take an irrevocable step without earnest prayer that He would keep you from making a mistake; and reveal to you His will.

It is not enough to think and pray this way when a new affection has already flung its spell over you. It is the highest importance that these subjects be made a matter of prayer and thought in the earlier stages of life, when a supreme affection is, as yet, an ideal and a dream. Let mothers speak of them to their daughters; and fathers to their sons—as Isaac did to Jacob (28:1–2). Let young men, whenever they think of these matters, turn their thoughts into prayers that God would guide them—as He did Abraham's servant—to the woman whom He has chosen to be their helpmeet. And let Christian women constitute themselves the wards of God: leaving Him to choose for them.

1. THE FOUR CONDITIONS OF A TRUE HOME.

a. *There must be a supreme affection.* This was clearly a love-match. "Jacob loved Rachel" (v. 18) is a sufficient explanation. If there is true love, then, though one has been taken from the other by death before they stand together at the marriage altar, yet in the sight of God those two are one forever.

It is needless to show how the necessity of the presence of a supreme love is the ground and justification of monogamy, the union of two. You have no right to marry if this love is absent.

b. *Marriage must be "only in the Lord."* Jacob's was so. He might have taken a wife of the daughters of Heth, as Esau did, steeped in the idolatries and impurities that cursed the land. But, guided by his parents' counsels, he crossed the desert to obtain a wife who had been reared in a home in which there still lingered the memory of the worship of the God of Abraham, of Nahor, and of their father Terah (31:53).

The Bible rings from end to end with warnings against mixed marriages. "Be ye not unequally yoked together with unbelievers" (2 Cor. 6:14). A mixed marriage is a prolific source of misery. In the course of a considerable pastoral experience, I have never known one to result in perfect happiness. Believers, in such unions, do not lift their unbelieving partners up to Christ; but are themselves dragged down to infinite misery and self-reproach. How can there be sympathy in the deepest matter? Each feels that there is one subject on which they are not agreed; and this is a fatal barrier to perfect union. The ungodly partner despises the Christian for marrying in the teeth of principle. The Christian is disappointed because the apparent influence gained before marriage is dissipated soon after the knot is irrevocably tied. Many a Christian girl has married an unbeliever, in the hope of saving him, and has bitterly regreted her choice.

c. *A true home should be based on the good will of parents and friends.* There is the halo of a brighter promise encircling the union of two young hearts, when it is ratified amid the congratulations of rejoicing friends. It is wise and right, where practicable, for children to consult, in such matters, those whose love has made them the eager guardians of their opening life; and to do so by courtesy, even when mature years have given them the right to choose and act for themselves. But if parents would have such confidences when their children are old, they must make themselves their confidants while they are young.

d. *There should be some prospect of suitable livelihood.* In the broad wealthy land where Jacob found himself, there was not much difficulty about that. It is a much more complicated matter amid the conditions of our crowded modern life. Yet there ought to be some security of a competence. Young man, select as your partner one who, with refinement and culture, is not above turning her hands to the practical details of household management, and who knows what to do and how to do it. Young women, give your hearts to men who love you well enough to earn you through years of faithful and steadfast courtship, if so it must be. Anyone can do one deed of gallantry; it takes a true man to serve for seven long years.

2. THE EXPULSIVE POWER OF SUPREME AFFECTION. "Jacob served seven years for Rachel; and they seemed unto him but a few days, for the love he had to her" (v. 20). That sentence always charms us for its beauty and its truth. Love has the power of making a rough road easy, and a weary waiting time short. It makes us oblivious to many things, which, for lack of it, would be insupportable.

Do you find it hard to deny yourself, to make the required sacrifices for doing His will, and to confess Him? Go to the Holy Spirit, and ask Him to shed the love of Christ abroad in your heart, and so teach you to love Him who first loved you. Then, as the tides of that love rise within your heart, they will constrain you to live, not for yourself, but for Him; then burdens will be light that once crushed; roads will be pleasant that once strained and tired; hours will fly that were once leaden-footed; years will seem as a day. Love's labor is always light.

3. SOME CLOSING WORDS. Are you unmarried? Do not bewail yourself, as if your life must be incomplete. Yours is not a higher state, as celebicy has falsely taught, but it is neither a failure nor a shame. Cease to measure yourself by human standards. Find rest in being just what your heavenly Father wills you to be. It may be that you have been kept free from the limited circle of a home, in order to pour your love on those who have no one else to love them.

Are you disappointed? Jacob was disappointed in poor Leah; and she spent many a bitter hour of anguish. Her father had forced her on a man who did not love her, and who wanted to be rid of her. She had a woman's heart, and pined for love that never came. There are few stories more touching than the secret history of Leah, as revealed in the names she gave her boys, and her reasons in giving them. Yet remember, she had her compensations in the love of those strong, healthy sons who greeted her with the title, "Mother," so dear to a woman's heart. There are, doubtless, compensations in your lot, if you are not too bitter to see them. And this is the best of all: "The Lord will look upon your affliction" (v. 32). Meanwhile, do not flinch from doing your duty as in His sight.

Are you happily married? Then beware lest you make an idol of your happiness; or suppose that there is no further need to watch. Is it not remarkable that Jacob's dearest wife was the source of his defeat and disgrace, in later years, because she hid in her baggage the household idols of her father?

Have you become a Christian since you were married to an unbeliever? Then do not seek, in any way, to alter your relations (1 Cor. 7:13–14); but expect, in all assurance, that you will be the happy means of winning that beloved one to Christ. And seek this, not so much by frequent speech but rather seek it by the beauty and consistency of your life: "That if any obey not the word, they may without the word be gained by your manner of life beholding your behavior" (1 Peter 3:1).

7

The Mid-Passage of Life
Genesis 30

In our last chapter, we saw how Jacob built for himself a home. But ah—what a home! The presence of the two sisters there was fatal to its peace. They who had been happy enough as sisters before he came, could not now live in such close quarters, as wives of the same husband, without incessant jealousy. Each had her own grievance. Poor Leah knew that Jacob had never loved her, and that she was not the wife of his choice; and though God compensated her by giving her that pride of Oriental women, a family of sons, yet even this was a new source of anguish to her; for Rachel envied her. She was frightfully desolate in the home, and the names of her sons are like so many landmarks of her misery. But Rachel must have been equally miserable: true, she had her husband's love, but she could not be sure of keeping it; and she had the mortification of seeing her sister's children growing up as her husband's heirs. How eagerly she prayed, and fretted, and proudly chafed!

What wonder, then, that the children grew up wild and bad? Reuben, unstable as water, excitable and passionate; Simeon, quiet to obey, but quick to desperate cruelty; and Levi, a willing accomplice in his crime. When children turn out badly, it is often the fault of their home training; and it is more often the result of what they see than of what they are taught. Whatever Jacob may have been—the impressions received in the woman's tents, of high words and evil passion, would be enough to ruin any child.

But it is not so much Jacob's home life, as his business dealings, that we have now to consider.

He served fourteen years, as a dowry for his two wives; and at the time when Rachel gave birth to her firstborn, Joseph, that period had elapsed. As soon as mother and child were able to undertake so long and fatiguing a journey, Jacob declared his intention of returning to Canaan; and this resolve was perhaps precipitated by a message from Rebekah saying that there was now no further reason for his absence.

This proposal alarmed Laban, who had learned to value Jacob's services; and was much too astute to let him go, without making an effort to retain so valuable a servant. Jacob at once caught at the opportunity of making an independent provision for his large and increasing family; and the bargain was struck.

Eastern sheep are almost wholly white; the goats black; the multicolored rare. Jacob proposed, therefore, that all the brown and speckled should be at once removed; and that all of that color, which the flock produced afterward, should be his wage. There was no harm in this, unless he had already made up his mind to take the unfair advantage of Laban, which is a dark blot on his name. But whether this was premeditated in the first instance or not, it is certain that Jacob acted as a cheat and a rogue. Laban entrusted his flocks to his care without supposing for a moment that he would tamper with the usual course of nature. Jacob, on the other hand, did not hesitate to use every art to secure his own advantage at Laban's cost; taking means to procure for himself the produce of the strongest of the flock, and to leave to Laban the enfeebled and the weak.

It is surprising to find how eagerly some of the older commentators try to vindicate Jacob in this. I feel no temptation to do so.

Let us draw near, and remonstrate with Jacob, as he sits beside his flocks in the scorching Eastern sun, and let us carefully notice his excuses and pleas.

He might urge, first, the necessity of self-protection. "My uncle is bent on defrauding me, and keeping me down; and, if I did not do this, he will succeed. You must meet a man on his own ground; and, as he has chosen to play the rogue with me, I cannot see the harm of turning his own weapons on himself." This reasoning did not die with Jacob: it is still passed round the world in act and word; and good men are sometimes sorely tempted to make use of it. But if you really believe in the almighty God, you can be sure that falsehood must ultimately fail, and righteousness finally win; and you will meet fraud by faith, cunning by conscience, and violence by a divine virtue. Remember how the Lord has said: "I will keep thee." Your competitors may do mean and dirty tricks; but you will live to see them trapped in their own pits, and pierced by their own swords; while if you continue to do right, you will go steadily forward to success.

He might urge, as a second plea, the familiar formula, Business is business. It is strange to hear professing Christians speak this way. They have one standard of morality for the Lord's Day, and another for the other six. They permit things in business that are contrary to the spirit and letter of the Word of God, and which they would not sanction for a moment in the ordinary dealings of daily life. And they quiet their conscience by the easy motto, Business is business. If this were the case, the larger part of the life of most men would be outside the circumference of God's commands. But it cannot be. The moralities of the gospel resemble the law of gravitation, which determines the pathway of a grain of dust on the autumn breeze, as well as the march of worlds.

But Jacob might urge, as his third plea, that this was the general practice. "Other shepherds practice it. Laban must know all about it; or he might know. When you are with Chaldeans, you must do as Chaldeans do. I am not worse than others." But a universal practice does not condone sin; this is the difference between God's laws and man's. Let all men break a human law and it stands abrogated on the statute book; it cannot be enforced. But though all men break a divine law, it will exact its penalty from all.

Jacob might urge, as his fourth plea that chicanery was necessary to obtain bread. "A man must live, you know." But the plea cannot stand. There is no *must* about it. Where would we be today if all the martyrs had argued that it was more important to live than to do right? Every man has to choose between these two. He may be well content to suffer the loss of all things, and to die, if he may keep inviolate the priceless jewels that God has entrusted to his care.

Jacob's double-dealing appeared to be a success. "The man increased exceedingly; and had much cattle, and maidservants, and menservants, and camels, and asses." But that which men call success, and which is sometimes a very superficial and temporary thing, proves nothing as to the rightness or wrongness of a life. Many a noble life in the sight of God has been a sad failure when judged by human standards. And many a failure in the judgment of man has been a royal success in the estimation of the angels.

I demur to the common use of the phrase, "Honesty is the best policy." If we are simply going to be honest because it pays, we are basing the fabric of our lives on too low a level; and our foundation may give way in days of storm. We must be honest—not because of good policy, but because of good principle; because it is right, and noble, and God-like; yea, because it pleases God.

Do not draw a line of separation between the house of God and the house of business. The office and the factory may be as much the house of God as the holiest shrine. A devout soul will abide with God in every calling in which it is called. If you cannot have the companionship of Jesus in the paths of daily business, by all means abandon them. But if they are at all legitimate, you will find Him at your side, though His presence is veiled from all other eyes.

Do what you have to do in the name of the Lord Jesus. In that name you are wont to pray. In that name learn to do your work. Speak that name over the most menial tasks; and they will glisten with heavenly beauty. Speak it over difficulties; and the iron gates will own the spell, and open to you of their own accord.

Take the Lord Jesus into your partnership. Consult Him before branching out into new directions, or consigning goods to fresh customers, or making large purchases. Let every transaction and every entry be freely open to His eye. And be sure to divide with Him the profits, which are His due. A business life, with such sanctions, could never fall on the shoals of bankruptcy.

8

The Stirring-up of the Nest
Genesis 31

In that sublime song with which the great lawgiver closed his words to Israel, we are carried through the steeps of air, to stand beside an eagle's nest, perched amid the inaccessible cliffs. The young eaglets are old and strong enough to fly, but they cling to the familiar nest. They dare not venture forth upon the untried air, or trust their fluttering wings. But they *must* learn to fly. There are joys awaiting them in the wide oceans of space, which far outweigh those of the rude nest in which they have been nurtured. And so the eagle stirs up the nest, and drives them forth. What anguish the young birds feel as they see that nest destroyed; and themselves thrust forth, as it might seem, to certain destruction! But when once they are launched upon the upbearing air, and learn by glad experience the freedom, the ecstasy of flight—how grateful they should be to the parent bird, who did not flinch from the unwelcome task; and who still swoops and flies beneath them, ready to catch them up if their powers should flag. There, in mid-heaven, she lets them fall again; and again she catches them, and thus, each moment they increase in confidence and strength. They develop powers of sustained flight, of which they were unconscious when they lingered by the nest.

It is a beautiful parable of human life. We all cling to the old nest—the old home where we were born. We say, with eager petulance, "Let us stay here forever. Do not speak to us of that great outer world; we are content; let us stay." But the great love of God has provided some better thing for us. He knows that there are heights and depths of life hidden from us till we go forth. Sharp may be the agony of the moment in which we see the nest stirred up, and find ourselves flung forth into a strange element. But it is not worthy to be compared with the glory instantly revealed; the glory of a faith that poises itself on the unseen; the glory of a hope that breasts the thundercloud; the glory of a love that soars ever upward to the sun.

These thoughts give the key to the next experience in Jacob's troubled life. Though he could not have guessed it at the time, yet, as we look back, we can easily understand why his residence at Haran was suddenly closed, and his home broken up. He was driven across the desert, as a fugitive, hotly pursued—much as he had been years before, only in the reverse direction.

In point of fact, Jacob was becoming too contented in that strange land. He was fast losing the pilgrim spirit; his wives, infected with the idolatry of their father's house, were in danger of corrupting the minds of his children. It was evident that his nest must be broken up in Haran; that he must become a stranger and a sojourner, as his fathers were. And this was another step nearer the moment when he became an Israel, a prince with God. This may be your destiny; and, if it be, accept meekly the discipline that forces you toward it. It is the hand that was pierced with nails that breaks up the next of the past, and beckons you to the untried but blessed realities in front.

1. THE SUMMONS TO DEPART. "And the LORD said unto Jacob, Return unto the land of thy fathers, and to thy kindred; and I will be with thee." Whether there was voice audible to the outward ear I cannot tell, but there was certainly the uprising of a strong impulse within his heart.

There are many kinds of voices in the world, and none of them is without significance; but the more truly we partake of the nature of "His own sheep," the more unerringly will we detect the voice of the Good Shepherd. If you are not quite sure, wait until you are. The only necessity is to be willing to do His will so soon as it is clearly seen. If you are in doubt, wait in faith until every other door is shut, and one path only lies open before you.

God's voice to the heart is generally corroborated by the drift of outward circumstances. "Jacob beheld the countenance of Laban, and, behold, it was not toward him as before." For some time their relations had been strained. Ten times in six years Laban had altered the method of computing his wages; and now there were symptoms of open rupture.

It is bitter to behold a change passing over men and women in their behavior toward us; a change we cannot avert. And yet God is undoubtedly in all this. Take heart: it is only part of the process of making you a prince; in no other way can your mean Jacob-nature be replaced by something better.

2. THE TENACITY OF CIRCUMSTANCES. When the pilgrim-spirit attempts to obey the voice of God, the house is always filled with neighbors trying to dissuade him from the rash resolve. There was something of this in Jacob's case.

He was evidently afraid that his wives would hinder his return. It would have been natural if they had. Was it likely that they would at once consent to his proposal to tear them from their kindred and land? This fear may have greatly hindered Jacob. He at least thought it necessary to fortify himself with a quiverful of arguments, in order to carry his point. But God had been at work before him; and had prepared their hearts, so that they at once assented to his plan, saying: "We have no further ties to home; now then, whatsoever God hath said unto thee, do."

In Laban's endeavors to retain Jacob, we have a vivid picture of the eager energy with which the world would retain us when we are about to turn away from it forever. It pursues us, with all its allies, for seven days and more (v. 23). It asks us why we are not content to abide with it (v. 27). It professes its willingness to make our religion palatable by mingling with it its own evils (v. 27). It appeals to our feelings, and asks us not to be too cruel (v. 28). It threatens us (v. 29). It mocks us with our sudden compunction, after so many years of contentment with its company (v. 30). It reproaches us with our inconsistency in making so much of our God, and yet harboring some cunning sin. "Wherefore hast thou stolen my gods?" (v. 30). Ah, friends, how sad it is, when we, who profess so much, give occasion to our foes to sneer, because of the secret idols which they know we carry with us! Sometimes it is not we who are to blame, so much as our Rachels—our wives, or children, or friends. But we should never rest until, so far as we know, our camp is clear of the accursed thing.

O that you might break away from that life of worldliness in which you have tarried too long! Make a clean break with it! Call your friends to witness your solemn act; above all, call God to witness your resolve—that never again shall the world, the flesh, or the devil, come over to you, or you pass over to them. This is the true Mizpah of the Lord's watch.

3. THE DIVINE CARE. Well might Jacob have thrilled with joy, as he said to his wives, "The God of my father has been with me." Blessed is he for whom God fights. He must

be more than a conqueror. So Jacob found it; and, at the end of his encounter with Laban, he was able to repeat his assurance that the God of his father had been with him (v. 42).

At the head of his flocks and herds, with wives and children and slaves, he struck across the Euphrates and the desert, at the utmost speed possible to his encumbered march; but God's angels accompanied him. He met their radiant hosts afterward (32:1). His flight remained unsuspected for three days; then Laban set off with swift camels in pursuit, and overtook them, while they were still threading their way among the richly wooded and watered hills of Gilead. It was a moment of real danger; and it was then that God interposed. "God came to Laban the Syrian by night." That dream laid an irresistible spell on Laban, which prevented him from carrying out his design to do Jacob hurt.

Jacob was an erring and unworthy child; but God did not leave or forsake him. Thus He was able to throw His protection around His erring child; and this was part of the loving discipline that was leading Jacob to a goal of which he never dreamed.

Jacob conceived that he was a model shepherd (v. 38), but he little realized how lovingly he was being protected by the shepherd-care of Him who keeps Israel, and who neither slumbers nor sleeps. That protection may be ours.

9

The Midnight Wrestle
Genesis 32

On the morning after his interview with Laban, Jacob broke up his camp on the heights of Gilead, and slowly took his journey southward. He little knew that that day was to be the crisis of his life.

This wondrous scene does not, in my opinion, correspond to that change that we call conversion. That was determined, surely, by the angel vision at Bethel. But it may rather be compared with that further blessing, which sometimes comes to a Christian after some years of religious experience and profession. There is no reason, in the nature of things, why it should be so. There is no reason why, at the moment of conversion, we should not at once step into the realization and enjoyment of all the possibilities of Christian living. But still, as a matter of fact, it often happens that some years of wilderness wandering do intervene between the deliverance of the Passover and the passage across the Jordan into the land of promise, and rest, and victory. Many a child of God who has no doubt of acceptance and forgiveness, is conscious of a broken and fitful experience: He passes into a climate that brings into glorious fruitage the seed-germs that were lying in his nature undeveloped. Such an experience fell to Jacob's lot after that memorable night.

Three events are narrated in this chapter, corresponding to morning, afternoon, and night of that memorable day.

1. IN THE MORNING, we are told that the angels of God met him. Those words tremble with mystic and indescribable beauty. How did it take place? Did they come in twos or threes? Or, as he turned some corner in the mountain pass, did he see a long procession of bright harnessed angels, marching four abreast, with golden bands girding

about them their lustrous robes, while the music of heaven beat time? Would it not remind him of Bethel, that lay across the chasm of twenty-five years? Would it not nerve and prepare him for coming danger?

Doubtless these angel-bands are always passing by us; only our eyes are shut so that we not see them. But whether we see them or not, we may always depend on their being at hand—especially when some heavy trial is near.

2. AS THE DAY WORE ON TO AFTERNOON, Jacob's spirit was shaken to the center by ominous tidings. He had sent messengers to announce to Esau his return, and to ascertain his mind. The messengers now returned in breathless haste to say that Esau was coming to meet him, with four hundred men at his back. Jacob was panic-stricken; and well he might be. His all was at stake—wives and children; herds and cattle; the careful gains of six laborious years. The Mizpah-tower barred the way back; his bridge was, so to speak, burned behind him. Around him were robber tribes, eager to seize on the rich booty, if he showed the least sign of vacillation or fear. But to go on seemed to involve a risk of inevitable ruin. There was just one alternative—which most men will only turn to when all other expedients have failed—he could at least pray; and to prayer he betook himself. It may have been a long time since he prayed like this.

There are many healthy symptoms in that prayer. In some respects it may serve as a mold into which our own spirits may pour themselves, when melted in the fiery furnace of sorrow.

He began by quoting God's promise: "Thou saidst." Be sure, in prayer, to get your feet well on a promise; it will give you purchase enough to force open the gates of heaven, and to take it by force.

He next went to confession: "I am not worthy." There passed before his mind his deceit to his aged father; his behavior to Esau; his years of trickery to Laban. All the meanness of his heart and life stood revealed, as a landscape is revealed when the midnight sky is riven by the lightning flash. "I am not worthy." Great soul-anguish will generally wring some such cry from our startled and stricken hearts.

Then he passed on to plead for deliverance: "Deliver me, I pray thee, from the hand of my brother, from the hand of Esau." It was, of course, quite right to pray this, but I cannot feel that it was a wholehearted prayer; for he had hardly finished it when he reverted to the plan on which he had been busy before he turned aside to pray. We are all so apt to pray, and then to try and concoct a plan for our own deliverance. Surely the nobler attitude is, after prayer, to stand still for God to develop His plan, leading us in ways that we had never guessed. The blessed life of our Lord was absolutely planless.

3. IT WAS MIDNIGHT. Jacob had already sent across the Jabbok his property, his children, even his beloved Rachel. "He caused them to pass over the brook and Jacob was left alone." There, alone, he considered the past; and anticipated the future; and felt the meanness of the aims for which he had sold his soul. He saw the wretched failure of his life, and so, suddenly, he became aware that a mysterious combatant was at his side, drawing him into a conflict, half literal and half spiritual, which lasted till break of day.

Was this a literal contest? There is no reason to deny it. It would have been as possible for the Son of God to wrestle literally with Jacob, as for Him to offer His hands to the touch of Thomas after His resurrection. The physical must have been largely present because, when he resumed his journey, Jacob limped. It was a physical fact, physically commemorated by the Israelites to this day, for they abstain from eating of that part in animals that corresponds to the sinew that shrank in Jacob's thigh. Men do not become lame in imaginary conflicts. But, in any case, the outward wrestling was only a poor symbol of the spiritual struggle that convulsed the patriarch's soul.

Remember that the conflict originated not with Jacob, but with the angel: "There wrestled a man with him." This passage is often quoted as an instance of Jacob's earnestness in prayer. It is nothing of the sort. It was not that Jacob wished to obtain something from God, but it was that He—the angel Jehovah—had a controversy with this double-dealing and crafty child of His. He was desirous to break up his self-sufficiency forever, and to give scope for the development of the Israel that lay cramped and coffined within.

Has not "this man" who wrestled with Jacob found you out? Have you not felt a holy discontent with yourself? Have you not felt that certain things, long cherished and loved, should be given up, though it should cost you blood? These convulsive throes, these heaven-born strivings, these mysterious workings—are not of man, or of the will of the flesh, but of God. It is God who works in you, and wrestles with you. Glory be to Him for His tender patience, interest, and love!

At first Jacob held his own. "He saw that he prevailed not against him." The strength that, years before, had rolled the stone from the well for Rachel's sheep, was still vigorous; and he was in no humor to submit. And thus we do all resist the love of God. Each one of us is dowered with that wonderful power of holding our own against God; and He knows, sorrowfully, that He cannot prevail against us, without taking some severe measures that will give us no alternative but to yield.

Then the angel touched the hollow of his thigh. Whatever it is that enables a soul, whom God designs to bless, to stand out against Him, God will touch. And beneath that touch it will shrink and shrivel; and you will limp to the end of life. Remember that the sinew never shrinks except beneath the touch of the Angel-hand—the touch of tender love. This is why your schemes have miscarried; God has touched the sinew of your strength, and it has dried up. Oh, you who are still holding out against Him, make haste to yield, lest some worse thing come upon you!

Then Jacob went from resisting to clinging. As the day broke, the Angel wanted to leave; but He could not because Jacob clung to Him with a death grip. The request to be let go indicates how tenaciously the limping patriarch clung to Him for support. He had abandoned the posture of defense and resistance, and had fastened himself on to the Angel—as a terrified child clasps its arms tightly around its father's neck. That is a glad moment in the history of the human spirit, when it throws both arms around the risen Savior, and hangs on to Him and will not let Him go. Have you reached the point of self-surrender? If not, ask God to show you what sinew it is that makes you too strong for Him to bless you; ask Him to touch it so that you shall be able to hold out no more. And then you will discover the threefold blessing that is yours.

a. *The changed name.* In Jacob's time names were given not for euphony, or by caprice, but for character. Now, when Jacob came into the attitude of blessing the Angel immediately said, "What is thy name?" And he said, "Jacob. By nature I am a supplanter, a rogue, and a cheat." Never shrink from declaring your true character: "My name is Sinner." "And he said, thy name shall be no more Jacob, but Israel: a prince with God." The changed name indicates a changed character. Jacob was clothed with the name and nature of a prince. There is only one way to princeliness—it is the thorn-set path of self-surrender and of faith. Why should you not now yield yourself entirely to God and give Him your whole being? It is only a reasonable service.

b. *Power.* The better rendering of these words would be: "As a prince hast thou power with God; and with man thou shalt prevail." We sign for power but we must obtain it from the Creator. The man who would have power with men must first have it with God; and we can get power with God only when our own strength has failed, and we limp. Oh, for the withered sinew of our own strength, that we may lay hold on the strength of God!

c. *The beatific vision.* "I have seen God face to face." Our moments of vision come at daybreak, but they are ushered in by the agony of dread, the long midnight vigil, the extreme agony of conflict, the shrinking of the sinew. The price is dear, but the vision is more than worth it all. The sufferings are not worthy to be compared with the glory revealed.

This is life: a long wrestle against the love of God that longs to make us royal. As the years go on, we begin to cling where once we struggled; and as the morn of heaven breaks, we awake to find ourselves living, and face to face with God—and that is heaven itself.

10

Failure
Genesis 33–34

That midnight wrestle, which last engaged our thoughts, made an epoch in Jacob's life. It was the moment in which he stepped up to a new level in his experience—the level of Israel the prince. But let us remember that it is one thing to step up to a level like that; it is quite another to keep it. Some, when they touch a new attainment, keep to it. Some, when they touch a new attainment, keep to it, and are blessed evermore; others, when they have stood there for a moment, recede from it. Jacob, alas! soon stepped down from that glorious level to which the Angel had lifted him.

This descent is indicated by the retention, in the sacred record, of the name Jacob. We should have expected that it would have been replaced by the new title, Israel—as Abram was by Abraham—but it is not so. How could he be called Israel when he had so soon reverted to the life of Jacob; and had gone back to the cringing, crafty, scheming life that he had been leading all too long? The time will come when Israel will become his habitual designation; but not yet—not yet.

We have to consider now the three evidences of failure that are recounted in these chapters.

1. THE FIRST FAILURE WAS IN HIS MANNER OF MEETING ESAU. As the morning broke, "Jacob lifted up his eyes, and looked; and, behold, Esau came, and with him four hundred men." Such is life. It is filled with sharply varied experiences.

How often do we find that a great blessing—like that which came to Jacob by the fords of the Jabbok—is sent to prepare us for a great trial. God prevents us, and prepares us, with the blessings of His goodness. Do not be surprised or discouraged if a time of fiery trial should follow a season of unusual blessing; indeed, you may be rather surprised if it does not. But when it comes, be sure to do as Jacob did not do—and draw heavily on all those resources of strength and comfort that have been stored up during the previous days of clear shining and peace.

There are two ways of meeting troubles: the one is the way of the flesh; the other, of the Spirit. The flesh anticipates them with terror; prays in a panic, and then cringes before them—as Jacob, who bowed himself to the ground seven times until he came near his brother. The way of faith is far better. She clings to God; she hears God say, "I am with thee, and will keep thee"; she believes that He will keep His word; she reviews the past, when the hands of Laban were tied, and argues that God can do as much again.

Some who read this may be dreading a meeting with their Esaus tomorrow; some creditor, some demand for payment, some awkward problem, some difficulty. And you are today worrying, planning, scheming, and contriving, as Jacob did, in arranging his wives and children, and servants, while tomorrow you will go cringing and creeping toward it.

Listen to a more excellent way. Do not lift up your eyes and look for Esaus. Lift them higher—to Him from whom our help comes. Then you will be able to meet your troubles with an unperturbed spirit. Those who have seen the face of God need not fear the face of man that will die.

Besides all this, when prayer has preceded trial, the trial turns out to be much less than we anticipated. Jacob dreaded that meeting with Esau, but when Esau came up with him, he ran to meet him, and embraced him, and fell on his neck, and kissed him; and they wept. The heroic Gordon used to say that in his lonely camel rides he often in prayer encountered and disarmed hostile chiefs, before he rode, unaccompanied, into their presence. None can guess, if they have not tried it for themselves, what a solvent prayer is for the difficulties and agonies of life.

It is beautiful to see that, in this, God was better to Jacob than his fears, or his faith. While he was foreboding the worst, his heavenly Friend was preparing deliverance.

2. THE SECOND FAILURE WAS IN THE SUBTERFUGE TO WHICH JACOB RESORTED, TO FREE HIMSELF FROM ESAU'S COMPANY. When Esau offered him the protection of his armed men, he was at once in a panic, for he dreaded them even more than the Bedouins of the wilds. He tried to evade the proposal by making many excuses, especially explaining that his flocks and his children could not keep up with their more rapid pace. And finally, still further to reconcile Esau to the separation, he promised to come at last to Seir, where Esau had fixed his abode.

Now I do not believe that Jacob really meant to go to Seir, for as soon as he had seen the rear of Esau's retiring forces, he journeyed in the opposite direction to Succoth. All such subterfuge and lying were utterly unworthy of the man who had seen God's angels face to face.

What wretched failure was here! The bright dawn was all too speedily overcast and if it had not been for the marvelous tenderness of God, there is no telling how much further Jacob would have drifted, or how indefinitely distant the day would have been in which he should be worthy to bear the name of Israel.

3. THE THIRD FAILURE WAS IN SETTLING AT SHECHEM. God had not said, Go to Shechem; but, "I am the God of Bethel." Bethel, rather than Shechem, was his appointed goal. But we are all too ready to fall short of God's schemes for our elevation and blessedness. So Jacob came to Shalem, a city of Shechem.

But he did worse; he pitched his tent before the city—as Lot did when he pitched his tent before Sodom. What took him there? Whatever may have been his reason, there stands the sad and solemn face that Jacob pitched his tent *before the city.*

Aren't many Christians still doing the same thing today? They live on the edge of the world, just on the border. They are far enough away to justify a religious profession, yet near enough to run into it for sweets. They choose their church, their pastimes, their friendships, on the sole principle of doing as others do; and of forming good alliances for their children. What is all this but pitching the tent toward Shechem?

But Jacob did still worse. Not content with pitching his tent before the city, he bought the parcel of ground "where he had pitched his tent." Abraham bought a parcel of ground in which to bury his dead, and this was no declension from the pilgrim spirit—it rather placed it in clearer relief. But Jacob was abandoning the pilgrim spirit and the pilgrim attitude, and was *buying* that which God had promised to *give* to him and to his seed. The true spirit of faith would have waited quietly, until God had made good His repeated promise.

It may be that Jacob sought to conciliate his conscience by building the altar, and dedicating it to the God of Israel. But where the altar and the world are put in rivalry, there is no doubt as to which will win the day: the Shechem gate will appeal too strongly to our natural tendencies, and we will find ourselves and our children drifting into Schechem—while the grass of neglect grows up around the altar, or it becomes broken down and disused.

"And Dinah, the daughter of Leah, which she bare unto Jacob, went out to see the daughters of the land." It is a startling announcement, but it contains nothing more than might have been expected. Poor girl! Was she lonely, being the only girl? She went along a path that seemed to her girlish fancy ever so much more attractive than the dull routine of home. She took no heed to the warnings that may have been addressed to her. And it all ended—as it has ended in thousands of cases since—in misery, ruin, and unutterable disgrace.

She fascinated the young prince, and fell. It is the old story that is ever new. On the one hand—rank, and wealth, and unbridled appetite; on the other—beauty, weakness, and dallying with temptation. But to whom was her fall due? To Schechem? Yes. To herself? Yes. But also to Jacob. He must forever reproach himself for his daughter's murdered innocence. And all this came because Jacob stepped down from the Israel level back to his old unlovely self.

Let us understand the causes of Jacob's relapse, and see how we may guard against it.

It arises, first, from trusting in the impulse received at a given moment, as though that were sufficient to carry the soul forward through all coming days; and there is therefore a relaxation of watchfulness, and prayer, and Bible study. We are all so apt to substitute an experience for abiding fellowship with the Son of God; to dwell in the past, instead of in the living present. This mistake can be obviated only by careful cultivation of the daily, hourly, friendship of the living Savior. And even this can be attained only by the grace of the Holy Spirit.

Second, it may arise from the energy of the self-life, which the apostle Paul calls *the flesh.* Before regeneration we attempt to justify ourselves; being regenerate, we attempt to sanctify ourselves. There must be more of God in our lives.

Third, these failures arise because we are conscious of the subsidence of the keen emotions that once filled our hearts, and suppose that in losing these we have really lost that spiritual attitude we then assumed. All the deepest experiences in Christian life consist in acts of the will, which may or may not be accompanied by emotion, and which remain when the glow of feeling has passed. God, therefore, withdraws the life of emotion that He may train us to live by faith, and in our wills.

Whatever failure comes may also be associated with our reluctance to confess to others the blessing that has irradicated our inner life. We should not hesitate to tell those with whom we are most intimate what great things the Lord has done for us. To withhold confession, is often to staunch the flow of blessing.

If you are conscious of having failed in any of these respects, ask to be forgiven and restored; and trust Him, who is the keeper of the faithful soul, trim you as the light of the sacred temple lamps.

11

Back to Bethel
Genesis 35

In itself, Bethel was not much. Imagine a long range of broken hills running north and south. The eastern slopes, bleak and tempest-riven, descend to the Jordan. The western slopes lie toward the more thickly-peopled parts of Palestine. In the valley at their foot runs the main thoroughfare of Palestine, which has been trodden by centuries of travelers—a rough, broken mountain roadway, following the uneven course of the valley, and intersected by innumerable watercourses. From this track and upward the mountain slopes are strewn with large sheets of bare rocks. No house is within sight, no cultivated lands break the stretch of mountain pasture, no domestic animals share the rule of the eagle, the wild goat, and the rabbit.

But to Jacob, Bethel was the most memorable and sacred spot in all the earth. It was there, on the first night of his flight from home, that the mystic ladder had seemed to link earth to heaven, thronged by angels engaged in holy ministry.

Many years had passed since then—years of searching discipline, which had revealed the meanness, the craft, the weakness of his nature. He had fallen far below the promise of his early vows; and of late it would seem that even worse symptoms had begun to show themselves. He seems even to have winked at the idols that were in common request among his people, and of the presence of which he was perfectly well aware (v. 2). Alas! what a fall was this for the man who had built so many altars to Jehovah, and was the chosen depository of those truths for which the world was waiting! For the world's sake, and for his own, it was essential that he should be compelled to regain the ground he had so grievously lost. It was then that he said to his household, "Let us arise, and go up to Bethel."

A voice (shall I not call it an instinct, within him?) cried: Go and dwell for a season at Bethel; gaze once more on the familiar scene; put your head down again upon that stone you set up for a pillar; and review the way in which the Lord your God hath led you.

But his untoward circumstances gave a further reason. He was in terrible trouble. He had settled himself down, and sunk a well for his supply, which became so famous as to be known through all succeeding time as Jacob's Well. He was intimately identified for several uneventful years with the life of the locality, and then his sons had made his name a stench among the inhabitants of the land by the frenzied passion with which they had revenged their sister's dishonor. He was in imminent danger of destruction from the infuriated tribes around him. He had to go somewhere, and it was at this moment that the impulse came to him to go up to Bethel.

But, above all, that impulse originated in God Himself. "God said unto Jacob, Arise, go up to Bethel, and dwell there." Why did God wish Jacob to go back to Bethel? Because Bethel was associated with one of the most blessed spiritual experiences of his life. And the summons to go back to Bethel was equivalent to an invitation to return to that fervor, that devotion, and those holy vows that had made that bare mountain pass the very house of God and the gate of heaven. "Come back; and be as near to Me as you were when you first set up that stone, and anointed it with oil."

There are some words that cannot be spoken in our ears without arousing in us an immediate response. So must the word Bethel have sounded in the ear of Jacob. "Then Jacob said unto his household, and to all that were with him, Put away the strange gods that are among you, and be clean, and change your garments: And let us arise, and go up to Bethel."

And so he came to Bethel, protected by God's watchful care; and he built there an altar, and God appeared to him again.

1. MANY CHRISTIANS ARE SUFFERING FROM SPIRITUAL DECLENSION. They hardly realize it for it has crept on them so quietly; but they have drifted far away from their Bethel and Peniel. Gray hairs are on a man before he knows it. Summer fruit begins to rot within, long before its surface is pitted with specks. So insensibly have you been slipping back, until you are infinitely farther from God than you were in the sacred, happy days that are past.

2. IDOLS ARE THE INEVITABLE SYMPTOM OF INCIPIENT DECAY. Go at autumn into the woods, and see how the members of the fungus tribes are scattered plentifully throughout the unfrequented glades. Where the shade is deepest, and the soil most impregnated with the products of corruption, they love to pitch their tents. Similarly, whenever there has set in upon the spiritual life the autumn of decay, you will be sure to find a fungus growth of idols.

You may hide your idols, like Rachel; but they will not remain hidden. They will work their way forward, until what was hidden as a sin becomes paraded as a boast. It may be that some backslider will read these lines, conscious that things are not now what they were between him and God. Such a one will bear witness from his own bitter experience, that in proportion to the decay of the inner life there has been the growth of some idol-love. You have set your heart on making a reputation, or a fortune; and as your energies have waxed in this direction, they have waned in the other.

3. THESE IDOLS MUST BE SURRENDERED BEFORE THERE CAN BE VICTORY OR PEACE. The reason for Jacob's flight before those alien tribes was, of course, the censurable and merciless action of his sons; but above and beyond this, lay the fact that Jacob had been giving some measure of countenance to the existence of idolatry in the camp. I always find, in Christian experience, that failure and defeat indicate the presence of some idol

somewhere, and the need of more complete consecration to God. Get down on your knees; search out the idols; ransack all the camel-baggage, in spite of all that Rachel may say; bring out the accursed things, and bury them.

How wise it was for Jacob to bury those idols right away! If he had kept or carried them with him, he might have been tempted to bring them out again. It was so much better to leave them right there, under the oak in Shechem, before he started for Bethel. We cannot be surprised at the mighty work of God in Ephesus after the splendid *auto-da-fé* that took place in the marketplace (Acts 19:19).

This, then, is our closing message: put away your idols, and get back to Bethel. Repent, and do the first works. Pray as you used to pray. Study the Bible as you used to study it. Spend the Lord's day as you used to spend it. Build an altar now on the same site on which you built it years ago. Give yourself again to God. Forget the things that are behind; stretch forward to those that are before. And God will appear to you again; and will renew the princely name and the princely blessing to which you might have thought that you had forfeited all right. Moreover, He will promise you marvelous fruitfulness in service, and far-reaching possessions in the land of promise (vv. 11–12). All these things are in store for you, if only you will bury your idols, and go up to Bethel, and dwell there.

12

The School of Sorrow
Genesis 35–42

I am never surprised to hear men date an unusual amount of trial from the moment in which heaven seemed nearer, and Christ dearer, than ever before. It must be so: or the blessing they had obtained would fade from their soul—as the photograph fades from the plate, unless it has been "fixed" in the dark chamber.

We are told that when, having left his idols behind, Jacob had got back to Bethel, and had built again the altar of renewed consecration, "God appeared unto him again, and blessed him." Are all the readers of these lines conscious that the blessing of the Almighty is resting upon them? Has God revealed Himself to you again, after the long, sad lapse of fellowship and communion? If not, would it not be wise to do as Jacob did? Ask God to show you what your idols are. Tell Him that you want to be only, always, all for Him. Put away not only your sins, but your weights—i.e., anything that hinders you in the Christian race. If you cannot do this yourself, tell Him that you are willing, tell Him that you are willing to be made willing. And when you have thus surrendered your will, give yourself again to Him. It may be that He will appear to us at once, flooding our spirits with the old unspeakable joy; or He may keep us waiting for a little. But it matters comparatively little, if only we can say, with the assurance of an unwavering faith, "We are His; nothing shall henceforth separate us from the love of God."

It was a great blessing, indeed, that God vouchsafed to Jacob. "God said unto him, Thy name is Jacob: thy name shall not be called any more Jacob; but Israel shall be thy name." Israel, the Prince. But this was not all: God constituted him father of nations and kings; and promised to give to him the land in which he was a wonderer, as his fathers before him. Now these two items of fruitfulness and possession are only possible to those who have passed through the school of suffering.

We need not dwell further, then, on the probable reasons why, from this moment, Jacob's path was draped in the gathering shadows of outward sorrow. But we may notice what those shadows were. And we may interest ourselves in remarking how, as the sorrows gathered, there was a fuller life, and fruitfulness, and royalty. Jacob is increasingly replaced by Israel, the Prince.

There are four burials in one chapter (Gen. 35), including that of the idols in Shechem. These were the beginning of sorrows.

First, Deborah died; the old favorite nurse, who had accompanied her young mistress when, long years before, she had left her home across the Euphrates to become Isaac's bride. What a link she must have been with that sacred past! It must have been a sad experience to Jacob to lay the remains of his mother's closest friend beneath that oak in Bethel. The grief occasioned by her death was evidently quite unusual; since even the oak became known, in later years, as "the oak of terrors."

But a worse sorrow was in store. They journeyed from Bethel, and there was but a little way yet to Ephrath. The foremost ranks of the march were eagerly pressing on for the camping ground. But suddenly a summons from the rear bade them halt. The beloved Rachel could not go another step. The tidings of her extreme agony and peril silenced the motley groups of drovers and slaves, and servants and sons.

But all the agony of those devoted hearts could not stay that departing spirit: the mother lived only long enough to see her second babe, and to enshrine her sorrow in its name; and then she died, and was buried there in the way to Ephrath, which is Bethlehem. It was a matter of evident regret to Jacob, later, that she did not lie, with the rest of her kin, in Machpelah's ancient cave; but he could never forget that lone spot on the way to Ephrath (48:7). Even to this day travelers turn aside to visit Rachel's tomb.

Yet another heartache was measured out to that much-tried man. We suffer keenly through the sins of those we love; and when the father saw his Reuben and his Judah stained with the soul of nameless impurity, he drank perhaps the bitterest cup of his life.

Nor was this all. He lived to see dissension and hatred rend his home. The elder brethren envied and hated their younger brother, Joseph; the son of the beloved Rachel, and the child of his old age. His partiality most certainly added fuel to the flame. It was a great mistake to confer the costly coat that indicated the heir and prince of an Eastern clan, but we can easily understand how naturally the old man would turn to the promising lad, whose dreams bespoke his regal future.

But there was worse to follow. One day the sons brought home the coat he knew so well; but it was bedaubed with blood, and stained. "This have we found; know how whether it be thy son's coat or no." It may be that a suspicion even then crossed his mind that there had been foul play. But if it did, he kept it to himself, and only let it slip afterwards in the bitterness of his grief (42:36). He at least professed to believe that an evil beast had devoured the beloved body, and that Joseph had been rent in pieces. How he mourned only those know who have passed through similar anguish.

But another sorrow was in store. Jacob was next called upon to see his aged father breathe his last; and perhaps once more to hear those trembling lips pronounce the blessing that had cost so much. "Isaac gave up the ghost and died, and was gathered unto his people." He joined the great gathering of his clan, and the two sons buried him. Esau came from Edom—the successful man of the world, who had anticipated this moment years before, as likely to suit his purpose for slaying Jacob; but who was sweetened and softened by the mellowing influence of time. And Jacob—limping in his step; broken by hard toils; stricken by his recent losses—came to help him. There they stood for a moment: the twins whose lives had been such a struggle and such a contrast, reconciled in the presence of the great silence of the grave; and soon to take these several ways, never again to meet, but to tread ever diverging paths, both they and their children, and their children's children.

On the heels of bereavement came out of those terrible famines to which Eastern countries are subject, and which sweep them bare of people. The family of Jacob was not exempt. The sons seem to have sat down in the solid indifference born of long privation; and were aroused only by their father's appeal. "Why do ye look one upon another?" They went down into Egypt—in all ages the granary of the world; and after an agonizing interval of suspense returned. But Simeon was not with them; and to get him, and more corn, Jacob must risk the son of his right hand—the lad who had cost him so much in Rachel's death.

In addition to all this, there was growing upon him a realization that his life was closing; that He must prepare to follow his father into the unseen. His years had been few in comparison with those of his forefathers, and he had the weary sense of failure in that he had "not attained" (47:9). Such sorrows fell to Jacob's lot: they fall to our lot still; and when they do, let us learn how to receive them.

1. DO NOT JUDGE BY APPEARANCES. Jacob said, "*All* these things are against me." It was a great mistake. Joseph was alive—the governor of Egypt; sent there to preserve their lives, and to be the stay of his closing years. Simeon was also alive—the blessed link was drawing and compelling his brothers to return into the presence of the strange Egyptian governor. Benjamin would come safely back again. All things, so far from being against him, were working together for good for him. Cultivate the habit of looking at the bright side of things. If there are only a few clouds floating in your sky, do not say that the whole is overcast; and if all the heaven is covered, save one small chink of blue, make much of that; do not exaggerate the darkness.

2. BE SURE THAT GOD HAS A PURPOSE IN ALL YOUR SORROW. The apparent aimlessness of some kinds of pain is sometimes their sorest ingredient. We can suffer more cheerfully if we can clearly see the end that is being slowly reached. If we cannot, it is hard to lie still and be at rest. But the believer knows that nothing can come to him, save by the permission of God's love. Each calamity has a specific purpose, and the Almighty varies His method of dealing with us: He ever selects the precise trial that will soonest and best accomplish His purposes; and He only continues it long enough to do all that needs to be done. I commend that precious promise to those who think their sorrows past endurance. They will not last forever; they will be suited to our peculiar needs and strength. They will accomplish that on which the great Husbandman has set His heart.

3. REMEMBER THAT NOTHING CAN SEPARATE YOU FROM THE LOVE OF GOD. When Jacob reviewed these dark passages of his life from the serene heights of his dying bed, he saw, as he had never seen it before, that God had shepherded him all his life long; and His Angel had redeemed him from all evil (48:15–16). We do not realize this at the time; but there is never an experience in life without the watch of that unsleeping Shepherd-eye,

never a peril without the interposition of that untiring Shepherd-hand. Take heart, you who are descending into the dark valley of shadow, the Good Shepherd is going at your side, though you do not see Him. His rod and staff will comfort you: yes, His own voice will speak comfortably to you. Fear not!

4. ANTICIPATE THE "AFTERWARD." Look not at the things that are seen; but at those that are not seen. Cast into the one scale your sorrows, if you will; but put into the other the glory that will presently be the outcome of the pain. Anticipate the time when every vestige of Jacob shall have been laid aside, and Israel is become the befitting title for your soul. Will that not repay you—because you will have been brought into a oneness with Christ which shall be heaven in miniature?

13

Glimpses of the Israel-Nature
Genesis 47

As a brook runs, it clears itself. It was so with Jacob's life. The discipline of life, like a refining fire, did not fail in its purpose. The dross of his nature was at last nearly worked out, and the nobler Israel-nature became more and more apparent. This change is marked by the change in the name by which he is designated on the inspired page. The old term, Jacob, is used but sparingly, and for the most part Israel is the title of his nobility.

Before we can study the traces of his increasing princeliness of character, we should do well to notice that the name Jacob, though used sparingly, is not wholly dropped. We can never forget what we were. We can never forget what we might be, were it not for the restraining grace of God. The Jacob-nature keeps breaking on the Israel-life; yet, as the years passed on, and the habit of fellowship becomes a permanent possession, these irruptions become less and less frequent, so that at last the Israel-nature has almost undisputed sway in the life.

We have to notice some manifestations of this Israel-nature in Jacob. For more than twenty years Jacob mourned for Joseph as dead. The monotony of those years was broken only by new misfortunes; we catch a few sobs from that stricken heart. On first seeing the bloodstained coat, "I will go down into the grave mourning"; on learning the first tidings about the rough governor, the lord of the land, "Me have ye bereaved of my children"; on the appeal of his sons to spare Benjamin, "My son shall not go down with you, lest ye bring down my grey hairs with sorrow to the grave"; on their renewed appeal, "Wherefore dealt ye so ill with me as to tell the man ye had a brother?" on giving his final consent, in addition to his direction that they should take some delicacies from their almost emptied stores, he said sadly and almost despairingly, "God Almighty give you mercy before the man, that he may send away your other brother, and Benjamin. If I be bereaved of my children, I am bereaved."

But the night of weeping was followed by the morning of joy. What emotion must have filled his heart when the completed band of his sons stood once again before him with such amazing tidings! Benjamin was there, and Simeon. Love had welded them together in the furnace of sorrow, like a twelve-linked chain, no link of which would ever again be missing. And, above all, Joseph was yet alive; and he was governor over all the land of Egypt. What wonder that the aged heart stood still, and its machinery almost threatened to break down beneath the pressure of sudden rapture. At first he could not believe it all. But the sight of the wagons convinced him. Then there came forth a gleam of the royal spirit of faith—the spirit of Jacob revived, and *Israel* said, "It is enough: Joseph my son is yet alive; I will go and see him before I die."

Before he left Canaan, he had one final interview with his almighty Friend. It happened at Beersheba—the last haltingplace amid the green pasture lands of the Land of Promise, and before they struck into the sand-waste that lay between them and Egypt. Everything there reminded him of his own early life that was spent there. He could find the ruins of his father's altar, and the well that his father had sunk, and "he offered sacrifices unto the God of his father Isaac." His mind was engaged in eager debate as to the path of duty. On the one hand, love to Joseph and his necessities drew him to Egypt; on the other, the memory of how much evil had befallen his ancestors whenever they went down to Egypt, made him question whether he was justified in going. God made his path clear; "Fear not to go down into Egypt; for I will there make of thee a great nation: I will go down with thee into Egypt; and Joseph shall put his hand upon thine eyes." How comfortably our God speaks to us when we are sore perplexed.

1. THERE IS A GLIMPSE OF THE ISRAEL-NATURE IN HIS MEETING WITH JOSEPH. How feverishly the old man anticipated it!—and when, on the confines of Egypt, he learned that the second chariot in the land was bringing his long-lost son to his embrace, he roused himself to meet him; not as the Jacob of olden days, but as Israel the Prince. "And Israel said unto Joseph, Now let me die, since I have seen thy face, because thou art yet alive."

2. THERE IS YET ANOTHER GLIMPSE OF THE ISRAEL-NATURE IN HIS BLESSING OF PHARAOH. Joseph might almost have been ashamed of his aged father, and left him in the background. He was old, and decrepit, and lame. He had spent all his life in tents and sheep farms, and was totally ignorant of the manners of a court. He was an exile, an emigrant, a man who had failed. His very presence there was due to his ruinous losses. What a contrast between him and the glorious Pharaoh, whose court teemed with science and wit, with soldiers and priests, with wealth and splendor! And yet, when Jacob stood before Pharaoh, there was so much moral grandeur about him that the greatest monarch in the world bent eagerly beneath his blessing. "How old art thou?" was the kind inquiry of the mighty monarch, to commemorate whom a massive pyramid, destined to outlast his race, was in course of erection. The reply was sad enough; and it was the Jacob-nature that uttered it. "My life has been a pilgrimage; its days have been few and evil." *Few*, in comparison with those of Terah, Abraham, and Isaac. *Evil*, in comparison with that of Esau, who stood at the head of a great kingdom, the progenitor of a line of kings. And yet, with this confession ringing in his ears, Pharaoh was blessed by those outstretched trembling hands, and by that quavering voice. Esau never could have done that.

God can endow a human spirit with such moral splendor as to compel the world's conquerors to confess themselves conquered before its power. You may be crafty, mean, and bargain-loving; yet if you will but yield yourself to God, and submit to His loving discipline, He will make you truly royal, and give you the moral power that masters all other power beside.

3. THERE IS YET ANOTHER GLIMPSE OF THE ISRAEL-NATURE IN HIS SOLEMN INJUNCTIONS TO JOSEPH ABOUT HIS BURIAL. "The time drew nigh that *Israel* must die: and he called his son Joseph, and said unto him . . ." (47:29). It is the death scene that shows the true nature of a man; and its darkness set Jacob's better nature in full relief.

He was evidently a man of faith. He knew the ancient promise made by God, that their seed should inherit Canaan. He was sure, therefore, that his people would not always abide in Egypt—however fertile its Goshens, or friendly its peoples. The trumpet would sound the summons for their departure. He must be where his people were. To him, there, burial in the most splendid mausoleum that was ever constructed was not for one moment to be compared with burial in Machpelah's solitary and humble cave; which at that time was a mere outpost in a distant and hostile land. And he desired it, not only because the mortal remains of Abraham and Sarah, of Isaac and Rebekah, and of Leah lay there; but because he foresaw the time when it would be surrounded by the teeming myriads of his children.

He could see this only by faith. Faith made him royal; as it will ennoble the coarsest and commonest nature, lifting the beggar from the dunghill, and making him sit among princes.

4. THERE IS YET ANOTHER GLIMPSE OF THE ISRAEL-NATURE IN HIS DEALINGS WITH JOSEPH'S SONS. In the chapter that records that solemn scene, it is almost entirely on Israel that our attention is fixed. "Israel strengthened himself on his bed." "Israel beheld Joseph's sons." "Israel stretched out his right hand." "Israel said unto Joseph."

The sands of time had nearly run out in that aged and battered body, and when Joseph arrived at his dwelling, the gift of his own munificence, the dying man seems to have been lying in the extreme of physical exhaustion. But the sound of the beloved name of "Joseph" rallied him; and, with that wonderful accuracy of memory that is so remarkable in the dying, he reviewed the past. The vision of the wondrous ladder, with its troops of angels; the precious words of promise, which one hundred years could not obliterate from the tablets of memory; the scene on the hilly road to Bethlehem, where he buried Rachel; the successive instances of the guardian care of the Angel who had tended him all his life long until that day—all passed before his eye, dim with age, but bright with memory and hope.

Amid this reverie, the old man became aware of the presence of Joseph's two sons, and inquired who they were; and when he knew, he asked that they might be brought near enough for him to give them an old man's blessing. He did this with great affection and solemnity. He kissed and embraced them; and was led by prophetic insight to distinguish between them, crossing his hands, and laying his right on the head of the younger, whom Joseph had placed before his left; and his left on the head of the elder, whom the father had placed before his right. When Joseph remonstrated with him, thinking it was a mistake due to his age and blindness, the old man still held to his choice, as one conscious of a prerogative in which not even Joseph must interfere.

This touching interview ended by the gift to Joseph of the parcel of ground that he had wrested from the Amorites in Shechem. It had long ago returned to its original owners, but he saw down the vista of the future that there would be a reversion of the whole to him and his—and it was of that future that he spoke in faith.

The whole of this scene is replete with a dignity, born of moral greatness, and worthy of Israel, the Prince.

14

Rest and the Rest-Giver
Genesis 49

There is much of interest in these dying words of Jacob, through which Israel the Prince shines so conspicuously.

It would, for instance, be interesting to mark their accuracy. Reuben, though the firstborn, never excelled; no judge, prophet, or ruler, sprang from his tribe. Simeon was almost absorbed in the nomad tribes of southern Palestine. The cities in which the sons of Levi dwelt were scattered throughout all the tribes. Vestiges of terraced vineyards still attest to how well the hilly province assigned to Judah suited the culture of the vine. Zebulun embosomed the lake of Galilee, and stretched toward the coast of the blue Mediterranean. Esdraelon, the battlefield of Palestine, where Assyria from the North and Egypt from the South often met in deadly feud, lay within the limits of Issachar. Dan was small as an adder but, like it, could inflict dangerous wounds on any invader who had to pass by it toward the heart of the country. Gad, much pressed by border war; Asher, notable for fertility; Naphtali, famous for eloquence; Benjamin, cruel as a wolf. As these justified the prophecy of their dying ancestor, while the mighty tribes of Ephraim and Manasseh sprung from the sons of Joseph, inherited the blessings to the full.

It would be interesting to mark the close connection between the awards and the character of the bearded sons who stood around the withered, propped-up body of that dying man, while his spirit was flaming out in one last splendid outburst of prophetic and princelike glory, too much for the frail tenement to endure. Reuben, for example, had committed a nameless sin years before; he might have hoped that it was all long since forgotten, but no, here it reappears, dragged into inevitable light. That sin deprived him of the primacy—*that one sin*. Was this not arbitrary? Not so, since it was the index of his character, and was the unerring evidence of an unstable nature, for sensuality and instability are one.

But there comes, in these dying words, the announcement of a personality, mysterious, ineffable, sublime, which dwarfs all others, before which that aged spirit bows in worship, illumining the withered face with a light not born of earth. What does he mean by those mystic words, describing the Shiloh, His coming, and the gathering of the peoples to Him? There is a power in them that strangely stirs our spirits. We feel instinctively that we are face to face with Him before whom angels bow, veiling their faces with their wings. Again the words ring in our hearts: "The sceptre shall not depart from Judah, nor a lawgiver from between his feet, until Shiloh come; and unto Him shall the gathering of the peoples be."

1. LET US TRY TO UNDERSTAND THEM. The primacy of Israel, forfeited by Reuben, was transferred to Judah. The scepter, or staff, surely indicates legislative authority; the

lawgiver, some kind of legislator, and the drift of meaning in the verse is that Judah should retain the primacy of the tribes; and should not fail to have some kind of government, and some kind of governor, until One came, of whom Jacob spoke as Shiloh.

And who is this Shiloh? The greatest modern Hebrew critics tell us that it is like the German *Frederick*—rich in peace; the rest-giver; the man of rest. And of whom can this be true, but of One? The true Shiloh can be none other than the Son of God who, standing among earth's toiling millions, said, "Come unto me, all ye that labour and are heavy laden, and I will give you rest."

I have sometimes wondered where Jacob learned this most sweet and true name of our Lord Jesus. Was it flashed into his heart, at that moment, for the first time? It may have been. But there is another supposition, which has often pleased me. You will remember that at Peniel, Jacob asked the mysterious combatant His name. What answer did he receive? The angel simply said: "Wherefore is it that thou dost ask after my name? And He blessed him there." I have sometimes thought that, as He blessed him, He whispered in his ear this lovely title, which lingered in the old man's mind as the years went on, and became invested with ever fuller and richer meaning. This is the universal order of Christian living: first the resistance, then the shrunken sinew, then the yielding and clinging, and finally rest.

2. LET US NOTE, ALSO, THEIR LITERAL FULFILLMENT. For long centuries, Judah held the proud position assigned by the dying chieftain. The lion of the tribe of Judah brooked no rival. Jerusalem lay in his territory. David sprang from his sons. Throughout the long captivity, princes still claimed and held their right; for we are told that when Cyrus issued the proclamation that gave them liberty, "there arose up the chief of the fathers of Judah, and numbered unto them Sheshbazzar, the prince of Judah." It was Judah that returned from the captivity and gave the title *Jew* to every member of the race.

3. LET US REALIZE THEIR TRUTH. What a variety of weary eyes will read these words—weary eyes, aching heads, tired bodies, breaking hearts. Would to God that each of these could understand that Jesus Christ, the true Shiloh, is able to give them, now and forevermore, rest! "Come unto me, *all* ye that are heavy laden, and I will give you *rest.*"

It is a royal word. If this were the only scrap of His words, we would feel Him to have been the most royal man that ever trod our world. What certainty is here—no doubt, or question, or fear of failure; no faltering in that clear voice; no hesitancy in that decisive accent. We may trust Him brothers and sisters. It will not take Him longer to give you rest, than it took Him to still the waves: *"immediately* there was a great calm."

The Shiloh-rest is not for heaven. We need not ask for the wings of a dove to fly away to it. We would not find it hereafter, if we did not first find it here.

The Shiloh-rest is not in circumstances. That thought lies at the root of the teaching of the Epicurean, the Stoic, the worldly philosopher. But circumstances will never bring it, any more than change of posture will bring permanent relief to the pain-racked body.

The Shiloh-rest is not in inaction. In heaven, though they rest, yet they do not rest. They rest in their blessed service. There is the strenuous putting forth of energy, but no strain, no effort, no sense of fatigue. And such is the rest He gives. Does He not speak of a "burden" and a "yoke" in the same breath as He speaks of rest?

And it is not hard to get it. See! He *gives* it; He shows just where to look for and it is easy enough to *find* a thing if we know just where it lies. There seem to me but three conditions to be fulfilled by us.

a. *Surrender all to Him.* As long as you try to wield that scepter, or permit your will to be the lawgiver of your life, the Shiloh cannot come to you. You must give up your own efforts to save yourself—your own ideas of getting right with God; your own choice; your own way; your own will. You must hand over your sinful spirit to be saved by Him; you must surrender the keys of every room in your heart; you must be willing for Him to be supreme monarch of every province of your being. So only can you expect rest. And if you cannot bring your nature into this posture, ask Him to do it for you.

b. *Trust Him, by handing over all to Him.* Hand over to Him all your sins and all your sorrows. Do not wait till sins have accumulated into a cloud or a mountain. Do not delay till you are alone. But as swiftly as you are conscious of any burden, pass it on to Jesus; cast all your care on Him, for He cares for you. His heart is large enough to hold the troubles of the world. As soon as you give, He takes; and what He takes He also undertakes. This is the blessed rest of faith; the Land of Promise into which our Joshua waits to lead all who trust Him.

c. *Take His yoke, and learn of Him* i.e., do as He did. What was His yoke? A yoke means submission. To whom did He submit? To the Father's will. This was the secret of His rest. To live in the will of God—this is rest. Be ever on the outlook for it, and whenever you see it, *take it.* Do not wait for it to be forced on you, as a yoke on a heifer unaccustomed to it, which struggles till a deep wound is cut in its flesh. But *take* the yoke; be meek and lowly; imitate Him who said, "The cup which my Father hath given me, shall I not drink it?" If you can say that, you have learned the secret of rest; and Shiloh has already come to you.

15

Home: At Last
Genesis 50

The end has come at last! And we stand with those stalwart men in that hieroglyph-covered chamber, silent with the hush of death, to see the wayworn pilgrim breathe his last. His life has been a stern fight; his pathway not strewn with roses, but set with flints; few and evil the days of the years of his pilgrimage. Compared with the brilliant career of Esau, his life might be almost considered a failure. Better a hundredfold to be Israel the Prince, though an exile; than Esau, the founder of a line of dukes. The name of Israel will be an unfailing inspiration to those who, conscious of untold weakness and unlovableness, shall yet strive to apprehend that for which they were originally apprehended by Christ Jesus.

Before the mind of the dying patriarch three visions seemed to float in that solemn hour. He was thinking of the City of God, of the gathering of his clan, and of that lone and distant cave in Canaan where his fathers lay, and which he had so often visited.

1. THE CITY OF GOD. We are expressly told in the Epistle to the Hebrews that Jacob was one of those "who died in faith." He was the heir of promise. The land promised to

Abraham and Isaac had not as yet passed into his possession; it was still held by the wandering and settled tribes who had eyed his journeyings with such evident suspicion. All he had was the assured promise that in the coming days it would be his through his seed. He clung tenaciously to the blessed promise, so often reiterated to Abraham, that the land would become his people's, and his assurance that God would keep His word flung a radiance over his dying moments. Oh, glorious faith! What cannot faith do for those whom God has taught to trust!

As it became clear to Jacob that *he* was not to inherit Canaan, he seems to have fixed his mind with increasing eagerness on heaven. He felt that if God had not destined for him an earthly resting place, yet He had prepared for him a city. And it was for that glorious city, the city of the saints, that his pilgrim spirit now yearned. It was his close proximity to it that stirred his aged spirit, and drew it on with breathless eagerness and rapid steps.

The sacred writer employs a beautiful similitude when he says of Jacob and the rest of the patriarchs, that they greeted the promises from afar (Heb. 11:13). So Jacob, as he neared the city of God, so dear to faithful hearts, approved his kinsmanship with the elect spirits of all ages, by reaching forth toward it his aged, trembling hands.

Modern commentators have wrangled fiercely as to how much or how little of the future life was realized by these ancient saints. Into that controversy I have no desire to enter. But Jacob and the men of his type desired "the better country, that is, a heavenly." The future was less indistinct to them than we sometimes suppose. They, too, stood on Pisgah-heights and beheld a Land of Promise. On such a Pisgah-height Jacob was standing; and as all earthly objects, even the face of Joseph, grew indistinct to his dimming eyes, those rapturous and celestial scenes grew on his spiritual vision and beckoned to him.

In what relation do you stand to that city of God? Do not imagine that it will gladden your dying gaze, unless it has often been the object of your loving thought in the days of health and vigor. Do you feel the *pull* of that city, as the sailor does of the anchor that keeps him from drifting with the tide? If so, it will gladden your dying moments.

2. THE GATHERING OF THE CLAN. "I am to be gathered unto my people." When the dying patriarch spoke this way, he meant something more than that his dust should mingle with all that was mortal of his forefathers. He surely looked upon the city as the gathering-place of his clan; the *rendezvous* of all who were *his* people, because they were the people of God.

What as to the intermediate state? At the best "we know not what we shall be." We cannot penetrate the veil that only opens wide enough to admit the entering spirit. It is clear that our spirits will not reach their full consummation and bliss till the morning of the resurrection, when body and spirit will be reunited; but it is equally clear that they will not be unconscious, but will enter into the blessed presence of our Lord.

There is no accent of uncertainty in the New Testament. As soon as the tent is taken down, the mansion is entered (2 Cor. 5:2). Absent from the body, the believer is present with the Lord. Do not puzzle over useless questionings: be content to know that death is not a state, but an act; not a resting place, but a transition to the palace.

What as to the recognition of the departer? It would not have been an object of anticipation to Jacob to be gathered to his people, if he would not know them when he reached their blest society. When the Jew thought of the unseen world, he expected to meet the saints, of whom he had heard from childhood, and especially Abraham. Was not the Jew wiser than most Christians? Has the body powers of recognition, and the spirit none? Can that be a Father's home, where the brothers and sisters do not know each other?

We shall be gathered to our people. Throughout the ages the elect souls of our race have been gathering there. Are they our people? Can we claim kinship with them? There is but one bond, as we are taught in Hebrews 11. Wherever it is found, it designates the owner to be one of those who can claim kinship with the saintly inhabitants of the city of God. The test question of qualification for the franchise of the New Jerusalem is: "Do you believe in the name of the only-begotten Son of God?"

3. THE CAVE OF MACHPELAH. "Bury me with my fathers in the cave that is in the field of Ephron the Hittite." For seventeen years Jacob had lived in Egypt, surrounded by all the comforts that Joseph's filial love could devise, and his munificence execute. But he must be laid where Abraham and Sarah, Isaac and Rebekah, and the faithful Leah awaited resurrection.

This was something more than the natural sentiment that impels us to request burial in some quiet spot in God's acre, where our family name is inscribed on many of the gravestones around. Jacob felt that Machpelah's cave was the first outpost in the land that was one day to belong to his people; and he wanted, as far as he might, to be there with them, and to share in the land of promise.

The last word was spoken, the last commission given, and he knew the end was come. "He gathered up his feet into the bed;" i.e., he met death quietly, calmly, manfully. He quietly breathed out his spirit, and was gathered to his people. And at that moment sorrow and sighing, which had been his close companions in life, fled away forever.

How calm and noble that face looked, fixed in the marble of death! The Jacob-look had vanished from it; and it was stamped with the smile with which the royal Israel-spirit had molded it in its outward passage.

What wonder, then, that Joseph fell on his father's face, and wept on him, and kissed him! He had borne the strain as long as he could; and now nature had to vent herself in manly, filial grief.

The body was carefully embalmed. No time, or pains, or cost, were spared. Egypt herself mourned for him for seventy days. Then one of the most splendid funeral processions that ever gathered to lay saint, or sage, or hero to his rest, carried that precious casket in solemn pomp from Egypt up to Canaan. And the signs of mourning were so great as to impress the inhabitants of the land, the Canaanites.

The stone was rolled away, and Jacob's remains laid on their appointed niche. Many a storm has swept over them—Assyrian, Egyptian, Babylonian, Grecian, Roman, Saracenic, and Mohammedan. But nothing has disturbed their quiet rest; and they hold the land in fee, till God shall fulfill in all its magnificence, the promise that He made and has never recalled—that He would give the land to Jacob's seed for an everlasting inheritance. So rest thee, ISRAEL THE PRINCE!

16

The God of Jacob
Psalm 46

It is comforting to discover in how many parts of Scripture God calls Himself the God of Jacob. He seems to take special delight in the title that links His holy nature with one who, so far from giving promise of saintship, was naturally one of the meanest of men. We would not have been surprised to find Him speaking of Himself as the God of Israel, the Prince, but it is as startling as it is reassuring to find Him speaking of Himself still more often as the God of Jacob.

He has not changed since He took Jacob in hand; and He is ready to do as much for all who are conscious of being equally worthless by nature, and who are willing to put themselves into His gracious hands.

There is little doubt that God would do as much for all the readers of these lines, if only they would be willing. And it is the object of this closing appeal to urge my readers to let Him have His gracious way with them. As we have studied together Jacob's life and character, have you not been keenly conscious of similarities between him and yourself? *You* too may be cunning, crafty, and deceitful; or you may be prone to outbursts of ungovernable temper; or you may be cursed by unholy desires that honeycomb your better nature; or you may be constantly brought into captivity to some tyrannous sin. There is no need for this to be your hapless lot for one moment longer, if only you will hand yourself over to the mighty God of Jacob. If God could make a prince of Jacob, He can do as much for anyone.

1. CULTIVATE A HOLY AMBITION. There is no tendency of the unrenewed heart more subtle or dangerous than ambition. And yet, if it is properly curbed and kept, ambition plays a useful part among the motive-forces of human life. And it is well to cultivate a holy ambition to be all that God can make us.

Do not be content to be always a Jacob. Let this be deeply engraved on your heart, as the sacred page is turned—that every promise is for you; and then look up to Him, and claim that He should do as He has said.

2. MAKE A COMPLETE SURRENDER TO GOD. Before God will begin His gracious work on a human spirit, it must be entirely surrendered to Him. Every province of the life must be placed under his government.

Some time ago, I saw a notice in the window of a most dilapidated shop. "This shop will shortly be opened under entirely new management." And as I stood for a moment there, it seemed as if the whole building put on a kind of hopeful smile, as much as to say, "I am so glad that I am to be put under an entirely fresh management." Several days afterward, as I passed that way again, I found a small army of carpenters and decorators at work; and on the next occasion, the change in management was evident to the most casual eye, for the whole place had a clean, sweet look about it that was quite attractive.

Now this is just what you require—you with the Jacob nature. You have been trying to manage yourself all too long. A change is evidently needed; but it must be complete. Do not be afraid of giving all up to the lovely will of Him who is love. Should there be things in your life that you find it hard to abandon, tell God that you give them over to Him; and that you are willing to have His will done, if He only will bring it to pass in His own good time and way. And if you cannot say as much as that, tell Him *that you are willing to be made willing.*

There is even a more excellent way than any, which is within the reach of the feeblest hand, and that is to ask the Lord to come into your life *to take* that which you do not feel able to give.

3. BE CAREFUL NOT TO THWART GOD'S GOOD WORKMANSHIP. Of course, there is a sense in which we cannot resist or impede the execution of His sovereign will. And yet, on the other hand, we may hinder and counterwork His loving purposes. Let us be on the guard against this disastrous resistance; and be ever on the alert to work out that which God is working in us, "both to will and to do."

I do not deny that God will fulfill His purpose in us, even though we hinder Him; but it will be carried through, as it was in the case of Jacob, at a terrible expenditure of agony and the shrivelling of the sinew of our strength. It is always better to *take* the yoke of divine purpose, offered by our Lord as His: "Take *my* yoke."

4. SEEK THE FULLNESS OF THE SPIRIT. If we would have His nature, we must have His Spirit: not in drops, but in rivers; not as a zephyr breath, but as "a rushing mighty wind."

This is the dying need of the Christian church in this day. We have learning, rhetoric, fashion, wealth, splendid buildings, and superb machinery; but we are powerless, for lack of the power that can be obtained only through the fullness of the Spirit. We have too largely forgotten the exhortation: "Be filled with the Spirit." We have thought that the fullness of the Spirit was a speciality for the apostolic age, instead of being for all time. And thus the majority of Christians are living on the other side of Pentecost. We can never be what we might be until we return to apostolic theory and practice in respect to this all-essential matter.

Seek this blessed filling. It is possible only to emptied hearts, but as soon as a vacuum has been created by the act of entire surrender, there will be an instantaneous filling by the Holy Ghost in answer to expectant desire and eager faith. So shall you be an Israel, and have power with God and man.

Life is no child's play to those who enter into God's purposes, and in whom He is fulfilling His sublime ideals. But when the discipline is over, we will be more than satisfied with the result; and, taking our stand among the princes of the royal blood, we will ascribe eternal glory to Him who loved us in spite of all, and washed us from our sins in His own blood, and out of Jacobs made us KINGS UNTO GOD.

JOSEPH

1

Early Days
Genesis 37

It is a great mission to rescue truth from neglect; to play the part of Old Mortality, who, chisel in hand, was wont to clear the mold of neglect from the gravestones of the Covenanters, so that the legend might stand out clearly. It is something like this that I attempt for this exquisite story. We think we know it, and yet there may be depths of meaning and beauty which, by their very familiarity, escape us. Let us ponder together the story of Joseph, for in doing so we shall get a foreshadowing of Him who was cast into the pit of death, and who now sits at the right hand of Power, a Prince and a Savior.

1. THE FORMATIVE INFLUENCES OF HIS EARLY LIFE. Seventeen years before our story opens, a child was borne by Rachel, the favorite wife of Jacob. The latter was then living as manager for his uncle Laban, on the ancient pastureland of Charran, situated in the valley of the Euphrates and the Tigris, from which his grandfather Abraham had been called by God. The child received an eager welcome from its parents.

But what a history has passed in that interval! When yet a child he was hastily caught up by his mother and sustained in her arms on the back of a swift camel, urged to its highest speed in the flight across the desert that lay, with only one oasis, between the bank of the Euphrates and the green prairies of Gilead. He could just remember the panic that spread through the camp when tidings came that Esau, the dread uncle, was on his march with four hundred followers. Nor could he ever forget the evening full of preparation, the night of solemn expectancy, and the morning when his father limped into the camp, maimed in body, but with the look of a prince on his face.

More recently still, he could recall the hurried flight from the enraged idolaters of Shechem, and those solemn hours at Bethel where his father had probably showed him the very spot on which the foot of the mystic ladder had rested, and where the whole family formally entered into a new covenant with God. It may be that this was the turning point of his life. Such events make deep impressions on young hearts.

These impressions were soon deepened by three deaths. When the family reached the family settlement, they found the old nurse Deborah dying. She was the last link to those bright days when her young mistress Rebekah came across the desert ot be Isaac's bride; and they buried her with many tears under an ancient but splendid oak. And the child could never forget the next event. The long caravan was moving slowly up to the narrow ridge along which lay the ancient village of Bethlehem: suddenly a halt was called, the beloved Rachel could go not another step, and there as the sun was sinking she died. This was the greatest loss he had ever known. A little later the lad stood with

111

his father and brethren before Machpelah's venerable grave, to lay Isaac where Abraham and Sarah and Rebekah awaited him, each on a narrow shelf; and where, after twenty-seven years, he was to place the remains of his father Jacob.

2. The Experiences of his Home Life.

a. *Joseph was endowed with remarkable intelligence.* The rabbis describe him as a wise son, endowed with knowledge beyond his years. It was this, combined with the sweetness of his disposition, and the memory of his mother, that won for him his father's peculiar love. "Israel loved Joseph more than all his children."

b. *And this love provided the coat of many colors.* We have been accustomed to think of this coat as a kind of patchwork quilt, and we have wondered that grown men should have been moved to so much passion at the sight of the peacock plumes of their younger brother. But the Hebrew word means simply a tunic reaching to the extremities, and describes a garment commonly worn in Egypt and the adjacent lands. Imagine a long white linen robe extending to the ankles and wrists, and embroidered with a narrow stripe of color round the edge of the skirt and sleeves, and you will have a fair conception of this famous coat.

Now we can understand the envy of his brothers. This sort of robe was worn only by those who had no need to toil for their living. All who had to win their bread by labor wore short, colored garments that did not show stain, or cramp the free movement of the limbs. Such was the lot of Jacob's sons, and such the garments they wore. They had to wade through morasses, clamber up hills, carry wandering sheep home on their shoulders, fight with robbers and beasts of prey; and for such toils the flowing robe would have been unfit. But when Jacob gave such a robe to Joseph, he declared in effect that from such hardships and toils his favorite son should be exempt. When, therefore, they saw Joseph dressed in his robe of state, the brethren felt that in all likelihood he would have the rich inheritance, while *they* would have to follow a life of toil. "And when his brethren saw that their father loved him more than all his brethren, they hated him, and could not speak peaceably unto him."

c. *The case was aggravated by his plain speaking.* "He brought unto his father their evil report." At first sight this does not seem a noble trait in his character. But there may have been circumstances that justified, and even demanded, the exposure. It is sometimes the truest kindness, after due and repeated warning, to expose the evil deeds of those with whom we live and work. If they are permitted to go on in sin, apparently undetected, they will become hardened and emboldened, and eager to go to greater lengths. But this was enough to make them hate him.

d. *Joseph dreamed that he should become the center of the family life.* All young people dream. Joseph's dreams foretold not only his exaltation, but his brother's humiliation. If he was the central sheaf, their sheaves had to do obeisance by falling to the earth around it. If he was on the throne, sun, moon, and stars had to do him homage. This was more than the proud spirits of his brethren could brook, and "they hated him yet the more."

Joseph was carried through the hatred and opposition of his foes; and his dreams were literally fulfilled later in the golden days of prosperity, just as Jesus was eventually seated at the right hand of God, as Prince and Savior. And your time, sufferer, will come at length, when God will vindicate your character and avenge your sorrows.

2

The Pit
Genesis 37

To the casual reader the story of Joseph's wrongs and of his rise from the pit to vice-regal power is simply interesting, for its archaic simplicity and the insight into the past that it affords. But to the man on whose heart the cross is carved in loving memory there is a far deeper interest. It is Calvary in miniature. It is the outline sketch of the Artist's finished work. It is a rehearsal of the greatest drama ever enacted among men.

1. JOSEPH'S MISSION. *"Jacob dwelt in the land* of his father's sojournings." After Jacob had buried his old father he continued to reside in the Vale of Hebron, where Isaac had dwelt for nearly two hundred years, and where Abraham abode before him. This was the headquarters of his vast encampment. But rich as the pastures of Hebron were, they were not sufficient to support the whole of the flocks and herds. The sons were compelled to drive these by slow stages to distant parts of the land. They were even forced, by stern necessity, to brave the anger of the people of Shechem, whom they had grievously wronged, and who had vowed vengeance on them for their foul behavior.

It was this that gave point to Jacob's question, "Do not thy brethren feed the flock in Shechem?" He had heard his sons speak of going there in search of pasture; now long weeks had passed since he received tidings of their welfare, and the memory of the past made him anxious about them. And this solicitude became so overpowering that it forced him to do what otherwise would never have entered his thoughts.

He was alone in Hebron with Joseph and Benjamin. They were his darlings; his heart loved them with something of the intense devotion he had felt toward their mother. Joseph was seventeen years old and Benjamin was younger. The old man kept them with him, reluctant to let them from his sight. But the old man yearned with anxious love over his absent sons; and at last, after many battlings and hesitations, he suddenly said to the dearly-loved Joseph, "Come, and I will send thee unto them . . . go, I pray thee, see whether it be well with thy brethren, and . . . bring me word again."

On Joseph's part there was not a moment's hesitation. In the flash of a thought he realized the perils of the mission—perils among false brethren, who bitterly hated him. But as soon as he knew his father's will, he said, "Here am I." "So, Jacob sent him . . . and he came."

a. *Is not all this suggestive of a yet loftier theme?* Our Lord never wearied of calling Himself the Sent of the Father. There is hardly a page in the Gospel of John in which He does not say more than once, "I came not of Myself, but My Father sent Me." Thus it became a constant expression with the New Testament writers, "God sent forth his Son"; "The Father sent the Son to be the Saviour of the world."

b. *It must have cost Jacob something to part with the beloved Joseph.* But who can estimate how much it cost the infinite God to send his only-begotten Son, who had dwelt in His bosom, and who was His Son from everlasting? Let us not think that God is passionless. If His love is like ours (and we know it must be), He must suffer from the same causes that work havoc in our hearts, only He must suffer proportionately to the strength and infiniteness of His nature. How much, then, must God have loved us, that

He should be willing to send His Son! Truly God *so* loved the world! But who shall fathom the depths of that one small word?

c. *But our Savior did not come solely because He was sent.* He came because He loved His mission. He came to seek and to save those who are lost. If you could have asked Him, as you met Him traversing those same fields, "What seekest Thou?" He would have replied in the same words of Joseph, "I seek my brethren." Nor was He content with only *seeking* the lost; He went after them *until* He found them. "Joseph went after his brethren [until] he found them in Dothan."

2. JOSEPH'S RECEPTION. "They saw him afar off, even before he came near unto them, [and] they conspired against him to slay him." He would doubtless have been ruthlessly slain, and his body flung into some pit away from the haunts of men, if it had not been for the merciful pleadings of Reuben, the eldest brother. "And it came to pass when Joseph was come unto his brethren, that they stripped Joseph out of his coat, his coat of many colours . . . and they took him, and cast him into a pit."

The historian does not dwell on the passion of the brothers, or on the anguish of that young heart, which found it so hard to die, so hard to say goodby to the fair earth, so hard to descend into that dark cistern, whose steep sides forbade the hope that he could ever scramble back into the upper air. But years later they said one to another, "We are verily guilty concerning our brother, in that we saw the anguish of his soul, when he besought us, and we would not hear." What a revelation there is in these words! We seem to see Joseph; he struggles to get free; he entreats them with bitter tears to let him go; he implores them for the sake of his old father, and by the tie of brotherhood.

a. *Unforgiven sin is a fearful scourge.* Year passed after year, but the years could not obliterate from the memories of the brothers that look, those cries, that scene in the green glen of Dothan. They tried to lock up the skeleton in their most secret cupboard, but it contrived to come forth to confront them even in their guarded hours. The old father, who mourned for his son as dead, was happier than were they, who knew him to be alive. One crime may thus darken a whole life. God has so made the world that sin is its own Nemesis—sin carries with it the seed of its own punishment. And the men who carry with them the sense of unforgiven sin, will be the first to believe in a vulture forever tearing out the vitals, a worm that never dies, a fire that is never quenched.

b. *But Joseph's grief was a true anticipation of Christ's.* "He came unto his own, and his own received him not" (John 1:11). They said, "This is the heir, come let us kill him, and the inheritance shall be ours." "They caught him, and cast him out, and slew him." "They parted his raiment among them." They sold Him to the Gentiles. They sat down to watch Him die. The anguish of Joseph's soul reminds us of the strong cryings and tears wrung from the human nature of Christ by the near approach of His unknown sufferings as the scapegoat of the race. The comparative innocence of Joseph reminds us of the spotlessness of the Lamb who was without blemish, and whose blamelessness was again and again attested to before He died.

c. *Here, however, the parallel ends.* Joseph's sufferings stopped before they reached the point of death; Jesus tasted death. Joseph's sufferings were personal; the sufferings of Jesus were substitutionary and mediatorial: "He died for us"; "He gave himself for me." Joseph's sufferings had no efficacy in atoning for the sin that caused them, but the sufferings of Jesus atone not only for the guilt of his murderers, but for the guilt of all.

3. JOSEPH'S FATE. "They sat down to eat bread." With hardened unconcern they took their midday meal. Just at that moment a new and welcome sight struck their gaze. They were sitting on the plain at Dothan, a spot that still retains its ancient name, and anyone stationed there, would be able to trace the main road that led from the fords of the Jordan toward the coast of the Mediterranean. Along this road at that moment a caravan was traveling. The brothers could readily make out the long string of patient camels moving slowly up the valley toward them.

The sight of these traveling merchants gave a sudden turn to the thoughts of the conspirators. They knew that there was in Egypt a great demand for slaves, and that these merchantmen were in the habit of buying slaves in their passage and selling them in that land. Why not sell their brother? It would be an easy way of disposing of him. It would save them from fratricide. So, acting on the suggestion of Judah, they lifted Joseph out of the pit, and sold him for twenty rings of silver—about eight ounces.

It was the work of a few minutes, and then Joseph found himself one of a long line of fettered slaves bound for a foreign land. Was not this almost worse than death? What anguish still rent his young heart! How eager his desire to send just one last message to his father! Little did he think then that hereafter he should look back on that day as one of the most gracious links in a chain of loving providences; or that he should ever say, "Be not grieved, nor angry with yourselves . . . God did send me [here] before you."

Joseph was betrayed by his brothers; Jesus by His friend. Joseph was sold for money; so was our Lord. Joseph followed in the train of captives to slavery; Jesus was numbered with transgressors. The crime of Joseph's brothers fulfilled the divine plan; and the wicked hands of the crucifiers of Jesus fulfilled the determinate counsel and foreknowledge of God.

God will "make the wrath of man to praise him."

3

In the House of Potiphar
Genesis 39

The Midianite merchantmen, into whose hands his brethren sold Joseph, brought him down to Egypt—with its riband of green pasture amid the waste of sand. In some great slave market he was exposed for sale, together with hundreds more, who had been captured by force or stealth from the surrounding countries.

He was bought by Potiphar, "the captain of the guard," who was, in all likelihood, the chief of the royal bodyguard, in the precincts of the court. The Egyptian monarchs had the absolute power of life and death, and they did not scruple to order the infliction of a variety of summary or sanguinary punishments, the execution of which was entrusted to the military guard.

Potiphar was an Egyptian grandee; a member of a proud aristocracy; high in office and in court favor. He would no doubt live in a splendid palace, covered with hieroglyphs and filled with slaves. The young captive must have trembled as he passed up the pillared avenue, through sphinx-guarded gates, into the recesses of that vast Egyptian palace where they spoke a language of which he could not understand a word, and where all was so new and strange. But "God was with him"; the sense of the presence and guardianship of his father's God pervaded and stilled his soul, and kept him in perfect peace. Who would not rather, after all, choose to be Joseph in Egypt with God, than the brothers with a blood-stained garment in their hands and the sense of guilt on their souls?

Let us consider how Joseph fared in Potiphar's house.

1. JOSEPH'S PROMOTION. "The LORD was with Joseph; and he was a prosperous man." The older versions of the Bible give a curious rendering here: "The Lord was with Joseph; and he was a lucky fellow." Everything he handled went well. Success followed him as closely as his shadow, and touched all his plans with her magic wand. Potiphar and his household got to the place where they expected this strange Hebrew captive to untie every knot, disentangle every skein, and bring to successful issues the most intricate arrangements. This arose from two causes.

a. *Though stripped of his coat, he had not been stripped of his character.* He was industrious, prompt, diligent, obedient, reliable. He did his work, not because he was obliged to do it, but because God had called him to do it. He said to himself, as he said in afterlife, "God did send me before you." He felt that he was the servant, not so much of Potiphar, as of the God of Abraham and Isaac. There, in the household of Potiphar, he might live a devout and earnest life as truly as when he spent the long, happy days in Jacob's tent: and he did. And it was this that made him so conscientious and careful, qualities that in business must ensure success.

When his fellow-servants were squandering the golden moments, Joseph was filling them with activities. When they worked simply to avoid the frown or the lash, he worked to win the smile of the great Taskmaster, whose eye was ever upon him. They often pointed at him with envy, and perhaps said, "He is a lucky fellow." They did not think that his luck was his character; and that his character meant God. There is no such thing as luck, except that luck means character. And if you wish to possess such a character as will insure your success in this life, there is no true basis for it but Jesus Christ.

b. *The Lord made all that he did to prosper.* "The LORD blessed the Egyptian's house for Joseph's sake; and the blessing of the LORD was upon all that he had in the house, and in the field." Such blessing would often be ours if we walked as near to God as Joseph did. Let us see to it that we live so that God may be with us.

c. *These words may be read by employees of various kinds.* They will surely be helped by the example of this noble youth. He did not give himself to useless regrets and unavailing tears. He girded himself manfully to do with his might whatsoever his hand found to do. He was "faithful in that which was least," in the most menial and trivial duties of his office. He believed that God had put him where he was; and in serving his early master well he felt that he was really pleasing his great heavenly Friend. This is the spirit in which all work should be done. "Whatsoever ye do, do it heartily, as to the Lord, and not unto men." Our lots in life are much more even than we think. It is not so important what we do as how we do it.

d. *These words may be read by employers.* We cannot estimate the worth of a true Christian servant. The Egyptian Potiphar must have been agreeably surprised at the sudden tide of prosperity that came to him. All things went well with him—his cattle throve in the field; his affairs prospered in the house. "The LORD blessed the Egyptian's house for Joseph's sake"; He paid him handsomely for His servant's keep. So it is still.

Ungodly masters owe many a blessing to the presence of some Christian servant or employee beneath their roof. When we reach heaven, and are able to trace the origin of things, we will find that many of the choicest blessings of our lives were procured by the prayers or presence of very obscure and unrecognized people who were dear to God.

2. JOSEPH'S TEMPTATION. Years passed on, and Joseph became the steward and bailiff in his master's house. "He left all that he had in Joseph's hand; and he knew not aught he had, save the bread which he did eat." And it was just here that Joseph encountered the most terrible temptation of his life.

a. *We may expect temptation in days of prosperity and ease rather than in those of privation and toil.* It is easy to keep the armor on when we ascend the desolate mountain pass, struggling against the pitiless blast, and afraid that any boulder may hide an assassin. It is hard to keep it buckled close when we have reached the happy vally, with its sultry air. But unless we keep armed there, we are lost.

b. *Temptation is hardest to resist when it arises from the least expected quarter.* Egyptian women in those days enjoyed as much liberty as our women do now: this is conclusively proved by the Egyptian monuments, which also testify to the extreme laxity of their morals. It may be that Potiphar's wife was not worse than many of her sex, though we blush to read of her infamous proposals. The sudden appeal to his passions invested the temptation with tenfold force. For the most part, the sailor is warned against the coming storm; but alas for him if he is caught by a sudden squall! Christian, beware of sudden squalls!

c. *Policy and conscience are often at variance* in respect to temptation. It seemed essential to Joseph to be in good stead with his master's wife. To please her would secure his advancement. To cross her would make her his foe, and ruin his hopes. How many would have reasoned that, by yielding for only a moment, they might win influence which they could afterward use for the best results! The only armor against policy is *faith* that looks to the long future, and believes that in the end it will be found better to have done right, and to have waited the vindication and blessing of God. Well was it for Joseph that he did not heed the suggestions of policy. Had he done so, he might have acquired a little more influence in the home of Potiphar; but it could never have lasted—and he would never have become prime minister of Egypt, or had a home of his own, or have brought his sons to receive the blessings of his dying father.

d. *There were peculiar elements of trial in Joseph's case.* The temptation was accompanied by opportunity: "there was none of the men of the house there within." It was well timed, and if he had yielded, there was not much fear of detection and punishment; the temptress would never publish her own shame. The temptation was also repeated day by day. How terrible must have been that awful persistency! The temptation that tires to win its way by its very importunity is to be feared most of all.

e. *Yet Joseph stood firm.* He reasoned with her. He referred to his master's kindness and trust. He held up the confidence that he dared not betray. He tried to recall her to a sense of what became her as his master's wife. But he did more. He brought the case from the court of reason to that of conscience, and asked in words forever memorable, and which have given the secret of victory to tempted souls in all ages: "How then can I do this great wickedness, and sin against God!"

If history teaches anything, it teaches that sensual indulgence is the surest way to national ruin. Society in not condemning this sin condemns herself. It is said that the temptations of our great cities are too many and strong for the young to resist. Men sometimes speak as if sin were a necessity. Refuse to entertain such thoughtlessness and dangerous talk. A young man *can* resist; he *can* overcome; he *can* be pure and chaste. We must, however, obey the dictates of Scripture and common sense. Avoid all places, books, and people that minister to evil thoughts. Remember that no temptation can master you unless you admit it *within* your nature; and since you are too weak to keep the door shut against it, look to the mighty Savior to place Himself against it. All hell cannot break the door open which you entrust to the safe keeping of Jesus.

f. *What a motto this is for us all!* "How can *I* do this great wickedness?" *I*, for whom Christ died. "How can I do this great *wickedness?*" Others call it "sowing wild oats." I call it SIN. "How can I do this *great* wickedness?" Many wink at it; to me it is a *great* sin. "How can I sin *against God?*" It seems only to concern men; but in effect it is a personal sin against the holy God.

g. *It might have been better if Joseph had not gone into the house to do his work;* but probably he had no choice except to go. He took care not to be with her (v. 10) more than he could help. We have no right to expect God to keep us if we voluntarily put ourselves into temptation. But if we are compelled to go there by the circumstances of our life, we may count on His faithfulness.

h. *Joseph did a wise thing when he fled.* Discretion is often the wisest part of valor. Better lose a coat and many a more valuable possession than lose a good conscience. Do not parley with temptation. Do not stay to look at it. It will master you if you do. "Escape for thy life; look not behind thee, neither stay in all the plain."

i. *There is no sin in being tempted.* The sinless One Himself was tempted of the devil. The will is the citadel of our manhood; and so long as there is no yielding there, there is none anywhere. I cannot be accused of receiving stolen goods, if I am simply asked to take them in—a request which I indignantly repudiate. The sin comes in when I assent, and acquiesce, and yield.

May we have grace and faith to imitate the example of Joseph, and above all, of our stainless Lord. We may be quite sure that no temptation will be permitted to assail us but such as is common to man, or that we are able to resist. Never forget that we who believe in Jesus are seated with Him at the right hand of power; nor that Satan is already, in the purpose of God, a defeated foe beneath our feet. Open your whole being to the subduing grace of the Holy Spirit. And thus we will be more than conquerors through Him who loves us.

4

The Secret of Purity
Genesis 39. *See also* Proverbs 4:23; 1 Peter 1:5; 2 Timothy 1:12

Joseph learned hundreds of years before our Savior taught it from the Mount of the Beatitudes, the blessedness of the pure in heart. There is nothing that we more earnestly admire than purity. Men familiar with the secret of self-control always attract to themselves the admiration and reverence of others.

We must always bear in mind that there is no part of our nature, no function of our human life, which is in itself common or unclean. But when man sinned in the glades of

Paradise, he changed the pivot of his being from God to self. And from that time man's highest law has consisted in the indulgence of appetite, the only restraint being imposed by the fear of disastrous consequences in name or position; in mind, body, or estate.

We must take into account the operation of the great law of heredity, by which we have become possessed of appetites and tendencies, which, however pure in their original intention, have been vitiated through the abuse of the many generations from which we have sprung. It is inevitable, therefore, that we should begin life under serious disadvantages, since we are closely related to a race which, through history, has been tainted by the poison of self-will, and swept by the storms of passion. And is not this what is meant by the theological term, *original sin;* and by St. Paul's phrase, "the law in the members"?

To guard against all possible misinterpretation, we reiterate that we do not hold sin to consist in a merely physical state or act, but that we are predisposed to sin by the very nature we have inherited, and no philosophy of the inner life can be satisfactory that does not recognize the presence of this body of flesh, which is not in itself sin, but which so readily lends itself to evil suggestion.

So long, therefore, as we are in the body, we cannot say that we stand where Adam stood when he first came from the molding hand of God. There is a great difference between us and him, in that at that moment his nature had never yet yielded to evil; while ours has done so thousands of times, both in those from whom we have received it, and in our own repeated acts of self-indulgence.

Is there then no deliverance in this life from that bondage? Surely there is. The one-sufficient power by which the promptings of our evil nature can be held in check is by the indwelling and infilling of the Holy Spirit.

Never in this life will the tempter cease to assail; and so long as we tabernacle in this body, we will carry with us that susceptibility to evil that is the bitter result of Adam's fall. But when the Holy Spirit fills us, the tempter may do his worst, and our nature will not respond to the solicitations that are made to it. And when the Spirit is in mighty power within, He will take away the very desire to yield to sin, so that we shall loathe and shudder at things that we formerly chose and reveled in.

And in many cases, where He is trusted to the uttermost, He does His work so quietly and effectually in keeping the sinful tendencies in the place of death, that the happy subject of His grace supposes that they have been extracted from the nature. They are as if they were not, and this blessed experience continues, just so long as the soul lives in the full enjoyment of the blessed Spirit's work.

Would that it might be the happy portion of each reader of these lines!

5

Misunderstood and Imprisoned
Genesis 39, 40. *See also* Psalms 102:17–19

When Potiphar heard the false but plausible statement of his wife, and saw the garment in her hand, which he recognized as Joseph's, his wrath flamed up; he would hear no words of explanation, but thrust Joseph at once into the state prison, of which he had the oversight and charge.

Joseph

1. THE SEVERITY OF HIS SUFFERINGS. It was not a prison like those with which we are familiar—airy, well-lit, and conducted by humane men. To use Joseph's own words, in the Hebrew, it was a miserable "hole." "I have done nothing that they should put me into the 'hole'." Two or three little rooms, crowded with prisoners, stifling in air, fetid with ill odors, perhaps half-buried from the blessed sunshine—this was the sort of accommodation in which Joseph spent those two miserable years.

Imagine a large gloomy hall, with no windows, paved with flags black with filth, no light or air, except what may struggle through the narrow grated aperture, by which the friends of the wretched inmates, or some pitying strangers, pass in the food and water which are the sole staff of life. No arrangements of any kind have been made for cleanliness, or for the separation of the prisoners. All day long there is the weary clank of fetters around manacled feet, as the victims slowly drag themselves over the floor, or resolve again and again around the huge stone columns that support the roof, and to which their chains are riveted. In some such sunless "hole" must Joseph have been confined.

a. *And this was hard enough for one who was used to wandering freely on the broad Syrian plains.* Confinement is intolerable to us all, but especially to youth, and of all youth most so to those in whose veins flows something of that Arab blood that dreads death less than bondage. We do not realize how priceless freedom is, because we have never lost it. And Joseph never valued it as he did when he found himself shut up in that stifling "hole."

b. *There was the constant clank of the fetter.* He was bound, and his feet were hurt by fetters. True, he enjoyed the favor of the keeper of the prison, and had exceptional liberty within the gloomy precincts so as to reach the inmates; but still, wherever he moved, the rattle of the iron reminded him that he was a prisoner still.

c. *His religious beliefs added greatly to his distress.* He had been taught by Jacob that good would come to the good, and evil to the bad; that prosperity was the sign of divine favor, and adversity of divine anger. And Joseph had tried to be good. Had he not, in the full flush of youthful passion, resisted the blandishments of the beautiful Egyptian, because he would not sin against God? And what had he gained by that? Simply the stigma that threatened to cling to him of having committed the very wickedness it was so hard not to commit; and, in addition, an undeserved punishment. Had he not always been kind and gentle to his fellow prisoners, listening to their stories, speaking comfort to their hearts? And what had he gained by that? To judge by what he saw, simply nothing; and he might as well have kept his kindness to himself.

Was it of any use, then, being good? Was there a God who judges righteously in the earth? You who have been misunderstood, who have sown seeds of holiness and love, to reap nothing but disappointment, loss, suffering, and hate—*you* know something of what Joseph felt in that wretched dungeon hole.

d. *Disappointment poured her bitter drops into the bitter cup.* What had become of those early dreams, those dreams of coming greatness? Were these not from God? He had thought so—yes, and his venerable father had thought so too. Were those imaginings the delusions of a fevered brain? Had God forsaken him? Had his father forgotten him? Did his brothers ever think of him? Would they ever try and find him? Was he to spend all his days in that dungeon, and all because he had dared to do right? Do you wonder at the young heart being weighed almost to breaking?

e. *And yet Joseph's experience is not alone.* You may never have been confined in a dungeon, and yet you may often have sat in darkness and felt around you the limitation that forbade you doing as you wished. You may have been doing right, and doing right may have brought you into some unforeseen difficulty; and you are disposed to say, "I have been too honest." Or you may have been doing a noble act to someone, as Joseph did to Potiphar, and it has been taken in quite a wrong light. Who does not know what it is to be misunderstood, misrepresented, accused falsely, and punished wrongfully?

2. THESE SUFFERINGS PROVED TO BE VERY BENEFICIAL.

a. Taken at the lowest point, *this imprisonment served Joseph's temporal interests*. That prison was the place where state prisoners were bound. There court officials who had fallen under suspicion were sent. Chief butler and chief baker do not seem much to us, but they were titles for very august people. Such men would talk freely with Joseph; and in doing so would give him a great insight into political parties, and a knowledge of men and things generally, which later must have been of great service to him.

But there is more than this. Psalm 105:18, referring to Joseph's imprisonment, has a striking alternative rendering, "His soul entered into iron." Put it in our language, and it would read, *Iron entered into his soul*. Is there not a truth in this, that sorrow and privation, the yoke borne in youth, are conducive to an iron tenacity and strength of purpose, which are the indispensable foundation and framework of a noble character? Do not flinch from suffering. Bear it silently, patiently, resignedly; and be assured that it is God's way of infusing iron into your spiritual makeup.

As a boy, Joseph's character tended to softness. He was spoiled by his father. He was too proud of his coat. He was given to tell tales. He was too full of his dreams and foreshadowed greatness. None of these were great faults, although he lacked strength, grip, power to rule. But what a difference his imprisonment made in him! From that moment he carried himself with a wisdom, modesty, courage, and manly resolution, that never fail him. He acts as a born ruler of men. He carried an alien country through the stress of a great famine, without a symptom of revolt. He holds his own with the proudest aristocracy of the time. He promotes the most radical changes. He had learned to hold his peace and wait. Surely the iron had entered his soul!

b. *It is just this that suffering will do for you*. God wants iron saints, and since there is no better way of imparting iron to the moral nature than by letting his people suffer, He lets them suffer. Are you in prison for doing right? Are the best years of your life slipping away in enforced monotony? Are you beset by opposition, misunderstanding, disgrace, and scorn. Then take heart; the iron crown of suffering precedes the golden crown of glory. And iron is entering into your soul to make it strong and brave.

Is some aged eye perusing these words? If so, the question may be asked, Why does God sometimes fill a whole life with discipline, and give few opportunities for showing the iron quality of the soul? Ah, that is a question that goes far to prove our glorious destiny. There must be another world somewhere, a world of glorious ministry, for which we are training. And it may be that God counts a human life of seventy years of suffering not too long an education for a soul that may serve Him through the eternities. It is in the prison that Joseph is fitted for the unknown life of Pharaoh's palace. If only we could see all that awaits us in the palace of the Great King, we should not be so surprised at experiences that befall us in earth's darker cells. You are being trained for service in God's Home.

3. JOSEPH'S COMFORT IN THE MIDST OF THESE SUFFERINGS.

a. *"He was there in the prison; but the LORD was with him."* The Lord was with him in the palace of Potiphar; but when Joseph went to prison, the Lord went there too. The only thing that severs us from God is sin: as long as we walk with God, He will walk with us, and if our path dips down from the sunny upland lawns into the valley with its clinging mists, He will go at our side. The godly man is much more independent of men and things than others. If he is in a palace he is glad, not so much because of its delights as because God is there. And if he is in a prison he can sing and give praises, because God is there and because the God of his love bears him company. To the soul that is absorbed with God, all places and experiences are much the same.

b. *Moreover, the Lord showed him mercy.* Oh, wondrous revelation! The Lord showed him a great sight—He showed him His mercy. That prison cell was the mount of vision from which he saw, as never before, the panaroma of divine loving kindness. It was well worth his while to go to prison to learn that. Whenever you get into a prison of circumstances, be on the watch. Prisons are rare places for seeing things. It was in prison that Joseph saw God's mercy. God has no chance to show His mercy to some of us except when we are in some sore sorrow. The night is the time to see the stars.

c. *God can also raise up friends for his servants* in most unlikely places, and of most unlikely people. "The LORD . . . gave him favour in the sight of the keeper of the prison." He was probably a rough, unkindly man, quite prepared to copy the dislikes of his master, the great Potiphar, and to embitter the daily existence of this Hebrew slave. But there was another Power at work, of which he knew nothing, inclining him toward his ward, and leading him to put him in a position of trust.

d. *There is always alleviation for our troubles in ministry to others.* Joseph found it so. It must have been a welcome relief to the monotony when he found himself entrusted with the care of the royal prisoners. A new interest came into his life, and he almost forgot the heavy pressure of his own troubles amid the interest of listening to the tales of those who were more unfortunate than himself.

There is no soothing for heart-sorrow like ministry to others. If your life is woven with the dark shades of sorrow, do not sit down to deplore in solitude your hapless lot, but arise to seek out those who are more miserable than you are. And if you are unable to give much practical help, you may largely help the children of bitterness by imitating Joseph in listening to their tales of woe or to their dreams of foreboding. If you can do nothing else, listen well, and comfort others with the comfort wherewith you yourself have been comforted by God. Out of such intercourse you will get what Joseph got—the key that will unlock the heavy doors by which you have been shut in.

e. *And now some closing words to those who are suffering wrongfully.* Do not be surprised. You are the followers of One who was misunderstood from the age of twelve to the day of His ascension; who did not sin, and yet was counted as a sinner. If they spoke evil of the Master of the house, how much more concerning the household!

f. *Do not get weary in well-doing.* Joseph might have said, "I give up; of what profit is my godliness? I may as well live as others do." How much nobler was his course of patient continuance in well-doing!

g. *Above all, do not avenge yourselves.* When Joseph recounted his troubles, he did not recriminate harshly on his brethren, or Potiphar, or Potiphar's wife. He simply said: "I was stolen away out of the land of the Hebrews: and here also have I done nothing that they should put me into the [hole]."

> *He sent a man before them,*
> > *Even Joseph, who was sold for a servant,*
> *Whose feet they hurt with fetters;*
> > *He was laid in iron,*
> *Until the time that His word came:*
> > *The word of the Lord tried him.*
> *The king sent and loosed him,*
> > *Even the ruler of the people,*
> > *And let him go free.*
> *He made him lord of his house,*
> > *And ruler of all his substance;*
> *To bind his princes at his pleasure,*
> > *And teach his senators wisdom.*

PSALM 105:17–22.

6

The Steps of the Throne
Genesis 41

The fact of Joseph's exaltation from the prison cell in which we left him, to the steps of Pharaoh's throne, are so well known that we need not describe them in detail. We will dwell briefly on the more salient points.

1. HOPE DEFERRED. "[Remember] me when it shall be well with thee." It was a modest and pathetic prayer that Joseph made to the great officer of state, to whose dream he had given so favorable an interpretation. Some, however, have said he had no right to ask this man to plead with Pharaoh, when he himself had access to the King of kings, and could at all times plead his case at His court. But if at this moment Joseph eagerly snatched at human help, who of us can condemn him? Who of us can help sympathizing with him? Who of us would not have behaved in like manner?

The great man no doubt readily acceded to his request. "Remember you," he said, "of course I will." And, doubtless, in the fullness of his heart, he resolved to give Joseph a place among the assistant butlers, or perhaps in the vineries. And as he left the prison, we can imagine him saying, "Goodby; you will hear from me soon." But he "forgot." Oh, that word "forgot"! How many of us know what it means! Day after day Joseph expected to receive some token of his friend's remembrance and intercession. Week after week he watched for the message of deliverance, and often started because of some sudden knock that made him think that the warrant for his release had come. But at last it was useless to hide from himself the unpalatable truth, which slowly forced itself upon his mind, that he was forgotten.

Hope deferred must have made his heart sick. But if he was disappointed in man, he clung the more tenaciously to God. Nor did he trust in vain for, by a chain of wonderful providences, God brought him out of prison, and did better for him than could have been done by the chief butler of Pharaoh's court.

123

2. THREE BRIEF PIECES OF ADVICE TO THOSE IN SIMILAR CIRCUMSTANCES.

a. *Cease ye from man, whose breath is in his nostrils!* We cannot live without human sympathy and friendship. But men fail us; even the best prove to be less able or less willing than we thought.

b. *Turn from the failure and forgetfulness of man to the constancy and faithfulness of God!* "He abideth faithful." But at last He will say, "O man, O woman, great is thy faith: be it unto thee even as thou wilt."

c. *Wait for God!* We are too feverish, too hasty, too impatient. It is a great mistake. Everything comes only to those who can wait. You may have had what Joseph had when still a lad—a vision of power and usefulness and blessedness. But you cannot realize it in fact. All your plans miscarry. Every door seems shut; the years are passing over you. Now turn your heart to God; accept His will; tell Him that you leave to Him the realization of your dream. He may keep you waiting a little longer; but you will find Him verify the words of one who knew by experience His trustworthiness: "The salvation of the righteous is of the LORD: he is their strength in the time of trouble. And the LORD shall help them, and deliver them" (Ps. 37:39–40).

3. THE LINKS IN THE CHAIN OF DIVINE PROVIDENCE. First, the wife of Potiphar makes a baseless charge, which leads to Joseph's imprisonment; then, the young prisoner ingratiates himself with the keeper of the prison, and is allowed to have free access to the prisoner. This happens at the very time that two state officials are thrown into jail on suspicion of attempting to poison their royal master. Then the verification of Joseph's interpretation of their dreams shows that he is possessed of no common power. After that, the department of memory in which Joseph's face and case are hidden becomes sealed, and then, after two full years, the king of Egypt dreams.

The dream was repeated twice, so similarly as to make it evident that something of unusual importance was intended. The scene in each case was the river bank; first, the green margin of grass, next, the rich alluvial soil. To say the least, it was a bad omen to see the lean cows devour the fat, and the withered ears devour the full. Nor can we wonder that the monarch of a people who attached special importance to omens and portents would hurriedly send for the priests, who on this occasion were reinforced by all the wise men, adepts in this branch of science. But there was no one who could interpret the dream of Pharaoh.

Then the butler suddenly remembered his prison experiences, and told the king of the young captive Hebrew. Pharaoh eagerly grasped at the suggestion. He sent for Joseph; and they brought him hastily out of the dungeon—the margin says, "they made him run." Still the king's impetuous speed was compelled to wait until Joseph had shaved himself and changed his prison garb. Perfect cleanliness and propriety of dress were so important in the eyes of Egyptians that the most urgent matters were postponed until they were properly attended to. How sad that men are so careful of their appearance before one another, and so careless of their appearance before God! Many a man who would not think of entering a room if his clothes were not clean and pressed is content to carry within his breast a heart as black as ink.

It is beautiful to notice Joseph's reverent reference to God in his first interview with Pharaoh. "It is not in me: God shall give Pharaoh an answer of peace." When the heart is full of God, the tongue will be obliged to speak of Him; such references will be easy and natural as flowers in May. Oh, that our inner life were more full of the power and love and presence of Jesus! Joseph was not ashamed to speak of his God amid the throng of idolaters in the court of Egypt: let us not flinch from bearing our humble witness in the teeth of violent opposition and supercilious scorn.

This position of recognizing Jehovah being assumed and granted, created no difficulty in interpreting the consumption of the seven good cows by the seven lean cows, and of the seven full ears by the seven empty ears, blasted by the east wind; or of indicating that the seven years of great plenty should be followed by seven years of famine, so severe that all the plenty would be forgotten in the land of Egypt, and that famine would consume the land.

So, in the presence of the thronged and breathless court, the young Hebrew interpreted the royal dream. That dream was framed in a thoroughly Egyptian setting, and was connected with the Nile. The sight of horned cattle coming up out of a river would not be a rare occurrence; and Joseph had no difficulty in carrying his audience with him, when he said that these seven cows—as also the seven ears of corn on one stalk, after the nature of that species of bearded wheat still known as Egyptian wheat—were emblems of seven years of great plenty throughout all the land of Egypt.

But perhaps that which gave Joseph most influence in that court was not his interpretation, but the wise and statesmanlike policy on which he insisted. As he detailed his successive recommendations: the appointment of a man discreet and wise with this exclusive business as his life work; of the creation of a new department of public business for the purpose of gathering up the resources of Egypt in anticipation of the coming need; of the vast system of storage in the cities of the land—it was evident that he was speaking beneath the glow of a spirit not his own, and with a power that commanded the instant assent of the monarch and his chief advisers. "The thing was good in the eyes of Pharaoh, and in the eyes of all his servants. And Pharaoh said unto his servants, Can we find such an one as this is, a man in whom the Spirit of God is?"

When Joseph had interpreted the dream and given his advice—little thinking as he did so that he was sketching his own future—Pharaoh said to his servants, "Can we find such an one as this is, a man in whom the Spirit of God is?" Then he turned to Joseph and said, "Forasmuch as God hath shewed thee all this, there is none so discreet and wise as thou art: thou shalt be over my house, and according unto thy word shall all my people be ruled: only in the throne will I be greater than thou. See, I have set thee over all the land of Egypt."

It was a wonderful ascent, sheer in a single bound from the dungeon to the steps of the throne. Joseph's father had rebuked him; now Pharaoh, the greatest monarch of his time, welcomes him. His brethren despised him; now the proudest priesthood of the world opens its ranks to receive him by marriage into their midst, considering it wiser to conciliate a man who was from that moment to be the greatest force in Egyptian politics and life. The hands that were hard with the toils of a slave are adorned with a signet ring. The feet are no longer tormented by fetters; a chain of gold is linked around his neck. The coat of many colors torn from him by violence and defiled by blood, and the garment left in the hand of the adulteress, are exchanged for vestures of fine linen drawn from the royal wardrobe. He was once trampled upon as the offscouring of all things; now all Egypt is commanded to bow before him, as he rides forth in the second chariot, prime minister of Egypt, and second only to the king.

All this happened because one day, for the sake of God, Joseph resisted a temptation to one act of sin. If he had yielded, we should probably never have heard of him again; no happy marriage, no wife, no child, no honour or usefulness, or vision of the dear faces of his kin, would ever have enriched his life with their abundant blessing. What a good thing it was that he did not yield!

I admire the names that Joseph gave to his sons. They show the temper of his heart when in the zenith of his prosperity. Manasseh means "forgetting"—God had made him forget his toils. Ephraim means "fruitfulness"—God had caused him to be fruitful. Be true! *You* will forget your sorrow and long waiting; *you* will be fruitful. Then be sure to give God the praise.

4. THE PARALLEL BETWEEN JOSEPH AND THE LORD JESUS. It is surely more than a coincidence. Joseph was rejected by his brethren; Jesus by the Jews, His brethren according to the flesh. Joseph was sold for twenty pieces of silver to the Ishmaelites; Jesus was sold by the treachery of Judas for thirty pieces, and then handed over to the Gentiles. Joseph was cast into prison; Jesus abode in the grave. Joseph in prison was able to preach the gospel of deliverance to the butler; Jesus went and preached the gospel to the spirits in the prison. The two malefactors of the cross find their counterpart in Joseph's two fellow prisoners. Joseph, though a Jew by birth and rejected by his own brethren, nevertheless was raised to supreme power in a gentile state, and saved myriads of them from death; Jesus, of Jewish birth and yet disowned by Jews, has nevertheless been exalted to the supreme seat of power, and is now enthroned in the hearts of myriads of Gentiles, to whom He has brought salvation from death, and spiritual bread for their hunger. The very name that Pharaoh gave to Joseph meant "Savior of the world"—our Savior's title. Yes, and we must carry the parallel still farther. After Joseph had been for some time ruling and blessing Egypt, his brethren came to him for forgiveness and help; so in days not far away we shall see the Jews retracing their steps and exclaiming "Jesus is our Brother."

5. THE WORLD'S NEED FOR CHRIST. You remember Pharaoh's dream. Seven cows, which had escaped from the torturing heat into the comparative coolness of the water, came up on the banks and began feeding on the grass. Shortly after, seven lean cows came up and, finding nothing left for them to eat, by one of those strange transformations common to dreams, swallowed up their predecessors. So the seven shrivelled ears devoured those that were rank and good. This is a symbol of a fact that is always happening.

It may be that seven years of famine have been passing over you, devouring all that you had accumulated in happy bygone times, and leaving you bare. Do you not guess the reason? There is a rejected Savior transferred to some obscure dungeon in your heart. There never can be prosperity or peace as long as He is there. Seek Him out. Ask Him to forgive years of shameful neglect. Give the reins of power into His hand, and He will restore to you the years that the cankerworm has eaten.

7

Joseph's First Interview With His Brothers
Genesis 42

The life of Joseph, as the Prime Minister of Egypt, was a very splendid one. Everything that could please the sense or minister to the taste was his. His palaces would consist of numberless rooms opening into spacious courts, where palms, sycamores, and acacia trees grew in rare luxuriance. The furniture would be elegantly carved from various woods, encrusted with ebony and adorned with gilding. Rare perfumes rose from vases of gold and bronze and alabaster; and the foot sank deep in carpets, covering the floors, or trod upon the skins of lions and other ferocious beasts. Troops of slaves and officials ministered to every want. Choirs of musicians filled the air with sweet melody.

But though one of rare splendor, *his life must have been one of considerable anxiety.* He had to deal with a proud hereditary nobility, jealous of his power, and with a populace mad with hunger. During the first seven years of his premiership he went throughout all the land of Egypt superintending the dykes and ditches that should utilize as much as possible the unusual rise of the Nile. He built vast granaries and bought up a fifth of the vast profusion of grain. "The earth brought forth by handfuls. And Joseph gathered corn as the sand of the sea, very much, until he left numbering; for it was without number." All this must have involved a great deal of anxiety; it must have been difficult for this young foreigner to carry out his wide-reaching plans in face of the stolid apathy or the active opposition of great officials and vested interests.

He was, however, *eminently qualified for this work,* for there was something in him that could not be accounted for by any analysis of his brain. As Pharaoh had said most truly, "He was a man in whom was the Spirit of God." Oh, when will men learn that the Spirit of God may be in them when they are buying and selling, and arranging all the details of business or home? May God send us all the simple reverent spirit of this man, who amidst the splendor and business of his proud position set God always before his face! At last, when the days of famine came, Joseph was able, as he later said, to be a "father" to Pharaoh, and to save the land.

All these events took time. Joseph was a lad of seventeen summers when he was torn away from his home; and he was a young man of thirty when he stood for the first time before Pharaoh. Seven years for the golden time of plenty must be added and perhaps two more while the stores of the granaries were being slowly exhausted. So probably twenty-five years had passed between the tragedy at the pit's mouth and the time of which we are thinking now. During those years the life in Jacob's camp had flowed uneventfully and quietly through the same unchanging scenes. The chief sign of the number of the slow passing years was the growing weakness in the old father's step and the increasing infirmity of his form. He pathetically speaks much of his "grey hairs." The sons of Israel had need to "carry Jacob their father." This was not simply the result of age but also of sorrow. Jacob bore in his heart the scars of many wounds, the chief of which was grief for his beloved Joseph. It was grief that he was compelled largely to nurse alone; and it was, perhaps, the keener because of the suspicions of foul play that seem to have suggested themselves to his mind. He went step by step down toward the grave "mourning for his son." He never could forget the sight of the blood-spattered coat, the dear relic of one whose face he never thought to see again.

Meanwhile, the sons had become middle-aged men, with families of their own. They probably never mentioned that deed of violence to each other. *They did their best to banish the thought from their minds.* Conscious slept. Yet the time had come when God meant to use these men to found a nation. And in order to fit them for their high destiny it was necessary to bring them into a right condition of soul. But it seemed almost impossible to secure repentance in those obtuse and darkened hearts. However, the Eternal brought it about by a number of wonderful providences. This, then, is our theme: God's gracious methods of awakening the consciences of these men from their long and apparently endless sleep.

1. THE FIRST STEP TOWARD THEIR CONVICTION WAS THE PRESSURE OF WANT. There was dearth in all lands; and the famine reached even to the land of Canaan. Often before, in the lives of the patriarchs, they had been driven by famine down to Egypt; and Jacob aroused his sons from the hopeless lethargy into which they were sinking by saying, "Why do ye look one upon another? Behold, I have heard that there is corn in Egypt: get you down and buy for us, from thence; that we may live, and not die. And Joseph's ten brethren went down to buy corn in Egypt."

It is so that God deals with us. He breaks up our nest. He loosens our roots. He sends a mighty famine that cuts away the whole staff of bread. Later those men look back on that time of difficulty as the best thing that could have happened to them: nothing less would have brought them to Joseph. Yes, and the time is coming when you will bless God for your times of sorrow and misfortune. You will say, "Before I was afflicted I went astray; but now have I kept Thy Word."

2. THE SECOND STEP WAS THE ROUGH TREATMENT THEY RECEIVED AT THE HANDS OF JOSEPH. It would seem that in some of the larger markets he superintended the sale of the corn himself. He may even have gone there on purpose; he may have even cherished, and prayed over, the fancy that his brethren might come themselves. At last the looked-for day arrived. He was standing as usual at his post, surrounded by all the confusion and noise of an Eastern bazaar, when his attention was attracted by those ten men. He looked with a fixed, eager look for a moment, his heart throbbing quickly all the while; and he needed no further assurance: "he knew them."

Evidently, however, they did not know him. How should they? He had grown from a lad of seventeen to a man of forty. He was clothed in pure white linen, with ornaments of gold to indicate his rank, a garb not altogether unlike that famous coat, which had wrought such havoc. He was governor of the land, and if they had thought of Joseph at all when entering that land (and no doubt they did), they expected to see him in the gangs of slaves manacled at work in the fields, or sweltering in the scorching brickyards, preparing material for the pyramids. So, in unconscious fulfillment of his own boyish dream, they bowed down themselves before him with their faces to the earth.

Joseph saw that they failed to recognize him, and partly to ascertain if his brethren were repentant, partly in order to know why Benjamin was not with them, he sought to test them. He spake roughly to them. He accused them of being spies. He refused to believe their statements, and put them in prison until they could be verified. He kept Simeon bound.

In all this, I believe *he repeated exactly the scene at the pit's mouth;* and indeed we may perhaps see what really happened there, reflected in the mirror of this scene. It is not unlikely that when they saw him coming toward them, in his prince-like dress, they had rushed at him, accusing him of having come to spy out their corrupt behavior, and take back an evil report to their father, as he had done before. If so, this will explain why he now suddenly accused them of being spies. No doubt the lad protested that he was no spy—that he had only come to inquire after their welfare; but they had met his protestations with rude violence in much the same way as the rough-speaking governor now treated them. It may be that they had even thrust him into the pit with the threat to keep him there until his statements could be verified, in much the same way as Joseph now dealt with them; and Simeon may have been the ringleader. If this were the case—and it seems most credible—it is obvious that it was a powerful appeal to their conscience and memory, and one that could not fail to awaken both.

And as those men, each in his dungeon, considered the treatment they had received, it must have vividly brought to their minds their treatment of that guileless lad, many years before.

a. *Memory is one of the most wonderful processes of our nature.* It is the faculty that enables us to record and recall the past. If it were not for this power the mind would remain forever in the blank condition of childhood, and all that had ever passed before it would leave no more impression than images do upon the plain surface of a reflecting mirror. But it has a universal retentiveness. Nothing has ever passed across it that has not left a record.

You may have been brought up in a house surrounded by an old-fashioned country garden, but you have not thought of it for years until you happened to see a plant or smell a scent peculiarly associated with it, and that brought it all back to your recollection. So is it with sin. Long years ago, you may have committed some sin; you have tried to forget it. It has not been forgiven and put away; you have almost succeeded in dropping it from your thoughts: but believe me, it is still there; and the most trivial incident may at any moment bring it all back upon your conscience, as vividly as if committed only yesterday. If sin is forgiven, it is indeed forgotten: God says, "I will remember it no more." But if only forgotten, and not forgiven, it may have a most unexpected and terrible awakening.

b. *This was the case with Joseph's brethren.* They said to each other as they heard the reiterated demand of this unusual governor for evidence that they were not spies, "We are verily guilty concerning our brother; in that we saw the anguish of his soul, when he besought us, and we would not hear; therefore is this distress come upon us."

3. THE THIRD STEP TOWARD CONVICTION WAS THE GIVING OF TIME FOR THEM TO LISTEN TO GOD'S SPIRIT, SPEAKING TO THEM IN THE SILENCE OF THE PRISON CELL. Without the work of the Holy Ghost they might have felt remorse, but not guilt. It is not enough to feel that sin is a blunder and a mistake, but not guilt. This sense of sin, however, is the prerogative of the Spirit of God. When He is at work, the soul cries out, "Woe is me, I am a sinful man!" "We are verily *guilty* concerning our brother."

a. *Will not these words befit some eyes that read these pages?* Are *you* not truly guilty? In early life you may have wronged some man or some woman. And now others seem to be treating you as you treated the associates of earlier days. You now are eager for salvation; and you learn the bitterness of being ridiculed, thwarted, tempted, and opposed. You recall the past; it flashes before you with terrible intensity. You cry, "God forgive me! I am guilty concerning that soul whom I betrayed or wronged." And this is the work of the Holy Spirit. Let Him have his blessed way with you!

b. *There is at least one Brother whom you have wronged.* Need I mention His name? He is not ashamed to call you brother; but you have been ashamed of Him. He did not withhold Himself from the cross; but you have never thanked Him. He has freely offered you the greatest gifts; but you have trampled them beneath your feet, and done despite to Him, and crucified Him afresh. "We are verily guilty concerning our Brother." These words may also be humbly and sorrowfully appropriated by many of us.

While these men spoke these words, Joseph stood by them. There was no emotion on those compressed features, no response in those quiet eyes. "They knew not that Joseph understood them."

There is a curious contrast in the twenty-fourth verse. First, we learn that "he turned himself about from them, and wept"; and next we are told that he "took from them Simeon, and bound him before their eyes." The brethren saw only the latter of these two actions, and must have thought him rough and unkind. How they must have trembled in his presence! But they did not know the heart of tender love that was beating beneath all this seeming hardness. Nor could they guess that the retention of Simeon was intended to act as a silken cord to bring the brothers back to him, and as part of the process of awakening the memory of another brother, whom they had lost years before.

c. *There were alleviations also in their hardships.* The sacks were filled with corn; provision was given for the journey home, so they did not need to dig into the supplies they were carrying back for their households; and every man's money was returned in his sack's mouth (v. 25). All this was meant in tender love, but their hearts failed them with fear as they emptied their sacks and saw the bundles of money fall out among the corn. God's dealings with us brim with blessing, and are working out a purpose of mercy that will make us rejoice all our days.

8

Joseph's Second Interview With His Brothers
Genesis 43

We will now deal with that affecting scene when Joseph caused everyone to leave him while he cast aside his dignity, stepped down from his throne, and fell on the necks of his brethren and wept. We have a lesser task just now, yet full of interest; we have to consider the successive steps by which that wayward family was brought into a position in which its members could be forgiven and blessed.

1. THERE WAS THE PRESSURE OF POVERTY AND SORROW (43:1). Jacob would never have turned his thoughts to Egypt if there had been plenty in Canaan. The famine drove the sons of Israel into Egypt to buy corn. And even though poor Simeon was bound in Egypt, the brothers would not have gone a second time if it had not been for the rigor of necessity. At first the aged father strongly opposed the thought of their taking Benjamin, even if they went themselves; and his children lingered.

There is a touching picture given of the conversation between Jacob and his sons, a kind of council of war. Reuben seems already to have lost the priority that his birthright would have secured, and Judah held the place of spokesman and leader among the brethren. He undertook to deal with his father for the rest of his brothers. At the outset, Jacob's request that they should go down to buy food was met with the most distinct refusal, unless Benjamin was permitted to accompany them. And when Jacob complained of their having betrayed the existence of another brother, all of them vindicated their action, and declared that they could not have done otherwise. At last Judah made himself personally responsible for the lad's safety, a pledge which, as we shall see, he nobly redeemed. And so, at last, Jacob yielded, proposing only that they should take a present to mollify the ruler's heart, double money to replace what had been returned in their sacks, and he uttered a fervent prayer to the Almighty on their behalf. Thus God in His mercy closed every other door but the one through which they might find their way to plenty and blessedness. There was no alternative but to go down to Egypt.

a. *So is your life.* You have had all that this world could give. But have you considered your ill-treatment of your great Elder Brother? Have you set your affections on things above? You know you have not. So God has called for a famine on your land. You have lost situation and friends. Your business is broken. Beauty, youth, health—all have vanished. Joseph is gone; Simeon is gone; and Benjamin is on the point of being taken away. Everything has been against you.

b. *It is a severe measure: how will you bear it?* In the first burst of the tempest, you say stubbornly, "I will not go down; I will not yield; I will stand out to the last." But, beware! God will have His way at last if not at first. The famine must continue until the wanderer arises to return to the Father, with words of penetent contrition on his lips. Oh that your word might be!—"Come, and let us return unto the Lord; for He has torn, and He will heal us; He has smitten, and He will bind us up."

2. THERE WAS THE AWAKENING OF CONSCIENCE. For twenty years conscience had slept. And as long as this was the case there could be no real peace between Joseph and his brothers. *They* could never feel sure that he had forgiven them. *He* would always feel that there was a padlock on the treasure-store of his love. Conscience must awake and slowly tread the aisles of the temple of penitence. This is the clue to the understanding of Joseph's behavior.

a. *Joseph, to arouse their dormant consciences, repeated as nearly as possible to them, their treatment of himself.* This has already engaged our thought. "Ye are spies" was the echo of their own rough words to himself. The prison, in which they lay for three days, was the counterpart of the pit in which they placed *him.* Men will best learn what is the true nature of their own iniquities when they experience the treatment they have meted out to others. And Joseph's device was a success. Listen to their moan, "We are verily guilty concerning our brother."

b. *Here again is a clue to the mysteries of our own lives.* God sometimes allows us to be treated as we have treated Him, that we may see our offenses in its true character, and may be obliged to turn to Him with words of genuine contrition. Your child has turned to Him with words of genuine contrition. Your child has turned out badly. You did everything for him, now he refuses to do what you wish and even taunts you. Do you feel it? Perhaps this will reveal to you what God feels, in that, though He has nourished and brought you up, yet you have rebelled against Him. Your neighbor, when in trouble, came to you for help, and promised to repay you with interest. Now he prospers and you ask him to repay you, but he either laughs at you or tells you to wait. Do you feel it? Ah, now you know how God feels, He who helped you in distress, to whom you made many vows, but who reminds you in vain of all the past. That conscience must indeed be deep in sleep that does not awaken at such appeals.

3. THERE WAS THE DISPLAY OF MUCH TENDER LOVE TOWARD THEM. As soon as Joseph saw them he invited them to his own table to feast with him. The brothers were brought into his house where every kindness was shown to them. It was as if, instead of being poor

shepherds, they were the magnates of the land. Their fears as to the return of the money were allayed by the pious, though misleading, assurance of the steward that if they had discovered it in their sacks it might have been put there by God, because the payment for their corn was in his hands. And when Joseph came they prostrated themselves before him in striking fulfillment of his own boyish dream. He asked them tenderly about the well-being of their father, and there must have been a pathos in his words to Benjamin that would have revealed the whole secret if they had not been so utterly unprepared to find Joseph beneath the strange guise of the great Egyptian governor.

What an inimitable touch that tells us how Joseph's heart welled up into his eyes, so that he needed to hurry in order to conceal the bursting emotions that threatened to overmaster him. "He sought where to weep; and he entered into his chamber, and wept there. And he washed his face, and went out, and refrained himself, and said, Set on bread."

The rejected Brother may seem strange and rough. He may cause sorrow. He may bind Simeon before our eyes. But beneath all, He loves us with a love in which is concentrated the love of all parents for their children, and of all friends for their beloved. And that love is constantly devising means of expressing itself. It puts money into our sacks; it invites us to its home and spreads banquets before us. Jesus feels yearnings over us which He restrains, and does not dare to betray until the work of conviction is complete and He can pour the full tides of affection on us, without injury to others or harm to ourselves.

4. THERE WAS THE DESTRUCTION OF THEIR SELF-CONFIDENCE. They thought their *word* was good; but when they told their family history, Joseph refused to believe it, and said it must be proved. They were confident in their *money*. But when they reached their first resting place on their way home, "as one of them opened his sack to give his ass provender . . . he espied his money; for, behold, it was in the sack's mouth. And he said unto his brethren, My money is restored; and, lo, it is even in my sack: and their heart failed them, and they were afraid, saying one to another, What is this that God hath done unto us?"

a. *How often this happens in the experience of sinful men!* They want to stand right with God, but they like to do so in their own way. Like Cain, they bring the fruit that their own hands have raised. Like these men, they bring their hard-earned money. No! the mercy of God is not to be bought by anything we can bring; it must be received as a gift without money and without price. Jacob said, "Peradventure it was an oversight": but it was not; it was part of a deeply-laid plan, designed and executed for a special purpose. There is no oversight, and no peradventure, in the life of anyone.

They were confident also in their *integrity*. Little knowing what was in the sack of one of them, when the morning was light they started on their return journey for the second time. They were in high spirits. Simeon was with them; so was Benjamin, notwithstanding the nervous forebodings of their aged father. They were evidently in high favor with the governor, or else they would not have been treated to so grand a feast on the previous day. Their sacks were as full as they could possibly hold. But they had barely got clear of the city gate when they were arrested by the steward's voice. "Why have ye rewarded evil for good?" And they said, "Wherefore saith my lord these words? Behold, the money, which we found in our sacks' mouths, we brought again unto thee . . . how then should we steal out of thy lord's house silver or gold?" And, so sure were they of their integrity, that they went further and said: "With whomsoever of thy servants [thy master's cup] is found, both let him die, and we also will be my lord's bondmen." "Then they speedily took down every man his sack to the ground, and opened every man his sack." And the steward searched them there on the bare road, beginning with the eldest to the youngest, "*and the cup was found in Benjamin's sack.*" Well might Judah and his brethren come to Joseph's house and fall before him on the ground, and say, "What shall we say unto my lord? what shall we speak? or how shall we clear ourselves? God hath found out the iniquity of thy servants." They were stripped of every rag of self-confidence, and were closed to his uncovenanted mercy.

b. *Some people resemble Benjamin.* They are naturally guileless and beautiful. Some faint traces of original innocence linger about them. Their type is shown forth in the young man whom Jesus loved, as he stood before Him breathless with haste, protesting that he had kept all the commandments blameless from his youth. Such people seem good, only because they are compared with sinners of a blacker dye. Compare them with the only standard of infinite purity, and they are infinitely condemned. You may think the linen clean as it hangs on the line, contrasted with the dingy buildings around; but when the snowflakes fall, you wonder that you never before discerned its lack of whiteness. So estimable characters pride themselves on their morality, only until they behold the seamless robes of Christ, whiter than any soap in earth could whiten them. But *these* must be taught their utter sinfulness; *they* must learn their secret unworthiness; *they* must be made to take their stand with the rest of men. Benjamin must be reduced to the level of Simeon and Judah. The cup must be found in *Benjamin's* sack. It is when the cup is found in Benjamin's sack that he, too, is brought to the feet of Jesus.

c. *There is a stolen cup in your sack,* my respectable, reputable, moral friend. You are probably unconscious of it. You pride yourself on your blameless life. You suppose that Christ Himself has no controversy with you. But if you only knew, you would see that you are robbing Him of His own. You use for yourself time and money and talents that He bought with his own precious blood, and which He meant to be a chosen vessel to Himself. But if you hide the unwelcome truth from yourself, you cannot hide it from your Lord.

d. *How then shall we act?* First, *do not linger.* "Except we had lingered, surely now we had returned this second time." If you had not lingered, you would have become an earnest, happy Christian. Make haste! The door is shutting; and when it shuts it will lock itself. The hourglass is nearly run out, and when its last grain has gone the court of mercy will close.

Second, *make full confession or restitution.* "They came near to the steward of Joseph's house and communed with him," and told him all about the finding of the money, and offered it back in full weight. Commune with Christ; tell Him all that is in your heart. Restore what you have taken wrongfully from Him or from others. Make full and thorough restitution. "He that covereth his sins shall not prosper: but whoso confesseth and forsaketh them shall have mercy" (Prov. 28:13).

Third, *throw yourself on the mercy of Christ.* Judah did not excuse himself or his brethren; he would have been wrong if he had. He adopted a wiser course—he pleaded for mercy. Mercy for their own sakes! Mercy for Benjamin's sake! Mercy for the sake of the aged father with his gray hairs at home! Try that plea with your Lord. You will find that it will not fail you. Say, as you beat upon your breast, "Be merciful unto me, *the* sinner!" He will not be able to refrain. He will say, "Come near Me; I am Jesus your Brother; your sins nailed Me to the cross, but God has overruled it for good, that I might save your lives by a great deliverance."

9

Joseph Making Himself Known
Genesis 45

"The cup was found in Benjamin's sack." What a discovery that was! But how did it get there? The brothers could not tell. They neither could nor would believe that Benjamin had known anything of it. Yet how to explain the mystery was a problem they could not solve. It seemed as if some evil genius were making them its sport, first in putting the money in their sacks, and then in concealing the cup there.

Each brother must have wished that the cup could have been found in any sack but than in Benjamin's. They all remembered their father's unwillingness to let him come. Jacob had seemed to have a premonition of coming disaster. When they first returned from Egypt he said decisively, "My son shall not go down with you; for his brother is dead, and he is left alone: if mischief befall him by the way in the which ye go, then shall ye bring down my gray hairs with sorrow to the grave." And when the pressure of famine compelled them, the last words of the stricken parent were, "God Almighty give you mercy before the man, that he may send away your other brother, and Benjamin. If I be bereaved of my children, I am bereaved." All the time his heart was filled with the presages of coming sorrow; and now those forebodings seemed about to be fulfilled. Oh, how different the road seemed to what it had been a little before! The same sun was shining; the same busy scene surrounded them—but a dark veil was spread over sky and earth. Let us study the scene that followed.

1. NOTICE THE CIRCUMSTANCES IN WHICH THEY FOUND THEMSELVES.

a. *Their conscience was now awakened, and it was ill at ease.* There was no need for them to mention that crime of twenty years before; and yet it seemed impossible for them to refrain from mentioning that which was uppermost in their minds. They were evidently thinking deeply of that dark deed by the pit's mouth. Their own sorrows had brought the sorrows of that frail young lad to their minds; and they could not but feel that there was some connection between the two. Thus the first words uttered by Judah their spokesman, as they entered the audience-chamber of Joseph, betrayed the dark forebodings of their thoughts: "What shall we say unto my lord? what shall we speak? or how shall we clear ourselves? God hath found out the iniquity of thy servants."

b. *God will always find out our iniquity.* "Be sure your sin will find you out" (Num. 32:23). Tens of years may pass over your life; and like these brethren you may be congratulating yourself that the sin is forgotten, and you are safe. Then a train of circumstances, little suspected, but manipulated by a divine hand, will suddenly bring the truth to light. And if all sin is not traced home to its authors in *this* world, at least there is enough to show how terrible that moment will be, when, at the "great white throne," the secrets of all hearts will be disclosed, and God will bring to light the hidden things of darkness.

c. *But, in addition, they were absolutely in Joseph's power.* There he stood, second to none but Pharaoh in all the land of Egypt. If he said that these men were all to be taken and imprisoned for life, or that Benjamin should be retained while the others were set free, there was absolutely no appeal: none could hinder him for a single moment. And the counterpart of this must surely be an alarming thought to the awakened sinner—that he is entirely at the mercy of the Judge of the quick and dead.

d. *Moreover, they saw that appearances were strongly against them.* There was no doubt that the cup had been found in Benjamin's sack, and though they were certainly innocent of the theft, yet they could not but feel that they were unable to clear or excuse themselves. As far as the evidence went, it pointed clearly and decisively to their guilt.

2. NOTICE THEIR BEHAVIOR.

a. *"They fell before him on the ground."* As they did so, they unconsciously fulfilled his own prediction, uttered when a boy. How vividly that memorable dream of the harvest field must have occurred to Joseph's mind! Here were their sheaves making obeisance to his sheaf, standing erect in the midst.

b. *But who was to be their spokesman?* Reuben had always had something to say in self-justification, and had been so sure that all would be right that he had pledged the lives of his children to his father for the safety of Benjamin; but *he* is silent. Simeon was probably the cruel one, the instigator of the crime against Joseph; but *he* dares not utter a word. Benjamin, the blameless one, the prototype of the young man whom Jesus loved, is convicted of sin, and has nothing to say. Who then is to speak? There is only one, Judah, who at the pit's mouth had diverted the brothers from their first thought of murder. And notice how he speaks. He throws himself helplessly on Joseph's mercy: "What shall we say unto my lord? what shall we speak? or how shall we clear ourselves?"

c. *We stand on surer ground than ever they did.* They had no idea of the gentleness of Joseph's heart. They did not understand why on one occasion he had hastened from their presence; they could not guess how near the surface lay the fountains of his tears. They only knew him as rough, and stern, and hard. "The man, who is the lord of the land, spake roughly to us." But we know the gentleness of the Lord Jesus. We have seen His tears over Jerusalem; we have listened to His tender invitations to come to Him; we have stood beneath His cross and heard His last prayers for His murderers, and His words of invitation to the dying thief. We then need not fear for the issue when we cast ourselves on His mercy.

d. *In all literature, there is nothing more pathetic than this appeal of Judah.* The eagerness that made him draw near; the humility that confessed Joseph's anger might righteously burn, since he was as Pharaoh; the picture of the elderly man, their father, bereft of one son, and clinging to this one, the only survivor of his mother; the recital of the strain that the governor had imposed on them, by demanding that they should bring their youngest brother down; the story of their father's dread, only overmastered by the imperious demand of a hunger that brooked no check; the vivid picture of the father's eagerness again to see the lad, in whose life his own was bound up; the heartbreaking grief at not seeing him among them; the heroic offer to stay there a slave, as Benjamin's substitute, if only the lad might go home; the preference of a life of slavery rather than to behold the aged man sinking with sorrow into his grave—all this is touched with a master-hand. But if a rough man could plead like this, what must not those pleadings be that Jesus offers before the throne! We have an Advocate in the Court of King's Bench who never lost a case: let us put ourselves into His hands, and trust Him when He says, "I have prayed for you."

e. *Thus Joseph's object was attained.* He had wished to restore his brothers to perfect rest and peace, but he knew that this were impossible as long as their sin was unconfessed and unforgiven. But it had now been abundantly confessed. Then, too, he had been anxious to see how they felt toward Benjamin. With this object in view he had given him five times as much as he had given them. Some think that he did this to show his special love. It may have been so, but there probably was something deeper. It was his dream of superiority that aroused their hatred against him: how would they feel toward Benjamin, if he, the younger, were treated better than them all? But notwithstanding the marked favor shown him, they were eager as before for his return with them. Besides, he wanted to see if they could forgive. It was Benjamin who had brought them into all this trouble: had they treated him in the spirit of former days, they would have abandoned him to his fate; but if so, they could not have been forgiven. But so far from showing malice, they tenderly loved and clung to him for the aged father's sake and his own. Evidently then all Joseph's purposes were accomplished; and nothing remained to hinder the great unveiling that was so near.

3. Notice the revelation and reconciliation.

a. *"Then Joseph could not refrain himself."* When Judah's voice ceased its pathetic pleading, he could restrain himself no more.

b. *And Joseph cried, "Cause every man to go out from me."* There was great delicacy here. He did not want to expose his brethren; and yet he wanted to say words that could not be understood by the curious ears of mere courtiers. His brethren, too, must have a chance to be themselves. "And there stood no man with him, while Joseph made himself known unto his brethren."

c. *And he wept aloud.* He began to weep so hard that the Egyptians heard the unusual sounds and wondered. Was this joy or grief? I am disposed to think it was neither. It was pent-up emotion. For many days he had been in suspense; so anxious not to lose them, so afraid that they might not stand the test. When from some secret vantage point he had watched them leave the city in the gray light, he may have chided himself for letting them go at all. His mind had been under great pressure; and now that the tension was removed, and there was no further necessity for it, he wept aloud. Ah, sinner, the heart of Christ is on the stretch for you!

And he said, "I am Joseph." He spoke in deep emotion; yet the words must have fallen on his brothers like a thunderbolt. "Joseph!" Had they been dealing all the while with their long-lost brother? "Joseph!" Then they had fallen into a lion's den indeed. "Joseph!" Could it be? Yes, it must be so; and it would explain many things that had sorely puzzled them. Well might they be troubled and terrified. Astonishment as at one risen from the dead, terror for the consequences, fear lest he would repay them the long-standing debt—all these emotions made them speechless. So he said again, "I am Joseph, *your brother*, whom ye sold into Egypt"; and he added very lovingly, "Be not grieved, nor angry with yourselves; for God did send me." Penitent sinner! in this way your Savior speaks to you. "I am Jesus, your Brother, whom you have sold and crucified; yet do not grieve for that. I was delivered by the determinate counsel and foreknowledge of God; though the hands have been none the less wicked by whom I have been crucified and slain. But if you repent, your sins will be blotted out.

d. *"And Joseph said unto his brethren, Come near to me."* They had backed farther and farther from him; but now he bids them approach. A moment more saw him and Benjamin locked in each other's arms, their tears freely flowing. And he kissed *all* his *brethren.* Simeon? Yes. Reuben? Yes. Those who had tied his hands and mocked his cries? Yes. He kissed them *all.* And after that they talked with him.

10

Joseph's Administration of Egypt
Genesis 47

While all the domestic details on which we have been meditating were transpiring, Joseph was carrying his adopted country through a great crisis—I might almost call it a revolution. When he became Prime Minister, the Egyptian monarchy was comparitively weak; but after he had administered affairs for some thirteen years, Pharaoh was absolute owner of all the land of Egypt; all the land became held in fee from the crown. The history of this change deserves more attention than we can give it now, but from first to last it was due to the statesmanship of the young Hebrew.

During the seven years of plenty, Joseph caused one-fifth of all the produce of every district to be hoarded up in its town, so that each town would contain, within immense granaries, the redundant produce of its own district. At last the years of famine came. "There was no bread in all the land; for the famine was very sore, so that the land of Egypt and all the land of Canaan fainted by reason of the famine."

The slender stores of the Egyptians were soon exhausted; and when all of Egypt was famished, the people cried to Pharaoh, saying: "Bread! bread! give us bread!" "Go unto Joseph; and what *he* saith to you, do." "And Joseph opened all the storehouses, and *sold* unto the Egyptians." This was right and wise. It would have been a great mistake to *give*. Joseph's policy was in exact accord with the maxims of modern political economy.

But the money was soon exhausted: it lasted just one year. What was to be done now? There was nothing left but persons and lands; the people were naturally loath to pledge these, but there was no alternative; and so they came to Joseph, and said, "Why should we die? Buy us and our land for bread." In other words, they became Pharaoh's tenant farmers, and paid him twenty percent, or one-fifth of their returns, as rent.

1. LET US STUDY THE SPIRIT OF JOSEPH'S ADMINISTRATION. He was "diligent in business, fervent in spirit, serving the Lord."

Of his *diligence in business* there is ample proof. When first raised to the proud position of Premier, "he went throughout all the land of Egypt." The granaries were built and the corn stored under his personal supervision. And when the famine came, the corn was sold under his own eye. The whole pressure of arrangements seemed to have rested entirely on his shoulders. Pharaoh wiped his hands of it, and sent his people to Joseph. Joseph gathered up all the money that was found in all the land of Egypt. Joseph bought all the land for Pharaoh; and Joseph superintended the removal of the people into the cities from one end of the country to the other for the easier distribution of food. Joseph made the laws. Young men, make Joseph your model in this. Choose a pursuit, however humble, into which you can rightly throw your energy, and then put into it all your forces without stint.

These are simple rules, but most important. *Make the most of your time.* The biggest fortunes the world has seen were made by saving what other men throw away. So be miserly over the moments, and redeem the gold-dust of time, and they will make a golden fortune of leisure. *Be punctual.* Some men are always out of step with old Father Time. They do not miss their appointments; but they always arrive five minutes late. It would seem as if they were born late, and have never been able to catch up their lost moments. *Be methodical.* Arrange, as far as you can, your daily work, subject always, of course, to those special calls that the Almighty may put in your way. *Be prompt.* If your work must be done, do it at once: well-earned rest is sweet. *Be energetic.* An admirer of Thomas Carlyle met him once in Hyde Park, and broke in on his reverie with an earnest request for a motto. The old man stood still for a moment, and then said, "There is no better motto for a young man than the words of the old book: 'Whatsoever thy hand findeth to do, do it with thy might.'"

But Joseph was also *fervant in spirit.* Love, joy, peace, long-suffering, meekness, goodness, self-control, all these were in him even to abounding. And it was, no doubt, owing to his fervor of heart. Would that more of our business people were "fervent in spirit"! There is too little of this. Time for the ledger, but none for the Bible. Time for the club or society, but none for the prayer meeting. Time to converse with friends, but none for God. And, as the result, we get to look wearied, tired, restless, and dissatisfied. Life bears a somber aspect. And men in this condition are not able to refresh weary souls that pass by. We must make time for private prayer and for the loving study of the Bible. Do not think that fervor of spirit is impossible to those who live amid the stir of business. It was not impossible to Joseph: it need not be impossible to any who will adopt the simple rules of the Bible and of common sense. It is not enough to light a fire—we must feed it. And yet how many of my readers may have gradually sunk into habits of carelessness in private devotion, such as are bound to reduce and extinguish fervor of soul!

But Joseph was also a *servant of God.* God was in all his thoughts. "I fear God," was his motto. "It was not you that sent me hither, but God: and he hath made me . . . ruler throughout all the land of Egypt." This was the inspiration of his life. In saying that, he showed that he felt accountable to God for all he was and did. Now we surely need a principle to bind together our daily life and our religious exercises. So many live in business on one set of principles—and put on another set with their Sunday clothes. Where is the principle that will bring all our life beneath one blessed rule? I know of no other principle than that laid down by the good centurion, when he said, "A man under authority." Obedience in everything to our Savior will simplify and regulate all things, and reduce the chaos of our life to one symmetrical and beautiful whole. If there is anything in your life that Christ cannot approve, it must be laid aside. The apostle invested with new dignity the existence of the poor slaves of his time, by saying, "Ye are servants of Christ: do service with a will, not as unto men, but as unto Christ." And it is of no consequence how menial your position is, you may do it for your dear Lord, whispering again and again, "This is for Thee, gracious Master, all for Thee." What a check this would put on hurried and superficial work! It would give a new dignity to toil, and a new meaning to life.

2. NOTICE THE CONFESSION OF THE EGYPTIANS. "Thou hast saved our lives."

As I see these Egyptians crowding round Joseph with these words on their lips, it makes me think of Him of whom Joseph was but a type. Joseph lay in the pit; and from the pit he was raised to give bread to the brethren who had rejected him, and to a nation of Gentiles. Jesus lay in the grave; and from its dark abyss He was raised to give salvation to His brethren the Jews, and to millions of Gentiles. The Egyptian name of Joseph meant, "the Savior of the world"; but the salvation wrought by him is hardly to be named in the same breath with that which Jesus has achieved. Joseph saved Egypt by wisdom; Jesus saved us by laying down His life. Joseph's bread cost him nothing; but the bread that Jesus gives cost Him Calvary. Joseph was well repaid by money, cattle, and land; but Jesus takes His wares to the market of the poor, and sells them to those who have no money or price. "Blessed are ye poor, for yours is the kingdom of heaven."

3. REMARK THE RESOLVE OF THESE EGYPTIANS. "Let us find grace . . . and we will be Pharaoh's servants." "You have saved our lives; and we will be your servants." How could we state better the great argument for our consecration to our Savior? He has saved us: ought we not to be His servants?

There are many arguments by which we might urge acceptance of the yoke of Christ. There is such *dignity* in it; there is such *happiness* in it; it is perfect freedom. To be free of Christ is to grind in slavery. To obey Christ is to go forth into the glorious liberty of the sons of God.

But I pass by these arguments now to present one more cogent, more pathetic, more moving. It is this: Jesus has saved you—will you not serve Him? Take Jesus moment by moment to be your Savior, Friend, and Lord; and yield to Him an obedience that will cover the entire area of your being, and will comprehend every second of your time. He deserves this. For you He lay in Bethlehem's manger. For you He was homeless and poor. For you He sweat the drops of blood and poured out His soul to death. For you He pleads in heaven. "I beseech you therefore, brethren, by the mercies of God, that ye present your bodies a living sacrifice . . . which is your reasonable service" (Rom. 12:1).

11

Joseph's Father
Genesis 47:1–11

We always turn with interest from an illustrious man to ask about his father and his mother. The father of Martin Luther and the mother of the Wesleys hang as familiar portraits in the picture gallery of our fancy. In the story of Joseph we are permitted to glance behind the scenes, and to consider the relations between him and his aged father, Jacob.

1. JOSEPH'S UNDIMINISHED FILIAL LOVE. From the first moment that Joseph saw his brothers in the grain market, it was evident that his love to his father burned with undiminished fervor. Those brethren little guessed how eager he was to learn if his aged

father was yet alive, nor what a thrill of comfort shot through his heart when they happened to say, "Behold, our youngest brother is this day with his father." Evidently, then, though twenty-five years had passed since he beheld that beloved form, his father was living still.

And when his brothers came the second time, Judah little realized what a tender chord he struck, and how it vibrated, almost beyond endurance, when he spoke again and again of the father at home, an elderly man, who so tenderly loved the young lad, the only memorial of his mother. He spoke of that father who had been so anxious lest mischief should befall him, and whose gray hairs would go down with sorrow to the grave, unless he came back safe. It was this repeated allusion to his father that wrought on Joseph's feelings so greatly as to break him down. "He could not refrain himself." And so the very next thing he said, after the astounding announcement, "I am Joseph," was, "Doth my father yet live?" And in the tumultuous words that followed, words throbbing with passion and pathos, sentences about the absent father came rolling out. "Haste ye, and go up to my father, and say unto him, Thus saith thy son Joseph, God hath made me lord of all Egypt: come down unto me; tarry not. . . . And ye shall tell my father of my glory in Egypt, and of all that ye have seen; and ye shall haste, and bring down my father hither."

The weeks and months that intervened must have been full of feverish anxiety for Joseph; and when at last he heard that his father had reached the frontier of Egypt, in one of the wagons that he had sent to meet him, he "made ready his chariot, and went up to meet Israel his father." Oh, that meeting! If the aged man was sitting in some recess of the lumbering wagon, weary with the long journey, how he would revive when they said, "Joseph is coming"! I think he would surely dismount, and wait, straining his aged eyes at the approaching company, from out the midst of which there came the bejewelled ruler to fall on his neck and weep there a good while. "Let me die," said Jacob, as he looked at Joseph from head to foot with glad, proud, satisfied eyes: "Let me die, since I have seen thy face; because thou art yet alive."

a. *But this was not all. Joseph loved his father too well to be ashamed of him.* When Pharaoh heard of the arrival of Joseph's father and brothers, he seemed very pleased, and he directed Joseph to see to their welfare. Then Joseph brought Jacob his father before Pharaoh.

We cannot but admire the noble frankness with which Joseph introduced his father to this great monarch, accustomed to the manners of the foremost court of the world. There was a great social gulf fixed between Egypt and Canaan, the court and the tent, the monarch and the shepherd. And if Joseph had been any less noble or simple than he was, he might have shrunk from bringing the two extremes together. But all these thoughts were forgotten in presence of another: this withered, halting, famine-pursued man was *his father*.

b. *In some cases the behavior of grown-up children to their parents is dishonorable.* With increasing money there comes a vast change in a man's social position. He lives in a fine house, and gives large parties. He sends his children to expensive schools. But what of his aged parents? He allows them a little that resembles an allowance annuity; but takes care to keep them out of his family—for, to tell the truth, he is rather ashamed of them. It is a false shame indeed! I prefer the noble magnanimity of Joseph, who seemed proud to introduce the withered, crippled patriarch to his mighty friend and liege lord. Young people, honor your parents!

2. PHARAOH'S QUESTION. "How old art thou?" This was Pharaoh's first inquiry, as Jacob entered his presence. It is a question that often rises to our lips, but it is suggested by a very false standard of estimating the length of a man's life. The length of a life is not measured by the number of its days; no, but by the way in which its days have been used.

Some live for many years, and at the end have little or nothing to show for them. Take out the wasted hours, and only a few hours of real life are left. There are men who will be seventy next birthday, but who have only lived six months out of their whole life. Our real life dates, not from our first birth, but from our second. All before that counts for nothing.

Others live for few years, but they have crowded them with strenuous, noble life: they have been punctual, industrious, methodical: they have redeemed the time; they have made the most of odd bits which others would have flung away as useless—and, as the result, they have much to show. What books they have read! What deeds they have done! What ministries they have set afoot! What friends they have made! What characters they have built up! They have lived long. They will be thirty next birthday, but in those few years they have lived the life which most men live in sixty years.

Permit a stranger to ask of each reader, "How old art thou?"

How old are you? *Seventeen?* That is indeed a critical time. It is the formative time: what you are now, you will be. You are leaving the sheltered bay of early life to launch out into the great ocean. Beware! it is winsome-looking, but it is treacherous. Be sure and take on board the great Master, Christ: none but He can pilot you through the shoals and quicksands that lie hidden on your course. Take on board none but those whom He chooses as the crew.

How old are you? *Twenty-one?* That is often described as the time of a man's majority, or independence. Never forget that there is at least One of whom you can never be independent.

How old are you? *Thirty?* It was at that age that our Lord emerged from obscurity: and think how many men have lived a great life and died before they reached this age. What are you doing in the world? Come, make haste! Your life will soon slip away. Take care, lest at the close you be constrained to say, "I have spent my life in laboriously doing trifles."

But this need not be your sad retrospect, if only you will yield your whole being to the Lord Jesus, asking Him to think in your brain, to live in your heart, and to work through your life.

How old are you? *Forty?* Take care! Very few are ever converted who have reached the downward slopes of forty. If you are not Christ's yet, the chances of your becoming His lessen at a tremendous ratio every week.

How old are you? *Fifty? Sixty? Seventy?* The snows are beginning to silver your head. Familiar pursuits must be abandoned. Familiar places must be visited no more. Affairs once your pride must be given over to the stronger nerve of others. Old friends, we look on you to teach us how to await our end, and how to die. It is a solemn question, "How old are you?"

3. JACOB'S ANSWER. "And Jacob said unto Pharaoh, The days of the years of my pilgrimage are an hundred and thirty years; few and evil have the days of the years of my life been, and have not attained unto the days of the years of the life of my fathers in the

days of their pilgrimage." Jacob's years had been *few* in comparison with those of his ancestors. Terah reached the age of 205; Abraham, 175; Isaac, 180. But "the whole age of Jacob was an hundred forty and seven years." They had been *evil*. As a young man he was wrenched from his dearest associations of home and friends, and went forth alone to spend the best years of his life as a stranger in a strange land. Arduous and difficult was his service to Laban, consumed in the day by drought, and in the sleepless night vigils by frost. He escaped from Laban with difficulty, and no sooner had he done so than he had to encounter his incensed and impetuous brother. In the agony of that dread crisis he met with the Angel Wrestler, who touched the socket of his hips so that he limped to the end of his life. These calamities had hardly passed when he was involved in extreme danger with the Canaanites of Shechem, and passed through scenes that have blanched his hair, furrowed his cheeks, and scarred his heart. Thus he came to Luz, and Deborah, Rebekah's nurse, died, and was buried beneath an oak, which was thereafter called the Oak of Weeping. "And they journeyed from Bethel; and there was but a little way to come to Ephrath," and Rachel (his favorite wife) bore a son. It came to pass, as she died, that she called his name "Ben-oni, the son of my sorrow." A little further on he came to Mamre, arriving just in time to bear the remains of his own father to the grave. And what sorrows befell him after that, have already touched our hearts, as we have studied the story of his son, Joseph. Reuben involved his name in shameful disgrace. Judah trailed the family honor in the mire of sensual appetite. To all appearance Joseph had been torn to pieces by wild beasts. The dissensions of his sons must have rent his heart. And even after his meeting with his long-lost son he was to linger for seventeen years a pensioner on the bounty of the king of Egypt: far from the glorious heritage that had been promised to his race.

Such was the exterior of Jacob's life. You would have called his life a failure. Compare it with the lot of Esau; and what a contrast it presents! Jacob obtained the birthright; but what a life of suffering and disaster was his! Esau lost the birthright; but he had all that heart could wish; wealth, royalty, a line of illustrious sons. The thirty-sixth chapter of Genesis contains a list of the royal dukes of his line. How often must Esau have pitied his brother!

And yet when this same Jacob stands before Pharaoh, the greatest monarch of the world bends eagerly to catch his blessing. "Jacob blessed Pharaoh." Jacob in his earlier life was crafty, a mere bargain-maker, a trickster; but all seems to have been eliminated in the fierce crucible of suffering through which he had passed; and he had reached a grandeur or moral greatness that impressed even the haughty Pharaoh. There is a greatness that is wholly independent of those adventitious circumstances that we sometimes associate with it. God Himself said, "Thy name shall be no more called Jacob, but Israel (a prince of God), for as a prince hast thou power with God, and with men."

Three things made Jacob royal; and will do as much for us.

a. *Prayer.* On the moorland, strewn with boulders, he saw in his dreams the mighty rocks pile themselves into a heaven-touching ladder. This struck the keynote of his life. Since that day he lived at the foot of the ladder of prayer, up which the angels sped to carry his petitions, and down which they came to bring blessing. Learn to pray without ceasing. It is the secret of greatness. He who is often in the audience chamber of the great King becomes kinglike.

b. *Suffering.* His nature was marred by selfish, base, and carnal elements. He took unlawful advantage of his famished brother; deceived his aged father; increased his property at the expense of his uncle; worked his ends by mean and crafty means. But sorrow ate away all these things and gave him a new dignity. So does it still work on those who have received the new nature, and who meekly learn the lesson that God's love designs to teach them.

c. *Contact with Christ.* "There wrestled a man with him until the breaking of the day." Who was He? Surely none less than the Angel Jehovah, whose face may not be seen, or His name known. It was the Lord Himself, intent on ridding His servant of the evil that had clung so long and so closely to him, sapping his spiritual life. And from that hour Jacob was "Israel." Ah, my readers, Jesus, the immortal lover of souls, is wrestling with you, longing to rid you of littleness and selfishness, and to lift you also to a royal life. Yield to Him, lest He be compelled to touch the sinew of your strength. If you let Him have His way, He will make you truly Princes and Princesses with God; and even those above you in this world's rank will gladly gather around you for the sake of the spiritual blessings you will bestow.

12

Joseph at the Deathbed of Jacob
Genesis 47:27–31

Jacob dwelled in the land of Goshen and there his sons led their flocks over the rich pasture-lands. "They grew, and multiplied exceedingly." So seventeen uneventful years went by. And as the elderly man became more and more infirm, his spirit was cheered and sustained by the love of Joseph. Evidently Joseph was the stay of that waning life, and it is not remarkable therefore that the patriarch summoned him not once, or even twice, but three times, to his deathbed. It is on those visits that we dwell now.

1. JOSEPH'S FIRST VISIT. "The time drew nigh that Israel must die." How inexorable is the "must" of death! There is no possibility of evading its summons. Jacob exceeded the ordinary span of modern life by many years, and, in spite of much hardship and privation, he had evaded the reach of death; but this could not be forever. The failing powers of his life gave warning that the machinery of nature was on the point of giving way. He must die. Long before our Lord walked this world, men cherished the hope of eternal life.

Daniel teaches in plainest language the truth of a general resurrection to endless life or endless shame. Ecclesiastes closes with an explicit statement of the spirit's return to its giver, and of final judgment. The Book of Job, whatever date may be assigned to it, has been called a hymn of immortality: he knew at least that his "Redeemer liveth, and that he shall stand at the latter day upon the earth: and though after my skin worms destroy this body, yet in my flesh shall I see God" (Job 19:25–26). In the Book of Psalms we have no uncertain evidence of the tenacity with which pious Jews clung to these hopes. "Thou wilt not leave my soul in [sheol]; neither wilt thou suffer thine Holy One to see corruption. Thou wilt shew me the path of life" (Ps. 16:10–11). And it is just this faith in and yearning after a life beyond the grave which is the true keynote of the lives of the three great patriarchs who lie together in Machpelah's ancient cave.

Why did they wander to and fro in the land of promise as sojourners in a strange land? Why were they content to have no inheritance—no, not so much as a place to put their feet on? Why did Abraham dwell with Isaac and Jacob in frail, shifting tents, rather than in towns like Sodom and Gomorrah? What did Abraham mean when he said to the sons of Heth, "I am a stranger and a sojourner with you"? And what was the thought in Jacob's mind when, in the presence of the haughty Pharaoh, he described his life as a "pilgrimage"? The answer is clearly given in the roll call of God's heroes contained in Hebrews 11: "They sought a country, a fatherland." And they were so absorbed with this one thought, that they could not settle to any inheritance in Canaan. Their refusal to have anything more than a grave in the soil of the Promised Land shows how eagerly they looked for the land that was very far off.

At first, no doubt, they thought that Canaan was to be the land of promise. But when they waited for it year after year, and still it was withheld, they looked into the deed of gift again, and instead of a city built by human hands, there arose before them the fair vision of the crystal walls and the pearly gates of the city which hath foundations, whose builder and maker is God.

This belief in "the city of God," of which later Augustine wrote on the coast of Africa, and which has sustained so many saintly souls, animated their lives, cheered them in death, and cast a bright ray across the gloom of the grave. "These all died in faith, not having received the promises, but having seen them afar off, and were persuaded of them, and embraced them." They "greeted them from afar," as the wanderer greets his longed-for home, when he sees it from afar. With what eagerness, with what earnest yearnings, with what fond anticipation, must these weary wanderers have looked for heaven!

a. *Jacob did not regard the future life as a mere state of existence* stripped of all those associations that make life worth the having. Indeed, in this he seems to have had truer thoughts than many who are found in Christian churches. He said, "I am to be gathered unto my people." For him the city to which he went was the gathering-place of his clan, the rendezvous of elect souls, the home of all who were *his* people because they were *God's*.

But it was not simply to express these hopes that the dying patriarch summoned the beloved Joseph to his side. The father wanted to bind the son by a solemn promise not to have him buried in the land of his exile, but to carry him back to that lone cave, which seemed an outpost in the hostile and distant land of Canaan. For seventeen years Jacob had been familiar with Egypt's splendid temples, obelisks, and pyramids; he had been surrounded with all the comforts that Joseph's filial love could devise or his munificence execute. But nothing could make him forget that distant cave that was before Mamre, in the land of Canaan. To him interment in the most magnificent pyramid in Egypt was not for a moment to be compared with burial in that solitary and humble sepulcher, where the mortal remains of Abraham and Sarah, of Isaac and Rebekah, and of the faithful Leah, lay waiting the day of resurrection.

b. *Human nature was not different then from what it is today.* Our truest home is still by the graves of the beloved dead. Many a warrior, dying in some distant land, has asked that his remains might be placed, but in the quiet country graveyard where the moss-covered tombstones repeat in successive generations the family name. It was natural, then, for Jacob to wish to be buried in Machpelah.

c. *But there was something more than natural sentiment.* He was a man of faith. He knew and cherished the ancient promise made by God to His friend, the patriarch Abraham, that Canaan should become the possession of his seed. That promise was the old man's stay. He knew that Canaan and not Egypt was the destined abiding place of his people. They would not always live in Egypt. If then, he was buried in Egypt, he would be left behind, a stranger among strangers. No, this could not be. If they are to leave, he must leave before them. If they are to settle in the land of promise, he will go first as their forerunner. And though he could not share the perils and pains and glories of the Exodus, he would be there to meet them when later descendants would enter on their inheritance.

"Bury me not, I pray thee, in Egypt: but I will lie with my fathers, and thou shalt carry me out of Egypt and bury me in their buryingplace." What son could resist that appeal? Can any of us resist the last appeals of our beloved? Joseph was too good and tender to hesitate for a single moment. "And he said, I will do as thou hast said." But the old man was not content with a mere promise. "And he said, Swear unto me. And he sware unto him. And Israel bowed himself upon the bed's head." So ended Joseph's first visit to his dying father.

2. JOSEPH'S SECOND VISIT. Tidings came to the Prime Minister of Egypt that his father was sick and wished to see him. And he went to him without delay, taking with him his two sons, Manasseh and Ephraim. When Joseph arrived at his father's dwelling, the aged patriarch seems to have been lying still, with closed eyes, in the extreme of physical exhaustion. He was too weak to notice any of those familiar forms that stood around him. But when one told him and said, "Behold, thy son Joseph commeth," the sound of that loved name revived him. He made a great effort, and, propped by pillows sat up upon the bed.

There was clearly no decay in his power of recollection, as the old man reviewed the past. And as his recollection embraced the past, it was also vividly alive to more recent incidents in the family history. He did not forget that Joseph, who leaned over his dying form, had two sons; and he announced his intention of adopting them as his own. "Thy two sons . . . which were born unto thee in the land of Egypt before I came unto thee into Egypt, are mine; as Reuben and Simeon, they shall be mine." By that act, while Joseph's name was obliterated from the map of Canaan, yet he became possessor of a double portion of his area, because Ephraim and Manasseh would from that day stand there as his representatives.

And when he had said so much, his mind wandered away. He saw again that scene on the hilly road to Bethlehem, just outside the little village, where his onward progress was suddenly halted, and all his camp was hushed into the stillness of a dread suspense, as the life of the beloved Rachel trembled in the balance. He could never forget that moment. His dying eyes could see again the spot where he buried her, "there in the way of Ephrath."

When the aged Jacob came back from his reverie, the first sight that arrested him was the presence of the awe-struck boys, who were drinking in every look and word, with fixed and almost breathless heed.

"Who are these?" said Israel.

"They are my sons," was the proud and immediate reply, "whom God hath given me in this place."

And Israel said, "Bring them, I pray thee, unto me, and I will bless them."

And so they were brought near, and the aged arms were put feebly around the younger and slender forms. And then again the dying man wandered back to a grief that had left as deep a scar as his sorrow for the beloved Rachel. Then turning to Joseph, he reminded him of the long years during which he thought he would never look again on his face. But now, God had shown him also his seed.

With prophetic insight he crossed his hands, as the two lads waited before him for his blessing, so that his right found its way to the head of the younger, while his left alighted on that of the elder. By that act he reversed the verdict of their birth, and gave the younger precedence over the elder. It was useless for Joseph to remonstrate, and to urge the claims of his firstborn. Jacob knew quite well what he was doing, and that he was on the line of the divine purpose. "I know it, my son, I know it; he also shall become a people, and he also shall be great: but truly his younger brother shall be greater than he, and his seed shall become a multitude of nations."

There was one thing only more to say, before this memorable interview ended. Years before, Jacob had become embroiled through the dastardly treachery of his sons, in conflict with the original inhabitants of Canaan, and had been compelled, in self-defense, to acquire by force a parcel of land, with his sword and with his bow. *This* he gave as an additional portion to his favorite son.

3. Joseph's third and last visit. Once more Joseph visited that death chamber. This was the third time and the last. But this time he stood only as one of twelve strong, bearded men, who gathered around the aged form of their father, his face shadowed by death, his spirit aglow with the light of prophecy. How intense the awe with which they heard their names called, one by one, by the old man's trembling voice, now pausing for breath, now speaking with great difficulty! The character of each is criticized with prophetic insight; the salient points of their past history are vividly brought to mind; and some foreshadowing is given them of their future.

This scene is an anticipation of the judgment seat where men shall hear the story of their lives passed under review, and a sentence passed, against which there shall be no appeal.

But the dying patriarch speaks with peculiar sweetness and grace when he comes to touch on the destiny of his favorite son. His words brim with tenderness and move with a stateliness and eloquence, which indicate how his heart was stirred to its depths. A few more sentences to Benjamin, and the venerable patriarch drew his feet up into his bed, and quietly breathed his last, and was gathered to his people. But that eager, much-tried spirit passed up into other scenes of more exalted fellowship and ministry, with no pause in his life, for in years to come God attested his continued existence and energy when He called Himself "the God of Jacob," for God is not God of the dead, but of the living. And Joseph fell on his father's face, and wept on him, and pressed his warm lips on the death-cold clay. He commanded the physicians to embalm his body, thus cheating death of its immediate victory.

13

Joseph's Last Days and Death
Genesis 50:24–25

"God will surely visit you, and ye shall carry up my bones from hence." These were the dying words of Joseph. And it is somewhat remarkable that these are the only words in his whole career that are referred to in the subsequent pages of the Scriptures. Of course, I refer to those words in Hebrews 11, where it is said, "By faith Joseph, when he died, made mention of the [exodus] of the children of Israel; and gave commandment concerning his bones."

Let us notice:

1. THE CIRCUMSTANCES UNDER WHICH THESE WORDS WERE SPOKEN.

a. *Joseph was now an old man.* One hundred and ten years had stolen away his strength, and had left deep marks on his form. It was ninety-three years since he had been lifted from the pit to become a slave. Eighty years had passed since he had first stood before Pharaoh in all the beauty and wisdom of his young manhood. And sixty years had left their papyrus records in the State archives since, with all the pomp and splendor of Egypt's court, he had carried the remains of his old father to Machpelah's ancient cave. He was old when he saw the bright young faces of his great-grandchildren: "they were brought up upon Joseph's knees." With long life and many days God had blessed His faithful servant. And now, stopping beneath their weight, he was fast descending to the breakup of natural life.

b. *But the shadows of his own decay were small compared with those that he saw gathering around his beloved people.* Sixty years before, when Jacob died, all was bright, and he was honored with a splendid funeral because he had given to the land of Egypt so great a benefactor and savior in the person of his son. But when Joseph died, all was getting dark, and the shadow of a great eclipse was gathering over the destinies of his people. No notice seems to have been taken in Egypt of his death. No impressive funeral services were voted to him at public expense. No pyramid was placed at the disposal of his sons. And he addresses his brethren gathered about him as being sorely in need of help. They needed an advocate at court, and an assurance of divine visitation.

Three hundred years before, the great founder of the nation had watched all day beside an altar, scaring away the vultures which, attracted by the flesh that lay upon it, hovered around. At length, as the sun went down, the watcher fell asleep—it is hard to watch with God—and in his sleep he dreamed. A dense and awful gloom seemed to enclose him, and to oppress his soul and on it, as upon a curtain, passed successive glimpses of the future of his race—glimpses which a divine voice interpreted to his ear. He saw them exiled to a foreign country, enslaved by the foreigner, and lingering there while three generations of men bloomed as spring flowers, and were cut down before the sharp sickle of death. And as he beheld all the terror of that enslavement, the horror of a great darkness fell on his soul. We know how exactly that horror was justified by the events that were so soon to take place. "The Egyptians made the children of Israel to serve with rigour: and they made their lives bitter with hard bondage, in mortar, and in brick, and in all manner of service in the field: all their service, wherein they made them serve, was with rigour" (Exod. 1:13–14). The first symptoms of that outburst of popular "Jew-hate" were already, like stormy birds, settling about the closing hour of the great Egyptian premier.

We cannot tell the precise form of those symptoms. Perhaps he had been banished from the councils of Pharaoh; perhaps he was already pining in neglect; perhaps the murmurs of dislike against his people were already rising; perhaps acts of oppression and cruelty were increasingly rife. In any case, the twilight of the dark night was gathering in; and it was this that made his words more splendid: they shone out as stars of hope.

c. *Moreover, his brethren were around him.* His forgiveness and love to them lasted till the testing hour by that great assayer, Death. Nor did *they* fail. From something narrated in the previous verses of this chapter, it would appear that, for long, his brethren, judging of him by their own dark and implacable hearts, could not believe in the sincerity and genuineness of his forgiveness. They thought that he must be feigning more than he felt, in order to secure some ulterior object, such as the blessing and approval of their aged father. And so they feared that, as soon as Jacob was removed, Joseph's just resentment, long concealed with masterly art, would break forth against them. It seemed impossible to believe that he felt no grudge, and would take no action at all with reference to the past; and they said, "Joseph will . . . certainly requite us all the evil which we did unto him." And Joseph wept when they spoke; wept that they should have so misunderstood him after his repeated assurances; wept to see them kneeling at his feet for a forgiveness that he had freely given them years before. "Fear not," he said in effect; "do not kneel there; I am not God: you thought evil against me; but God meant it for good, to save many people alive, as it is this day."

The Lord Jesus, who lights every man coming into the world, was in Joseph's heart, and his behavior was a foreshadowing of incarnate love. Reader! He waits to forgive you in this way. Though you have maligned, and refused, and crucified Him afresh, and put Him to an open shame; yet, for all that, He waits to forgive you so entirely, that not one of these things shall be ever mentioned against you again.

d. *Lastly, he was dying.* He had warded off death from Egypt; but he could not ward it off from himself. "I die." They were among the last words that he had caught from his father's dying lips (48:21), and now he appropriates them to himself. Yes, and in doing so, he touches the zenith of his noble confidence and hope. O that each of us may go on shining more and more each day until our last, and that, when heart and flesh are failing most conspicuously, the life of the spirit may flash out with its most brilliant lights.

It was under all these circumstances that Joseph said, "God will surely visit you, and ye shall carry up my bones from hence."

2. LET US INVESTIGATE THE FULL IMPORTANCE OF THESE WORDS. And we may do so best by comparing them with Jacob's dying wish: "Bury me with my fathers in the cave that is in . . . the field of Machpelah." This was most natural: we all love to be buried by the beloved dust of our departed. And Jacob knew that there would be no great difficulty in carrying out his wish. Joseph was then in the height of his power. There was no great faith therefore in asking for that which could so easily be accomplished. But with Joseph it was different. He too wanted to be buried in the land of Canaan; but not at once—not then! There were two things he expected would happen: the one, that the people would go out of Egypt; the other, that they would come into the land of Canaan. He did not know when or how; he was only sure that so it would be: "surely."

To Joseph's natural vision these things were most unlikely. When he spoke, Israel was settled in Goshen, and so increasing in numbers and in wealth that any uprooting was becoming daily more unlikely. And as to the oppression that was perhaps beginning to threaten them, what chance would they have of ever being able to escape from the detaining squadrons of Egypt's chivalry, supposing they wished to go? But his anticipation of the future was not founded on human foresight, but on the distinct announcements of the Almighty. He remembered how God had said to Abraham, "Look from the place where thou art northward, and southward, and eastward, and westward; for all the land which thou seest, to thee will I give it, and to thy seed forever" (Gen. 13:14–15). That promise was repeated to Isaac.

Again that promise was reiterated to Jacob as he lay at the foot of the shining ladder, "The land whereon thou liest, to thee will I give it, and to thy seed." These promises had been carefully treasured and handed on. Jacob on his deathbed reassured Joseph that God would certainly bring them to the land of their fathers; and now Joseph reanimated the trembling company that gathered around him with the same hope. Thus he commanded that his bones should be unburied, so that at any moment, however hurried, when the trumpet of exodus sounded, they might be ready to be caught up and borne onward in the glad march for Canaan.

What a lesson must those unburied bones have been to Israel! When the taskmasters dealt harshly with the people, so that their hearts fainted, it must have been sweet to go and look at the mummy case that held those decaying remains, waiting there to be carried forward; and, as they did so, this was doubtless their reflection, "Evidently then, Joseph believed that we were not to stay here always, but that we should sooner or later leave for Canaan: let us brace ourselves up to bear a little longer, it may only be a very little while!" Yes, and when some were tempted to settle down content with prospering circumstances, it was a check on them to think of those bones, and say, "Evidently we are not to remain here always: we should do well not to build all our hopes and comfort on the unstable tenure of our sojourn in this place." And, often, when the Israelites were ready to despair amid the difficulties and weariness of their desert march, those bones borne in their midst told them of the confident hope of Joseph—that God would bring them to the land of rest.

We have no unburied bones to animate our faith, or to revive our drooping zeal; but we have something better—we have an empty grave. It tells us that He is risen. It tells us that not death, but life, is to be the guardian angel of our desert march. It tells us that this world is not our resting place or home; it tells us that resurrection is not possible only, but certain; and that before long we will be where He is. He will go with us along the desert pathway, till we go to be with Him.

3. LET US REALIZE THE SPIRIT THAT UNDERLAY AND PROMPTED THESE WORDS. It was above all a pilgrim spirit. Joseph bore an Egyptian title. He married an Egyptian wife. He shared in Egyptian court life, politics, and trade. But he was as much a pilgrim as was Abraham pitching his tent outside the walls of Hebron, or Isaac in the grassy plains of the south country, or Jacob keeping himself aloof from the families of the land.

We sometimes speak as if the pilgram spirit would be impossible for us who live in this settled state of civilization. Our houses are too substantial; our movements too closely tethered to one narrow round. But if that thought should ever cross our hearts again, let us turn to Joseph, and remind ourselves how evidently he was animated by the spirit of those "who confessed that they were pilgrims and strangers on the earth." Ah, friends, what are we living for? Are our pursuits bounded by the narrow horizon of earth, and limited to the fleeting moments of time? Are we constantly engaged in lining as warmly as possible the nest in which we hope to spend our old age and die? Are we perpetually seeking to make the best of this world? I fear that these are the real aims of many professing Christians; and, if so, it is simply useless for them to claim kinship with that mighty stream of pilgrims bound to the city that has foundations, their true home and mother city. On the other hand, you may be at the head of a large establishment, engaged in many permanent undertakings, closely attached to the present by imperious duties; and yet, like Joseph, your heart may be detached from things seen and temporal, and engaged, in all its secret longings, to the things unseen and eternal.

a. *The pilgrim spirit will not make us unpractical.* Joseph was the most practical man in his time. Who are likely to be as prompt, as energetic, as thorough, as those who feel that they are working for eternity, and that they are building up day by day a fabric in which they shall live hereafter? Each day is character-building for better or for worse: each deed, well or ill done, is a stone in the edifice; each moment tells on eternity. We will receive a reward according to our deeds.

b. *But the pilgrim spirit will make us simple.* There are two sorts of simplicity: that of circumstances, and that of heart. Many a person sits down to bread and milk at a wooden table, with a heart as proud as pride can make it; while many others who eat off a golden plate and are as simple as Cincinnatus at his plough. The world cannot understand this. But here in Joseph is an illustration. Ah, my friend, it is not the unjewelled finger, nor the plain attire, nor the unfurnished room, that constitutes a simple unaffected life: but that vision of the spirit, which looks through the unsubstantial wreath-vapors of the morning to the peaks of the everlasting hills beyond and above.

What a contrast there is between the opening and closing words of Genesis! Listen to the closing words, "A coffin in Egypt." And is this all? Is all God's work to end in one poor mummy case? Stay. This is only the end of Genesis, the Book of Beginnings. Turn the leaf, and there you will find Exodus, and Joshua, and Kings, and Prophets, and Christ. God is not dependent on any one of us. We do our little work and cease, but God's work goes on. And it is enough for each of us, like Joseph, to have lived a true, pure, strong, and noble life—and to leave Him to see after our bodies; our beloved, whom we leave so reluctantly, and our work. Nor will He fail. "And Moses took the bones of Joseph with him," on the night of the Exodus (Exod. 13:19); "and they buried the bones of Joseph in Shechem: . . . and it became the inheritance of the children of Joseph" (Josh. 24:32).

MOSES

1

Our Standpoint
Hebrews 11:24

The writer of the Epistle to the Hebrews lays bare the secret of the marvels effected by the heroes of Hebrew story. We make a profound mistake in attributing to these men extraordinary qualities of courage, and strength of body or soul. But there was one characteristic common to them all, which lifted them above ordinary men, that they had a marvelous faculty of faith which, indeed, is but the capacity of the human heart for God. Four times over this is cited as the secret of all that Moses did for his people.

And what is this faith? It is not some inherent power or quality in certain men, by virtue of which they are able to accomplish special results unrealized by others. It is rather the power of putting self aside that God may work unhindered through the nature. It is, in brief, that capacity for God that appropriates Him to its uttermost limit, and becomes the channel or vehicle through which He passes forth to bless mankind. The believer is the God-filled, the God-moved, the God-possessed man; and the work that he effects in the world is not his, but God's through him.

There are, therefore, these necessary conditions of all true faith:

The sense of helplessness and nothingness.

An absolute assurance of being in God's plan.

Entire consecration, that He may work out His will through heart and life.

The daily food of promise.

A daring to act, in utter independence of feeling, on a faith that reckons absolutely on the faithfulness of God.

It will be our contention throughout our study of the remarkable life before us, that, though Moses may have had commanding features of mind and body, and have been versed in all the learning of his time, yet the marvelous outcome of his life work was not due to any of these qualities, but to the faith that knit his soul to God. His faith sufficed to do what all his other qualities, without his faith, must have failed in doing.

We hope to go further, and show that all the blessings that God in His mindfulness of His covenant bestowed on Israel, came through the channel of Moses' faith.

Each of the above-mentioned conditions of a mighty faith was fulfilled in the history of Moses.

He was allowed to make his first efforts for the emancipation of his people in the energy of his own strength, and to fail egregiously. Because of this he fled to Midian, spent exile, until it was with the greatest difficulty that he could be induced to undertake the divine commission. He was reduced to the last extreme of helpless nothingness when the burning bush flamed in his path, a symbol of his utter weakness, possessed and indwelt yet unconsumed by God, who is a consuming fire.

He was as thoroughly yielded to the purpose of God as the staff he held in his hand was to his own will. He fed daily on the promises of God, pleading them in prayer, and leaning his whole weight on them. And he often knew what it was to leave behind him the familiar and tried, for the strange and new. At the bidding of God he stepped out, though there seemed nothing to tread on, launching himself and three millions of people absolutely on the care of God, assured that God's faithfulness could not fail.

His faith made Moses all he was. Why should we not have it? It is certain that we can have his faith if we but pay the price of enduring his discipline. And if only we possessed his faith, why should we not see another Exodus—seas seamed with paths of salvation; foes defied; chains snapped; captives emancipated; and Jehovah worshiped with songs of triumph! Surely there is no limit to the possibilities of a life that has become the channel through which God can pour Himself forth.

Are you willing to die to your own strength; to forsake your own plans for God's; to seek out and do his will absolutely; to take up the attitude of entire and absolute surrender to his purposes; to feed daily on the promises of God, as a girl on the pledge of her absent lover; to step out in faith, reckoning, without emotion of any kind, on the faithfulness of God, only fully persuaded that He will perform all that He has promised? Then surely through you God will, here or hereafter, work as in the times of old, of which our fathers have told us.

2

His Mother's Faith
Hebrews 11:23

It was on a very unfriendly world that the little babe opened his eyes. Without, all was as fair as nature and art could make it. Near the little cottage, which for a brief space was to shelter him, the mighty Nile rolled between its reedy banks. Within the easy distance of a maiden's morning walk stood the great city of Memphis, metropolis of Egypt and seat of the Court; center of trade, and art, and war, and religion; the focus to which the national life converged.

Past that cottage home would go royal processions; priests from all parts of the land would pass it on their way to the mighty Temple of Phthah. You would also see the perpetual supply of leeks and melons and garlic, barley and wheat and rye, delicate fabrics from the loom, for which the Egyptians became so famous, spice and balm for the vast City of the Dead, and the multitudinous provision for the demands of a large and wealthy population. These must have covered the neighboring roads with an unceasing stream of camels and asses and caravans, and the river with an innumerable flotilla of boats, barges, and ships. Not far away, across the level sands, were the Pyramids, which even then were becoming venerable with age, and were destined to remain for forty centuries, witnesses alike to man's instinctive belief in his immorality, and to his selfish indifference to the anguish of his fellows. Amid these circumstances of wealth and splendor the little babe was born to an unkindly lot.

1. HE BELONGED TO AN ALIEN RACE. More than three hundred years before, the forefathers of his people had emigrated from the neighboring land of Palestine. The king had welcomed them as likely to be valuable allies, for he also belonged to a foreign race, and sat on an unstable throne. At his command they had settled in the best of the land, a strip of green called Goshen, situated amid vast tracks of sand. There they prospered

and multiplied, till they numbered near upon two million souls. But they remained as distinct a people as they are now in every nation under heaven, and as such were open to suspicious hate.

2. HE BELONGED TO AN OPPRESSED RACE. A different dynasty had succeeded to that which welcomed them, and one to whom the name of Joseph had no charm. At the time of which we write a tiny cloud of impending war trembled on the Eastern sky, and suggested to the reigning monarch the fear that there might be a coalition between his enemies and the Hebrew race, which had grown into such numbers and might, as to be very formidable. He resolved, therefore, to wear them out, and to reduce both their numbers and their spirit by the rigor of their lot.

Suddenly, the shepherds of Goshen found themselves drafted for service in the brickfields, under the eye and whip of cruel taskmasters, who exacted from them daily a certain number of bricks; or they performed service in the field, drawing water from the river for the irrigation of the land, and toiling in the cultivation of the soil. "And all their service, wherein they made them serve, was with rigor" (Exod. 1:14); as if every occasion was eagerly taken advantage of for dealing out cruel and merciless punishment.

The father of the little household was probably compelled to bear his share in the bondage and blows that made the existence of his people so bitter. From morning to night he would toil, naked, beneath the burning sun, returning often with bleeding wounds torn open by the scourge, and inclined to question the very existence of God and his character for mercy. Very dark was the night that lay heavily on the chosen people in these years of cruel enslavement.

3. HE WAS BORN AT A TIME OF UNUSUAL TROUBLE. The household consisted of father and mother, an elder sister, some fifteen years of age, and of a little brother, Aaron, three years of age. When the latter was born, there was apparently no special need of secrecy, for the king was trying to attain his object by the vigorous policy we have above described. But during the interval he had discovered that it was not stringent enough; and he had therefore added to it a scheme for the destruction of all the male children, by casting them into the river as they were born.

It is not likely that this decree was in active operation for more than a few months. It was a spasm of cruelty that was inspired by sudden fear, but was too utterly opposed to the better instincts of human nature to secure for itself a permanent position in the practice of Pharaoh's subordinates. But while it lasted, it was the bitterest element in all that bitter sorrow.

4. BUT HE WAS THE CHILD OF BELIEVING PARENTS. We know but little of them. The father is said to have been "a man of the house of Levi," and we learn afterward that his name was Amram, and he descended from Kohath, the son of Levi; but the tribe of Levi had then no special importance—in fact, it seemed destined to be divided in Jacob and scattered in Israel. The mother, Jochebed, belonged to the same tribe, and, indeed, was related to her husband in a closer consanguinity than was later permitted. They were humble folk, glad enough to receive "wages" from the hand of wealth and royalty, but they preserved the best religious traditions of their nation, and in this contrasted favorably with many of their race.

Dean Stanley has shown that the sojourn in Egypt had produced a very deleterious result on the children of Israel. "The old freedom, the old energy, above all, the old religion of the patriarchal age, had faded away." The Sabbath was forgotten; the rite of circumcision, the significant token of the covenant, fell into disuse; the comparative purity of their forefathers proved unable to resist the licentious attractions of heathen festivals, to which in after years they perpetually recurred.

But evidently there were some families who remained faithful amid the prevalent corruption. Among these was that into which this child was born. The sacred covenant between God and their race was reverently remembered, and held by a faith that dared to believe that, sooner or later, God must interpose.

But their religious life was still more manifested by their faith. "By faith Moses, when he was born, was hid three months of his parents, because they saw he was a proper child; and they were not afraid of the king's commandment." We have often been furnished with a picture depicting the anxiety with which his parents received their newborn babe, the distress of Amram, and the fears of Jochebed. Such a picture may be true of other Hebrew parents, but it is not true of them. "They were not afraid." When it was announced to Jochebed that she had borne a boy, she was enabled to cast the care of him on God, and to receive the assurance that he should come to no hurt.

She was not always on the *qui vive* for the step of officer or midwife. She would take all ordinary precaution; but she would never give way to excessive fear. Finally, the mother was led by the good Spirit of God to weave the papyrus rushes into a little ark, or boat, coating it with bitumen, to make it impervious to water. She put the child into the ark with many a kiss, closed the lid on its sweet face, with her own hands bore it to the water's edge, and placed it tenderly among the flags that grew there. She knew that Pharaoh's daughter came there to bathe, and it might be that she would notice and befriend the little foundling. Or, if not, the God whom she trusted would help her in some other way. Miriam was set to watch, to see "what would be done to him"; and Jochebed went back to her house, fighting a mother's natural anxiety by a faith that had enclasped the very arm of the living God, who could not fail her. That is faith. Can we wonder at the faith of the man who was born of such a mother, and nurtured in such a home?

3

"Come to Years"
Hebrews 11:24

It all happened according to the mother's faith. The princess, accompanied by a train of maidens, came to the river bank to bathe. She saw the ark among the flags, and sent her maid to get it. In the midst of the little group the lid was carefully lifted, and their eyes were charmed with the sight of the beautiful face, while their hearts were touched with the whimper of the babe, who missed its mother, and was frightened by its unwonted surroundings and the many unfamiliar faces.

Quickly the woman's heart guessed the secret. The neighborhood of Hebrew huts, the features and complexion of the babe, the unlikelihood of a mother forgetting her suckling child, the sudden recollection of the stern edict that her father had lately promulgated, all pointed to the inevitable conclusion, "This is one of the Hebrews' children." The sudden interposition of Miriam, who had eagerly and breathlessly watched the whole scene, with her naïve suggestion of fetching a Hebrew nurse, solved the problem of what should be done with the foundling almost as soon as it could have suggested itself. The child's mother soon stood before the princess, and received the precious burden from her hands; and as she did so, was there not something in her almost convulsive moment that revealed to that quick eye the secret of the little plot? Whether it were so or not, the story does not tell. But with what an ecstasy of joy would that mother pour out her heart when the door was closed on the little group? The child's life was secure beneath the powerful protection of Pharaoh's own daughter, who had said, "Nurse it for me." And the wages she had promised would do more than provide for all their need. God had done "exceedingly abundantly."

How long the boy stayed in that lowly home we do not know, but it was long enough to know something of the perils and hardships of his people's lot; to learn those sacred traditions of their past, and to receive into his heart the love of the only God, which was to become the absorbing passion and emphasis of his career. Priests, philosophers, and scholars, might do their best later, but these ideas had been built into the growing structure of his soul, never again to be disintegrated from its fabric. What an encouragement to mothers to make the most of the early years during which children are confided to their charge.

At last the time arrived when Thermutis claimed for her own the child she had rescued. The mother's heart must have suffered bitterly as she let her son go into the unknown world within the great palace gate; and very lonely must the little household have felt when the last kisses had been exchanged, the last instruction given, and the last prayer offered. But, amid all, faith rose preeminent, and believed that He who had delivered the child from the perils of the Nile, would keep him pure and sweet amid the evils and fascinations of the court.

What a magnificent land must Egypt have been in those days of which Herodotus and the hieroglyphic records speak! The atmosphere was rainless; the Nile brought from afar the rich alluvial soil that born corn enough to feed the world; the banks of the river were covered with cities, villages, stately temples, and all the evidences of an advanced civilization; while mighty pyramids and colossal figures towered to a hundred feet in height. Seven millions of people throve on this green riband of territory, and while the great mass of them were probably poor and ignorant, the upper classes, and especially the priests, were remarkable for their familiarity with much of which we know.

The cream of all this was poured into the cup of Moses. He was brought up in the palace, and treated as the grandson of Pharaoh. When old enough he was probably sent to be *educated in the college* which had grown up around the Temple of the Sun, and has been called "the Oxford of Ancient Egypt." How wonderfully was God fitting him for the years to come! Stephen says: "Moses was learned in all the wisdom of the Egyptians" (Acts 7:22). Much of it stood him in good stead when he became the founder of a new state.

But Moses was something more than a royal student: *he was a statesman and a soldier.* Stephen tells us that he was "mighty in words and deeds": mighty in words— there is the statesman; mighty in deeds—there the soldier. Josephus says that while he was still in his early manhood the Ethiopians invaded Egypt, routed the army sent against them, and threatened Memphis. In the panic the oracles were consulted, and on their recommendation Moses was entrusted with the command of the royal troops. He immediately took the field, surprised and defeated the enemy, captured their principal city, "the swamp-engirdled city of Meroë," and returned to Egypt laden with the spoils of victory.

Thus year followed year until he was forty years of age. Already the foremost positions of the State were open to him, and it seemed as if the river of his life would continue in the same bed, undiverted, only waxing ever broader and deeper in its flow.

But beneath all, another thought was always present with him, and gradually dwarfed all others as it grew within his soul. He could not forget that his parents were slaves; that the bondmen who were groaning in the brickfields beneath the lash of the taskmasters were his brethren. He never lost the thought of that God to whom his mother had taught him to pray: and he could not rid himself of the impression that his destiny did not lie amid such surroundings as those, but was in some way to be associated with the fulfillment of that promise that he had heard so often from his mother's lips.

He broke, as gently as he might, the news to his benefactress that he could no longer hold the position to which she had raised him, or be called her son, but must step back to the lowly lot which was his by birth.

1. NOTICE THE NOBLE INGREDIENTS IN THIS GREAT RESOLVE.

a. *It was made in the full maturity of his powers.* With nothing to gain and all to lose, he descended from the steps of the loftiest throne in the world.

b. *It was made when the fortunes of the children of Israel were at their lowest ebb.* They were slaves, were suffering affliction, and were reproached. For a palace there would be a hut; for luxury, hard fare and coarse food; for respect and honor, hatred and contempt; for the treasures of Egypt, poverty and want; for the society of the learned and *élite*, association with the ignorant and depraved. But with deliberate resolution he bowed his head beneath the yoke even though it was rough and heavy.

c. *It was made when the pleasures of sin seemed most fascinating.* There is nothing gained in saying that there are no pleasures in sin. There are. And Moses was not oblivious to all this; yet, in the heyday of his strength, in the prime of his manhood, in a court where continence and purity must have been unknown, he dared to forego it all.

d. *It was made decisively.* Many would have tried to retain the proud position and to benefit their enslaved brethren at the same time. But there was no trace of this in the great renunciation that cut Moses off from the least association with the fond and fascinating associations of early life.

2. THE THOUGHT WHICH LED TO IT. "By faith. Moses refused. . . . He believed God's promise to Abraham, that after four hundred years of bondage his people would come out; and he knew that that period had nearly expired. He believed that there was a destiny waiting for the chosen people in the long future. He believed that there was a recompense of reward awaiting them beyond the domain and limit of Egypt, more glorious than the dazzling splendor of its highest rewards and honors.

But he did what he did, because he saw by faith what eye had not seen, or ear heard, or the heart conceived; and these things—that wealth and that reward—being so much better than anything Egypt could offer, he cheerfully took the path of affliction, of self-denial and reproach, which led to them.

See, child of God, what is within your reach, if only you will dare to deny yourself and take up your cross! Is the renunciation hard? Do not forget that Christ is suffering with you in it all. He knows every step of the way, because He has so often traversed it in the experience of his own. There is no solace to the agonized soul so sweet as the perpetual mention of His dear name.

And who can estimate the result? The water streams from the smitten rock; an Exodus and the birth of a nation of freemen were the outcome of this great renunciation.

4

Deliverance by Main Force
Acts 7:24–25

There was true heroism in the act, when Moses stepped down from Pharaoh's throne to share the lot of his brethren. At the same time there was a great deal for him to learn. Later he was to be a hand nerved and used and empowered by God Himself (Ps. 77:20); but now he was acting in his own self-energy—rash, impetuous, headstrong. Years later he was to be the meekest and least obtrusive of men, conscious to a fault of his own weakness, and at every step looking up for guidance and help; but now he leaned wholly on his own understanding and, without taking counsel of God, thought to secure the emancipation of his people by the assertion of his will, and the putting forth of his might.

But there was the making of a saint in him even though it would take many a long year of lonely waiting and trial before this strong and self-reliant nature could be broken down, shaped into a vessel meet for the Master's use, and prepared for every good work.

1. THE FIRST ATTEMPT AT DELIVERANCE.

a. *It sprang largely from human sympathy.* As soon as Moses reached Goshen his first act was to visit his people in the midst of their toils, and to see them work amid conditions of severest hardship. Brick-making in clay pits must always be difficult work, but how much more so when an Egyptian sun shines vertically above you and a taskmaster stands by with his heavy whip to punish the least attempt to rest a moment. As he heard the nation sighing because of its bondage, and groaning under its accumulated sorrows, his soul was filled with tender pity. But it wasn't long before that pity for his people turned to indignation against their oppressors. Before he had gone very far, he came on one of the taskmasters cruelly beating a Hebrew; and as he witnessed the heavy blows falling on the unresisting, quivering body, he could restrain himself no longer, and killed the Egyptian, and buried his body in the nearest sands.

It was a chivalrous act, well meant, and at least significant of the strength of the emotions pent up within him, but the mere impulse of pity would never have been strong enough to bear him through the weary years of the desert march. Beneath the repeated provocations of the people it must have given way. Nothing short of a reception of the divine patience, could suffice for the demands that would be made on him in those coming terrible years.

Is there not a lesson here for many of God's workers? They have not learned to distinguish between passion and principle, between impulse and a settled purpose. If we undertake a definite work because He calls us to it, because it is put before us as a duty for His sake, or because we are channels through which the unebbing torrent of his divine pity is flowing, we have secured a principle of action that will bear us through disappointment, failure, and ingratitude. The way in which men treat us will make no difference to us, because all is done for Him.

b. *It was premature.* God's time for the deliverance of His people was not due for forty years. The iniquity of the Amorites had not reached its full, though it was nearing the brim of the cup (Gen. 15:16). Moses' own education was very incomplete; it would take at least forty years to drain him of his self-will and self-reliance, and make him a vessel meet for the Master's use. The Hebrew people had not as yet come to the pitch of anguish, which is so touchingly referred to, when the death of their principal oppressor seems to have brought matters to a crisis, and they forsook the false gods to which they had given their allegiance in order to return to the God of their fathers (Exod. 2:23).

We all know something of this haste. As Saul, in presence of the Philistine invasion, we suppose that we cannot last for another hour, and we force ourselves to offer the burnt offering. Then we are chagrined to see Samuel's figure slowly pacing up the mountain pass as the fire burns down to its last embers, and to hear from his lips the sentence of deposition for our impatience (1 Sam. 13:12–14).

One blow struck when the time is fulfilled is worth a thousand struck in premature eagerness. It is not for you, O my soul, to know the times and seasons that the Father has put in His own power; wait only on God. Wait at the gates of your Jericho for seven days; do not utter a sound till He says, "Shout"; but when He gives the signal, with the glad cry of victory you shall pass over the fallen wall into the city.

c. *It was executed in the pride of human strength.* It was natural that Moses should suppose that he could do something to relieve his people's lot. He would make that nation of oppressors reel before his blows, and of course he would be hailed by his people as their God-sent deliverer.

He was rudely surprised when one day he went out to continue his self-imposed task, and sought to settle a difference between two Hebrews, to find himself repulsed from them by the challenge, "Who made thee a prince and a judge over us?" He had never expected a rebuff from his own people. Evidently, then, God's time had not arrived; nor could it come until the heat of his spirit had slowly evaporated in the desert air, and he had learned the hardest of all lessons, that "by strength shall no man prevail." We must be brought to an end of ourselves before God can begin with us. But when once we have come to that point there is no limit to what may be wrought during a single life by the passage through it of His eternal power and Godhead.

d. *It was too apprehensive of the judgment of other men.* We are told that he looked this way and that way before he killed the Egyptian; and when he found that his deed of revenge was known, he feared and fled (Exod. 2:12). But suppose that he had felt he had been divinely commissioned to execute judgment on Egypt, would he have cared who was looking, and what was being said? He would have been perfectly indifferent to the praise or blame of men. Whenever men look this way and that to see what other men are doing or saying, you may be quite sure they do not know for certain their Master's plan.

There has been only one perfect Servant of God who has ever trodden our world. He never looked this way or that. He alone could say, "He that sent me is with me: the Father hath not left me alone; for I do always those things that please him" (John 8:29). Oh, for the single eye, that our whole body also may be full of light!

2. THE FLIGHT TO THE DESERT. The news of what Moses had done came to the ears of Pharaoh, and he sought to slay him. But Moses feared, and fled from the face of Pharaoh. Later, under similar circumstances, it is said, "He forsook Egypt, not fearing the wrath of the king" (Heb. 11:27). And when we ask the reason for his fearlessness, we learn that it was by faith he did so; for "he endured, as seeing him who is invisible." But if such were the case later, why was it not so at the time with which we are dealing? Why did he not exercise faith in the invisible God?

Faith is possible only when we are on God's plan, and stand on God's promise. It is useless to pray for increased faith until we have fulfilled the conditions of faith. Faith is as natural to right conditions of soul, as a flower is to a plant. And among those conditions this is the first—find your place in God's plan, and get on to it; and this is the second—feed on God's promises. When each of these is realized, faith comes of itself; and there is absolutely nothing that is impossible.

But Moses was out of touch with God, so he fled, and crossed the desert that lay between him and the eastern frontier. He threaded the mountain passes of the Sinaitic peninsula, through which in later years he was to lead his people; and at last sat down wearily by a well in the land of Midian. there his chivalrous interference was suddenly elicited on behalf of the daughters of the priest of Midian, who seem to have suffered daily from the insolence of shepherds appropriating the water that the shepherd-maidens had drawn for their flocks. That day, however, the shepherds met their match, and were compelled to leave the water troughs to the women, who hurried home, unexpectedly early, to tell of the Egyptian who had delivered them from the hands of the shepherds. It was a good deed that could not pass without repayment in that hospitable land, and it opened the door to the chieftain's tent; ultimately to marriage with one of those same shepherdesses; and finally to the quiet life of a shepherd in the calm open spaces of that wonderful land that, on more than one occasion, has served as a divine school.

5

The Marvellous Colloquy
Exodus 3:4

1. A MEMORABLE DAY. It began with an ordinary morning. The sun rose as usual in a dull haze over the expanse of sand, or above the gaunt forms of the mountains, seamed and scarred. As the young day opened, the sun began to shine in a cloudless sky, casting long shadows over the plains; and presently, climbing to the zenith, threw a searching, scorching light into every aperture of the landscape beneath. The sheep browsed as usual on the scant herbage, or lay panting beneath the shadow of a great rock. These things were as they had been for forty years, and as they threatened to be, after Moses had sunk into an obscure and forgotten grave. Then, all of a sudden, a common bush began to shine with the emblem of Deity, and from its heart of fire the voice of God broke the silence of the ages in words that fell on the shepherd's ear like a double knock: "Moses, Moses."

That voice still speaks to those whose hearts are hushed to hear. Insensibly to ourselves we contract the habit of thinking of God as the God of the dead, who spoke to the fathers in oracle and prophet; whereas the I AM is God of the living—passing through our crowded thoroughfares, brooding over our desert spaces, and seeking hearts that are still enough from their own plannings and activities to listen.

The main point for each of us is to be able to answer his summons with the response, "Here am I." If that summons were to come today, too many of us would have to ask for a moment's respite while we went to finish some neglected duty. Oh, for the free, untrammelled, unengaged spirit, to be ready to go at any moment the Lord may appoint.

2. A REMARKABLE ANNOUNCEMENT. Out of the bush came the voice of God, blending past, present, and future, in one marvellous sentence: *the past,* "I am the God of thy father, the God of Abraham, the God of Isaac, and the God of Jacob"; *the present,* "I have surely seen the affliction of my people which are in Egypt, and have heard their cry by reason of their taskmasters; for I know their sorrows, and I am come down to deliver them"; *the future,* "Come now therefore, and I will send thee unto Pharaoh" (Exod. 3:6–10).

3. DIVINE LONGSUFFERING UNDER PROVOCATION. In the first blush of youthful enthusiasm Moses had been impetuous enough to attempt the emancipation of his people by the blows of his right hand. But now that God proposes to send him to lead an exodus, he starts back in dismay almost petrified at the proposal. Moses, who had run before God in feverish impatience, now lags fainthearted behind Him.

a. *At first he expostulated:* "Who am I, that I should go to Pharaoh?" "And God said, Certainly I will be with thee." "I whose glory shines here, who am as unimpaired by the flight of the ages as this fire is by burning; who am independent of sustenance or fuel from man; who made the fathers what they were; whose nature is incapable of change—I will be with you." What an assurance this was! He seems to say: "Not an hour without my companionship; not a difficulty without my cooperation; not a Red Sea without my right arm; not a mile of wilderness journeying without the Angel of my Presence."

b. *In his next excuse* Moses professed his inability to answer if he were asked the name of God (v. 13); and this was met by the proclamation of the spirit-stirring name, JEHOVAH: "I AM THAT I AM." There we have the unity of God to the exclusion of the many gods of Egypt; the unchangeableness of God, who lives in an eternal present; the self-sufficiency of God, who alone is His own equivalent.

The term JEHOVAH was not wholly unknown to Moses, for it entered into his mother's name, Jochebed—*Jehovah my glory;* but now for the first time it was adopted as the unique title by which God was to be known in Israel. It slowly made its way into the faith of the people; and whenever employed, it speaks of the self-existent and redeeming qualities of the nature of God, and is forever enshrined in the precious name of our Savior, JESUS. The whole subsequent life of Moses and of Israel was inspired by this name.

And for us it is full of meaning. "This is my name for ever, and this is my memorial unto all generations" (v. 15). And as its full meaning opens to our vision, it is as if God put into our hands a blank check, leaving us to fill it in as we will. Are we dark? let us add to His I AM the words, *the true Light;* are we hungry? the words, *the Bread of Life;* are we defenseless? the words, *the Good Shepherd;* are we weary? the words, *Shiloh, the Rest-giver.*

c. *Moses' third excuse* was that the people would not believe him, nor hearken to his voice (Exod. 4:1). But God graciously met this also by showing him miracles that he might perform in Egypt, and that would read deep lessons to himself. "What is that in thine hand? And he said, A rod." It was probably only a shepherd's crook. What a history, however, awaited it! It was to be stretched out over the Red Sea, pointing a pathway through its depths, to smite the flinty rock and to win victory over the hosts of Amalek. A rod with God behind it is mightier than the vastest army.

At God's command the rod was cast on the ground, and it became a serpent. The serpent played a very conspicuous part in Egyptian worship, and as it wriggled on the sand and sought to do Moses harm, so that he fled from it, it was an emblem of the might of Egypt before which he had became a fugitive. But when God gave the word, it easily became once more a rod in his hand, as he fearlessly grasped the venomous animal by the tail.

The second sign was even more significant. His hand thrust into his bosom became leprous; and when he did it again it became pure and white. It was as if God met his consciousness of moral pollution and taught him that it could be put away as easily as his flesh was cleansed, through His forgiving grace.

And the third sign, in which it was promised that the water of the Nile should become blood on the dry land, was full of terrible omen to the gods of that mighty country, the people of which depended so entirely on its river, for they worshiped it as a god.

d. *The last excuse* that Moses alleged was his lack of eloquence. "O my Lord, I am not eloquent . . . I am slow of speech, and of a slow tongue" (v. 10). But God was willing to meet this also with His patient grace; and if only Moses had been willing to trust Him, it is probable that God would have added the gifts of a persuasive and splendid oratory to the other talents with which Moses was so copiously endowed.

But Moses would not believe it; so at length the Lord ended the conference by saying that He would send Aaron with him, to be his colleague and spokesman. Ah! better a thousand times had it been for him to trust God for speech, than be thus deposed from his premiership! Aaron shaped the golden calf and became a thorn in the side of the saint of God—and probably in the eyes of their contemporaries. Aaron took the greater attention, and had most of the honor and credit of the great deliverance.

4. THE FINAL ASSENT. It was a very grudging one. We seek every reason for evading the divine will, little realizing that He is forcing us out from our quiet homes into a career that includes, among other things, the song of victory on the banks of the Red Sea; the two lonely sojourns for forty days in communication with God; the shining face; the vision of glory; the burial by the hand of Michael; and the supreme honor of standing beside the Lord on the Mount of Transfiguration.

6

"To Egypt"
Exodus 4:20

The fire faded from the bush; the light above the brightness of the sun died away; the voice was still; and Moses looked around on the browsing sheep and the mighty mountains with the strange wonder of a man awaking from a trance. It had been the supreme hour of his life, for which all previous years had been preparing, and from which all future ones would date.

1. FIRST STEPS TOWARD RETURN. Slowly, thoughtfully, perhaps painfully, he prepared to obey the heavenly summons. Gathering his flock together, he conducted it from the backside of the desert, with its stern grandeur, its unoccupied spaces, its intense silence, to Midian, the seat of his clan, where human voices and interests could reassert themselves. "And Moses went and returned to Jethro, his father in law. . . . "Let me go, I pray thee, and return unto my brethren which are in Egypt, and see whether they be yet alive."

The request must have involved surprise and pain to Moses' entire family, for they seemed to have become so entirely one with themselves. And his going would involve that of wife and boys and of the infant son, who seems to have been but recently born. However, the permission he asked was granted in the laconic answer. "Go in peace."

But even then he lingered. It was needful for God to send a second summons into his life. "And the LORD said unto Moses in Midian: Go, return into Egypt: for all the men are dead which sought thy life."

Stirred up by this second summons, Moses prepared to start for Egypt.

Imagine, then, that departure. Zipporah sitting on the ass, perhaps nursing a little babe, while the husband and father walked beside. And in his hand was the sacred rod—only a shepherd's crook, but now the rod of God—destined to be employed for deeds of transcendent power, and always reminding him of what weak things could do when wielded by strong hands behind them. Three things happened on that journey.

2. A FURTHER REVELATION. "And the LORD said unto Moses . . ." (v. 21). And there followed a marvelous epitome of events that were to transpire within the next few months, from the making of the water into blood to the slaying of the firstborn.

This was in harmony with one of the greatest principles in the moral and spiritual realm. We only learn as we endeavor to obey. It may be that you are in darkness; disobedience is the cause. You have disobeyed the distinct word of the Lord. And you will never get back into the warm, blessed, circle of His manifested presence until you have gone back to the place where you dropped the thread of obedience, and, taking it up where you left it, do what you know to be the word and will of God. Then, as you start to obey, the voice of God will greet you once more with the old familiar tones.

3. A PREPARATORY RITE. In the inn Moses seems to have been attacked by sudden and dangerous illness, and was on the point of death. It would seem that for some reason Moses had neglected the rite of circumcision for one of his children, perhaps the one newly-born. And as he seemed to hang in the quivering balance between life and death, this was brought to mind, and he was compelled to insist that the rite should be performed.

It was a comparatively trivial thing, insignificant in the eyes of man, and yet there are no trifles in a man's dealings with God. And so Moses is kept waiting on the threshold of the great enterprise of his life because this rite of circumcision had not been administered to a little babe. We may be conscious of having been sent to do a great work for God, and yet be shrinking from some small known duty; and disobedience here will impede our progress, as does a stone in a traveler's shoe. It was because Moses was to be so eminently used that he came into God's most searching discipline. Take heart, suffering child of God! He chastens because He loves, and is about to use you.

The exhibition of incompatability displayed by Zipporah, when she had performed the rite, seems to have led Moses to feel that it would not be wise to take her with him; and, on the whole, it seemed better that she should abide quietly with her own people until the act of emancipation was wrought. In the after narrative we find that "Jethro, Moses' father in law, came with his sons and his wife unto Moses into the wilderness, where he encamped at the mount of God" (Exod. 18:5).

4. A BROTHERLY ALLIANCE. Moses recovered from his illness, but he was lonely because he sent back his wife and children. However, he started again on his journey, threading his way through those corridors of red sandstone by which he had passed some forty years ago. But how different all seemed! *He* was different. He was no longer a disappointed man, smarting with the sense of recent failure; but was strong in the Lord, conscious of a great mission and of the presence of an angel beside him who would be equal to every emergency.

And he knew that the same power that brought him forward was bringing toward him the brother whom he had not seen for forty years. God so contrived it that they met in the Mount of God, where the bush had burned, and the voice of God had summoned Moses from shepherding a flock to become shepherd of a host. Then what greetings! "He kissed him." What interchange of confidences! "Moses told Aaron all the words of the LORD who had sent him." What questionings, as the exile would ask tidings of those whom he had loved!

7

Failure and Disappointment
Exodus 5:22–23

In loving interchange of thought, the noble and venerable brothers reached Egypt: and in answer to the divine command proceeded to summon the elders of Israel to a conference, at which they presented their credentials, and related the divine message with which they had been entrusted.

1. THE INTERVIEW WITH THE ELDERS. It must have been a remarkable meeting, perhaps the first of the sort ever held. When all were gathered Aaron recited on behalf of Moses, who probably stood beside him without a word, the magnificent words spoken at the bush (Exod. 3:16–22). But we do not know how they were received.

At this juncture the brothers probably gave the signs with which God had provided them: the serpent was changed into a rod; the leprous hand was made natural and whole; the water of the river became blood as it was poured out on the land (Exod. 4:2–9). These won conviction, and from that meeting the tidings spread throughout the nation, whispered from hut to hut, and from slave to slave among the brick kilns.

2. THE AUDIENCE WITH PHARAOH. The next step for the brothers was to go to Pharaoh, with the demand that he should let the people go to hold a feast in the wilderness. This was according to divine direction (Exod. 3:18), and was moreover a reasonable request. It did not set forth all they wanted, but inasmuch as it was a foregone conclusion that Pharaoh would grant nothing, every care was taken to deprive him of the excuse of saying that their demands were preposterous.

The scene probably took place in an audience-room of some splendid palace. How mixed must Moses' feelings have been, entering as a suppliant the precincts in which he had played no inconspicuous part in those buried years! And then Aaron and he uttered the words which pealed as a thunderclap through the audience. "Thus saith the LORD God of Israel, Let my people go, that they may hold a feast unto me in the wilderness."

In order to appreciate the audacity of the demand, we must remember the unbridled power and authority that were claimed by the Egyptian monarchs. In addition, the present monarch had recently, through his generals, achieved great victories, and these successes had greatly enhanced his arrogant pride so that it was in a paroxysm of supercilious scorn that he answered the divine demand: "Who is the LORD, that I should obey his voice to let Israel go? I know not the LORD, neither will I let Israel go."

The point of the reply lies in that word *obey*. This stung him to the quick. He also was a god. Who was this other God who dared to issue such a summons! A God of whose existence till that moment he had been unaware! The God of a parcel of slaves! How dare they speak of their paltry Deity in his presence.

The brothers met this outburst with a reiteration of their message, telling how the God of the Hebrews had met with them; and requesting, in a softer tone, that they might be permitted to do as He had requested. But the king refused. Turning sharply on the two brothers, he accused them of hindering their people's toils, and commanded them to do their own share in the clay pit or the brick kiln: "Wherefore do ye, Moses and Aaron, let the people from their works? get you unto your burdens." What a bitter taunt there was in that last sentence! How the royal lip curled as it was uttered! And so the audience ended, and the brothers came down the crowded corridors amid the titter of the court. A very different scene was to be enacted a few months later when the news came of the overthrow of the monarch in the Red Sea.

3. FAILURE AND DISAPPOINTMENT. That same day a new order was issued from the palace, emanating from Pharaoh himself, to the taskmasters of the people. And probably, before the evening fell, the ominous word had passed from the taskmasters to the head men who were set over their fellow Hebrews, and were therefore responsible for the daily delivery of a certain number of bricks, that they must expect no more straw, though the daily returns had to be maintained.

Then followed a time of awful anguish. The Hebrew headmen told some of the people to scatter themselves over the country, collecting straw from every quarter, and to do it with all haste. And in the meantime they urged the rest of the people to compensate for the absence of the straw-gatherers by their added energy. Every nerve was strained to the uttermost. From early morning to the last ray of light the whole nation sought to do the impossible beneath the scorching sun, and with never a moment's pause. And yet as the number of bricks was counted it fell inevitably short. In vain did the taskmasters push them, saying, "Fulfill your works, your daily tasks, as when there was straw." In vain were the officers of the children of Israel, whom Pharaoh's taskmasters had set over them, of Israel, whom Pharaoh's taskmasters had set over them, beaten, and such beatings could mean death.

Finally, the Israelites could stand it no longer, and resolved to make an appeal direct to Pharaoh. "The officers of the children of Israel came and cried unto Pharaoh" (Exod. 5:15). It was a bitter day for the two brothers when the people took the matter into their own hands and, without using them as intermediaries, went directly to the king to get him to put them back to the point at which they stood before that well-meant, but disastrous interference. But it was evidently better that Moses and Aaron should wait outside the palace to learn the result of the interview (v. 20).

It happened just as it might have been expected, for the king would not listen to the appeal made to him. "He said, Ye are idle, ye are idle: therefore ye say, Let us go and do sacrifice to the LORD. Go therefore now, and work; for there shall no straw be given to you, yet shall ye deliver the tale of bricks" (vv. 17–18). And so they came from Pharaoh, at the very extreme of agony, dreading the lingering death from exhaustion and stripes which apparently awaited their whole nation; and as Moses and Aaron stood there they poured on them the bitterness of their spirit. It must have been a heartbreaking experience to hear from those lips the bitterest reproaches they could frame, cutting them as knives.—"The LORD look upon you, and judge; because ye have made our savour to be abhorred in the eyes of Pharaoh, and in the eyes of his servants, to put a sword into their hand to slay us."

It was necessary that Moses, Aaron, and the Hebrews should come to see that their case was desperate, so they would lean only on the arm of the living God and venture forth depending on Him alone. It was necessary that the people see that they could not better their position by any efforts of their own.

4. THE RESORT OF THE BAFFLED SOUL. "And Moses returned unto the LORD, and said, Lord, wherefore hast thou so evil entreated this people? why is it that thou hast sent me?" (v. 22). The agony of soul through which Moses passed must have been as death to him. He died to his self-esteem, to his castle building, to pride in his miracles, to the enthusiasm of his people, to everything that a popular leader loves. As he lay there on the ground alone before God, wishing himself back in Midian, and thinking himself misused, he was falling as a corn of wheat into the ground to die, no longer to abide alone, but to bear much fruit.

It is a lesson for us all. God must bring us down before He can raise us up. Emptying must precede filling. We must get to an end of ourselves before He can begin in us. But what a beginning He makes! "Then the LORD said unto Moses, Now thou shalt see what I will do to Pharaoh: for with a strong hand shall he let them go, and with a strong hand shall he drive them out of his land" (Exod. 6:1). And as those words of encouragement and promise broke on his ear, he must have forgotten the averted looks and bitter words of the people, and risen into a new world of restful expectation. Deliverance was sure, though he had learned that it did not depend on anything he could do, but on that all-sufficient God, who had announced Himself as the I AM.

8

The Love of God in the First Four Plagues
Lamentations 3:32

In despair Moses had thrown himself on God, pouring out the story of his failure and shame. "Wherefore hast thou so evil entreated this people? why is that thou hast sent me?" But there was no chiding, no rebuke, on the part of his strong and faithful Friend, who knew his frame, and remembered that he was but dust. "Then the LORD said unto Moses, Now shalt thou see what I will do to Pharaoh."

The emphasis lies in the words, *Then—Now,—I. Then*—when he had reached the lowest point of self-confidence. *Now*—since all human effort had been put forth in vain. *I*—the self-existent, ever-glorious Lord. He will not give His glory to another.

The time of depression with the discouraged servant of God is always a time of promise. Then God takes to Himself a new name (Exod. 6:3); then He gives a glimpse of the meaning of His dealings in the past (v. 4); then He reveals the sympathy of his heart, which can detect inarticulate groans (v. 5); then, since He can swear by no other, He pledges Himself with a sevenfold guarantee (vv. 6–8).

God always links obedience and promise. Promise is intended to spur to action. We hear, that we may pass on to others the words that have stirred our spirits; and therefore, Moses was recommissioned to speak, first to the children of Israel, and then to Pharaoh, king of Egypt. It must have been a very memorable day in which the summons came to him *in the land of Egypt,* as it had come before in the wilderness of Sinai (Exod. 6:28). God speaks not only in the stillness of the hermit's life, but also amid the stir of active engagement and the press of crowds.

It took more than usual courage for the two brothers to undertake this further ministry; their people were too broken with anguish of spirit and disappointed hope to care much what was said, especially when it was said by men who had been the cause of the increase of their burden. And as for Pharaoh, it was idle to suppose that he would be touched by lips that had no power to charm the ears of Hebrews. But it was not the time for parley. There was no doubt as to his duty, so there was to be no hesitation in his obedience.

At the outset of the interview Pharaoh, as was expected, asked for their credentials, which they gave as God had instructed them. But the evidence was neutralized by the magicians counterfeiting them. It was significant that Aaron's rod swallowed up their rods, but the great question would have to be settled on a wider arena, and by the series of more remarkable signs.

It is necessary that we should for a moment consider the underlying principle of God's dealings with Pharaoh, especially in the earlier plagues. And it will not be difficult to discern the operation of the external principles of divine justice and love in the staggering blows which the divine Power dealt to Pharaoh and his land.

1. THE LOVE OF GOD. Always and everywhere, God is Love. And surely we must believe that Pharaoh was included in the love that gave Jesus Christ to the world. It must be possible, therefore, to find a clue that will reconcile the love of God, which brooded over Pharaoh and his land, with the apparent harshness that inflicted the successive plagues. And it will help us if we remember that there is a marked difference between the first four plagues and the rest of them. In the beginning of God's dealings with the tyrant it would almost appear as if He set Himself to answer the question, "Who is the LORD, that I should obey his voice?" and to remove the ignorance of which he complained when he said, "I know not the LORD." It would have been impossible to expect that in a single week he should accept the commands of One whose name was, for the first time, uttered in his presence by the representatives of a nation of slaves. And so God set Himself to show that the gods of the heathen were no gods and that though He had winked at the days of past ignorance, the time had come when He commanded all

men everywhere—Pharaoh on his throne, the priest in his temple, the slave in his hut—to repent.

"Who is Jehovah?" He is the God of nature, at whose bidding the Nile no longer blesses, but curses, her devotees; at whose command the objects of Egyptian worship become a loathing and an abomination and make the land stink; at the expression of whose will the bodies of the priests are covered with the lice that deride all that razor or water can do for their extermination, and at whose summons the sacred beetle corrupts the land. "Not know Him?" He is the God who speaks through human voices; the God of the aged; the God of those groaning serfs; the God who could not run back from a covenant into which He had entered with that long-suffering people; the God of redemption and of eternity.

2. THE FAITH OF MOSES. Though it is true that the love of God was at work, seeking to reveal itself to Pharaoh by the ordering of the plagues; yet we must always remember that the faith of Moses played no inconspicuous part in respect to them. Throughout the conflict that issued in the emancipation of Israel, Moses was closely dealing with God. God was vividly present to the eye of his soul. He thought much more of the presence and power of Jehovah than he did of the majesty and might of the greatest king of the time. It was therefore through *his* faith, as the medium and instrument, that God acted with His mighty hand and outstretched arm. Just as electricity must have a wire to conduct it, so the almighty power of God demands the organ of our faith. That faith may be very slender; all the godhead may pass through the slender faith of a very unworthy man just as the ocean may pass through a very narrow channel. It is with such thoughts in our mind that we consider the first four plagues, and how God showed His love in them.

3. THE PLAGUES. *The river of blood*—One morning, shortly after the events already described, Pharaoh, accompanied by high officials, court functionaries, and priests, came down either to perform his customary ablutions or to worship. On the river's brink he found Moses waiting for him. There was no hesitation now in the peremptory summons. "The LORD God of the Hebrews hath sent me unto thee, saying, Let my people go, that they may serve me in the wilderness." Then follow words which bear out what has been already said of God's purpose in the plagues, "In this thou shalt know that I am the LORD."

The summons was met by the curled lip of scorn or imperturbable silence; and as there was no alternative, Aaron smote the water with the rod in the presence of the court. An instantaneous change passed over the appearance and the nature of the water. It became blood. From bank to bank, the tide of crimson gore swept on, hour after hour, day after day, until a week had passed. The fish died and floated on the surface. The air reeked with corruption. And the effects of the visitation extended throughout all the pools, and reservoirs, and cisterns, in places of public resort, as well as in the homes of the people. There was no water in all the land, except the scanty supplies obtained by digging shallow wells, and collecting the brackish surface water.

The magicians in some way counterfeited the marvel; and Pharaoh probably thought that Moses and Aaron were practicing some sort of trickery.

Frogs—It may have been but a few days after the first plague that Moses and Aaron renewed their demand for emancipation, and told the king the penalty of refusal. But there was no response, no proposal, and the inevitable blow fell.

The land suddenly swarmed with frogs. They came up from the river in myriads, till the very ground seemed alive with them, and it was impossible to walk far without crushing scores of them. Frogs in the houses, frogs in the beds, frogs baked with the food in the ovens, frogs in the kneading-troughs worked up with the flour; frogs with their monotonous croak, frogs with their cold, slimy skins, everywhere—from morning to night, from night to morning—frogs. And the aggravation of the plague consisted in the fact of the frog being the emblem of the goddess of fertility, so that it was sacrilege to destroy it.

This plague elicited from Pharaoh the first symptom of surrender. He sent for the brethren and implored their prayers that the scourge might be removed, promising that compliance with his request would secure deliverance: "I will let the people go." To make the supremacy and power of God more manifest, Moses bade the monarch fix his own time for the staying of the plague, and then went to cry to the Lord: "Moses cried unto the LORD . . . and the LORD did according to the word of Moses."

It is remarkable that though the magicians counterfeited the coming of the frogs, they were evidently unable to remove them; and, indeed, the king does not appear to have appealed to them for help. But what a lesson was taught to Pharaoh—that Jehovah was above all gods, and that He alone could do according to His will!

Lice—The Egyptians were scrupulously clean in their personal habits, anticipating the habits of our own time. And the priests were specially so. They bathed themselves repeatedly, and constantly shaved their bodies so that no uncleanliness might unfit them for their sacred duties. What horror, then, must have taken hold of them when the very dust of Egypt seemed to breed lice and they found that they were not exempted from the plague, which was as painful as it was abhorrent to their delicate sensibility.

Perhaps there is something more than appears at first sight in the words, "there was lice in man and *in beast*." Not only on the bodies of the priests, but on those of the sacred beasts, was there this odious pest. Each revered shrine boasted its sacred bull or goat, whose glossy skin was cleansed with reverent care; and it was an unheard-of calamity that it should become infested with this most disgusting parasite. Thus upon the gods of Egypt did God execute judgment. The magicians themselves seem to have felt that this plague was a symptom of the working of a higher Power than they knew, and even they urged Pharaoh to consider that it was the finger of God.

The beetle—It is not certain what is meant by the word translated "flies." And though it is possible that it is rightly rendered "flies," it is quite as likely that it stands for a peculiar kind of beetle, which was the emblem of the sun-god. Their most powerful deity seemed now to have turned against them. The bettles covered the grounds, swarmed into the houses, and spoiled the produce of their land.

That it was no mere natural visitation was made clear by a division that was made in this plague between the land of Egypt and that of Goshen, where the Israelites were found. And perhaps this worked on Pharaoh's heart as nothing else had done, for he was prepared to allow the Israelites to sacrifice in the land. It was a concession that Moses could not accept, for the Israelites would be obliged to sacrifice as victims animals that the Egyptians considered sacred, and irritated feeling might provoke some terrible outbreak of violence. Pharaoh yielded to this reason, and promised to let them go if they did not go very far, on the condition that Moses should secure the removal of the plague. "And the LORD did according to the word of Moses."

9

How the Character of Moses Grew
Hebrews 3:2

If we were engaged in telling the story of the Exodus, it would become us to study carefully the account of the succeeding plagues. But it is on Moses that our attention must be focused and it is marvelous to trace the growth of this man, in perhaps a few months, from the diffidence and hesitancy of Midian to the moral sublimity that made him "very great in the land of Egypt," in the sight of the great officials of the court, no less than of the mass of the common people (Exod. 11:3).

We can trace this development of character through the remaining plagues, and as we do so we will inevitably discover that the secrets of growth consist in an instant and unquestioning obedience, an utter indifference to human opinion, strength of purpose, unfailing patience, indomitable courage, persevering faith and prayer.

Murrain—In the earlier part of his ministry Moses had repeatedly asked questions of God before he set about the performance of the divine commissions. "Who am I, that I should go in unto Pharaoh?" "How shall Pharaoh hear me who am of uncircumcised lips?" It needed much persuasion and entreaty before he would fulfill Jehovah's word.

But all that had vanished now. Though he had been in the royal presence at least seven times, and each time the bearer of heavy tidings, he was increasingly abhorred by Pharaoh and his court. Though his appearances there so far had been unsuccessful in securing the great purpose that God had set before him, yet there was no hesitancy or questioning when for the eighth time, the Lord told him to present himself in the palace to demand the emancipation of the people on pain of a murrain on the beasts.

The murrain came at the fixed time, "and all the cattle of Egypt died." The cattle that fed on the green meadows of the Nile; the horses of the wealthy, for which Egypt was famous; the asses of the poor; the camels that bore the merchandise of Egypt afar, in exchange for spices and balm and myrrh (Gen. 37:25); the oxen that ploughed the fields; the sheep that constituted so large a proportion of their wealth—on all of these the murrain fell. The land was filled with death; the rich landowners were greatly impoverished; the poor suffered severely; thousands of shepherds and teamsters were thrown out of work; the routine of business communication was seriously interrupted; and evidence was given of the increasing severity of the plague: while God's care for His own was clearly shown in the cordon of protection that He placed around Goshen, concerning which it is said, "Of the cattle of the children of Israel died not one."

Boils and Blains—In estimating a man's work we must always consider the character of the man himself. It must have been a much greater effort for Moses to be the medium of such judgments, and the object of so much bitter hatred, than for many. A man who had kept sheep for forty years would be likely to acquire a tender shepherd heart. And it must have been no small effort to be the instrument for inflicting pain.

But he did not flinch. It was not for him to aspire to be more pitiful than God, and therefore when Aaron and he were told to take ashes and fling them broadcast on the air, to become a boil breaking forth with blains on man and on beast, he did not hesitate. Taking in his hands handfuls of ashes, he accosted Pharaoh on some public occasion, when he and his court of magicians were assembled in the open air, and sprinkled the light gray dust up toward heaven. It had such immediate effect that "the magicians could not stand before Moses because of the boils, for the boil was upon the magicians, and upon all Egyptians" (Exod. 9:11).

The Hail—As the plagues advance, Aaron increasingly drops out of sight. In the first three plagues the Lord said distinctly to Moses, "Say unto Aaron" (7:19; 8:5, 16). In the fourth (8:20) and fifth (9:1), the word was to Moses only. In the sixth the command is to them both (9:8), but in the seventh, the command is given exclusively to Moses again. "The LORD said unto Moses, Stretch forth thine hand toward heaven, that there may be hail" (v. 22). And so with the plagues of locusts (10:12), and of the darkness that might be felt (10:21). Why this was we are not told. It does not appear that Aaron had in any way forfeited his position by misconduct. In any case, Moses came increasingly to the front as the wielder of the miracle-working rod and as the emancipator of Israel.

In the present instance, also, he seems to have acquired to a surprising extent the power of speech. Those stammering lips became the channels of unwonted eloquence, and were kindled by unexpected fire. It was as if he had suddenly felt able to lay aside the mediation of Aaron, and to claim those words which the Almighty had promised to put into his mouth.

The warning given to Pharaoh in that early morning was a solemn one, but it was in vain. He had deliberately hardened himself so often that now both warning and appeal even tended to harden his heart still more.

And so the storm broke. As the rod was uplifted, vast thunderclouds drifted up from the sea and covered the land. They poured out their contents in thunder, hail, and fire. Storms of any kind are rare in Egypt, and this was "very grievous, such as there was none like it in all the land of Egypt since it became a nation." But from all these the land of Goshen was free.

Through the pelting storm, Moses and Aaron were summoned into the royal presence to hear for the first time from those proud lips the confession of sin (Exod. 9:27), and also urgent entreaty that the mighty thunderings and hail which were then shaking palace and city might cease. Passing uninjured through the storm, he went beyond the city gates into the open country. With outspread hands he interceded for the land of the oppressors of his people, and God hearkened to his request so that the thunders and hail ceased, and the rain no longer poured out on the earth (v. 33).

The Locusts—The tone of Moses rose with every plague. Up to now he had been content with repeating his demand, but now the failure of the king to keep his word had altered the relations between them. Pharaoh had forfeited all claim to his respect. He had made repeated promises and broken them. Moses altered his tone, not now treating him as a sovereign, but as a sinner, and dealing directly with his proud and obstinate heart: "Thus saith the LORD God of the Hebrews, How long wilt thou refuse to humble thyself before me?" The penalty of further delay was to be an infliction of locusts.

The Egyptians well knew what a plague of locusts might mean, and therefore the servants of Pharaoh pleaded with the king to acquiesce in the demand of the Hebrew leaders. Better lose a nation of slaves, they said, than imperil the land.

Pharaoh, at his servant's suggestion, proposed a compromise. He was willing to let *the men go*, and threatened them with evil if they did not accept this proposition. But there was no hesitation in its instant refusal by the brothers. It could not be. The young and old must go, sons and daughters, flocks and herds—*all*. None was to be absent in that great convocation, which was to assemble somewhere in the desert to hold a feast to Jehovah. The court had never heard the great Pharaoh so addressed, nor could he endure that dauntless speech. So, at a signal from him, they were driven from his presence.

But the locusts came with an east wind which, blowing straight from the desert, had set in on the land for a whole day and night. "When it was morning, the east wind brought the locusts." Their numbers filled the air, and literally covered the earth. Its green surface was darkened by their brown forms, and every trace of green in the fields, on the fruit trees, and among the plentiful herbs, of which the Egyptians were so fond, instantly disappeared. The animals had perished, and now the produce of the earth. Surely the next visitation must sweep away all human life. Panic-stricken, the king sent for the men whom shortly before he had driven from his presence. He confessed that he had not only sinned against Jehovah, but also against them; and entreated that this death might be removed. In answer to Moses' intercession, "the LORD turned a mighty strong west wind which took away the locusts, and cast them into the Red sea; there remained not one locust in all the coasts of Egypt" (v. 19). But again Pharaoh went back on his word.

The Darkness—Unannounced, the darkness fell like a pall on the land, "even darkness [that could] be felt." "They saw not one another, neither rose any from his place for three days." All the activities of the land were paralyzed. The stoutest hearts were dismayed.

When the plague passed away, the monarch summoned the brothers for the last time, and made a final desperate effort at compromise. The nation might go, he said, but the flocks and herds had to remain. But Moses penetrated the craft of the proposal, and tore it to shreds. "Our cattle also shall go with us, there shall not an hoof be left behind." Clearly they would be required for sacrifice (v. 25). Once again the proud spirit of the king, uncowed by repeated misfortune, untaught by the stern discipline of pain, broke vehemently forth, and he said, as if exasperated beyond endurance, "Get thee from me, take heed to thyself, see my face no more; for in that day thou seest my face thou shalt die" (v. 28).

Moses answered with calm dignity, as became the ambassador of God. "And Moses said, Thou hast spoken well; I will see thy face again no more" (v. 29). But as he turned to leave the royal presence, he said; "Thus saith the LORD, About midnight will I go out into the midst of Egypt: and all the firstborn in the land of Egypt shall die" (11:4–5).

Thus the bowing reed of Midian became as a rock on which the tempest expends its force in vain; the man who had left that palace in fear, strode its courts as a king; and the faith that fled before the serpent-rod became strong enough to wield the thunderbolts of heaven, and to bring the land of Egypt to the brink of destruction.

10

Preparing for the Exodus
Exodus 12:41

The first three plagues fell equally on the children of Israel as on the Egyptians, but when the brothers threatened Pharaoh with the fourth, they were commissioned in the name of God to utter this added message: "I will sever in that day the land of Goshen, in which my people dwell" (Exod. 8:22). And from that hour the children of Israel were exempted from the terrible inflictions by which Egypt was desolated. No murrain swept off their beasts. No boils broke out on their persons. No tempest swept their fields. No locusts destroyed their crops. No darkness obscured to them the sun. Thus, the Hebrews had ample time to prepare for that Exodus that Moses at least knew was so near.

As we study that strange and marvelous episode, we must never forget the light thrown on it by the memorable verse that tells us that "through faith [Moses] kept the passover, and the sprinkling of blood, lest he that destroyed the firstborn should touch them" (Heb. 11:28). The importance of this verse lies in the fact that it attributes the keeping of the Passover, the sprinkling of blood on the lintels of the Hebrew houses, and the immunity of the Hebrew people, to the effect of the heroic faith that burned so steadily in the soul of this simple-hearted man; the entirety of whose obedience was only equalled by the absoluteness of the unquestioning faith that dared to take God at His word.

1. HIS FAITH WAS BASED ON PROMISE. On the tenth of the following month the head of each family, whether slave or elder, was to select a firstling lamb, free of disease and defect. Only if the family was too small to need a lamb for itself might it join with a neighboring household. The lamb was to be kept from the tenth to the fourteenth of the month, and killed on the fourteenth day, toward the end of the afternoon. The blood, as it gushed warm from the wound, was to be carefully caught in a basin, and sprinkled on the two side posts and lintel of the houses where the Israelites dwelled: the carcass was to be roasted whole and eaten with unleavened bread and bitter herbs.

The whole family was to be gathered around the table, from the gray-headed grandfather to the newborn babe. The men were to have their waist girded as for a long journey, and were to grasp their staves. The women were to have their dough and kneading troughs bound up in little bundles, with their clothes, so they could be easily carried on their shoulders. All were to have their feet sandalled. The meal was to be eaten in haste. And thus, with ears intent to catch the first note of the trumpet, the whole nation was to await the signal for its Exodus, sheltered by blood; while strength was stored for the fatigues that must be endured before the land of bondage was left behind forever.

Moses at least must have felt that God was in effect saying to His people that they were not less guilty, in some respects, than the Egyptians around them. Had they not forgotten His Sabbaths and turned to serve other gods? For these things, at least, they were held guilty in His sight, and were liable to lose the firstborn of their homes, unless they kept the sprinkling of blood.

And when all the provisions had been fulfilled, Moses reposed his faith: "I will pass through the land of Egypt, and will smite all the firstborn in the land of Egypt, both man and beast . . . and when I see the blood, I will pass over you, and the plague shall not be upon you to destroy you, when I smite the land of Egypt" (vv. 12–13).

2. HIS FAITH LED TO ACTION. It is a glorious thing for men and angels to see a faith which, with no outward appearance to warrant it, will yet step out on a path of literal obedience. Moses simply obeyed, believing that there could be no mistake, no shadow of turning in Him to whom he had given the allegiance of his soul.

Oh, that such faith was ours! Not arguing, nor questioning, nor reasoning, but believing that the promises of God are Yea and Amen in Christ.

And such faith becomes contagious. The faith of Moses had kindled faith in three million people who stood ready to plunge the knife into the fleecy victim that awaited it, to sprinkle the blood, to start on the distant march, but with no fear that the firstborn of the house should be left as a corpse. No father eyed his son with anxiety; no mother trembled to hear the rustle of the angel-wing; no boy shuddered at the near approach of death. It was enough that God had said, that, when He saw the blood, He would pass over. The Israelites knew the blood was there to speak for them, and they believed therefore that all must be well. And though no one knew exactly their destination, nor how they would reach it, they had no misgivings as to the issue.

3. HIS FAITH WAS VINDICATED. Who can depict that night, ever memorable in the history of our race—when, indeed, as Bunsen says, history itself was born—the night when God brought Israel out of the house of bondage! All was still with an almost preternatural silence; but suddenly the stillness was interrupted by a scream of anguish, as a mother rushed out into the night to announce that the Angel of Death had begun his work, and she was presently answered by the wail of a mother in agony for her firstborn; and this by another, and yet another. There was not a house where there was not one dead—even Pharaoh's palace was not exempt. The news spread like wildfire that the heir to the throne was dead. "And there was a great cry in Egypt."

"And Pharaoh rose up in the night, he, and all his servants, and all the Egyptians; and . . . he called for Moses and Aaron by night, and said, Rise up, and get you forth from among my people." There was no attempt at conference. They, their people, their children, and their property, were to be gone. And the bidding of the palace was repeated by ten thousand tongues. The one eager desire of the Egyptians was to get rid of the Israelites at all speed, and at all cost. They were glad to give them anything they asked, and thus bestowed some payment for their long unremunerated labor; and even Pharaoh, the haughty monarch, begged them to bless him before they went.

And so the host stepped forth into freedom. For the first time the Israelites realized that they were a nation, and drank the rich deep draught of liberty. A mere horde of slaves, they suddenly crystallized into a people. The spirit of their leader inspired and thrilled them. Then their mouth was filled with laughter, and their tongue with singing. What faith did for them it will do for you and me. O soul enslaved by a worse tyranny than Pharaoh's. If only you would claim deliverance you can have it. Only claim your freedom, and you will tread on the lion and adder; the young lion and dragon shall you trample under foot.

11

The Passage of the Red Sea
Exodus 14:29–30

It was not long after the hour of midnight before the entire Israelite host was on the move. From different points the vast host—which, judging from the fact that the number of the men amounted to six hundred thousand, and the total could not have been less than two and a half millions—converged toward the central meeting place at Succoth.

Succoth would be about fifteen miles down the road, and there they made their first prolonged halt. They baked unleavened cakes of the dough that they had brought with them; the weary women and children rested in leafy tabernacles hastily improvised from the foliage of that region, so that the whole host, heartened and refreshed, was able to undertake its second stage, which was Etham, on the edge of the wilderness, where the green vegetation of Egypt fades into the wilderness, where the green vegetation of Egypt fades into wastes of sand. There is one episode that we must not forget to mention, and which shows how largely the whole Exodus was wrought in faith. "And Moses took the bones of Joseph with him" (13:19). This great ancestor of their race had been dead some four hundred years, but on his deathbed he had made his brethren swear that when God visited them, as He most surely would, and brought them out of Egypt, they should carry his bones with them in their march. In his death, and through that weary waiting time, he had been the prophet of the Exodus; and how often those unburied bones must have been the theme of conversation in Hebrew homes! And now that they were accompanying their march, all the people realized that the anticipations of generations were being fulfilled.

1. THE GUIDING PILLAR. As that Hebrew host broke away from the land of bondage, a majestic cloud gathered in the pure morning atmosphere at the head of the vanguard, never again to desert that pilgrim band until the Jordan was crossed and it had settled down to brood over the house of God. But all through the years, when night fell, it burned with fire at its heart; fire, which was always the symbol and sign of the presence of God.

This served many purposes. It was the guide of their march; it was a shadow from the burning heat of a vertical sun, and at night it provided them with a light as it watched over them like the Eye of God. On one occasion, at least, as we shall see presently, it rendered important service by concealing the movements of Israel, lying between them and the pursuit of their foes.

In the thought of Moses, that cloud by day and night must have been full of reassurance. And it is touching to learn that "He took it not away," as if neither sin, nor murmuring, nor disobedience, could ever drive away Him who loves us, not because we are good, but to make us so; and who cannot leave or forsake those whom He has taught to lisp, "Abba, Father."

2. THE ROUTE. The easiest route to Canaan lay through the Isthmus of Suez and the land of the Philistines. A journey of a little over one hundred miles would have conducted them to their destination. But God did not permit them to go that way, lest the sight of embattled hosts should unnerve them. Years later, when the education and revelations of the desert were finished, they might behold those scenes undismayed. But as yet they must not know war till they had been more deeply taught in the might and care of God. So is our journey ever adapted to our strength. God is always considering what we are able to bear; never leading us into dangers before which heart and flesh would succumb. "God led them about."

It must have been a great disappointment when the cloud altered its course and led them due south. On one side of them was Migdol (the modern Muktala) and impassable wastes of sand; on the other was the Red Sea. East of them or, as it might be, in front, was the impassable range of Baal-Zephon.

It was a perfect cul-de-sac. There was no egress from it except the way by which they had entered. Loud and deep must have been the murmurs and protestations of the people. "Is this the way to Canaan? We know better! How dare you presume to lead us, when your very first tactics prove you to be wholly untrustworthy?"

Such reflections and reproaches are not easy to bear. They can be borne only by a man who has learned utterly to trust his God. They made no impression on Moses. He had learned to obey Him implicitly, and to see himself always completely vindicated. Oh, for more of this simple trust in God, which rests so distinctly in His guidance and help!

Often God seems to place His children in positions of profound difficulty—leading them into a wedge from which there is no escape; contriving a situation which no human judgment would have permitted had it been previously consulted. The very cloud leads them. You may be thus involved at this very hour. It does seem perplexing and mysterious to the last degree, but it is perfectly right. The issue will more than justify Him who has brought you to this place. You have only to stand still and see His salvation, which is prepared as the morning.

3. THE PURSUIT. No sooner had Israel gone than Pharaoh was sorry. The public works stood still for lack of labor. Vast territories were suddenly unoccupied. The labor of this enslaved people was missed on every side, in city and field. There was a sudden loss of revenue and service that he could ill dispense with. And his pride forbade that he should quietly acquiesce in their unhindered Exodus. Besides, in their mad haste to be rid of this people, the Egyptians had loaded them with jewels of silver, and jewels of gold, and raiment; so much so that it is distinctly said, "they spoiled the Egyptians." It is clear from the contributions afterward made to the building of the Tabernacle, that Israel was carrying off a large amount of treasure and valuables. "And the heart of Pharaoh and of his servants was turned against the people, and they said, Why have we done this, that we have let Israel go from serving us?" (14:5-6).

At this juncture the king heard of the extraordinary movement southward which seemed to have thrown them again into his power. "But the Egyptians pursued after them, all the horses and chariots of Pharaoh . . . and overtook them" (14:9).

And so as the afternoon closed in, of perhaps the fifth day of the Exodus, the outposts of the fugitive host beheld the dreaded forms of the Egyptian warriors coming over the ridges of the desert hills; and as the night fell they were aware that the whole Egyptian host was encamped in their vicinity, only waiting for the morning light to swoop down on them, involving them either in a general massacre or, in what was perhaps more dreadful, a return to slavery.

It was an awful plight. Terrible, indeed, was the breaking of that news on those craven hearts. They immediately turned on Moses and spent their fear and anguish on his heart. "Wherefore hast thou dealt thus with us? Were there no graves in Egypt? Better to have perished there than here! Why did you not leave us alone? Where is your God?" And then that noble spirit rose up in the might of its faith. He was not fearful nor dismayed; he was standing still to see God's salvation. He knew that Jehovah would fight for them, and redeem them, and vindicate His word.

12

The Song of Victory
Exodus 15:21

From his chariot-cloud their Almighty looked down on the cowering crowd of fugitives in their great fear as they cried to Him.

It would almost seem, from an expression in the Psalms, that the children of Israel yielded to more rebellion at the Red Sea than appears from the narrative of Moses. We are told distinctly that they "provoked him at the Sea, even at the Red Sea," because "they remembered not the multitude of [his] mercies"; so that God saved them in spite of their rebelliousness, for his Name's sake, and "that he might make his mighty power to be known" (Ps. 106:7–8).

The one man who seemed unmoved amid the panic of the people was their heroic leader, whose faith was the organ of their deliverance. And therefore it is that in all after-allusions to this great event his hand is always referred to as the instrument through which the might of Jehovah was seen. By his faith they passed through the Red Sea as by dry land.

1. THE ROD. There is a limit to prayer. This was not the time for heartrending supplication, but for action; Moses had to give to the people the word of advance. Over the sea, he had to stretch out his rod; and by his faith he had to afford the power of God a channel through which it could pass to cleave the mighty waters.

That rod had already done many things: it grew first in some watered glade of the Sinaitic peninsula, knowing little of its destiny until it was cut down by the shepherd for the purpose of guiding his flock, or clubbing some beast of prey; it was in his hand when God first met with him, and cast on the ground it became a serpent, the emblem of Egyptian pride. It had already figured in many of the Egyptian plagues; stretched over the waters of the river to turn them to blood; lifted toward heaven to summon the storm, extended over the land to turn the very dust to lice, hereafter it was to win victory over Amalek and to open streams from the heart of the rock. Everywhere it was emphatically "the rod of God." But never in all of its history had it done, nor would it do, such marvels as awaited it that night, when at the bidding of God, it was stretched over the waters of the Red Sea.

As the rod was in the hands of Moses, so Moses was in the hand of God; and so may each of us be, if only we would yield ourselves implicitly to Him for service.

2. THE CLOUD. Until now the pillar of cloud had swept in majestic glory through the heaven, but at this juncture it settled down on the ground like a great wall of billowy vapor, standing for a fence between the camp of Egypt and the camp of Israel. To the former it was dark and menacing, forbidding progress, and enshrouding the movements of the fugitives; to the latter it gave light, casting a sheen on the sand and sea, and indicating, with unerring accuracy, the path that soon appeared. All night through, those heaven-lit beacon fires burned brightly.

3. THE PASSAGE. A terrific storm broke on the scene. The earth shook and trembled; from out the darkness brooding overhead came the repeated flash of the lightning,

followed by the long reverberation of the thunder. The Most High uttered His voice, which was followed by the pelt of the hailstones and the fall of fireballs. The east wind rose in fury, driving before it the retreating waters, then catching them up in its hands it piled them, wave on wave, until they stood up a wall of foam and tumult, from base to top, fretting, seething, fuming, held steadily and always by the pressure of that mighty blast, that gave them no respite, but held them as in a vise; and all the water behind, backed up, leaned on that rampart, so strangely built, so marvelously maintained.

Shelving down from the shore between these two walls of water, a broad thoroughfare lay outspread, and at that moment the word that had sprung from the lips of the leader, and had been caught by those who stood closest to him, passed like prairie fire, though in a whisper, from lip to lip. "Speak unto the children of Israel, that they go forward"; and immediately, without precipitate haste but with glad obedience, the ransomed host stepped down, rank after rank, and passed between the walls of glass and fire amid the rattle of the storm, which made the withdrawal of their hosts inaudible to their foes. Imagine, if you can, that triumphal march: the excited children restrained from exclamations of wonder by the perpetual hush of their parents; ashamed or confounded that they had ever mistrusted God or murmured against Moses.

4. THE PURSUIT. As soon as the Egyptians became aware that Israel was escaping, they followed them, and went on after them into the midst of the sea. When the host was between the walls of water, the whole force of the storm seemed to spend itself on them. A sudden panic seized them; their heavy chariots could make but little progress in the ooze of the sea bottom, and the wheels themselves became clogged and bound so that they could not move; and they turned to flee, conscious that a greater than Israel was engaged against them.

At this juncture the morning light began to break, and at the bidding of God Moses stretched out his hand over the sea from that far shore which he and Israel had by this time gained, and the sea returned to its strength. The Egyptians fled against it in vain; they were overwhelmed in the sudden rush of water toppling down on them from either side. They sank as lead in the mighty waters, and in less time than it takes to tell the story not a trace of Pharaoh's proud army remained.

5. THE SONG OF MOSES. "Then sang Moses." The morning dawn revealed one of the most memorable spectacles of history. A nation of slaves, fleeing from their masters, had suddenly became a nation of freemen, and stood emancipated on the shores of a new continent. The chivalry of Egypt was overwhelmed in the midst of the sea, for there remained not so much as one of them left; and all along the shore lay the bodies of the dead, cast up from the depths of the tide. Here there was given to Israel for all subsequent time an evidence of the trustworthiness of God, which compelled belief, not only in their great Deliverer, but also in his servant Moses.

And from that ransomed host, congregated there in one vast throng, an anthem broke forth. There is no thought of anyone or anything but the Lord throughout the entire piece. It was *He* who had triumphed gloriously, and cast horse and rider into the sea. It was *His* right hand that had dashed in pieces the enemy. It was because *He* blew with *His* wind, that they sank as lead in the mighty waters. It was through the greatness of *His* excellency that they who had risen against Him were overthrown.

And the ease of his victory was clearly accentuated. The waters were piled as walls

179

by his breath. He blew with his wind, and a whole army sank as a stone into the depths. He had but to stretch out His right hand, and the sea swallowed the flower of the greatest army of the time.

The women, led by Miriam, replied in a noble refrain, "Sing ye to the Lord, for he hath triumphed gloriously; the horse and his rider hath he thrown into the sea." So God turns our anxieties into occasions of singing—weeping endures for a night, but joy comes in the morning.

13

Marah and Elim
1 Corinthians 10:11

The peninsula of Sinai, on the shores of which the ransomed people stood, and which for forty years was to be their schoolhouse, is one of the wildest, grandest, barest countries in the world. It has been described as a tangled maze of mountains, piled in inextricable confusion, and gradually rising in height. Between the Red Sea and the lowest outworks of these mighty citadels of rock there is a plain of gravel; and from there the way climbs slowly upward through long avenues and passes composed of purple granite or brilliant sandstone, giving a richness to the landscape unknown to our bleaker and grayer hills.

Though not expressly stated, there must have been a division of the Israelite host, from the point where their first encampments were pitched in the strange new land of freedom. The flocks and herds, as is the custom with modern Arabs, were dispersed far and wide over the country, to crop the scanty "pastures of the wilderness." It was there that their flocks and herds were preserved, while the main body of the people marched with Moses.

How marvelous the change! No longer the ceaseless pulse of movement of Egypt; no longer the green valley of the beneficent Nile, where water never failed, and luscious vegetables, melons, leeks, and garlic, charmed away thirst; no longer the majestic glory of sphinx, and pyramid, and temple: but instead, a silence so intense that the Arabs say they can make their voices heard across the Gulf of Akaba, a waste so waterless, that they might count themselves fortunate if they met a spring in a day's march.

1. THE COURAGEOUS FAITH OF MOSES. He knew that desert well; he knew, too, that if they were to follow the northern route it would not take them very long to reach the land of the Philistines, "which was near," and where they would be easily able to procure all necessary supplies either by force or purchase. But we are told that he deliberately led them southward and entered the wilderness. "So Moses brought Israel from the Red sea, and they went out into the wilderness of Shur." He could not do otherwise because the cloud went that way; but even with that indication of God's will before his eyes, it must have required a heroic faith to lead two million people directly into the wilderness (Exod. ·13:17; 15:22).

2. THE TESTING OF HIS FAITH. "They went three days in the wilderness, and found no water" (Exod. 15:22). The first day's journey was, doubtless, very distressing—the blinding sand-storms, the glare of the sun reflected from the white limestone plains, the

absence of shade, of tree, of water. And the water they carried in their waterskins must have become hot and unrefreshing.

The second day was not less trying. The sea was now far behind them, and there was nothing to break the monotony of the treeless, lifeless, waterless horizon. Surely as they pitched their black tents for the night it was difficult to repress some discontent, or at least anxiety, as to what the morrow might bring to their blistered feet and fevered lips. Their supplies of water were also getting low, if they were not exhausted.

The third day broke. Perhaps Moses, knowing that pools of water were not far away, encouraged his people to persevere; and every eye was eagerly strained to catch the first sight of palm tree and living verdure. And when at last, toward the close of the day, they sighted them in the far distance, how glad their shouts, how buoyant their hearts, how ready their expressions of confidence in Moses! Their fatigues and complaints and privations were all forgotten, as with quickened pace they made for the margin of the wells. But ah, how great was their disappointment and chagrin when the first long draught filled their mouths with bitterness, and they discovered that the water was too nauseous to drink! As long as there was none to be had, they had managed to endure; but this sorrow was harder than they could bear, and they turned on Moses and murmured, "What shall we drink?"

3. MOSES' RESOURCE. "He cried unto the Lord." How much better this than to rebuke the people, or to threaten to give up his appointment, or to sit down in despondency as utterly out of heart! Beside each bitter Marah pool there grows a tree which when cast into the waters, makes them palatable and sweet. And of what is that tree the type, if not of the cross of Jesus—which is the symbol, not only of our redemption but of a yielded will? It was there that His obedience to the will of His Father reached its supreme manifestation. He became obedient to death, even the death of the cross. Nor is there anything that will so take the bitterness out of disappointment, and so make it palatable and even life-giving, as to look up from it to the cross, and to say, "Not my will, but Thine be done. Thy will is my happiness. In Thy will is my bliss."

What a constant lesson Moses was learning from day to day! And gradually he must have come to feel that the whole responsibility of the pilgrimage was on the great, broad shoulders of his Almighty Friend.

4. ELIM. There are more Elims in life than Marah, and we *encamp* by them. We are not required to tarry at the one but we may spend long blessed days at the other. How refreshing the shadow of those seventy palm trees! How sweet the water of those twelve wells! How delightful those long restful days! You say that they will never come to you? Yes, but they will! They come to all tired souls. There is no desert march without an Elim at last. We must tread the desert, or we can never come to Elim. But the desert lends the Elim much of its bliss. Do not stay murmuring at Marah; press on! our Elim is within sight. Hope in God, for you shall yet praise Him.

At Marah Moses received from God a glad, fresh revelation, that He would be the healer of His people in their wilderness march, securing them from the diseases of Egypt. And Elim was the vindication of the promise. What a God is ours! He overthrows our foes in the sea, and disciplines His people in the desert. He leads us over the burning sand, and rests us in luxuriant glades. He permits disappointment at Marah, and surprises us at Elim. He proves by Marah, and at Elim recruits us.

14

The Gift of Manna
Exodus 16:14-16

We may encamp at Elim, and stay for long happy days in its green bowers, but we may not live there; at least the majority may not. Few characters are able to reach their highest and noblest excellence amid the genial conditions through which at times each life is permitted to pass. Therefore it is that, though the cloud of the divine guidance broods at Elim long enough to recruit us, it soon gathers up its folds, leaving us no alternative but to strike our tents and follow. So it is said that "they took their journey from Elim, and all the congregation of the children of Israel came unto the wilderness of Sin, which is between Elim and Sinai" (16:1).

There are things about God and His ability to supply all needs of the soul of man that could not be learned in any Elim, with all its beauty; and can only be acquired where its bowers are exchanged for those long corridors of rock that lead to the foot of Sinai. It is well, then, to leave Elim; beyond it lie Sinai, Pisgah, and Canaan.

1. THE DESERT MURMURINGS. It was a great aggravation of the responsibilities that already lay heavily on the heart of Moses, to have to encounter the perpetual murmurings of the people whom he loved so well. It only drove him continually back on his Almighty Friend and Helper. But the repeated outbreak of these murmurings all along the wilderness route only sets in more conspicuous prominence the beauty of his gentle meekness, and the glory of his faith, which probably was the one channel through which the power of God wrought for the salvation and blessing of His people.

a. *Murmurers are short of memory.* It was only one short month since the people had come forth out of Egypt—a month crowded with the wonders which the right hand of the Lord had wrought. The chronicler specially notes that it was the fifteenth day of the second month, and adds, "The whole congregation of the children of Israel murmured against Moses and Aaron in the wilderness; and the children of Israel said unto them, Would to God we had died by the hand of the LORD in the land of Egypt, when we sat by the fleshpots, and when we did eat bread to the full; for ye have brought us forth into this wilderness to kill this whole assembly with hunger" (vv. 2-3). They could well remember the sensual delights of Egypt, but they forgot the lash of the taskmaster and the anguish of heart with which they worked at the kneading of the clay.

Whenever a murmuring fit threatens, let us review the past and recount the Lord's dealing with us in bygone years. Did He deliver in six troubles, and is He likely to forsake us in the seventh? When the psalmist complained, and his spirit was overwhelmed, he tells us that he considered the days of old, the years of ancient times; he remembered the years of the right hand of the Most High.

b. *Murmurers are short of sight.* They fail to see that behind all the appearances of things there lie hid the presence and providence of God. Moses called the attention of the people to this fact, which enhanced so gravely the magnitude of their offense. They thought that they were only venting their frustrations on a man like themselves. Annoyed and apprehensive, it was some relief to expend their spleen on the one man to whom they owed everything. But their faithful leader showed them that their insults were directed not against himself, but against Him whose servant he was, and at whose bidding everything was being wrought. "The LORD heareth your murmurings which ye murmur against him: and what are we? your murmurings are not against us, but against the LORD" (v. 8).

c. *Murmurers are short of faith.* The pressure of want had begun to make itself felt but very slightly, if at all, on the host. It was not so much the hardship that they were at that moment experiencing, but that which they thought to be imminent. Provisions were running short; supplies were becoming exhausted. It was thus that they came to Moses and murmured.

Too many of God's children despair because of what they dread, and break into murmurings that they think certain things will happen to them: If they were to stop to think for a single moment, they would see that God is pledged by the most solemn obligations to provide for them. Why do you murmur? It is because you doubt. Why do you doubt? It is because you look out on the future, or consider your circumstances, apart from God.

How different to this murmuring life was that of our blessed Lord, who also was led into the wilderness and was without food for forty days! But He did not complain. And even when He hungered, and the devil suggested that hunger was not becoming to the newly-designated Son of God, He meekly said that it was enough for Him to have His Father's will. The Son never for a moment questioned his Father's right to follow any line of procedure He chose, and was apparently perfectly satisfied. And in this divine patience He has shown how murmurings may find no foothold, and how the soul may be braced to endure hardship.

2. THE WILDERNESS FOOD. It is not for us to tell here the whole story of the manna. It is enough to remember:

a. *To look up for our supplies.* "He gave them bread from heaven to eat." For the believer there are five sources from which help may come, for in addition to the four quarters of the winds he looks up to the heavens. There came *from heaven* the sound of the rushing of a mighty wind. Look higher, child of God, to the heart and hand of the Father!

b. *To feed on the heavenly bread daily and early.* "They gathered it every morning . . . and when the sun waxed hot, it melted." There is no time like the early morning hour for feeding on the flesh of Christ by communion with Him, and pondering His words. How different is that day from all others, the early prime of which is surrendered to fellowship with Christ! Nor is it possible to live today on the gathered spoils of yesterday. Each man needs all that a new day can yield him of God's grace and comfort. It must be daily bread.

c. *To feed on Christ is the only secret of strength and blessedness.* If only believers in Christ would realize and appropriate the lesson so clearly taught in this narrative, as well as in the wonderful discourse our Lord founded upon it (John 6:22–58), they would find themselves the subjects of a marvelous change.

Let us unceasingly make our boast in the Lord, as we step out onto the unknown and untried. And who shall lament the beauty of Elim, or the fleshpots of Egypt, or the frugal meals of Jethro's tent, when such lessons are to be learned in the society of our eternal Friend, who can never fail those who dare to trust Him; and who gives to the uttermost capacity of our faith, that we may in turn give as much as they need to those poor friends of ours, who beseige us with entreaties for help and bread (Luke 11:5–9).

15

Rephidim
Exodus 17:1–15

If you hope to lead men, you will sooner or later come to a Rephidim. It was according to the commandment of the Lord that the children of Israel journeyed "by stages" (v. 1, *marg.*) from the wilderness of Sin, and pitched in Rephidim. The character of the worker is as dear to God as the work he is doing. Do not be surprised then, Christian worker, if you find yourself landed in Rephidim. There are lessons to be learned there of incalculable worth.

1. THERE WE LEARN THE LIMIT OF OUR ABILITY. Few of us can stand great or long-continued success. To stand on the height, with none to rival, with nothing left to scale, the wonder and the envy of a host—ah! this is a task in which the brain reels, the step falters, and the heart gets proud. God will not permit His power to be employed for the inflation of human pride, or to minister to the exaltation of the flesh.

We can easily suppose that Moses was in danger of a fall. For the last few months his career had been an uninterrupted line of success. He had brought the proudest monarch of his time to his knees with the cry of a suppliant. He had become great in the eyes of priesthood and court. He had led the greatest Exodus the world had seen or would see. The parted ocean, the submerged host, the song of victory, the fall of the manna, the evidence of his statesmanship and sagacity as a born leader of men—all combined to place him in an unparalleled position of authority and glory.

It was therefore probable that God brought Moses to Rephidim to counteract and check all uprisings of self-sufficiency; to teach him the narrow limits of his resources and ability.

Whatever Moses may have begun to think, all self-confidence must have vanished like a wreath of mist among the hills when he found himself face to face with that infuriated mob. They broke through every barrier erected by gratitude, or memory of past deliverances, and with violence demanded water. "The people did chide with Moses, and said, Give us water that we may drink" (Exod. 17:2). And such was their irritation that they seemed ready to stone him. No wisdom or power of his could help in such a situation and "he cried unto the LORD, saying, What shall I do?"

It is a blessed position to which the providence of God reduces us when we find ourselves face to face with an overmastering necessity. Then we learn the limit of our sufficiency. We confess that we are not sufficient of ourselves, to account anything as from ourselves; but our sufficiency is from God. When we reach the end of self, we have reached the beginning of God. It is from the low threshold of the door that the life-giving stream gushes on its heaven-sent way.

2. THERE WE LEARN MUCH ABOUT GOD. This always follows the other lesson. We are brought to know ourselves that we may be prepared to know God. So at Rephidim the need that abases us and drives us to God, reveals God.

a. *We learn His patience.* Not a word of reproach or remonstrance breaks on the still desert air. If the people had been exemplary in their humble trust, they could not have met with more tender willingness to supply their need. The people, and perhaps

Levi especially, proved Him at Massah, and strove with Him at the waters of Meribah, asking whether the Lord were among them or not, though the cloud brooded overhead, and the manna lay each morning around the camp: yet there was no word of rebuke, only directions for the immediate supply of their need.

b. *We learn the reality of His spiritual presence.* "I will stand before thee there upon the rock in Horeb" (v. 6). The people had just threatened to stone Moses; but God, in effect, bade him not to fear. It was as if He said: "Pass on before them, no harm shall come to you; and this will be a sign that I am actually there on the rock, it will gush with watersprings." Never before had God been more real to His servant than He was that day, when He rose up as a rampart to protect him from the infuriated crowd with their threatening stones. It is when men turn against us most, that the Lord stands beside and says, "Fear not!"

c. *We learn God's secret storehouses.* "Thou shalt smite the rock, and there shall come water out of it." This is strange! A rock would seem the last place to choose for the storage of water. But God's cupboards are in very unlikely places. Ravens bring food. The Prime Minister of Egypt gives corn. Cyrus lets go the people of Israel from Babylon. The Jordan heals the leper. Meal makes poisoned pottage wholesome. Wood makes iron swim. A Samaritan binds up the wounds and saves the life of the pillaged traveler. Joseph of Arimathaea buries the sacred body in his own new tomb. There can be no lack to them that fear Him, and no fear of lack to those who have become acquainted with His secret storehouses.

That smitten rock was a type of Christ. A Rock, indeed—stable amid upheavel, permanent amid change. A smitten Rock! And the soldier's spear set flowing the blood and water that have issued to heal the nations and quench their thirst. "They drank of that spiritual Rock that followed them, and that Rock was Christ." There is no water that will so satisfy thirst as this crystal Rock-water.

3. THERE WE LEARN THE POWER OF PRAYER. The tribe of Amalek was probably descended from Esau and, like him, was wild and fierce and warlike. Were they likely to submit tamely to the intrusion of a new people into their pasture lands and strongholds that they had succeeded in holding against Egypt? According to Josephus, this power tribe gathered to this spot all the forces of the desert, from Petra to the Mediterranean; and "they smote the hindmost of the Israelites, even all that were feeble among them, when they were faint and weary."

If Egypt represents the power of darkness, Amalek is a type of the flesh which, though thoroughly defeated and broken, is always apt to crop up in moments of weakness and carelessness.

Moses entrusted the troops to Joshua, here first brought into prominence, while he climbed the hill with the sacred rod in his hand. There he surveyed the battle and stretched out his hands in prayer—fought with unseen combatants the entire day, and won the victory by intercessions, of which those steady arms were the symbol. It is a beautiful picture. Three elderly men in prayer. Two staying up the third!

In Rephidim we learn the lesson that prayer will do whatever impossible. In earlier days Moses would never have thought of winning a battle except by fighting. He now learns that he can win it by praying.

As to the prayers of a church so are the success. If they are maintained, the banner floats on to victory; if they are languid and depressed, the foe achieves a transient success. Let us then learn to pray, filling our Rephidims with strong crying and tears, obtaining by faith for ourselves and other victories that no prowess of our own could win. What deliverances might we win for our dear ones, and all others who are strongly molested by the flesh, if only we were found more often on the top of the hill with the uplifted rod of prayer in our steadied hands!

16

The Godward Aspect
Exodus 18:19

When the Israelite host had left Rephidim, they began to climb up from the coast of the Red Sea into the heart of the mountain range of Sinai. Their route has been compared to a stair of rock. Before them, through the pure air, floated the majestic cloud leading them they knew not where. They only knew that they had no option but to follow, since their supply of manna and water depended on absolute obedience to its movement.

Tidings in the desert fly fast, and the aged priest, in the strongholds of Midian, had been kept fully informed of the wonderful series of events of which his relative had been the center. When, therefore, tidings came of the arrival of the vast host in the vicinity of Sinai, he took Zipporah, Moses' wife, and her two sons and brought them to Moses. The day closed with a solemn feast and sacrifice, and the following day seems to have been a rest day. On that day an incident took place that was destined to have important issues on the history of the great leader as well as of the people whom he led. "It came to pass on the morrow, that Moses sat to judge the people: and the people stood by Moses from the morning unto the evening" (v. 13).

1. MOSES' HABITUAL PRACTICE. We get a sudden glimpse, here into the kind of life Moses was leading at this time. When the host encamped, and there was a day at liberty from the weariness of the march, he seems to have sat on a judgment seat, to which all the people came who had any disputes, or grievances, or matters about which they desired to obtain advice and divine counsel. Despite all their murmurings they looked on him as the organ for the voice of God, and sought from his lips an authoritative declaration of the divine will.

We can imagine him going to God each day with long lists of questions for one and another of the mighty host. This and the other cause he laid before Him for counsel, quoting names and circumstances, arguments and reasons on either side, and waiting for the message he was to carry back. What variety! What directness! What reality must have pervaded his prayers! How vividly must he have realized that he was, indeed, in partnership with the Most High, a fellow worker and yokefellow.

This "being for the people to Godward" became more and more characteristic of the life of Moses. Whenever the people cried to him, he prayed to the Lord. When the spirit of revolt spread through the camp, he fell on his face. When it seemed likely that the whole nation had to perish for their sin, he stood in the breach, and besought the Lord, and turned away the destruction that hung over them like a lurid cloud. Twice for forty days their interests detained him in the holy mount. And many years later he is classed with Samuel as one who had stood before God for his people.

2. THE TAX ON MOSES' STRENGTH. Work like this cannot be done without severe expenditure of all that is most vital to man. It drains the sympathies, taxes the brain, wearies the heart charged with the anxieties and sorrows, the burdens and needs of a throng of perplexed and troubled souls. And it therefore became apparent to the keen eye of Jethro's loving solicitude that both Moses and the people were being worn away in his attempt to meet all their demands.

We do not always see the cost at which we are doing our work. We are sustained by the excitement and interest of it. Some men get weary of forbearing; they cannot live slowly; they must expend themselves, pouring their lives out as a libation from a bowl. And it is an act of benevolence when some Jethro is prompted to interpose and suggest a mitigation of the fever, a slackening of the eager rush. The Jethros seldom prevail with us. They get scant thanks for their pains. We have to learn by some terrible collapse. But they have, at least, deserved well by us.

3. MOSES' ASSENT TO JETHRO'S PROPOSAL. It cannot be God's will that any of His servants should wear away. No hard taskmaster is He, driving His slaves beyond the limit of human endurance. The burden of responsibility that He lays on their shoulders may be heavy; but it is not too heavy. The bell never summons a servant to a duty concerning which God does not say to him, "My grace is sufficient for you; as your day so shall your strength be."

Sometimes God's workers made the mistake of burdening themselves with work that others could do just as well, and indeed, it would be if they did it. This seems to have been the case with Moses. He appeared to think that he alone could judge, manage, and administer the affairs of Israel. And this monopoly of the administration was working adversely. It was overtaxing him, it was wearing out the people; it was delaying the course of justice; and it was allowing a large amount of talent to lie unused. Jethro's advice was therefore most timely; that Moses should provide out of all the people able men, with the three important qualifications that they should fear God, love truth, and hate unjust gain. These were to deal with the small matters, while the greater ones would still be brought to Moses. It was much better to set all these men to work than to do all their work. It evoked talent; it ennobled them by placing them in positions of responsibility before their fellowmen; it drove them to personal dealings with God; it inspired them with a fellow-feeling with Moses; it turned critics into sympathizers and companions; it educated them for positions for which they might be required in the emergencies of the future.

Is there not a thought here for many of the Lord's workers who may read these words? Are we not dissipating our energies over too wide an area? Do we not attempt to embrace in our life many things that others could do as well as ourselves? We should live on the greatest side of our nature, reserving ourselves for that; not careless of minor details, if there is no one else to manage them, but prepared to hand them over to "able men," even though they may first have to learn their duties at a cost of some mistakes and failures. The prophet and priest, the man of God, the teacher, these are especially in these directions, cultivate such endowments to the uttermost—they are rare enough—leaving some details to be cared for by others who may be cast in a more practical mold.

17

At the Foot of Sinai
Exodus 19:18

From Rephidim the children of Israel marched slowly and laboriously through the great thoroughfare of the desert now known as the Wady-es-Sheykh, the longest, widest, and most continuous of those vast desert valleys. It must have been an astonishing exchange from the flat alluvial land of Egypt, where the only hills were those raised by the hands of man. On either side of the pilgrim host lofty and precipitous mountains reared their inaccessible ramparts of red sandstone and variegated granite, without verdure, or gushing rills, or trace of any living thing. There was nothing to allure them or arrest their steps amid the awful desolation and grandeur of those inaccessible precipices. They would sometimes be almost overwhelmed by the bare sterility of the scene, and by the awful silence that was stirred to resent the intrusion of such a multitude upon its ancient reign. But their course was always onward; and a deepening awe must have grown on their souls.

At last it broke on them. After a march of eighteen miles from the Red Sea, they came out on a perfectly level plain of yellow sand, some two miles long, and half-a-mile wide, nearly flat, and dotted over with tamarisk bushes. The mountains that gather around this plain have for the most part sloping sides, and form a kind of natural amphitheater; but toward the south there is one pile of jagged cliffs that rise upward in wild precipitousness, while behind lies the granite mass of Gebel Mousa, deeply cleft with fissures, and torn, as though it had fought a hard battle with earthquake, storm, and fire. This pile of rocks is called Ras Sufsafeh, and was probably "the mount that might be touched and burned with fire." It rises from the plain below as a huge altar, and all that transpired on its summit would have been easily visible to the further limits of the camp of two million souls pitched beneath.

Such was the chosen scene for the giving of the Law. There the hosts of Israel remained stationary for long weeks and there, while clouds veiled the heights, and fire played from peak to peak, God met with His people and gave them His Law, writing His name not on tablets of stone merely, but on the entire course of human history.

1. GOD'S OBJECT AT SINAI. At the time of the Exodus the world was almost wholly given to idolatry. The first objects of idolatrous worship were probably simply the sun and moon and heavenly bodies, or other conspicuous objects of creative wisdom and power. Later, the Deity was supposed to reside in men, and even beasts. In dealing with this deluge of idolatry, God acted as He did with the deluge of water that drowned the ancient world. He began with a single family, teaching them the sublime lessons concerning Himself. Then when they had understood the lessons, they were to teach others.

Let us notice the successive steps.

a. *First step*. God chose from the masses of heathendom one man, "called him alone," and led him to follow Him into a strange land. There, shut away from surrounding peoples, He began to teach him about Himself. Jehovah spared no time or pains with the first great Hebrew, so that he, being blessed, might be the means of blessing to the race.

b. *Second step*. God welded the Hebrew people together into one that they might be able to receive and retain as a part of their national life those great truths with which they were to be entrusted. This welding was accomplished by the tie of common parentage, of which they were justly proud; by the bond of a common occupation that kept them to themselves as shepherds, apart from the busy traffic of cities and marts of commerce; and last, by the pressure of a common trial, which together with the marvelous deliverance that was granted them, remained fresh and indelible in all later generations. So perfectly did God do this work, that while other nations have risen, reigned, and fallen, and their disintegration has been utter and final, the children of Abraham endure, like an imperishable rock, undestroyed by the chafe of the waves or the fret of the ages.

c. *Third step*. God revealed His existence. Into the midst of their bondage tidings came that the God of their fathers was a living God; that He had met one of their number in the desert and had called him by name, and had promised to intercede in their behalf.

d. *Fourth step*. God showed by the plagues that He was stronger than the gods of Egypt. Can you not imagine the children of Israel saying, "Our God is great, but perhaps He is not so strong as Isis, or Osiris, or Serapis, or the sacred bull"? But the wonders that were wrought on the gods of Egypt settled that question forever.

e. *Fifth step*. God excited their love and gratitude. You can do anything you like with those you love: but to get, you must give; to excite love, you must declare it. Hence they were touchingly reminded of what He had done: "Ye have seen what I did unto the Egyptians, and how I bare you on eagles' wings, and brought you unto myself" (Exod. 19:4).

f. *Sixth step*. God set Himself to teach them concerning certain of those great qualities, the knowledge of which lay at the foundation of all right dealings between the people and Himself. And in order to achieve His purpose, He made use of outward significant signs.

g. *Seventh step*. God clearly designated Moses to be the organ and channel of His communications to man. "Lo, I come unto thee in a thick cloud, that the people may hear when I speak with thee, and believe thee for ever" (v. 9).

2. THE LESSONS OF SINAI.

a. *The majesty of God*. The natural scenery was sufficiently majestic; but it became more so as the incidents of the third day were unfolded. Meanwhile the clouds dropped water, and there were showers of tropical rain. And it was amid such scenes that God spoke. Could any combination of natural phenomena have given grander conceptions of the majesty of the divine nature?

b. *The spirituality of God*. What was their God like? On that memorable occasion, "when Moses brought forth the people out of the camp to meet God," they saw no likeness. He was there, for He spoke. But there was no outward form for the eye to discern. It has not been easy for mankind to learn this lesson so clearly taught on Sinai, that God is a Spirit.

c. *The holiness of God*. This primal lesson was also taught in striking fashion by outward signs that impressed the sense. Bounds were erected to keep the beasts from grazing on the thin herbage of the lower slopes: whoever touched the Mount must die, all clothes were to be carefully washed against that third day, absolute purity was to be observed in heart and life, Moses alone was called up to the top of the Mount, and when he had climbed there, he was sent all the way down again for the express purpose of charging the people, and even the priests, not to break through to gaze on the Lord, lest God should break forth on them. All these significant acts converged to give outward and sensible manifestation of the holiness of God.

d. *The royalty of God.* The Jewish state was a kingdom, and God was King. And the reality of His government appeared in the way in which Moses himself obeyed his behest. It was a sight never to be forgotten to see how their great leader Moses was absolutely subservient to the command issued from God's pavilion. At the best he was only God's executor, "the passive instrument of the divine will." The Decalogue was spoken by God Himself "out of the midst of the fire, of the cloud, and of the thick darkness, with a great voice" (Deut. 5:22). Every ordinance of the Law, every custom and provision for domestic and civil life, every item in the construction of the sanctuary and in the ordering of the priests, was due to the direct will of God, spoken from His mouth. How clear was the testimony to the supremacy of the Most High! Such were some of the lessons taught at Sinai.

The life of fellowship with God cannot be built up in a day. It begins with the habitual reference of all to Him, hour by hour, as Moses did in Egypt. But it moves on to more and longer periods of communion. And it finds its consummation and bliss in days and nights of intercession and waiting and holy intercourse. Ah, what patterns are seen on the Mount! Alas for us that we move so far from it! Or at the best are admitted to stand only with the elders, and set paved work of sapphire stone beneath God's feet! Oh, for the closer access, the nearer view, the more intimate face to face intercourse, such as is open still to the friends of God!

18

The Vision of God and Its Effect
Exodus 34:29

We are justified by the highest authority in deriving spiritual lessons from this incident in the life of the great lawgiver. The apostle expressly refers to it when he says that we all may, with unveiled face, behold the glory of the Lord, and be transformed (2 Cor. 3:13–18). That blessed vision which of old was given only to the great leader of Israel, is now within reach of each individual believer. "We *all* . . . are changed."

1. THE DESIRE TO SEE GOD CARRIES WITH IT THE PLEDGE OF ITS GRATIFICATION. For many years the desire had been growing in the heart of Moses to see the face of God. "Show me now thy way, that I may know thee"; "I beseech thee, show me thy glory." If we garner every opportunity, cultivate every faculty, and keep our faces ever toward the mountain of communication, we shall infallibly find that the heart that yearns for the vision shall see that vision realized. "And the LORD said unto Moses, I will do this thing also that thou hast spoken: for thou hast found grace in my sight. . . . be ready in the morning, and come up in the morning unto Mount Sinai" (Exod. 33:17; 34:2).

2. THE GRATIFICATION OF DESIRE DEPENDS ON FULFILLMENT OF CERTAIN CONDITIONS.

a. *We must learn to obey.* Obedience was the great characteristic of Moses. He was faithful in *all* God's house as a servant. The repeated refrain of the books of the Pentateuch is the phrase that sounds deep and often: "as the LORD commanded Moses, so did he." God could always depend on him. And it was to him, rather than to the disobedient hearts of the people, that God revealed Himself.

Clearly, obedience is the stepping stone to vision. We must be servants before we can be friends. The path of literal obedience, even though it is rough and steep, is the only path to the mountain summit with its marvelous revelation.

Do not be disobedient to heavenly visions; never turn aside to your own preferences from the narrow path of unswerving loyalty to the voice of God. Dare to do right, though you stand alone among the recreant hosts; and you will thus fulfill one prime condition of the vision of God.

b. *We must be willing to pass through the thick cloud.* "God called unto Moses out of the midst of the cloud . . . and Moses went into the midst of the cloud" (Exod. 24:16, 18). Thick banks of dense cloud, dark in their earthward aspect, though insufferably bright on their inner side, shut out the light of sun and the spectacles of earth, and shut him in with God. But he would not have seen the vision if he had not been willing to pass through the cloud and to stand beneath the shadow of the divine hand.

The garden, the cross, and the grave, are the only way to the Easter morning. The walls must be toned to a neutral tint on which masterpieces of painting are to be exhibited. And it seems indispensable that we should pass into the shadow of bereavement, temptation, and distress, if we are to emerge into God's marvelous light and estimate its brilliance.

c. *We must dare to be alone.* When we read those solemn words, "Be ready in the morning, and come up in the morning unto mount Sinai, and present thy self there to me in the top of the mount. And no man shall come up with thee, neither let any man be seen throughout all the mount; neither let the flocks nor herds feed before that mount" (Exod. 34:2–3)—they seem to echo to us in other but similar tones. "When thou prayest, enter into thy closet, and when thou hast shut thy door, pray to thy Father which is in secret" (Matt. 6:6).

Valuable as are the opportunities for Christian culture and service they will be disastrous if they rob us of the time that we should otherwise spend with God. Let the first moments of the day, when the heart is fresh, be given to God. Never see the face of man until you have seen the King. Dare to be alone often on the Mount.

3. WHEN THE CONDITIONS ARE FULFILLED, THE VISION IS SURE. Perhaps Moses, as he entered the cloud, expected that the Almighty would pass before him, riding on a cherub, flying on the wings of the wind, girt with rainbow and storm, while the thunder rolled as drums in his march. But lo! he seemed to stand in a ravine, on a ledge of rock, shadowed by a hand, while through that mountain ravine passed the divine procession; and a still, sweet, penetrating voice told that God was love.

Mark the progress of revelation to the adoring soul. In Horeb, Moses had stood in the outer court, to learn that God is changeless. In the giving of the Law he had stood in the glory of the Holy Place, to learn that God is righteous. Now he was admitted to the inner shrine, to learn that the Lord God was merciful and gracious, longsuffering, and abundant in goodness and truth.

No one who waits for Him will be ashamed. He will satisfy desires that He has Himself implanted. As to Fletcher of Madeley, to Catherine of Siena, and to hundreds of others, so to you, when least expecting it, will come the beautific vision, perhaps constraining you to cry, as John Tennant did: "Hold, Lord, it is enough! or the frail vessel will break beneath the weight of glory."

4. SUCH VISIONS LEAVE UNMISTAKABLE TRACES. The face of Moses shone; and did not his heart and life shine also? Could it have been otherwise? Linen in which the housewife has laid sachets will smell fragrantly: ordinary iron placed near a magnet becomes magnetic; and it is impossible for us to be with God often without becoming godly.

The old legends of the saints tell of those who, by long meditation on the crucifixion of the Lord, received in their very flesh the marks of His wounds. There is certainly a spiritual counterpart of this in the long, fixed gaze of the soul on the vision of God, by which the details or elements of the divine beauty pass into the life, and light it up with a loveliness that is not of earth.

5. SUCH TRACES ARE NOT PERCEIVED BY THOSE WHO PRESENT THEM. "Moses wist not that his face shone." He was glorious in all eyes but his own.

True Christian excellence is as unconscious of its beauty as Moses was; whenever it becomes self-conscious it loses its charm. The possessor of the genuine article never talks about it, never thinks about it, and would be almost overwhelmed to hear of any such thing being ascribed to him. It is like the bloom on a peach, the pearls of dew on the morning lawn, or the stillness of the surface of a mountain pool.

19

The Broken Sentence
Exodus 32:32

This is one of the most pathetic verses of the Bible and bears on its face the evidence of its genuineness. It could not have emanated from the mind or pen of some later scribe, because it is so entirely unexpected, so strange, and yet so likely. It is the fragment of a sentence of which we would have given much to hear the conclusion, but who can presume to finish that which in this supreme hour was choked by a paroxysm of grief, a sob of irrepressible emotion?

1. THE PROBLEM WITH WHICH MOSES HAD TO DEAL.

a. *The idolatry of his people.* After the utterance of the ten great words of Sinai, the people, frightened by the thunderings and lightnings, and the voice of the trumpet, and the smoke of the mountain, urged Moses to act as their daysman and mediator. "They said unto Moses: Speak thou with us, and we will hear; but let not God speak with us, lest we die" (Exod. 20:19). The great lawgiver and leader, acting on their request, thereupon withdrew himself into the divine pavilion, and was absent for about six weeks. After awhile, they became uneasy and restless. "Where is he? He did not take food enough with him to sustain him for so long. Has he met with some mishap on those lonely steeps?" "As for this Moses, the man that brought us up out of the land of Egypt, we wot not what is become of him" (Exod. 32:1). And then turning to Aaron, the man of words, sure that neither he nor twenty like him could fill the gap which the loss of Moses had caused, they cried. "Up, make us gods, which shall go before us."

We may notice in passing the essential nature of idolatry, for in this marvelous chapter we have its entire history. We start from the first cry of the soul, which betrays a yearning for an idol, to the draining of the last bitter dregs with which, when ground to powder, the idolater has to drink its very dust. The idolater does not—in the first instance, at least—look on his image as God, but as a representation or manifestation of God. It is an attempt on the part of the human spirit, which shrinks from the effort of communion with the unseen and spiritual, to associate God with what it can own and handle, so as to have a constant and evident token of the presence and favor of God.

This was the case of Israel. It was only three months since they had stood by the Red Sea and seen its waters roll in pride over the hosts of Pharaoh. Every day since then God's love had followed them. And even at the time with which we are dealing the entire summit of the mount was crowned by the pavilion of cloud, which was the emblem of His presence in their midst. But notwithstanding all, they were carried away before that imperious craving of the human heart, which cries out for a sensible image for its worship.

Their idolatry, then, was a violation, not of the first, but of the second commandment. They did not propose to renounce Jehovah—that was left for the days of Ahab; but they desired to worship Jehovah under the form of a calf, and in distinct violation of the emphatic prohibition which said, "Thou shalt not make unto thee any graven image, or any likeness of any thing that is in heaven above, or that is in the earth beneath; thou shalt not bow down thyself to them, nor serve them." This was the sin also of Jeroboam.

b. *Their degradation.* There can be no doubt that the worship of the calf was accompanied by the licentious orgies that were a recognized part of Egyptian idolatry. This is implied in the narrative: "The people sat down to eat and to drink, and rose up to play." A striking emendation is given of verse 25: "Moses saw that the people were broken loose; for Aaron had let them loose for a derision among their enemies." And from this we may infer that the bonds of continence, that had restrained them since the Exodus, had been suddenly slackened, with the result that they broke from all restraint, and gave themselves up to their unholy riot.

c. *The claims of God.* There was every reason to believe that God would exact the full amount of penalty, not because He was vindictive, but because the maintenance of His authority seemed to demand it. The righteousness of His career, the inviolability of His oath, the authority of the Ten Commandments, so recently given, combined to make it necessary that He should do as He had said.

And yet, on the other hand, there was the fear that if, to use the language of men, God's anger waxed hot and He consumed them, the Egyptians might say, "For [evil] did he bring them out, to slay them in the mountains, and to consume them from the face of the earth." And thus Jehovah's character might be misunderstood and maligned among the neighboring nations.

How could God maintain His character with His own people without imperilling it with the Egyptians? If He spared the people, they would begin to think that neither His threats nor His promises were worth their heed. And if He destroyed them, His glory would be dimmed; and He might seem to have become unmindful of the oath that He swore by Himself to His servants. Abraham, Isaac, and Israel that He would multiply their seed, and give the land of Canaan to them as a heritage forever. So greatly did these considerations weigh with Moses, that he refused the divine offer to make him the only survivor of the host, and the progenitor of a great nation.

2. THE EMOTIONS WITH WHICH HIS SOUL WAS STIRRED. In the mount he acted as intercessor. When God told him all that was transpiring in the plain below, and showed the glittering sword of justice suspended over the guilty nation by a thread, he pleaded for the people he loved.

On his way down from the mount, when he came near enough to see the calf and the dancing, peering over some overhanging ledge of rock, the old impetuous vehemence that had characterized him in earlier life, broke out with all its early intensity. "Moses' anger waxed hot, and he cast the tables out of his hands, and brake them beneath the mount."

When he reached the camp, he seems to have walked into the astonished throng, broken up their revelry, and overturned their calf, ordering it to be destroyed and the fragments mingled with the water they drank. But as this was not enough to stop the inveterate evil, he was compelled to use more drastic measures, and by the sword of Levi to extinguish it with the lifeblood of three thousand men.

Then when the next day came, when the camp was filled with mourning over those new graves, when the awful reaction had set in on the people and himself, the tide seems to have turned. His indignation was succeeded by bitter sorrow and pity. The pitiable state to which their sin had reduced them aroused his deepest compassion; and he said unto the people, "Ye have sinned a great sin: and now I will go up unto the LORD; peradventure I shall make an atonement for your sin" (v. 30); but he did not tell them the purpose that was in his heart, nor the price he was planning to pay.

3. THE OFFER THAT HE MADE. He returned quietly and thoughtfully to the chamber of God, as the people stood observing. He felt that the sin was very great. He could not see how God could go back from His solemn threatenings. He was convinced that if the merited judgments were averted, it must be in consequence of an atonement. Yet, what atonement could there be? Animals could not avail, though they were offered in slaughter. There was only one thing he could suggest—he could offer himself. This was the secret that he locked in his breast as he climbed the mountain. And it was this that made him say, "Peradventure." He could not be sure that the ransom price would be large enough.

It may be asked how he came to think of atonement. But we must remember that there probably had already been much talk between God and himself about the sacrifices the people were to offer. Again and again the word *atonement* had been employed. He had learned that by suffering one could redeem others. He had seen the deep possibilities in the law of substitution, and it seemed a natural thing therefore to propose that he, the chosen servant, the prince and leader of the people, should be weighed in the scale against the nation, and that God should accept his blood as a ransom for their life.

Moses confessed his people's sin to God, and added: "Yet now, if thou wilt forgive their sin—." He would not finish that sentence. He could not trust himself to depict the blessed consequences that would ensue, if only God would forgive.

But the dark fear oppressed him that free pardon was too much to expect. Ah, how little did he realize the love of God in Jesus Christ our Lord! And he therefore added: "And if not, blot me, I pray thee, out of thy book which thou hast written" The proposal was either that he should then and there die, and not see the good land beyond Jordan; or that he should cease to be numbered with God's people.

How the heart of God must have moved toward the faithful servant, whose proposal recalled another scene in the faraway ages of eternity when the Son of God undertook to redeem man by making an atonement through the shedding of His own blood!

Of course, the offer was not accepted. No one can atone for his own sin, much less for the sins of others. Yet the people were spared. The passing by of their transgression was rendered possible by the propitiation that was to be offered in the course of the ages on the cross (Rom. 3:25).

20

God's Presence Our Rest
Exodus 33:14

This assurance of rest is as applicable to the present age as that of the Exodus. No, perhaps there is a special message in it for these feverish days, so filled with discord, confusion, and strife. But that rest must be sought deeper down than in circumstances. It must begin at the center of our being, and in its accord with the being of God.

1. THE CIRCUMSTANCES BY WHICH THIS ASSURANCE WAS CALLED FORTH.

a. *Moses was a very lonely man.* Perhaps more lonely in the midst of the two million people he was leading as a flock, than he had been amid the solitudes of the desert, tending the flock of Jethro. The contrast between his lofty enjoyment of divine communion, and the people, always set on sensual pleasure, must have lent intensity to the isolation of his spirit. "And Moses said unto the LORD, See, thou sayest unto me, Bring up this people: and thou hast not let me know whom thou wilt send with me." What a sigh there is here for companionship!

It is certain that these words will be read by many whose lives are outwardly solitary. Some are left during long hours to bear the burden of the home or of suffering, or of some service like a sentry on night duty at a lonely post. It is to that state of mind that the assurance of the text was given.

b. In addition to this, *the hosts were soon to leave the mountain region of Sinai,* with which Moses had been familiar during his shepherd life, in order to take the onward road through unknown deserts, infested by daring and experienced foes. So what if the pillar and cloud led them slowly along those desert pathways, and at night shed a broad flood of light on the clustered tents of the desert encampment; yet the prospect of that journey through the great and terrible wilderness was sufficient to disturb the stoutest heart.

Are there not times with many of us when we have reason to fear that, in consequence of some sad failure or sin on our part, the Lord may be obliged to withdraw the conscious enjoyment of His love? Such thoughts quicken the pace of the soul as it goes to His footstool.

2. The place where this assurance was given. The earlier intercourse between the servant, "faithful in all his house," and He who had appointed him, seems to have been on the mountain summit. But after the outburst of the people's sin, a change was made that did not necessitate such prolonged or distant absences from the camp. Indeed, he was absent for only one other period of forty days (34:28) until the time of his death, some thirty-eight years later.

During the prolonged interview that he had been permitted to enjoy, God had spoken to him much about the Tabernacle that was shortly to be built. A tent was therefore selected; and was pitched "without the camp, afar off from the camp, and called it to the Tabernacle of the congregation. And it came to pass, that every one which sought the LORD went out unto the tabernacle of the congregation, which was without the camp" (v. 7).

But its special benefit was obvious in the case of Moses Himself. It was no longer necessary for him to climb to the mountain summit; he was able to transact all necessary business by going out to the tent. And when it was rumored through the camp that he was about to do so, "all the people rose up" to see the marvelous spectacle, "and stood, every man at his tent door," looking after him. They did this because as soon as he entered the tent, the pillar of cloud descended from its position in mid-heaven, and stood at the door of the tent, the vehicle and emblem of the divine presence. Thus "the LORD spake unto Moses face to face, as a man speaketh unto his friend"; and Moses spoke to his Father, who is in secret, with the freedom of a child.

It was there that this amazing colloquy took place. Moses spoke of his loneliness, and asked who was to be associated with him in his great task. Then it seemed as if that faithful heart suddenly caught sight of a blessing more transcendent in glory than any he had yet dared to ask. His petition was couched in great humility, but he ventured to suggest that God should Himself show him his ways, that he might know Him. It was as if he said, Will You be my comrade and companion—my referee in difficulty; my adviser in perplexity; my friend in solitude?

And God's answer came back on his spirit with music and balm. "My presence shall go with thee, and I will give thee rest" (v. 14). Nothing was said as to the people. The promise of the divine presence was made apparently to Moses alone.

But faith gets bolder as it mounts, and Moses not only took the assurance of the divine presence for himself, but asked that it be extended to include the people.

In this request also he was successful. "And the LORD said unto Moses, I will do this thing also that thou has spoken: for thou hast found grace in my sight" (v. 17). There are moments of holy intercourse with God, rapturous, golden moments in the lives of all His servants. When next they visit us let us plead, not only for ourselves, but also for others, asking for them an equal blessedness.

3. The blessedness this assurance guaranteed. There was, first, the divine presence; and there was, second, the promised Rest—not the rest of Canaan, for this Moses never saw, but a deeper and more blessed inheritance, which may be the portion of all faithful souls. But at their heart these two are one. The divine presence is rest.

The conscious presence of God with us is possible only on three conditions.

First, we must walk in the light, as He is in the light, for He will have no fellowship with the unfruitful works of darkness, or turn aside to go with us on any crooked path of our own choosing.

Second, we must recognize that the blood of Jesus Christ His Son constantly cleanses us from all sin, not only that which we judge and confess, but that also which is seen only by His pure and holy eyes.

Third, we must claim the gracious aid of the Holy Spirit, to make real that presence, which is too subtle for the eye of man, unless it be specially enlightened.

When these conditions are fulfilled, the blessed soul enters on an experience of the presence of God, and the sense of that presence is rest.

21

Tabernacle Building
Exodus 25:9, 40

The heart of the Jewish people was the tabernacle, around which their tents circled, and the movements of which determined the journeyings of the host. The tabernacle also taught them some of the deepest thoughts about God, in a kind of picture language.

We must remember that the children of Israel did not possess a language like our own, with many words and a rich vocabulary, capable of expressing all kinds of abstract ideas such as love, wisdom, purity, spirituality, holiness. So before making His revelation God had to provide language for His thoughts. This He did largely in the construction of the tabernacle.

1. THE CONCEPTION OF THE TABERNACLE. The pattern in the mount! Then clearly there must have been some visible phenomenon, some bright apparition, some glorious picture cast on the clouds or built on the old rocks. There may have been stakes and curtains, cherubs and lamps, gold and silver, altar and candlestick; but they would not bear the touch—they existed as a beautiful dream.

But it is almost inconceivable that God did not at the same time explain to Moses those wonderful conceptions of His own nature, and His relations to men, which were intended to be set forth in this material structure. They were as follows:

a. *God's willingness to share man's life.* If the people had only seen the devouring fire on the top of Sinai, the pavilion of God's presence, they would never have dared to think that there was any community of interest between Him and them. To their minds, He would always have seemed distant and unapproachable. So God said, "Let them make me a sanctuary; that I may dwell among them" (v. 8).

Thus it was ordained that this larger tent should be pitched among them, only differing from their own in its proportions and materials; but standing on the same level sand, struck and pitched at the same hour with theirs, and enduring the same vicissitudes of weather and travel. Did this not say, as plainly as words could, that the tabernacle of God was with men, and that He was willing to dwell with them and become their God? Did it not teach that Jehovah had become a pilgrim with the pilgrim host, no longer a God afar off, but a sharer in their national fortunes?

b. *The greatness of God.* To this, too, a visible expression was to be given. The tabernacle must have cost an immense sum for that fugitive nation of slaves. The silver pedestals placed at intervals along the sand to hold the upright boards; the gorgeous tapestry that composed ceiling and walls; the golden furniture, of which the seven-branched candelabra alone weighed one hundredweight of gold; the brass wrought into sixty brazen pillars, with their silver capitals and hooks, from which were suspended curtains so thin that people could see all that was transpiring in the outer court. How costly these were!

On that new year's day, the anniversary of the Exodus (Exod. 40:17), as it stood forth completed in the desert sunshine, it must have furnished new and enlarged conceptions of the divine majesty.

c. *God's unity.* All around them the nations were under the spell of idolatry. But the tabernacle, with all its differing parts, and materials, and accessories, was one. One ark; one incense altar; one altar of burnt offering; one sacred purpose in every order and rite for the putting away of uncleanness. It stood therefore among men as a perpetual protest against idolatry, and as an emphatic witness to the unity of God. "Hear, O Israel; The LORD our God is one LORD." Such was the perpetual message that floated on the desert air from that unique structure.

d. *God's spirituality.* The concept that God was a Spirit was conveyed to the people in that most striking form.

Enter the holy place; your eye is arrested by the heavy but magnificent curtain, covered with cherubim, that cuts off six feet of the length of the entire structure. Pull that aside, and you pass into a chamber that is a perfect cube, a miniature of the New Jerusalem, whose length, and breadth, and height, are equal. In the Egyptian temple this apartment would contain the crocodile or ibis; but here there was only a box, over which forms of exquisite beauty bent with outspread wings, and between them a light shone that was not borrowed from sun or stars. Could anything more significantly convey the idea that God was a Spirit?

This absence of any visible form in the inner shrine most astonished the rough soldier Pompey, who strode with eager curiosity across the floor, which had never before been pressed by anything but the unsandalled foot of the high priest once a year. He expected to find some visible embodiment of Jehovah, and turned contemptuously away deriding the empty void. But to Moses it must have been an unparalleled conception, overpowering his thoughts.

e. *God's purity.* The impression of this was produced by a series of comparisons. First, the tabernacle stood within a courtyard fenced from public approach, the outer part could be trodden only by those men who had passed through certain rites of purification; and as to the inner part, it could be trodden only once a year by the high priest, carefully cleansed by many rites, and clad in garments of special design, while the blood of slain animals, selected out of the herds for their freedom from any blemish or speck, was sprinkled around. All was done to impress upon the people the care with which they should approach God; and in this way impressions of His holiness were wrought into the national mind.

And throughout these arrangements, and notably by these repeated references to the blood of sacrifices that was to be shed and sprinkled, Moses became familiarized with the philosophy of the Atonement.

Such thoughts as these must have penetrated the soul of Moses as he waited before God, oblivious to the flight of time, the waning love and idolatry of his people, or the demands of the body for food. And as we behold the great spectacle of that rapt and spellbound soul, we get some conception of one part at least of the engagements of eternity, and we are stirred to seek after a more intimate knowledge of God.

2. THE REPRODUCTION OF THE PATTERN. There is a special interest to us all in this. We are not called to build the Tabernacle again, after that old pattern that has served its purpose and fallen into disuse because it was superseded by the clearer revelations of the Gospel. Yet there is an analogy that is full of instruction and inspiration in the life of every true believer, and deserves our attention for a moment.

As the tabernacle dwelled in the mind of God before it was reproduced on the desert sands, so does the life of each one exist, as a conception of that same infinite intelligence.

When a child is born into the world, there is in the mind of God a perfect picture of what that life may become, an ideal to which it may be conformed. There is a clear anticipation of what it will be, but side by side there is a distinct prevision of what it might be. And if only that pattern could be seen and literally reproduced, if only that life could attain to the divine ideal, there would be no room for regret or disappointment. It would fulfill its complete purpose as a thought of the divine mind, and attain its perfect consummation and bliss. Alas, that with so many of us, as the years have passed, we have wrought our own evil will and followed our own design!

a. *God's pattern was comprehensive.* No tassel, nor socket, nor tiny detail, was left to the fancy or ingenuity of the artificers; all was comprehended in the divine pattern. Of every detail God had a plan, because in each some purpose was hidden and the symmetry of the whole depended on the perfection of each part. So in life God's thought covers all details. Nothing is too trivial to be made a matter of prayer and supplication.

b. *God's plan was unfolded gradually.* Probably the account of the revelation of the successive parts of the tabernacle is an exact transcript of the method by which the divine design was unfolded to Moses' thought. Line upon line, precept upon precept— such is ever the divine method.

We will not be able to see far in front, nor the whole completed plan of our life, but as we complete one thing another will be revealed, and then the next and the next. It may be that we will not understand the divine purpose, but at the end of life we will see that it was one complete and exquisite structure, of which no part was wanting.

c. *God's plan was commensurate with the people's resources.* As the pattern was there on the Mount, there were also the materials for its realization in the possession of the people below—the gold and silver and precious stones, the blue and purple and scarlet, the fine linen and goats' hair, the rams' skins and badgers' skins, the genius of the artificers, and the willingness of the people.

God never gives a man a pattern without making Himself responsible for the provision of all materials needed for its execution. If the materials are not forthcoming, you may seriously question whether you are not working on a plan of your own. God will not provide for a single tassel of your own addition to His Scheme.

d. *God's plan must be resolutely obeyed.* Again and again in the last chapter of Exodus we are told that all was done, "as the LORD commanded Moses." This was his supreme joy and satisfaction, that he had not added to or diminished from the divine command and so the work was finished.

e. *God's plan is always progressive.* In pursuing the earlier stages of the divine tuition, Moses was especially occupied with elaborating the elementary idea of sacrifice, as in the case of the Paschal Lamb. The next stage was the building of the tabernacle, with which we have now been engaged. But this was not the final form of the divine revelation to which he was called to give visible shape. Years later, when disease was mowing down thousands of victims throughout the camp, as a judgment on the murmurings of the people, their leader was summoned to make a serpent of brass and place it on a pole, that all who looked might live.

In that supreme moment, Moses caught sight of the dying Lord, and discerned not only the fact but also the method of His death. To no other Old Testament seer, so far as we can learn, was it given to know that Jesus must be lifted up on a cross. But this was permitted to him who had faithfully wrought out the divine plan in its earlier stages; and he too was privileged to set forth, so graphically and simply, the nature of saving faith. "As Moses lifted up the serpent in the wilderness, so must the Son of man be lifted up; that whosoever believeth in him should not perish, but have everlasting life" (John 3:14–15).

Thus is it always. As we climb the hill, the horizon expands; as we do God's will more thoroughly, we know His doctrine more completely.

22

The Start From Sinai
Numbers 10:29

Israel sojourned under the shadow of Sinai for about eleven months. What a change had been produced in their condition! They arrived there a fugitive and unorganized people; they left in a mighty nation in battle array, provided with a sacerdotal system that was to last for centuries as a type of the priesthood of Christ and his saints; and furnished with a code of laws and sanitary enactments that have been a model for the most civilized peoples of the world.

The very appearance of the camp indicated this marvelous change. In the midst the sacred tent with its brooding cloud, and around it the goodly tents of the people. The priests and Levites pitched around it, in the inner circle; and around them again the twelve great tribes, three toward each point of the compass, guarding the tabernacle as a most sacred charge, and as the center of their national life.

It was a marvelous spectacle also, when the cloud was taken up, and the priests, through the silver trumpets, gave the signal that the camps on the east side should begin to lead off the march. Judah passed on first, followed by Isaachar and Zebulun; the sons of Gershom and Merari, with their six wagons bearing the heavier portions of the tabernacle (Num. 7:1–9) came next; and after these Reuben, followed by Simeon and Gad; then the long lines of Kohathites, carrying on their shoulders the vessels of the Holy Service; and last, the remaining six tribes in two great divisions, the one led by Ephraim and the other by Dan.

All was beautifully ordered, and though we may not attribute the mighty revolution that had been thus effected to the unaided genius of Moses, we cannot but feel that, as God for the most part gave His teachings through minds competent to receive and transmit them, so the mental endowments of Moses must have been of no mean order. But side by side with this colossal intellect there was still a weak, human heart that betrayed itself in the proposal he made to Hobab.

1. Moses' PROPOSAL. During their stay at Sinai, Hobab, chieftain of a tribe closely related to Moses by marriage, visited the people. Of course, he knew the country well,

every foot of it—where the springs lay, and the pastures, and the safest shortest routes; and so Moses approached him with the request that he would go with them, to give them the benefit of his practical knowledge.

This request was most natural. Moses was a very lonely man, as we have seen, and it was pleasant to have someone bound to him by a blood affinity, to unburden himself to in any special crisis.

At the same time it was at variance with the general custom, which even then must have begun strongly to assert itself of Israelite exclusiveness. The Jew made no intermarriages with neighboring peoples on pain of death; he dressed in a special garb, and differed from all other men to the very dressing of his beard.

Yet it was an unusual thing for the great lawgiver to go out of his way to utter this winsome invitation to a Midianite prince. And there must have been a strong reason that prompted it. Because Moses had never gone that way before he was so eager to obtain Hobab's company. How blessed to have a Hobab who knows the ground!

We seek our Hobabs in the advice of sage, gray-haired counselors; in the formation of strong, intelligent, and wealthy committees; in a careful observance of precedent. Now, in one sense, there is no harm in this. We have neither right nor need to cut ourselves adrift from others who have had special experience in some new ground on which we are venturing. But there is also a great danger that we should put man before God; that we should become unmindful of the true Guide and Leader of souls. When we have given Him his right place, He will probably restore our judges as at the first, and our counselors as at the beginning; but the first necessity is that the eye should be single toward Him so that the whole body may be full of light.

2. THE FAILURE OF HOBAB, AND THE DIVINE SUBSTITUTE. The desert chieftain was by no means enamored of the proposal. The result of it all was that in reply to Moses' request, Hobab said bluntly, "I will not go; but I will depart to mine own land, and to my kindred" (v. 30). Moses urged and entreated him further, but whether he succeeded or not is doubtful; though there are some reasons for thinking that the second request prevailed because the descendants of the Kenite are numbered among the chosen people (Judg. 1:16).

But it would seem as if his aid was rendered needless by the provision of guidance immediately promised. Up to this moment the position of the ark had been in the midst of the host, in front of Ephraim, Benjamin, and Manasseh; but after that it went three days' journey in front of the people, "to seek out a resting place for them." Far behind, at a distance of miles, followed the camp with its tumult, its murmur of many voices, the cries of little children, the measured tramp of armed bands. But none of these intruded on the silence and solemnity which, like majestic angels, passed forward with that courier group accompanying the ark, over which cherubic forms were bending. That Moses was there is indubitable, for the august sentences are recorded with which he announced its starting forth and its stopping. In the one case, looking into the thin air, which seemed to him thronged with opposing forces of men and demons, he cried, "Rise up, LORD, and let thine enemies be scattered; and let them that hate thee flee before thee"; and in the other he cried, "Return, O LORD, unto the many thousands of Israel" (vv. 35–36). Thus God Himself superseded the proposal of Moses by an expedient which more than met their needs.

Let us not anticipate God's guidance or press on Him unduly. "He that believeth shall not make haste." Let there be an interval between the ark and your steps, so that you may see, as far as possible, what God would have you do; and then deliberately, thoughtfully, but with fixed determination, follow. *He* will "be to us instead of eyes."

And oh, the bliss of knowing that Jesus is not "three days' journey" away; but near, so that He is ever between us and our foes.

23

Noble to the Core
Numbers 11:29

Uninterrupted success is hard to bear, much more so than perpetual trial. If it should be debated as to whether sunshine or storm, success or trial, were the more severe test for character, the shrewdest observers of human nature would probably answer that nothing so clearly shows the real stuff of which we are made as prosperity.

For some two years Moses had been borne along on a flowing tide. Through faith in the living Jehovah, he had vanquished the proudest monarch of his time; had conducted nearly three million people through the wilderness wastes without a settled commissariat; had disciplined an unorganized multitude into a mighty host, with a code of legislation and ritual that is the admiration of all thoughtful men. This was success enough to turn the head of any ordinary man, nor could we have wondered if he had shown signs of undue elation and pride. But the two incidents that we are now to consider show how absolutely simple and humble he had remained amid a number of success.

1. ELDAD AND MEDAD. In condescension to his weakness, his almighty Friend appointed seventy colleagues to bear with him the burden of the people.

In each case of those thus anointed, the accession of spiritual force was marked by the sudden breaking forth of prophecy. For the sixty-eight of them the power of utterance was only spasmodic and temporary. They prophesied, but only for awhile. Two of the selected number who, for some reason, had remained in the camp, suddenly became conscious of their reception of that same spirit, and they, too, broke out into prophecy, and appear to have continued to do so. Instantly a young man, jealous for the honor of Moses, carried to him the startling tidings, "Eldad and Medad do prophecy in the camp"; and as he heard the announcement, Joshua, equally chivalrous, exclaimed, "My lord Moses, forbid them!" eliciting the magnificent answer, "Enviest thou for my sake? would God that all the LORD's people were prophets, and that the LORD would put his Spirit upon them!"

This is the spirit of true magnanimity. Whenever the eye is single for the glory of God and when the spirit is centered in one eager and intense desire to see His will done, the faithful servant is willing to be anything or nothing, if only the divine purpose would be accomplished.

2. MIRIAM. What did she not owe to Moses? But for him she would have been an unknown slave girl, mated to a toiler in Pharaoh's brickfields, the mother of slaves. But now she was free, and the representative woman of an emancipated race, through the

brother whom she had rocked in her arms. It was sad that at the age of ninety she should turn against him whom she had tended and loved; and that she should poison the mind of the elder brother who had been his spokesman and right hand.

They spoke against Moses because of the Ethiopian woman he had married. Some have thought that Moses had married a second time, but it seems wiser, since the death of Zipporah is not mentioned, to consider the reproach as applicable to her, especially as she probably bore in her complexion the brand of another race. "Cushite" means black, or dark-complexioned. She had come to the camp recently; and for some time Miriam may have been carefully watching her, with the result that her entire woman's nature revolted from the thought of having to resign her primacy to such as she was. It is always difficult to see another filling the place that we have looked on as ours, especially if we are conscious of being able to fulfill its duties better.

We can imagine her talking to Aaron and to the women with whom she was intimate, about these "Cushites," until she had raised quite a storm of feeling. This was bad enough in her, but how much worse in Aaron, who held the proudest position in the camp. The function of Moses was temporary, and would pass away with his life; whereas that of Aaron was permanent to himself and his heirs. Yet Aaron could not but feel how vast was the gulf between him and his brother. And out of this there sprang the jealousy that made Zipporah its excuse. "And they said, Hath the LORD indeed spoken only by Moses? Hath he not spoken also by us?"

But how did Moses act—he who, years before, had felled an Egyptian with one blow of his fist? Did he call on God to strike them down in his anger? Nothing of the sort. He answered not a word; for "the man Moses was very meek, above all the men which were upon the face of the earth" (Num. 12:3). In his bearing he reminds us of Christ in the judgment hall, who, "when he was reviled, reviled not again."

Was this weakness, as some would say? No, instead it was the exhibition of colossal spiritual strength. Only the strong man can be perfectly still under provocation, holding himself in, and turning the vehemence of his soul into the heat of an intense love.

It may be well to give some closing rules as to the attainment of this meek and quiet spirit.

a. *Let us claim the meekness of Christ.* This, of course, was not possible for Moses in the direct way in which it is for us. And yet doubtless, in his case also there was a constant appeal for heavenly grace. The humility of Jesus did not forbid His proposing Himself as our model for meekness. "Learn of Me," He said, "for I am meek and lowly in heart." In moments of provocation there is nothing better than to turn to Him and claim His patience and meekness, saying, "I claim these, my Lord, for the bitter need of my spirit."

b. *Let us cultivate the habit of silence.* Express a thought, and you give it strength and permanence; repress it, and it will wither and die. Utterance will give it vigor, and will sow another crop that will soon fruit again. Silence will kill it; as ice kills fish when there are no vent holes by which they can come up to breathe.

Learn to be still; to keep the door of the lips closed; to give an answer when it is asked, and an explanation when it is needed to correct a misapprehension. "Let every man be swift to hear, slow to speak, slow to wrath" (James 1:19).

c. *Next consider the harm done by the aggressors to themselves.* The cloud moved from over the tent, as if it must leave the very spot where the culprits stood; and behold, Miriam was leprous, white as snow. There is a piece of profound instruction here—you cannot say unkind or bitter things about someone else without hurting yourself more than you hurt that person. Like the boomerang of the savage, curses come back to the spot from which they start.

d. *Let us allow God to vindicate our case.* Moses trusted God to vindicate him. The Lord heard all that was said, and spoke suddenly to the three, and told them that while He would speak to others in visions and dreams, it was to Moses only that He would speak face to face, so that he might behold Jehovah's form. "Wherefore then," He said, "were ye not afraid to speak against my servant Moses?" (Num. 12:8).

c. *Let us give ourselves to intercessory prayer.* Moses cried to the Lord, saying, "Heal her now, O God, I beseech thee" (v. 13). When we pray for those who have despitefully used and persecuted us, it is marvelous how soon the soul becomes calm and tender. We may begin to do it as a duty, in obedience to the command; we soon discover it to be as snow on a fevered forehead, cooling and soothing the soul.

And the Lord heard His servant's prayer, and healed Miriam; but the whole host was delayed a week through her sin. We may be forgiven, but these outbreaks of sin always entail disaster and delay. Neither we nor others can be where we might have been had they not occurred.

24

A Bitter Disappointment
Numbers 14:25

It was a weary journey from Kibroth-hataavah to Hazeroth, and thence to Kadesh, probably the weariest of the entire route. Moses spoke of it afterward as "that great and terrible wilderness" (Deut. 1:19). But at last the hosts reached Kadesh-barnea, on the borders of the Land of Promise, within sight of the low hills, the flying-buttresses, so to speak, of the verdant tableland, which first arrests the eye of the traveler coming up from the vast limestone plain of the desert.

How welcome that spectacle, after the four hundred miles of journey that had occupied the people for the past fifteen months! It must have been especially gratifying to the eye of Moses.

1. HIS HOPES. As yet God had graciously veiled from him the weary journeys of the forty years that were to succeed. Moses had no idea what to expect. From the way in which he spoke to the people, he evidently counted on a comparatively brief struggle, sharp, but short, through which they would pass to their possession. These are the words he addressed to the people as they camped in sight of the rolling prairies of Canaan: "Ye are come unto the mountain of the Amorites, which the LORD our God doth give unto us. Behold, the LORD thy God hath set the land before thee: go up and possess it, as the LORD God of thy fathers hath said unto thee; fear not, neither be discouraged" (Deut. 1:20–21).

As he said these words there must have been deep in his heart a sigh of relief that now his task was almost done, and he could lay down his weighty responsibilities. And as for himself, surely there were in store some few happy years in which he could repose after the long toils of his life. After a few years spent in this manner, he might ask to to depart in peace and pass home from the Canaan of earth to the Sabbath-keeping of heaven.

But suppose it could not be so! What if He who loves us better than we love ourselves has marked our stations in a desert-march, that lead right up to the mount from which we are to ascend to our Father's home! What if we are to fight with Moab, and meet Balaam, and see every one of those with whom we began life fall around us! What if we are to lie down to die alone beneath His kiss, away from the prattle of children and the warm pressure of loving hands on some Pisgah height! This is precisely what came to Moses.

2. THE QUARTER FROM WHICH HIS DISAPPOINTMENT CAME. It came entirely from the people.

a. *Their first mistake was in desiring to spy out the land.* It is certainly said in these chapters that "the LORD spake unto Moses, saying, Send thou men, that they may search the land of Canaan" (Num. 13:1–2). But the proposal did not emanate from the Lord. It had another origin, which was disclosed by Moses himself forty years later in words that followed those quoted above, "And ye came near unto me every one of you, and said, We will send men before us, and they shall search us out the land, and bring us word again" (Deut. 1:22).

As in the case of Saul, the king of Israel, God gave them what they would have. Their self-will was a profound mistake. Had not God promised to give them the land, and could they not trust His choice? They had but, as Moses said, to go up and possess that which He had given.

b. *Their second mistake was in receiving the discouraging report of the majority of the spies.* Up to a certain point there was perfect agreement between them. "We came into the land whither thou sentest us, and surely it floweth with milk and honey; and this is the fruit of it." Then the ten said, "The people be strong, that dwell in the land, and the cities are walled, and very great; and, moreover, we saw the children of Anak there. . . . We be not able to go up against the people; for they are stronger than we" (vv. 28, 31). But the two, Caleb and Joshua, whose names alone linger on our tongues as household words, replied, "If the LORD delight in us, then he will bring us into this land, and give it us" (Num. 14:8).

The difference between the two lay in this, that the ten looked at God through the difficulties, as when you look at the sun through a reversed telescope, and it seems indefinitely distant and shorn of its glory; while the two looked at difficulties through God. And the people sided with the ten, and turned aside from the thought of God, to dwell long and sadly on the stupendous obstacles that hindered their occupation of the land. "We see that they could not enter in, because of unbelief" (Heb. 3:19).

c. *Their next mistake was in their murmuring, which proposed to substitute a captain for their tried friend and God-given leader.* "All the congregation lifted up their voice, and cried; and the people wept that night. And all the children of Israel murmured against Moses and against Aaron: and the whole congregation said unto them, Would God that we had died in the land of Egypt. . . . And they said one to another, Let us make a captain, and let us return into Egypt" (14:1–4).

This was perhaps the bitterest hour in Moses' life. The people whom he had loved with passionate devotion, whose very existence was due to his intercession on the Mount when they were on the point of being destroyed, had forgotten all he had done.

They actually proposed to supersede his authority, and if he would not go with them under their new-made captain, to leave him to his own devices there. And he fell on his face before all the assembly of the congregation. What unutterable agony rent his breast!—not only that he should be set aside in this way, but that the anger of God should be so provoked by the people he loved!

3. HIS REFUSAL TO ESCAPE THE DISAPPOINTMENT. The dream of Moses for a speedy entrance into the land might even yet have been realized. If all the people were cut off, and he spared to be a second Abraham, the founder of the nation, it might be possible even yet for him to pass into the good land, and like Abraham settle there. So God, knowing the hidden nobleness of his faithful servant, and eager that it should be revealed to all the world, suggested to him that He should smite the people with pestilence, and disinherit them, and make of him a nation greater and mightier than they.

There are few grander passages in the whole Bible than that in which Moses puts away the testing suggestion as impossible. "If thou shalt kill all this people as one man, then the nations which have heard the frame of thee will speak, saying, Because the LORD was not able to bring this people into the land which he sware unto them, therefore he hath slain them in the wilderness" (vv. 15–16). Moses would not have the rest he longed for at the sacrifice of a ray of God's glory, or of the people with whim his life was linked, though they had sadly plagued and disowned him. And so he turned away from the open gate into Paradise, and again chose rather to suffer with the people in their afflictions than enjoy the pleasures of Canaan alone.

4. A CONTRAST TO HIS ENDURANCE OF DISAPPOINTMENT. Little is said about the leader's bearing. He kept silence, and did not open his mouth. But the people's behavior throws his into strong relief.

When they heard that they were to wander in the wilderness for forty years, until their bodies fell in its wastes, to be interred in the sands as winding sheets, they rose up early in the morning and got up to the top of the mountain, saying "Lo, we be here, and will go up unto the place which the LORD hath promised. . . . Nevertheless the ark of the covenant of the LORD, and Moses, departed not out of the camp" (vv. 40, 44). By force of will and energy they sought to reverse the sentence just passed on them. Moses meekly bowed his head to it, and accepted the discipline of those long years.

25

Faithful Under Reproach
Numbers 16:22

Few men have had greater experience of the ingratitude of their fellowmen than had Moses. Here it broke out again, and this time in a formidable conspiracy led by Korah, with whom were associated two hundred and fifty princes, men of renown.

In the history of all workers for God there will come crises, when wrong motives will be imputed and unkind suggestions passed from mouth to mouth, even by those whose spiritual life has been due to their prayers and tears. One time it is jealousy of growing influence; then it is unwillingness to accept directions and fall in rank at the word of command; again it is the dislike of a carnal soul at the high spiritual demands that are in direct collision with its longings for milk and honey, fields, and vineyards. Such disaffection begins with one discontented sensual soul, but it spreads as fire in prairie grass.

1. LOOK ON YOUR POSITION AS GOD'S APPOINTMENT. Korah and his confederates suggested that Moses and Aaron had taken on themselves the offices they held, the one as king in Jeshurun, whenever the heads of the people gathered; the other, with his family, as priest. Why should these offices be exclusively vested in the two brothers? Were there not plenty of men as good as they? Was not all the congregation holy? It was a conspiracy of princes against the leader and prince, and of Levites against the priestly family.

Moses instantly fell on his face before God. But he made no further attempt to justify his position or Aaron's. He might have alleged his past services, his claims on the gratitude and loyalty of the people; he might have reminded them that their national existence was due, under God, to his faith, his prayers and tears, his intercessions and exertions on their behalf. But on all these points he held his peace, and took the whole matter into the divine presence, throwing the responsibility on his God.

a. *He reminded the malcontents that their own position had been assigned by the appointment of the Most High.* The God of Israel had separated them from the congregation of Israel, to bring them near to Himself, to do the service of the tabernacle of the Lord, and to stand before the congregation of Israel, to bring them near to Himself, to do the service of the tabernacle of the Lord, and to stand before the congregation to minister to them. It was distinctly *He* who had brought them near, and all the sons of Levi with them. There was therefore no cause for jealousy. Posts were assigned to men, and men to posts, by the distinct interposition of God. And they who had been so distinctly appointed surely should admit that an equally distinct divine appointment had been made in respect of Aaron and himself.

b. *This outpouring of anger was shown to be really directed against God Himself.* "Both thou and all thy company are gathered together against the LORD: and what is Aaron, that ye murmur against him?" (v. 11)

c. *Moses left the ultimate decision with God.* They were all to take censors, which were the ordinary prerequisites of the priests alone; and having charged them with fire and incense, were to present themselves before the Lord at the door of the tent of meeting. It would be then for God to choose who should be holy, and who should be invited to come near to Him.

Let us act as Moses, the faithful servant did, and refer all to the decision of our Master and Lord; and in the meanwhile be at peace. When difficulties come, as they will, they are His as much as they are ours. We have no right to carry His anxieties and care for His cares. He asks us to do His work; to obey His behests; and to transfer all the weary pressure and burden to Himself. If the people do not like us, it is for Him to determine whether He will keep us in our position; and if He chooses to do so, He must keep us there and give us favor with them. If our mission involves the assumption of leadership which is disputed by others, we cannot recede from it so long as we can say with Moses, "The LORD hath sent me to do all these works, for I have not done them of mine own mind" (v. 28). Thus pride and jealousy are alike impossible. We know we receive nothing except it be given us from heaven; and we refer all who disagree to Him who has put us where we are.

2. CHERISH KINDLY FEELINGS TOWARD THOSE WHO OPPOSE. How nobly Moses dealt with this murmuring crowd! When he first heard their contentious voices, he assumed the posture of intercession and began to plead for those who despitefully used and persecuted him. When it seemed, on the following morning, as if God would destroy not only the ringleaders, but all the congregation who assembled with them at the door of the tent of meeting, he fell on his face and pleaded with God not to punish all for the sin of one man. Dathan and Abiram, the sons of Eliab, were specially insulting; and, when Moses summoned them, they returned an insulting message, accusing him of betraying them with false representations and asking why he had not led them into the land of milk and honey. They went so far as to insinuate that they dared not come, lest he should bore out their eyes (v. 14). Moses was naturally very indignant and wounded by these bitter and undeserved reproaches, but he made no attempt to answer them, except in self-vindication before the Lord. And when asked he did not hesitate to go to them, with no trace of vindictiveness in his address.

And on the following day when the people, unawed by the terrible judgments that had befallen, murmured against Aaron and Moses, and accused them of having killed the people of the Lord, he again averted from them the judgment that was threatened—first by his prayers, and then by hastening Aaron to stand, censer in hand, between the plague-stricken and those as yet unreached by the sickle of death.

This is the true pastor's heart. He partakes of the spirit of the Good Shepherd, who loved those who taunted Him, and pleaded for the forgiveness of His murderers.

3. YOU MAY EXPECT GOD TO VINDICATE YOU. "And Moses said. . . . If these men die the common death of all men . . . then the LORD hath not sent me. But if the Lord [create a creation (*marg.*)], and the earth open her mouth, and swallow them up . . . then ye shall understand that these men have provoked the LORD. And it came to pass, as he had made an end of speaking all these words, that the ground clave asunder that was under them, and the earth opened her mouth and swallowed them up" (vv. 28–32). It was essential to the existence of the camp that the mutiny should be stamped out without mercy. There was no help for it.

26

How He Got Into Trouble
Numbers 20:11

It was but one act, one little act, but it blighted the fair flower of a noble life and shut the one soul whose faith had sustained the responsibilities of the Exodus with unflinching fortitude, from the reward that seemed so nearly within its grasp.

The wanderings of the forty years were almost over. The congregation that had been scattered over the peninsula had converged toward the given meeting place in Kadesh. There the encampment remained for some months, and there Miriam died. She was one of the few with whom that lonely spirit could still converse of that life that lay beyond the desert sands, the valleys of Sinai, and the waters of the Red Sea, in the distant mighty land of the Pharaohs and the Pyramids. Aaron, Caleb, Joshua (and perhaps the Levites), were the only relics and supervisors of that vast triumphant host, whose voices had rung out their challenge on the morning of emancipation.

1. How it happened. The demand of the people on the water supply at Kadesh was so great that the streams were drained. Because of this there broke out again that spirit of murmuring and complaint that had cursed the former generation, and was now reproduced in their children. Oblivious to the unwavering care of all the preceding years, the people assembled themselves together against Moses and Aaron, though it was against Moses that they principally directed their reproach.

They professed to wish that they had died in the plague that Aaron's censer had stayed. They accused the brothers of malicious designs to effect the destruction of the whole assembly by thirst. Although the cloud of God brooded overhead and the manna fell day by day, they cursed their abiding place as evil. They taunted Moses with the absence of figs, vines, and pomegranates. They demanded water.

However, he resumed his old position, prostrating himself at the door of the tent of meeting until the growing light that welled forth from the secret place indicated that the divine answer was near. Unlike the injunction on a similar occasion, which now lay back in the haze of years. Moses was urged, though he took the rod, not to use it, but to speak to the rock with a certainty that the accents of his voice, smiting on its flinty face, would have as much effect as the rod had had previously, and would be followed by a rush of crystal water.

Moses might have entered into these thoughts of God in quieter and more tranquil moments, but just now he was irritated, indignant, and hot with disappointment and anger. Therefore, when the assembly was gathered together in their thronging multitudes around him, he accused them of being rebels. He spoke as if the gift of water depended on himself and Aaron. He showed how irked he was at their demand, and then vehemently smote the rock with his rod twice. And as those blows reechoed through the still air, they shook forever the fabric woven by his dreams and hopes.

What a warning there is here, admonishing us that we sometimes fail in our strongest point, and that a noble career may be blasted by one small but significant and forever lamentable failure! "The Lord spoke unto Moses and Aaron, Because ye believe Me not, to sanctify me in the eyes of the children of Israel, therefore ye shall not bring this congregation into the land which I have given them" (v. 12).

The people did not suffer through their leader's sin. The waters gushed from out the rock as plentifully as they would have done if the divine injunctions had been precisely complied with. "The water came forth abundantly; and the congregation drank, and their beasts also."

2. The principle that underlay the divine decision.

a. *There was distinct disobedience.* There was no doubt as to the divine command; and it had been distinctly disobeyed. Moses was not to strike, but to speak; and he had twice smitten the rock. In this way he had failed to sanctify God in the eyes of the people. He who ought to have set the example of implicit obedience to every jot and tittle, had inserted his own will and way as a substitute for God's. This could not be tolerated in one who was set to lead and teach the people.

It is a solemn question for us all whether we are sufficiently obedient. It is a repeated burden of those sad chapters of Hebrews which tell the story of the wilderness wanderings—the cemetery chapters of the New Testament—that "they could not enter in because of unbelief." But throughout the verses the margin suggests the alternative reading of *disobedience;* because disobedience and unbelief are the two sides of the same coin—a coin of the devil's mintage. They who disobey do not believe; and they who do not believe disobey.

b. *There was unbelief.* It was as if Moses had felt that a word was not enough. He did not realize how small an act on his part was sufficient to open the sluice gates of omnipotence. A touch is enough to set omnipotence in action.

It is wonderful to hear God say to Moses, "Ye believed me not." Was this not the man by whose faith the plagues of Egypt had fallen on that unhappy land; and the Red Sea had cleft its waters; and the daily manna had spread the desert floor with food; and the people had marched for thirty-eight years unhurt by hostile arm? What had happened? Had the wanderings impaired that mighty soul, and robbed it of its former strength, and shorn the locks of its might, and left it like any other? Surely, something of this sort must have happened! One act could have wrought such havoc only by being the symptom of unsuspected wrong beneath. Oaks do not fall in a single storm unless they have become rotten at their heart.

Let us watch and pray lest there be in any of us an evil heart of unbelief; lest we depart in our most secret thought from simple faith in the living God; lest beneath a fair exterior we yield our jewel of faith to the solicitation of some unholy passion.

c. *There was the spoiling of the type.* "That Rock was Christ." It was from His heart, smitten in death on Calvary, that the river of water of life has flowed to make glad the city of God, and to transform deserts into Edens. But death came to Him, and can come to Him but once. "Christ was once offered to bear the sins of many" (Heb. 9:28). "For in that he died, he died unto sin once; but in that he liveth, he liveth unto God" (Rom. 6:10). "I am he that liveth, and was dead; and, behold, I am alive for evermore" (Rev. 1:18). These texts prove how important it was to keep clear and defined the fact of the death of Christ being a finished act, once for all. It is evident that for the completeness of the likeness between substance and shadow, the rock should have been stricken but once. Instead of that, it was smitten at the beginning and at the close of the desert march. But this was a misrepresentation of an eternal fact, and the perpetrator of the heedless act of iconoclasm had to suffer the extreme penalty, even as Uzzah died for trying to steady the swaying ark.

But there was something even deeper than these things. There was an eternal fitness in the nature of the case in Moses not being permitted to lead the people into the land of rest. Moses represented the Law. It came by him, and he therefore fitly stands before the gaze of the ages as the embodiment of that supreme law, whose eye does not wax dim or its force abate under the wear and tear of time. But the law can never lead us into rest. It can conduct us to the very margin and threshold, but no further. Another must take us in, the true Joshua—Jesus, the Savior and Lover of people.

3. THE IRREVOCABLENESS OF THE DIVINE DECISIONS. Moses drank deeply of the bitter cup of disappointment. And it seems to have been his constant prayer that God would reverse or mitigate his sentence. "I pray thee, let me go over, and see the good land that is beyond Jordan, that goodly mountain, and Lebanon" (Deut. 3:25). No patriot ever yearned more to tread the blessed soil of his fatherland as did Moses. With all the earnestness that he had used to plead for the people, he now pleaded for himself. But it

was not to be. "The LORD was wroth . . . and said unto me, Let it suffice thee; speak no more unto me of this matter" (v. 26).

At such times our prayer is not literally answered. By the voice of His Spirit, by a spiritual instinct, we become conscious that it is useless to pray further. Though we pray not three times but three hundred times, the thorn is not taken away. But there is a sense in which the prayer is answered. Our suffering is a lesson warning people in years to come. We are permitted from Pisgah's height to scan the fair land we long for, and are then removed to a better land. We have the answer given to us later, as Moses, who had his prayer gloriously fulfilled when he stood with Christ on the Transfiguration Mount.

27

Preparing for Pisgah
Deuteronomy 31:2

Moses' last year was as full of work as any he had known.

1. THERE WAS THE CONQUEST OF EASTERN CANAAN. Its original inhabitants had been expelled by the kindred tribes of Moab and Ammon but they, in their turn, had been dispossessed of a considerable portion of the territory thus acquired, by the two Canaanite chiefs, Sihon and Og.

The attack of the Israelites was justified because of the churlish refusal of Sihon to the request that they might march through his borders on their way to Jericho. He not only refused them passage, but gathered all his people together and went out against Israel on the front line between his territory and the wilderness. The song that commemorated the victory lays special emphasis on the prowess of the slingers and archers of Israel, afterward so renowned: "We have shot at them; Heshbon is perished" (Num. 21:30). These words suggest the probable reason for the overthrow of this powerful monarch, under the providence of God. The sword followed on arrow or stone, so that the army was practically annihilated; no further resistance was offered. The cities opened their gates; and this fertile region between the Arnon and the Jabbok, consisting of "a wide tableland, tossed about in wild confusion of undulating downs, clothed with rich grass, and in spring wavering with great sheets of wheat and barley," came into possession of the chosen people.

But this was not all. North of this lay Bashan, a rich and well-wooded country, abounding in noble forests of oak and of olive trees, interspersed with patches of corn in the open glades. Og, its king, was renowned for his gigantic stature. According to Josephus' narrative, he was coming to the assistance of Sihon, when he heard of his defeat and death. But, undaunted, he set his army in array against the hosts of Israel. The battle ended in the complete victory of Israel. The result is told in the strong, concise narrative of Moses. "They smote him, and his sons, and all his people, until there was none left him alive; and they possessed his land" (Num. 21:35).

Nothing could have accounted for the marvelous victories that gave Israel possession of these valuable tracts of country—with cities fenced with high walls, gates, and bars, together with a great many unwalled towns—but the intervention of God. He had said earlier, "Fear not! I have delivered him into thy hand": and so it happened.

Immense swarms of hornets, which are common in Palestine, seemed to have visited the country at this juncture, so that the people were driven from their fortresses into the open plains where they were less able to stand the assault of the Israelites.

Moses, at their urgent request, proceeded to allot this rich and beautiful territory to the Reubenites and Gadites and the half-tribe of Manasseh, after receiving their solemn pledge to bear their share in the conquest of western Palestine. "I commanded you," he said later, "ye shall pass over armed before your brethren the children of Israel . . . until the LORD have given rest unto your brethren, as well as unto you" (Deut. 3:18, 20).

2. HIS LAST CHARGE TO THE PEOPLE. This was delivered in a series of farewell addresses, which are contained in chapters 1–30 of the Book of Deuteronomy. This book is to the four preceding ones much what the Gospel according to John is to the other three. It is full of the most pathetic and stirring appeals. Well may it be said of Moses that he loved the people; and in these pages we may trace the course of the molten lava that poured from his heart. The key-phrases of that remarkable book are: "Keep diligently"; "Observe to do"; and, "The LORD shall choose."

3. HIS ANXIETY ABOUT A SUCCESSOR. Moses spoke to the Lord, saying, "Let the LORD, the God of the spirits of all flesh, set a man over the congregation, which may go out before them, and which may go in before them, and which may lead them out, and which may bring them in; that the congregation of the LORD be not as sheep which have no shepherd." In answer to this request, he had been directed to bring Joshua, the son of Nun, before Eleazar, the priest, and before all the congregation, and to give him a charge. This he seems to have done; but as death drew near he apparently gave him a second charge (cf. Num. 27:16–17, and Deut. 31:7–8).

What a striking scene it must have been when, on his one-hundred-and-twentieth birthday, the aged law-giver called to Joshua, and said to him in the sight of all Israel, "Be strong and of a good courage; for thou must go with this people unto the land which the LORD hath sworn unto their fathers to give them; and thou shalt cause them to inherit it. And the LORD, he it is that doth go before thee; he will be with thee; he will not fail thee, neither forsake thee: fear not, neither be dismayed" (Deut. 31:7–8). Immediately afterward the pillar of cloud stood over the door of the tabernacle, and Moses and Joshua were summoned to present themselves before God in its sacred precincts. There, in almost identical words to those that He had spoken by the lips of Moses, God gave Joshua his commission to bring the children of Israel into the land that He had sworn to give them, together with the promise that He would be with them.

4. HIS LAST ACTS WERE TO ARRANGE FOR THE CUSTODY OF THE LAW AND THE PERPETUATION OF ITS READING. He did the first by depositing the book, in which he had recorded the divine revelations made to him, in the side of the ark of the covenant. It was to be kept under the custody of the Levites; and passages were to be read from it at the end of every seven years, when all Israel appeared before God in the place He would choose.

And as to the second, Moses put his exhortations and entreaties into two magnificent odes, the one dealing out warnings against apostasy, the other dwelling seriatim on the characteristics of the tribes, and giving them a part blessing, after the fashion of the dying Jacob.

What glimpses we get of the inner life of this noble man! All that he wrought on earth was the outcome of the secret abiding of his soul in God. He was nothing: God was all. And all that he accomplished on the earth was due to that Mighty One indwelling, fulfilling, and working out through him, as His organ and instrument, His own consummate plans.

Thus Moses drew his life's work to a close. Behind him a long and glorious life, before, the ministry and worship of the heavenly sanctuary. Here, the shekinah; there, the unveiled face. Here, the tent and pilgrim march; there, the everlasting rest. Here, the Promised Land, beheld from afar, but not entered; there, the goodly land beyond Jordan entered and possessed.

28

The Death of Moses
Deuteronomy 34:5–6

The records of Scripture find little room for dying testimonies, words, or experiences; while they abound in stories of the exploits and words of those who have stormed and suffered and wrought in life's arena. This may explain why, contrary to human custom, the death of the great lawgiver is described with such brief simplicity.

But this simplicity is equalled only by the sublimity of the conception. After such a life it was proper that Moses should have a death and burial unparalleled in the story of mankind; and we do not wonder that poet, painter, and preacher have found in that lonely death on Pisgah's summit a theme worthy of their noblest powers.

1. ITS BEARING ON SIN. We cannot suppose that the sudden outburst of impetuous temper at Meribah—when his spirit was agitated by a fierce whirlwind of wrath, as a storm sweeping down some mountain rent on an inland lake—could remain long unforgiven. As far as the east is from the west, so far had that transgression been removed. But though the remission was complete, yet the result lingered in his life, and shut him out from an experience that should have been the crown of his career.

Nor does sin only entail loss and sorrow on the transgressor; it robs mankind of much of the benefit which otherwise had accrued from his life. If it had not been for his want of faith and his passionate behavior, Moses would have led his people across the Jordan, and served them for many years.

2. ITS BEARING ON DEATH.

a. *It's loneliness.* That majestic spirit had ever lifted itself, like some unscaled peak, amid other men. Into its secrets no foot had intruded, no human eye had peered. But its loneliness was never more apparent than when, unattended even by Joshua, he passed up to die amid the solitudes of Nebo. Alone he trod the craggy steep; alone he gazed on the fair landscape; alone he lay down to die.

But in that loneliness there is a foreshadowing of the loneliness through which each of us must pass unless caught up to meet the Lord in the air. In that solemn hour human voices will fade away, beloved forms will vanish, familiar scenes will grow dim to the sight. Silent and lonely, the spirit migrates to learn for itself the great secret. Happy the man who, anticipating the moment, can say: "Alone, yet not alone, my Savior is with me. He who went this way by Himself is now retreading it at my side."

b. *Its method.* We die, as Moses did, "according to the word of the LORD." Some still substitute "kiss" for "word"; so that it seemed as if the Almighty had kissed away the soul of his faithful servant, drawing it back to himself in a long, sweet, tender embrace.

Is not this the manner in which all saints die? Lit in the evening by the rays of a stormy sunset, piercing through the cloud-drift, the tired spirit sinks down, and He bends over it to give it its goodnight kiss, as in earliest days the mother had done to the wearied child.

c. *Its sepulcher.* We are told that "the LORD buried him in a valley in the land of Moab," in spite of the opposition of the evil one, who contended with the archangel sent to secure that noble deserted shrine. And so even a band of angels was not permitted to perform the sacred work of interment. We are told that *He* buried him; as if the Almighty would not delegate the sacred office to any inferior hand.

d. *Its purpose.* We are told that "the children of Israel wept for Moses in the plains of Moab thirty days"; and if we connect this statement with the fact of the unknown grave, we will be able to discern the divine purpose in its concealment. Is it not more than likely that, if the Lord had not concealed his grave, the valley of Bethpeor would have become a second Mecca, trodden by the feet of pilgrims from all over the world?

e. *Its vision.* From the spot on which he stood, without any extraordinary gift of vision, his eye could range over an almost unequalled panorama. At his feet, the faraway tents of Israel; to the north, the rich pasture-lands of Gilead and Bashan, bounded by the desert haze on the one hand, and on the other by the Jordan valley, from the blue waters of the Lake of Galilee to the dark gorge of the Dead Sea. And beyond the river he could sweep over the fair Land of Promise, from the snow-capped summits of Hermon and Lebanon to the uplands of Ephraim and Manasseh; with the infinite variety of cities perched on their pinnacles of rock, of cornfields and pasture lands, of oil, olives, figs, vines, and pomegranates. Immediately before him, looking west, was Jericho, in its green setting of palm trees, connected by the steep defile with Jerusalem; not far from which Bethlehem, on the ridge of the hills, gleamed as a jewel.

So to dying people still comes the vision of the beautiful land beyond the Jordan. It is not far away—only just across the river. May God grant us the blessedness of dying on the hilltop with that vision in our gaze.

3. THE BEARING ON DISPENSATIONAL TRUTH. The Law came by Moses; and Moses stands on the plains of history as the embodiment, as he was also the vehicle, of the moral law.

It was in perfect keeping with this conception that there was no decay in his natural vigor. His eye was as a falcon's, his step limber and elastic, his bearing erect. He did not die of disease, or amid the decrepitude of old age; "he was not, because God took him." Time had made him only venerable, but not weak. And thus he represents God's holy law which cannot grow outworn or weak, but always abides in its pristine and perfect strength, though it cannot bring us into God's rest.

This is the beautiful Land of Promise, which can be seen from afar only by those who know nothing except what Moses can teach them; but may be entered by those who follow the ark through the river of death to the self-life, and forward to resurrection ground.

JOSHUA

1

The Book of Joshua

There is a special inner meaning in the Book of Joshua which cannot be exhausted when we have learned from it the story of the extermination of the Canaanites; of the partition and settlement of Canaan; and of the noble simplicity and military exploits of Joshua. It is impossible to suppose that so much space should have been given to the record of these events unless there had been some deep and holy purpose, some deep spiritual truth required for the growth of holy souls throughout the ages.

The clue to this inner meaning is given by the writer of the Epistle to the Hebrews, the third and fourth chapters of which are all-important in determining the drift of our interpretation; and it is to the clearer appreciation of the true meaning of these chapters that we must attribute the increasing interest with which the church of God turns to this record of the simple, transparent, humble, and strong soldier.

A careful study of the chapters referred to shows us that though Canaan was not *the* rest of God, yet it was a vivid type of that blessed Sabbath-keeping into which we may enter here and now. "We which have believed *do* enter into that rest." Our Lord Jesus has entered into His rest, as God did into His. He is therefore the representative of His followers to whom He allots the ideal Land of Canaan as they believe. We are urged to give diligence to enter into that rest, that no man "fall after the same example of [disobedience]" (Heb. 4:11).

All these references go to establish the spiritual significance of this wonderful story that tells of that satisfaction of rest, wealth, and victory that may be enjoyed by those who have come to know the secret things that God has prepared for them who love Him, and who are revealed by His Spirit.

There is another book in the New Testament in deep spiritual accord with the story told in the Book of Joshua, the Epistle to the Ephesians, which rises above all the other epistles as the soaring cathedral tower rises above the maze of architecture beneath, and carries within its heart bells that ring out the wedding peal. Already in that epistle we can detect notes that are to announce the consummation of creation in the marriage of the Lamb. The Book of Joshua is to the Old Testament what the Epistle to the Ephesians is to the New.

The characteristic word of the Ephesians is *the heavenlies* (1:3, 20; 2:6; 3:10; 6:12). Of course, it does not stand for heaven, but for that spiritual experience of oneness with the risen Savior in His resurrection and exaltation which is the privilege of all the saints, and which is theirs in Him. It may help us to a better comprehension of this analogy between the "heavenly places" and the land of Canaan, if we trace it in the following five particulars.

1. EACH WAS THE DESTINED GOAL TO WHICH GOD'S PURPOSE LED HIS PEOPLE. When the Lord appeared to Moses at the burning bush, in the first sentence He spoke, He pledged

Himself not only to deliver His people out of the land of the Egyptians, but also to bring them up out of that land unto a good land flowing with milk and honey. Their emancipation from Pharaoh was only preparatory to their settlement in the Land of Promise.

The plagues of Egypt that struck the fetters from the wrists of an enslaved nation, the institution of the Passover and shedding of blood, the passage of the Red Sea and destruction of the hosts of Egypt—all must have been abortive had they not led on to, and been consummated in, the settlement of Israel in Canaan. In no other way could the divine promise to Abraham have been fulfilled.

Similarly, though so many of the Lord's redeemed seem ignorant of it, all the wonderful facts that lie behind the history of the church prepare all believers for the glad entrance into the blessed life. It will be a life of joy that must forever be a song without words, peace that passes understanding, love that passes knowledge.

It is remarkable how constantly the epistles point to this experience. The apostles write their glowing paragraphs for the perfecting of the saints, and the unfolding of the true conditions of holiness, victory, and power.

Let me here solemnly ask: Have you realized these conditions, and entered on those privileges? Are you still in the wilderness, or have you entered the Land of Promise? Test yourself by the promises made to Israel, which are types and shadows of eternal realities; and if they do not foreshadow facts in your spiritual experience, realize then that you frustrate the purpose of God in your redemption. Leave those things that are behind to reach forth to the goodly land beyond the Jordan, apprehending that for which you were apprehended of Christ Jesus.

2. EACH WAS IMPOSSIBLE BY MEANS OF THE LAW. The law of God can never bring the soul of man into the Land of Promise; not because of any defect in it, but because of human infirmity and sin. In that marvelous piece of self-analysis given us in the Epistle to the Romans, the apostle repeatedly affirms that the law is holy, and righteous, and good; he insists that he delighted in it after the inward man, but he tells us that he finds another law in his members, warring against the law of his mind, and bringing him into captivity. It is the presence of this evil law in our members that makes obedience to the law of God impossible, filling us with disappointment and unrest, ceaseless striving and perpetual failure. We must therefore leave the law as an outward rule of life behind us, so that the divine Joshua may lead us into the Land of Promise.

Just as the forgiveness of sins and eternal life are the free gift of God's grace, to be received by faith, so the fullness of the blessing of the gospel of Christ is bestowed only on those who, in the absence of all merit and effort, receive it with open and empty hands. We do not work up to our rest day, as the Jews did; but down from it.

3. EACH WAS ENTRUSTED TO A REPRESENTATIVE. It is a remarkable characteristic of the story of Joshua that God repeatedly addresses him for the people, and bestows on him what was destined for them. And it was for him to apportion it. These people were to inherit the land that He "sware unto their fathers to give them." All was put into the hands of Joshua, as the trustee of Israel, and we find it stated, at the close of the seven years' war, that "Joshua took the whole land, according to all that the LORD said unto Moses; and Joshua gave it for an inheritance unto Israel according to their divisions by their tribes" (Josh. 11:23).

How perfectly is this type fulfilled in our blessed Lord! To Him as the trustee and representative of His people has all spiritual blessing been given, and He holds it for us to claim. All power is given to Him in heaven and on earth. The Father has given Him to have life in Himself, that He might give us life more abundantly. He is full of grace and truth, that out of His fullness we all may receive. He received of the Father the promise of the Holy Ghost, that he might pour Him forth in Pentecostal fullness.

Let us diligently comprehend all the fullness of our inheritance in Jesus; and then let us go forward to apprehend it by faith. Whatever He has is in trust for us. Let us claim it!

4. EACH WAS MISSED BY MANY. They died in the wilderness so that the generation who cried "Would God that we had died in the wilderness!" did in fact die there.

Such scenes are still witnessed. And the state of His church must be a bitter sorrow to the heart of her Lord. Notwithstanding His agony and bloody sweat, His cross and passion; in spite of the earnest remonstrance of His word and Spirit; and though the fair land of Canaan lies within view—yet so comparatively few appear to have realized what He intended. All around us souls, redeemed by His blood, who have been numbered among His people, are perishing outside the land of blessedness in graves of worldliness, of self-indulgence, and masterful sin. We find here and there a Joshua, a Caleb, or a tribe of Levites. But the majority seem to have come short. See to it, reader, that you are not one of them! "Let us also fear."

5. EACH WAS INFESTED BY MANY ADVERSARIES. The seven nations of Canaan held the land with strongholds and chariots of iron; though the Lord caused them to be to His people as bread, which needs only to be eaten. They came against the invading hosts in all the pride of their vast battalions and the array of their warlike preparations; but at his rebuke they fled, at the voice of his thunder they hasted away.

The "heavenly places" also are not removed from the noise of conflict, or free from the presence of the foe. Those who are raised to sit there in Christ have to encounter the spiritual hosts of wickedness, principalities and powers of evil. They are conquered foes. Nevertheless they are terrible to behold and are certain to overcome, unless we are abiding in our great Joshua who has already vanquished them, and have taken to ourselves the whole armor of God.

Thus the land of Canaan and the heavenly places are one: and we may read into these ancient records the deepest thoughts of the New Testament.

2

The Divine Commission
Joshua 1:7

As Joshua stood on the threshold of his great work, he was repeatedly urged to be strong and of a good courage. Some little time before the death of his predecessor, a great convocation of all Israel had been summoned, at which Moses had solemnly transferred his office to his successor, and had given him a charge, saying, "Be strong and of a good courage; for thou must go with this people unto the land" (Deut. 31:7). And now the voice of God reiterates the charge and repeats the injunction.

At first this startles us. What! must all those whom God uses be strong? Because, if that be so, we who are like Ehud, left-handed; like Gideon, least in our father's house; or like Saul of Tarsus, painfully conscious of weakness, can never get beyond the rank and file in the army of the Lord.

When Moses first received the sentence of death on the other side of Jordan, no one could have been more deeply grieved than his faithful friend and attendant. But the thought of succeeding him never presented itself to his mind.

When therefore the call came to him to assume the office that Moses was vacating, his heart failed him, and he needed every kind of encouragement and stimulus, both from God and man. "Be strong" means that he felt weak; "Be of good courage" means that he was frightened; "Be not thou dismayed" means that he seriously considered whether he would not have to give up the task. He was a worm and no man: how could he deliver Israel?

It is when men are in this condition that God approaches them with the summons to undertake vast and overwhelming responsibilities. Most of us are too strong for Him to use; we are too full of our own schemes, and plans, and ways of doing things. He must empty us, and humble us, and then He will raise us up, and make us as the rod of His strength. The world talks of the survival of the fittest. But God gives power to the faint, and increases might to those who have no strength. He perfects His strength in weakness, and uses things that are not, to bring to nothing things that are.

Let us consider the sources of Joshua's strength.

1. A FAITHFUL PAST. "After the death of Moses the servant of the LORD . . . the LORD spake unto Joshua the son of Nun, Moses' minister" (Josh. 1:1). In his case, as always, the eternal rule held good, that faithfulness in a few things is the condition of rule over many things; and the loyalty of a servant is the stepping stone to the royalty of the throne.

The previous years of Joshua's past had been full of high and noble endeavor. For forty years, if Josephus is correct in his statement as to his age at the death of Moses, he shared the slavery and sorrows of a captive race. As a descendant of one of the leading families of Ephraim (Num. 13:8, 16), he may have taken some leading part in the marshalling of the Exodus, and there approved himself as worthy of all trust. His conflict with Amalek; his good report of the Land of Promise; his refusal to take any part in the disastrous attack on the Canaanites; his eagerness for the good name and fame of Moses; his patient endurance of the weary years of wandering—all prove that his was no common character. This summons of Joshua to the leader's place in Israel was the reward of more than eighty years of faithful service.

None of us can tell for what God is educating us. We fret and murmur at the daily task of ordinary life, not realizing that it is only in this way that we can be prepared for the high and holy office that awaits us. God's will comes to you and me in daily circumstances, in little things equally as in great: dignify the smallest summons by the greatness of your response, so the call will come to you as to Joshua, the son of Nun, Moses' minister.

2. A DISTINCT CALL. "Arise, go over this Jordan, thou, and all this people, unto the land which I do give to them. . . . Be strong and of a good courage: for thou shalt cause this people to inherit the land which I sware unto their fathers to give them." When a

man knows that he has been called to do a certain work, he is invincible. He is not unconscious of his own deficiencies, whether they are natural or intellectual. He is not insensible to difficulty; there are none so quick as he to see the great stones, the iron gates, the walled cities, the broad and flowing rivers. He is not invulnerable to the shafts of ridicule and adverse criticism, but for all these he looks steadily to the declared purpose of God and yields himself to be the channel through which it may operate.

Joshua's task was a difficult one. The people of Canaan were well versed in the arts and sciences of the time, acquired from commerce with the Phoenicians on the north and the Egyptians on the south. It seemed preposterous to suppose that a nation of a few years' existence was so soon to dispossess nations that had gained the country by conquest and were prepared to fight for every inch of territory by the most approved methods of warfare. It is clear that the reiterated assurance of God to settle Israel with his help must have been a great source of strength to him.

3. THE SENSE OF THE PRESENCE OF GOD. "As I was with Moses, so I will be with thee: I will not fail thee, nor forsake thee." There was one particular in which Joshua would always come far behind his great predecessor. Both were in necessary and constant communication with God, but Joshua had to seek counsel through the high priest, whereas Moses had enjoyed direct intercourse with God, speaking to Him "face to face, as a man speaketh unto his friend" (Exod. 33:11). Still, Joshua, the son of Nun, was equally sure of the personal companionship of his great ally, though he lacked the direct vision.

All through the arduous campaign that followed, nothing could daunt Joshua's courage while that assurance was ever ringing in his memory: "I will be with thee."

4. THE INDWELLING OF THE WORD OF GOD. "This book of the law shall not depart out of thy mouth; but thou shalt meditate therein day and night." We must meditate on the words of God because it is through the Word of God that the Spirit of God comes in fullness to be the mighty occupant of our inner man. This, after all, is the secret of strength—to be possessed of the strong Son of God, strengthened by His indwelling might, and filled by His Spirit.

We can do all things when Christ is in us in unthwarted power. The only limit lies in our faith and capacity or, in other words, in our absolute submission to His indwelling. Our risen Lord is charged with power.

Be strong in your weakness through the strengthening might of Christ. Take weakness, weariness, faintheartedness, and difficulty into His presence; they will melt as frost in the sun. You will make your way prosperous, and have good success; and you will lead a nation to inherit the Land of Promise.

3

Three Days' Pause
Joshua 1:11; 2

The whole land of Canaan was Israel's by deed of gift. As soon as Lot had separated from Abraham, choosing all the plain of Jordan, and pitching his tent toward Sodom, the Lord drew near His faithful servant, assuring him that He would not allow him to lose by his magnanimity. "The LORD made a covenant with Abram saying, Unto thy seed *have I given this land*, from the river of Egypt unto the great river, the river Euphrates" (Gen. 15:18).

But though this was so, each square mile of it had to be claimed from the hand of the people who possessed it. "The sole of the foot" had to be put down to claim and take. It is not difficult for us to realize these things, for spiritually we occupy precisely a similar position. God our Father has blessed us with all spiritual blessings in Christ Jesus, but they are not ours to enjoy until we have claimed and appropriated them by a living faith. They are ours only as we avail ourselves of them. Hence the need to "be strong and very courageous."

But now a new and unexpected delay took place. A three days' pause was called for. The officers informed the people that three days had to go by before they could go in to possess the land that the Lord their God was giving them to possess.

1. WHAT THIS PAUSE MEANT. "Three days" is a recognized period in Scripture for death and resurrection. It was therefore appropriate that this period should elapse before the people could pass through symbolic death over to resurrection ground.

But there was another and deeper reason for the delay, which closely touches one of the greatest principles of the inner life. When Israel reached its banks, the Jordan was in flood and was overflowing the low-lying lands on either side of its bed. It was the time of "the swellings of Jordan," which years later was employed as an expression for overwhelming trouble. Before the gaze of the assembled hosts, the turbid floods rushed on, swollen by melting snows from far away Mount Hermon, and carrying trunks of trees and other débris torn from the banks in their impetuous descent.

Across the river stood Jericho, enclosed by palms and tamarisks, in a very paradise of exquisite vegetation, with its aromatic shrubs and gardens scenting the air. But as the people beheld it, all their cherished hopes of taking it by their own energy or courage must have been utterly dissipated. What could they do in face of that broad expanse of rushing, foaming, turbulent waters? The Jordan, on the page of Scripture, is constantly associated with death—not the death of the body; but that baptism into death that signifies a pause in the energies of nature, and an entrance through faith on a higher and nobler level. But never in all its history did the Jordan more effectually pronounce the sentence of death than on that day when it taught the people that by no strength or energy of their own could they prevail.

Multitudes have come to the brink of that river, and have been left there, waiting on its banks, that they might consider the meaning of those impassable waters, and carry away the sentence of death in themselves.

What a marvelous expression concerning the faith of Abraham!—"And being not weak in faith, he considered not his own body dead . . . yet the deadness of Sarah's womb" (Rom. 4:19). Not many could have stood such considerations long without losing all the faith they ever possessed. There was one secret, however, that sustained him. He looked to the promise of God. Turning from the one to the other, he did not waver. These are the only conditions on which the vision of the river will not hurt us; if only we turn from it to the presence of the Captain of the Lord's host, and to the covenant that is ordered in all things and sure. Then we will continue strong through faith, and be fully assured that what God has promised He is able also to perform.

2. HOW THIS PAUSE WAS SPENT. During this space of three days, events transpired that are both interesting and typical. Among other things Jericho was entered by the two spies.

a. *Jericho may rightly stand for the world of men over which judgment is impending, but which goes on its way unheeding.* Within two weeks a blow was to fall from which the city would not rally for centuries.

The majority of the people were either bent on stubborn resistence, or boasted about their river and their walls. Their iniquity was full. But there was one soul in their midst who was capable of faith, and was already exercising it. And He who had nurtured Rahab, and led her to the point she had reached, was bent on perfecting what He had begun, and on leading her into the fullest light that that age possessed. This is ever God's way. Wherever there is a Rahab who, amid much sin and ignorance, is living up to the truth she has, and longs for more, God will take her hand and lead her to Himself.

Two references are made in the New Testament to Rahab's faith (Heb. 11:31; James 2:25). It was true faith, though it was exercised toward only a fragment of the truth. All that Rahab knew was that God had delivered His people from Pharaoh, and had promised to give them that land. She believed it, and it was counted to her for righteousness. And the evidences of her faith were quick to follow. She identified herself with Israel by the scarlet thread. She gathered her family under her roof; yet she was commended to the care of Israel and became a link in the ancestry of the Son of Man.

Rahab, the poor outcast of Jericho, who had this strange faith in God, entered in with the people to possess the land that flowed with milk and honey. She is thus the type of gentile sinners who are permitted to share in the unsearchable riches of Christ; to sit with Him in the heavenlies; to form part of that new race that is gathering around the true Joshua, the Lord from heaven. So then we are no more strangers or sojourners, but fellow-citizens with the saints, and of the household of God. Only let us avail ourselves of our heritage!

b. *During this brief pause Joshua also had an opportunity to determine the feelings of the two and a half tribes.* He discovered that they were fully prepared to discharge the obligation into which they had entered with Joshua, and to march with the other tribes to the conquest of Canaan. But they were equally set on returning to the rich pasturelands of Gilead and Bashan, which Moses gave them beyond the Jordan, toward the east. They had "much cattle" (Num. 32:2, 4, 19, 33).

Are not these the type of Christians to whom the Land of Promise is as freely open as to others, and who make an incursion into it with no thought of remaining? Are there not among us those who have spent seven years in the Land of Promise, and have had hallowed experiences of blessedness, rest, and power; but who have been swept off their feet and have been pulled back by the receding tide of worldliness?

The end of such is but too clearly suggested by the fate of those Eastern tribes. They had their much grass; but they gradually became cut off from the corporate life of Israel. They gave few great names to the roll of saints and heroes emblazoned on Israel's story. They were the first to fall beneath the invasions of Assyria, and were swept into captivity from which they never returned.

3. HOW THE PAUSE ENDED. On the third day the hosts seem to have come nearer the river's brink, and their tents were pitched for the night in close proximity to the rapid waters. It was then that Joshua said to the people, "Sanctify yourselves: for tomorrow

the LORD will do wonders among you." From this it would seem that the wonder-working power of God is dependent on the sanctification of His people. When we ask the old question, "Why art Thou as a mighty man that cannot save?" we get the answer that shows that *we* are to blame for the divine impotence, "He could do no mighty work there, because of their unbelief" (Matt. 13:58).

If only we would all sanctify ourselves, putting off the old man with his deeds, and putting on the new man, renewed daily in the image of Christ, we would find that wonders would begin and never cease; that the tomorrows would only unfold greater and better things than ever before; that Jordans would cleave, and Jerichos would fall. Then the Land of Promise would lie open with its immeasurable plenty, its oil and wine, its corn and honey, its precious, priceless stores.

4

Passing the Jordan
Joshua 3:10

There were several reasons why it was needful for God to drive out the seven nations that dwelled in Canaan. But the chief among them stands that suggested by the memorable interview held between Jehovah and Abraham, the ancestor of the chosen race, four centuries before—the iniquity of the Amorite was now full (Gen. 15:16).

In the first place, the nations of Canaan had given themselves to *the most abominable immorality*. The destruction of the people by the sword of Israel was only the hastening of the natural results of their shameful vice. The reasons that necessitated the deluge of water necessitated this deluge of blood. Plague spot as it was, Canaan would have infected the world had it not been passed through the fire.

In the second place, the Canaanites were *steeped in spiritualism*, and held close communications with the demons of the air, which have always been forbidden to men. When man opens a passage of communication with the fallen spirits around him, he exposes himself to God's direst wrath; and for the sake of the race these black arts must be stopped.

And this last thought gives a new complexion to this conflict. In driving out and destroying these demoralized races, God was in effect waging war with the evil spirits, who from their seat in the heavenlies were ruling the darkness of that land. And thus this old record is invested with a new interest. It is not simply the story of the conquest of Canaan, but it is a fragment from the chronicles of heaven, giving an episode in the eternal conflict between light and darkness, between heaven and hell. What an interesting additional analogy between the Book of Joshua and the Epistle to the Ephesians!

God graciously granted a sign of the ultimate issue of the war, so that through the seven years of coming conflict the people of Israel could be at rest as to the result. "Hereby ye shall know that the living God is among you, and that he will without fail drive out from before you the Canaanites, and the Hittites, and the Hivites, and the Perizzites, and the Girgashites, and the Amorites, and the Jebusites. Behold, the ark of the covenant of the Lord of all the earth passeth over before you into Jordan." The passage of the turbulent waters of Jordan was to be the heaven-appointed sign.

1. THE PASSAGE OF THE JORDAN. At the close of the three days of preparation there seems to have been a movement of the camp from Shittim, with its acacia groves, to a spot within a mile of the boisterous rush of the swollen floods. There Israel spent the last memorable night of pilgrimage and wandering. As the dawn broke, the officers again passed through the host, and bade the people watch and follow the movements of the ark. Only a short interval elapsed before the congregation pulled up their slight black tents, packed up their household goods, and adjusted their burdens, and stood in one great host, two and a half million strong, prepared to tread the untried path. The sun was rising behind them, its beams flashing on the Jordan, a mile of water wide, and setting in bold relief the white walls of the houses of Jericho; while all the adjacent hills of Canaan stood around veiled in morning mist, or robed in the exquisite garments of light.

At last the little group emerged from those densely-crowded hosts. It was the chosen band of priests, white-robed, barefooted, who slowly descended the terraced bank of the river, bearing on their shoulders the sacred ark, its golden lid and bending cherubim hidden beneath their covering of blue. How awesome the silence! How fixed the gaze that followed their every step! How hushed the wisecracks and the loud denials of the previous days that protested that the passage was impossible; and that it would be wiser to wait until the mile of water had dwindled to the normal width of thirty yards when the stream was four or six feet deep, and easily fordable!

Nearer the little procession came; but even when it was within a yard of the river brink its approach effected nothing. The waters showed no disposition to flee or fail. But when the feet of the priests touched the tiny wavelets, brown with mud, a marvelous change took place. They began to divide and shrink away. And as the priests pursued them, descending ever further toward the midst of Jordan, they fled before them as if panic-stricken. Nothing could account for so great a wonder except the presence of the God of Jacob, and that the ark of the covenant of the Lord of all the earth was passing through those depths.

Up the river some thirty miles, at Adam, the city that is beside Zaretan, the flow of the river had suddenly stopped, and the waters, unable to hurry forward, gathered into a heap and probably formed a vast lake that spread itself for miles. From that point and downward, the waters, no longer supplied from above, began to fail; they hurried toward the Sea of Death, and were swallowed up in its dark unwholesome depths. "They were wholly cut off." As there were none to follow, the river bed for miles was dry; and the people, hurrying down the bank, "hastened and passed over." The feet of the priests stood firm until every individual of the redeemed race had crossed the river.

And this was the promised sign, for He who could drive out the waters would drive out their foes. Having done so much, He would perfect that which He had begun.

2. THE TYPICAL SIGNIFICANCE OF THIS PASSAGE. "There shall be a space between you and [the ark]." Yes, the Lord Jesus preceded His church. He first passed through the grave in resurrection power. "Every man in his own order: Christ the firstfruits, afterward they that are Christ's" (1 Cor. 15:23). In all things, and therefore in this also, He must have the preeminence. "The priests that bare the ark of the covenant of the LORD stood firm . . . until all the people were passed clean over Jordan."

The waters of judgment may be accumulating for all who cling to the old Adam-stock, but they can never slip from their leash until every trembling laggard soul that will has passed into blessed rest. You may be young, or crippled, or ready to stop, or much afraid, but if you will but cast in your lot with the host of the ransomed, the Priest will lengthen out the dispensation, and hold the waters back for you.

3. THE BEARING OF THIS PASSAGE ON CHRISTIAN EXPERIENCE.

a. *We have already seen the effect produced on death by the death of the Lord Jesus.* It is appointed unto man *once* to die. And since we have died in Him, we shall find death robbed of its terrors. The darkness of the valley is only that of a shadow, but this is not all. By virtue of our union with Him, we have passed through death on to resurrection ground, and have become "the children of the resurrection." It is on this fact in our spiritual history that the apostles base many of their most powerful arguments and appeals. "How shall we that are dead to sin, live any longer therein?" (Rom. 6:2). "Forasmuch then as Christ hath suffered for us in the flesh, arm yourselves likewise with the same mind: for he that hath suffered in the flesh hath ceased from sin; that he no longer should live the rest of his time in the flesh to the lusts of men, but to the will of God" (1 Peter 4:1–2).

b. *With this truth we can foil the most enticing fascinations of the world.* We have passed out of it with our dear Lord. We have become citizens of the new Jerusalem, and if we still move amid the world's engagements, it is in the garb of strangers and foreigners—men from the other side of the river who speak the language and wear the attire of the heavenly Canaan—the language, *love;* the attire, *the white raiment,* pure and clean, washed in the blood of the Lamb.

There is no hope that we shall be able to cope with these things by any might or wisdom of our own. The opposition of that relative; the hatred of that persecutor; the strength of that passion; the tyranny of that habit; the untowardness of our circumstances—these are our Jordan. How easy life would be if only these were other than they are! Give me Canaan without its Jordan! But God permits the Jordans that He may educate our faith. Do not look at the troubled waters rushing past; but at the Priest, who is also the ark of the covenant.

When you come to the dreaded difficulty, be what it may, you will find that because his feet have been dipped in its brink, it has dwindled in its flow. Its roar is hushed; its waters are shrunken; its violence is gone. The iron gate stands open. The stone is rolled from the sepulcher. The river bed is dry. Jericho is within reach. "They passed clean over Jordan."

5

The Stones of Gilgal
Joshua 4:5

On the western side of Jordan, to which the host of Israel had now come, five miles from the river brink, the terraced banks reached their highest point. That was Gilgal. There the first camp was pitched, on the edge of a vast grove of majestic palms, nearly three miles broad and eight miles long, that stretched away to Jericho. In the midst of this forest could have been seen, reaching through its open spaces, fields of ripe corn, "for it was the time of the barley harvest"; and above the topmost trees you could see the high walls and towers of the city on the farther side, which from that grove derived its proud name, "Jericho, the City of Palms."

Gilgal was the base of operations in the war against the people of Canaan. There the camp remained, with the women and children (9:6; 10:6). It ranked with Mizpeh and Bethel among the holy places where Samuel exercised his sacred office (1 Sam. 7:16). It was the rallying point to which the people gathered at solemn times of national crisis (11:14). Saul had reason to remember it; and there Agag was hewed in pieces "before the LORD."

Probably to the last of the events and beyond, the twelve stones that had been pitched by Joshua as the lasting memorial of the passage of the river were visible.

At the time when the book was written, the other heap of stones, laid in the river bed, must have been clearly discernible when the stream, temporarily swollen by the spring floods, had retreated to its normal width (4:9); and there could have been no difficulty in fixing the hill of circumcision where, at the command of God, they had rolled away the reproach of Egypt, and from which the name Gilgal, or Rolling, was derived (5:9).

Gilgal was from the first "holy ground" (5:15); and as we traverse it again in devout thought, it will also give us themes for deep and holy meditation.

1. THE STONES ON THE BANK. At the divine bidding twelve men, one out of each tribe, went down into the river's bed. From the place where the priests' feet stood firm in Jordan, each man took a stone. For centuries these stones had laid there undisturbed; but now, piled together in a heap before the eyes of all men, they were to be a memorial of the passage of Jordan, as the song of Moses was of the passage through the Red Sea.

It is well that forgetful hearts like ours should be stirred up by way of remembrance. We are so apt to grow unmindful of the Rock that begot us, and to forget the God who gave us birth. Therefore it was necessary that these memorial stones be erected beside our Jordans, with their inscription, "Wherefore remember."

Consider those twelve stones on the further side of Jordan, and be sure that as they represented the entire people, and commemorated their marvelous transportation from the one side of Jordan to the other, so, in the New Jerusalem, the twelve foundation-stones bearing the names of the apostles, and the twelve gates inscribed with the names of the twelve tribes of Israel, are a standing memorial that the church as a whole is on resurrection ground; but her shame and sorrow are that she has not availed herself of her lofty privileges, or descended to earth girded with the power of the risen, living Jesus.

We have crossed the River. Our eternity is begun. In Jesus we are loved and accepted. We are more than conquerors; we occupy a position which, if we would only keep it, is unassailable by our foes. They can prevail only against us when they succeed in attempting us to abandon it. All things are ours in union with our raised and reigning Lord.

2. THE STONES IN THE BED OF THE STREAM. Not content with pitching a pile of stones on the river's bank, Joshua, at God's command, set up twelve stones in the midst of Jordan, in the place where the feet of the priests that carried the ark of the covenant stood. And often, as he came back to Gilgal, he must have gone out by himself to walk and meditate beside the river, turning the outward and the inward gaze to the spot where beneath the

flow of the current those stones lay hidden. They were the lasting memorial of the miracle that otherwise might have faded from memory, or seemed incredible. They were aids to faith. Where they lay the people had been, and the feet of the priests had been planted dry. And surely the power that had arrested the Jordan, and brought the people up from its bed, would not fail until it had worked out the whole purpose of God.

3. THE RITE OF CIRCUMCISION. Israel looked for nothing less than to be led from the river brink to the conquest and partition of the land. They suddenly discovered, however, that this was not quite the divine program for them. But they were required to submit to a painful rite, the seal of the covenant that was made originally to Abraham, and by virtue of which the land had been given to him and to his seed (Gen. 17:8–10).

During the wanderings of the desert—which were due to their unbelief, and practically disinherited them—the observance of this rite had been stopped because the operation of the covenant was for the time in suspense. But now that the new young nation was learning to exercise its faith, the covenant and its seal was again put into operation. "Their children, whom he raised up in their stead, them Joshua circumcised."

Even those comparatively unenlightened people must have realized that there was deep spiritual significance in the administration of that rite at that juncture. On more than one occasion they had heard Moses speak of circumcising the heart; and they must have felt that God meant to teach them the vanity of trusting to their numbers, or prowess, or martial array. The land was not to be won by their might, but to be taken from His hand as a gift. Self and the energy of the flesh had to be set aside that the glory of coming victory might be of God, and not of man.

We too must have our Gilgal. It is not enough to acknowledge as a general principle that we are dead and risen with Christ; we must apply it to our inner and outer life. If we died with Christ, we have to mortify our members, which are on the earth. The first effect of our appreciation of the meaning of Christ's death will be our application of that death to our members that are on the earth. We have no warrant to say that sin is dead, or that the principle of sin is eradicated; but we can say that we are dead to it in our standing, and are dead to it also in the reckoning of faith.

There is a sense in which all believers have been circumcised in Christ, but there is another sense in which it is needful for them to pass one after another through the circumcision of Christ that is not made with hands, and that consists in the putting off of the body of the flesh. To that all who would lead a life of victory and inherit the Land of Promise must submit. The process may be sharp, for the knife does not spare pain. But it is in the hands of Jesus, the lover of souls. Do not shrink from it! Let Him do all that He deems needful, though it may take many days before the wound is healed. And though it might appear that the circumcised life will always be a maimed life, it is not really so; the contrary is the universal testimony of this book. When the hand is cut off, we go maimed *into life*. When we mortify the deeds of the body, we begin to live. When the Lord our God has circumcised our hearts, then we love Him with all our heart and with all our soul—and we live.

You can never take Jericho, Christian worker, until you have been circumcised, until God has taken away your self-reliance, and has brought you down into the dust of death. Then, when the sentence of death is in you, you will begin to experience the energy of the divine life, the glory of the divine victory.

6

Three Successive Days
Joshua 5:10–12

In one of his sonnets, Matthew Arnold tells of an interview he had on a day of fierce August sunshine, in Spitalfields, with a preacher whom he knew, and who looked ill and overworked. In answer to the inquiry as to how he fared. "Bravely," he said, "for I of late have been much cheered with thoughts of Christ the *Living Bread.*" He is not the only human soul who, above the ebb and flow of London storm and tumult, has set up a mark of everlasting light to cheer, and to light its course through the night.

In this old record we may discover without effort the Living Bread under three aspects—the Passover; the corn of the land; the manna. Each of these was associated with one of three successive days.

1. THE PASSOVER. The Passover itself could never be repeated. But the Feast of the Passover, held in commemoration of that event, was destined to perpetual repetition until it gave place to a yet more significant symbol; which, in turn, is to fade into the marriage supper as the love of betrothal fades into that of marriage.

The Feast of the Passover was held at Sinai, but it was not held again until the forty years had elapsed. In fact, it could not be held while the nation, through unbelief and disobedience, was untrue to the covenant. Had it not been distinctly affirmed, amid other provisions, that no uncircumcised person should eat of it? But as soon as the circumcising of the people was completed there was no longer a barrier; and the Passover was kept between "the two evenings," as the sun of the fourteenth day of the month was flinging toward them long shadows from the palm trees and walls of Jericho.

There were two significant parts of the Passover as it was first instituted. First was the sprinkling of blood on the doors without. Second, the family gathered around the roasted lamb, eating it in haste. As years went on and conditions altered however, blood was no longer sprinkled on the lintel and door posts, but the drinking of wine was substituted for that ancient and significant act. And the family gathered around the table to the sacred feast, not merely with the girded loin and staff in hand as befitted pilgrims, but with the leisured restfulness of home. In point of fact it was a family meal at which the people reviewed the past with thankfulness, and talked together of that mercy that had been so remarkably displayed in their national history. On reaching the Land of Promise, the thoughts of the people were guided back to the great fact of redemption by blood that lay at the basis of their existence.

The other side of the Passover has also a counterpart in our experience. The Israelites feasted, they drank the light Eastern wine, and years later they chanted the Hallel and ate of the flesh of the lamb. The bread was unleavened and the herbs bitter, but joy exceeded sorrow. And this is the type of Christian life.

The Lord's Supper is not simply a memorial of what He did on Calvary, or is doing on the throne; it is a perpetual reminder to the believing heart of its privilege and duty to eat the flesh and drink the blood of the Son of Man in a spiritual way. We must eat His flesh or we will have no life in us. We must drink His blood or we will not dwell in Him, or He in us.

229

But let us always remember that as no uncircumcised person was permitted to partake of the Passover, so none who are living in willful sin can feed on the flesh and blood that were given for the life of the world. There must be a Gilgal before there can be a Passover in the deepest and fullest sense.

2. THE CORN OF THE LAND. "And they did eat of the old corn of the land on the morrow after the passover." There is no need for the adjective *old*. It would be sufficient to say that they ate of the corn of the land, though it is likely that it was the corn of the previous harvest, and not that which was then ripening throughout the land of Canaan, and ready for the sickle. The main point is that, with great thankfulness, the Israelites, the majority of whom had never tasted anything but manna, ate of the produce of the Land of Promise.

Is it not significant that on this very day the Lord Jesus arose from the dead, "the firstfruits of them that slept"? Surely, then, it is no straining of the parallel to say that the corn of the Land of Promise represents Him in risen glory. He fell as a seed of corn into the ground to die, but through death He has acquired the power of imparting Himself to all who believe. He was bruised, as all bread corn must be—the wheel of the cart of divine justice ground Him beneath its weight—but He has become thereby as the finest of the wheat to feed the needs of the world. We must feed on the Paschal Lamb and learn the full meaning of his cross and passion, His precious death and burial; but we must also feed on the corn of the heavenly land, and derive life and blessing from His glorious resurrection and ascension.

The church has in some measure learned to appreciate the importance of the Incarnation and Crucifixion. But it is comparatively seldom that we hear in treatise or sermon any adequate treatment of the Ascension from the lowest parts of the earth to that zenith point of glory from which He fills all things. Oh, to know what Paul meant by his emphasis when he said, *"yea rather*, that is risen again"; and to understand his thinking when he said that though he had known Christ after the flesh, he wished to know Him so no more, because he longed to understand the power of His resurrection. The Paschal Lamb is good; but the corn of the land includes the fruits, and honey, and bread-stuffs that grow on the soil of the resurrection life.

The ascension of Christ may be considered in many aspects. The majesty and triumph of the God-man, as He is raised far above all principality and power, whether of angels or of demons, and above every name that is named, whether in this world or that which is to come; the certainty that the same power that raised Him from the grave to the right hand of the Father waits to do as much for each of us; the belief that in His ascension He has received gifts for each of us, and the best of all gifts, the fullness of the Spirit, is for us to claim and receive. These are themes that stir our sluggish hearts and make them leap with gladness, which no increase of corn or wine can yeild to the men of this world. Happy indeed are they who also in heart and mind ascend, and *with Him dwell continually*. To do this is to eat of the corn and fruit of the land.

3. THE MANNA. "And the manna ceased on the morrow after they had eaten of the old corn of the land." There was no break between the two. The corn began before the manna ceased. The one overlapped the other as the thatch of a haystack or the feathers of a bird.

God does not desire that there should be those intervals of apparent desertion and the failure of supplies of which so many complain. It is likely that He may have to withdraw the extraordinary and exceptional, as represented by the manna; but He will wait until we have become accustomed to the ordinary and regular supplies of His grace, as represented by the corn.

We are constantly being forced from the familiar manna that came without anxiety or seeking on our part, to the corn that requires foresight and careful preparation. This is needful because in these we learn invaluable lessons of patience, and self-denial, and cooperation with God. But how we first shrink from the change!

How gracious then is the gentle, thoughtful kindness of God, who lets us see the new before He takes away the old. He allows us to become accustomed to walking before He removes the chair on which we had leaned so long.

This, then, is our main lesson. We must learn to live in such a way as to be nourished with the life of the Son of God. When we eat of Christ, we live by Him, as He lived by the Father; and as the Father, dwelling in Him, worked through His life, and did His wondrous works, so He, entering into us—the Word by His words—will do through us what had otherwise been impossible.

Do you long for more strength to do or suffer, to witness or turn the foe from the gate? Then feed on Christ, meditating on His word, communing with Him, filled by His Spirit, who takes of the things that are His and reveals them to us. "Blessed are they that hunger and thirst; they shall be filled." "He hath filled the hungry with good things." "Bread that strengtheneth man's heart."

7

The Warrior Christ
Joshua 5:13–15

"It came to pass." The time and exact location are not defined, but they are not that important in the presence of that marvelous episode that stands before the conquest of Canaan. As to the time, it was probably the day in which the manna had ceased, and the leader had realized that the land must now furnish what was needed. As to the place, it is enough to know that it was *by Jericho*.

Behind lay the Jordan, the furrow made by the passage of the host no longer discernible; though the fresh heap of memorial stones proclaimed the miracle of the dried river bed. Beneath, under the shadow of the hill, lay the camp, where the people were resting from their weariness, in the first glad realization that their long journeyings were ended. While five miles away, on the path to Canaan, towering above the palm groves, arose the strongly fortified walls of Jericho.

It must have been for Joshua, at least, a time of anxious suspense. It had been comparatively easy to cope with Amalek, and Og, and Sihon, because they had met Israel in open war upon the field of battle; but that was a different matter from attacking a city that was able to hold its own in a long siege. It was impossible to leave it in the rear, unsubdued, but it was also suicidal to sit down before it to starve it to surrender. As the weary months dragged on, the energy of the people would evaporate, and the armies of their foes would gather. Eagerly must the lonely chieftain have longed for one moment with Moses or, better still, with that Angel of the Presence of God, who had been promised when the camp was still pitched beneath the cliffs of Sinai.

Thinking much and deeply, Joshua wandered forth alone, and suddenly, "as he lifted up his eyes and looked, behold, there stood a man over against him with his sword drawn in his hand."

But who was this man? Joshua didn't know; but his heart was pure and clear, and therefore he did not hesitate to go up to him and challenge him with the inquiry, "Art thou for us, or for our adversaries?" Then came the majestic reply, "Nay; but as captain of the host of the LORD am I now come."

We cannot doubt who He was. Though bearing the semblance of a man, He was certainly neither man nor angel. We have to believe that He who spoke to Joshua on the threshold of Canaan was none other than Jehovah, the God of Israel, whose delights, long before the Incarnation, were with the sons of men, and who anticipated it by paying preliminary visits to our earth in corporeal form.

1. THE SPECIAL SIGNIFICANCE OF THIS VISION TO JOSHUA. It has been generally supposed that this divine Captain came to take Joshua's place in command, and to assume the supreme direction of the hosts of Israel; but that is not the deepest meaning here. "The LORD'S host" does not primarily allude to those Israelite armies encamped beside the overflowing waters of the Jordan, but to other and invisible hosts. Those troops of harnessed angels were the hosts of which this wondrous warrior was Captain.

There are several references in Scripture to the presence, near at hand, of angel-hosts. It is therefore in harmony with the tenor of Scripture to see those lines of warriors waiting within the curtains of the unseen to be led against the foes of God and Israel. And we read a new meaning into the ancient phrase, by which Jehovah became known. "Who is the King of glory?" "The LORD of hosts, he is the King of glory."

Is it therefore any cause for wonder that the walls of Jericho fell down, or that vast armies were scattered, without a blow being struck; or that the land was subdued in a campaign of seven years? These achievements were the earthly and visible results of victories won in the heavenly and spiritual sphere by armies that follow the Word of God on white horses, clothed in fine linen, white and pure. Those walls fell down because they were smitten by the impact of celestial hosts. Those armies fled because the dark powers with which they were in league had been put to the rout before the Lord God of Sabaoth. There was therefore deep significance in the words with which Caleb had sought to encourage his people forty years before. "Their defence is departed from them, and the LORD is with us: fear them not" (Num. 14:9). And we can better understand what the Lord meant when He said, "As captain of the host of the LORD am I now come."

2. THE SIGNIFICANCE OF THIS VISION TO THE CHURCH. Throughout the world of nature there are signs of conflict and collision. Everywhere armies meet in battle, and part to repair their losses or count their gains. The invisible molecules of the calmest air are in rapid motion all around us, jostling with each other, and fighting hard to keep their course, but they are hindered by a thousand kindred molecules that are fighting too, so that we move and work in a cyclone of whirling atoms. There is no pool, however tranquil; no forest glade, however peaceful; no island bathed by southern seas and set gem-like on the breast of ocean, however enchanting; no scene, however fascinating,

which is not swept by opposing squadrons contending for victory. The swift pursue their prey; the strong devour the weak; the fittest alone survive in the terrific strife.

For the student of God's ways all this leads up to a more tremendous struggle, between darkness and light, evil and good, Satan and our King. All through His earthly ministry our Lord encountered the dark powers. But the life and death of the man Christ Jesus turned the tide. And when He arose and ascended, it became established beyond a doubt that, though man in himself was no match for hell, yet man in Christ, in union with the Son of God, was more than a conqueror; he was able to do all things through Him who strengthens him, and is destined to overcome.

How sad that this truth has been so little appreciated! The church of Christ has too often either considered that she contained within herself all the resources necessary for victory over the evil of the world; or she stood paralyzed or aghast before the Jerichos of sin that have risen up to obstruct her path. The fenced cities of drink and lust, of self-indulgence or apathy, have refused to open their gates to her challenge, and have laughed defiance to her hosts. Then she has appealed to Caesar—to human methods, and alliances, and expedients. But in vain, for notwithstanding all, the walls have not fallen down, nor have her foes left her.

The saints of God have need to repent of their sins and failures in this direction. Let them realize that the Captain of the celestial hosts has already led His squadrons against their foes and His. Let them put away all that would imperil or impair the alliance. Let them raise a modification of the old battle cry, which was originally based on an acknowledgment of this great spiritual fact, and charge with the shout, "The sword of the Lord and of his people."

3. THE SIGNIFICANCE OF THIS VISION TO US. We sometimes feel lonely and discouraged. The hosts with which we are accustomed to cooperate are resting quietly in their tents. No one seems able to enter into our anxieties and plans. Our Jerichos are so formidable—the neglected parish; the empty church; the hardened congregation; the godless household. How can we ever capture these and hand them over to the Lord like dismantled castles for Him to occupy?

But in our hours of disappointment, when we have tried our best in vain, and have fallen—as the birds of the sea that dash themselves against the lighthouse tower fall to the foot with broken wing—it is well to go forth alone, confessing our helplessness, and waiting for the vision, for then we will be likeliest to see the Captain of the Lord's host. He will undertake our cause; He will marshal His troops and win the day; He will fling the walls of Jericho to the ground. Our cooperation may be employed, but only to walk around the walls, in the garb of priestly purity, and to blow the rams' horns.

But we must be holy, if we would cooperate with Him. We must put off the old man, with his affections and lusts; we must cleanse ourselves from all filthiness of the flesh and spirit; we must cast off the works of darkness, and array ourselves in the panoply of light.

The battle is not to the strong, nor the race to the swift; but each to those who are living lives separate from the world and dedicated to God. The vessels that are meet for the Master's use are pure ones. Cleanness, rather than cleverness, is the prime condition of successful service. May there be no partition between God's holiness and ours! Nothing to insulate us or shut off the current!

8

The Walls of Jericho
Joshua 6

Jericho was filled with faintheartedness. There was no issuing forth of the men of war; no sudden night attack on that hose that lay along the Jordan bank, the brown tents pitched around the central pavilion or tabernacle of God. It was as though some mysterious spell had fallen on king and people, unnerving them, impelling them to stand on the defensive and await the unfolding of events. "Their heart melted, neither was there spirit in them any more, because of the children of Israel."

Israel, on the other hand, was probably impatient, eager to be led to the conflict. The men of war, confident in their might, were eager to match themselves against the inhabitants of the land and to wipe out in blood the memory of their fathers' defeat at Hormah. Conscious that the passage of the Jordan had been due to the presence of the priests, it may have been that there was a secret desire in their hearts to show that the time had come for the priests to stand aside, while they approved their prowess and won the land by might.

But they had to learn that the land was a gift, to be received by faith, not won by effort. God required of them only to obey, and wait, and trust, while the divine Captain led His celestial hosts to the assault and achieved the victory. "And the Lord said unto Joshua, See, I have given into thine hand Jericho, and the king thereof, and the mighty men of valour. And ye shall compass the city, all ye men of war, and go round about the city once."

It certainly was the strangest spectacle ever witnessed by a beleaguered garrison. The besiegers did not make an assault, or rear mounds, or place scaling ladders againt the walls. Nor did they afford an opportunity for parley or discussion of terms of capitulation. On each side it seems to have been understood that the war would be to the knife—no quarter asked, no mercy shown. Without delay the host of Israel began encompassing the city.

It was but a little after dawn. The sun had mounted not far above the eastern horizon. Then from out of the camp of Israel a long procession began to unwind itself. First the men of war, marching beneath their tribal banners; then seven priests, white-robed, blowing with seven trumpets of rams' horns; next the ark of God, hidden by its coverings from the gaze of Israelite and Canaanite alike; and last the tribe of Dan, bringing up the rear.

Toward the city this strange procession made its way, preserving an absolute silence, except that the priests went on continually and blew with the trumpets. With that exception no other sound was heard. No challenge! No taunt! No cry as of those who shout for mastery! The entire host wound silently around the city as a serpent, and when the circuit was completed, to the surprise of the Canaanites, who probably expected an immediate assault, it returned quietly to the camp from which it had emerged some hour or two before. And the rest of the day passed without further incident. "So they did six days."

On the seventh day, the circuit of the walls was repeated seven times. And at the close of the seventh, Joshua's voice rang out on the still evening air the command, "Shout, for the LORD hath given you the city." Then the priests blew a blast on the trumpets; the people shouted with a great shout that reverberated through the hills around, and was perhaps answered by the feebler voices of the women and children from the camp; and the wall of Jericho fell down to the ground, so that the people could go up into the city, "and they took the city."

In various directions we may find a counterpart of this remarkable incident.

1. IN CHRISTIAN EXPERIENCE. If Egypt represents our conflicts with the world, and Amalek our conflict with the flesh, the seven nations of Canaan represent our conflict with the principalities and powers of wicked spirits who resist our entrance into the heavenlies and dull our practical realization of what Christ has wrought for us. Entrenched behind the ramparts of some stronghold of difficulty or habit, they defy us and threaten to arrest our progress in the divine life. Who is there among us, or who reads these lines, who does not know, or has not known, of something—a cherished indulgence, a friendship, a pernicious entanglement—reared as an impassable barrier to the enjoyment of those blessed possibilities of Christian experience which are ours in Christ, but which for that reason seem beyond our reach? That thing is a Jericho.

Again, it may be asked, who is there who has not stood, at some period or another, before a Jericho, right in the pass to Canaan? To all such there is comfort in the word spoken by the great Captain to Joshua, standing with bared foot on the holy ground, "See, I have given into thine hand Jericho, and the king thereof, and the mighty men of valour."

a. *Be still!* The hardest of all commandments is this! That our voice should not be heard; that no word should proceed from our mouth; that we should utter our complaints to God alone—all this is foreign to our habits and taste.

It is only the still heart that can reflect the heaven of God's over-arching care. Only when we have quieted ourselves as weaned babes can we reach that position in which God can interpose for our help. "Be still," says God, "and know that I am God." And that soul may well be still and wait, which has learned that the Lord of hosts is beside it, and the God of Jacob its refuge. To that Friend it hastens to pour out its secret agony. In that home it nestles as in the cover of a great rock, sheltered from the blast.

b. *Obey!* As in this story so in grace, there must be cooperation between God and man. The walls of Jericho could fall down only by the exercise of divine power, but the children of Israel had to encompass them. Only God can give a body as it has pleased Him to the seed corn, but man must plough, and sow, and reap, and thresh, and grind. Only God can remove the difficulties that stand in the way of an entirely consecrated and blessed life, but there are commands and duties which we must fulfill.

What are these? In some cases we are withholding obedience that we should give at once. There are things that we ought to do, but which we are not doing. And there is equal danger in doing more than we should—endeavoring to scale walls we are told to encompass; shouting before the word of command has been given; making the circuit of the city more often than the once each day prescribed by the divine ordering.

Whatever then is clearly revealed to us as the will of God, either for us to do or discontinue doing, let us immediately respond, and leave it to Him to do all the rest.

c. *Have faith!* Look from all your preparations, and even from your God-commanded acts to God Himself; and as you do so, your difficulties will melt away— that stone will be rolled from the mouth of the sepulcher; that iron gate will open of its own accord; those mighty walls will fall down.

Believe that He is working for you, and all who know you will be compelled to confess that the Lord has done great things for you. He has given you Jericho. Let your

235

heart dwell on that word. Though the walls are yet standing, they are as good as gone; and with their ruins behind you, you can go forward to possess the land.

2. IN CHRISTIAN WORK. The apostle speaks of strongholds that had to be cast down, and of high things that exalted themselves against the knowledge of God. He also asserts that he did not war against such things according to the flesh, and that the weapons of his warfare were not of the flesh, but were mighty before God for the casting down of strongholds, and for the bringing of every high and proud thought into captivity to the obedience of Christ.

What need there is for all Christian workers to ponder these pregnant words! The peril of our time is that we should get away from the simplicity of the early church, which went into the conflict with the mighty superstitions and flagrant sins of its age, with no weapons except those that may be found in symbol in this old-world incident. There were the white robes of priestly purity; the lifting up of the propitiation of Christ; the blowing of the ram's horn; the gospel message proclaimed with no silver cadence, but with rude and startling effect, as a summons to surrender.

With what dismay would the confessors and martyrs, the prophets and apostles of early Christianity view the methods with which we assail the monster forms of vice that confront us!

When confronted with all these things, we are apt to fight the world with weapons borrowed from its arsenals and to adopt methods that savor rather of the flesh than of the spirit. It is a great mistake. Our only hope is to act on strictly spiritual lines. If we can overthrow the dark spirits that abet and maintain, we will see the system that they support crumble as a palace of clouds before the wind.

Let us be pure and holy, giving time to heart searching in the presence of the Captain; let us lift up the sacrifice and work of Jesus; let us blow the gospel trumpet of alarm and summons to surrender; let us be much in silent prayer before God; let us cherish a spirit of unity and love, as the tribes of Israel forgot their differences in one common expedition against their foes; above all, let us believe in the presence and cooperation of God, and we will see the old miracle repeated, and the walls of Jericho fall down.

3. IN THE STORY OF THE CHURCH. This capture of Jericho is surely capable of being read as a parable of things that are yet to be. It may be that this narrative of the taking of Canaan is even a miniature anticipation of what is yet to transpire in that future that is probably so near. God has given the kingdoms of this world to His Son; but they will have to be engirdled by the sacramental hosts of His elect until He will have put down all rule, and authority, and power.

9

Arrest and Defeat
Joshua 7:1–2

The conquest of Canaan occupied seven years, and during the whole of that time Israel lost but one battle; indeed, the thirty-six men killed in headlong flight before the men of

Ai seem to have been the only loss their hosts sustained. The story of this defeat is told with great detail because it involved lessons of the greatest importance to Israel, and of incalculable value to ourselves.

The experience of defeat is far too common to the majority of Christians. They do not lie on their faces before God, eager to discover the cause of failure, to deal with it, and to advance from the scene of defeat to wider and more permanent success. If we but carefully investigated the causes of our defeats, they would be second only to victories in their blessed results on our characters and lives.

There were three causes for this defeat.

1. THEY WERE SELF-CONFIDENT BECAUSE AI WAS SMALL. Jericho was a heap of smoldering ruins. Man and woman, both young and old, and ox, and sheep, and ass—all had been utterly destroyed with the edge of the sword.

Fearing no attack from the rear, Joshua at once set his face toward the interior of the country, and chose a deep gorge or ravine, which lay a little toward the north, as the route for his army. Eight miles from its opening on the Jordan valley this ravine met another, and near the junction of the two stood the little town of Ai, with a population of twelve thousand persons. The proportion of fighting men has been calculated at about two thousand, but they were strong and commanded the pass, so that Joshua had no alternative but to mete out to Ai the same terrible fate as that with which he had visited Jericho.

Speaking after the manner of men, there was considerable force in the report of the spies sent up the valley to reconnoiter. The place was much smaller than Jericho, and would apparently require much less expenditure of time and strength for its capture. Jericho may have needed the entire host; but for Ai some three thousand men would surely suffice. "Make not all the people to toil thither; for they [*i.e*, the men of Ai] are but few."

But this recommendation went on the supposition that Jericho had been overthrown by the attack of the hosts of Israel; whereas actually they had had singularly little to do with it. They had walked around it and shouted—that was all. It had been taken by their great Captain and Leader, and by Him given into their hands. To speak as they did was to ignore the real facts of the case, and to argue as though the victory were due to some inherent qualities in themselves; with the inference that because they had conquered at Jericho they must therefore necessarily conquer at Ai.

There is no experience in the Christian life so full of peril as the hour when we are flushed with recent victory. Counting from our great triumph at Jericho, we despise such a small obstacle as Ai. Surely, we argue, if we have carried the one, we shall easily prevail at the other! And so it frequently happens that a great success in public is followed by a fall in private. We never so need to observe the injunction to "watch and pray" as when the foe is flying before us.

There is nothing small in Christian life—nothing so small that we can combat it in our own strength. The victories we have won in fellowship with God have imparted no inherent might to us; we are as weak as ever; and as soon as we are brought into collision with the least of our enemies, apart from Him, we shall inevitably go down before the shock. The faith, watchfulness, and fellowship with God, which availed before Jericho, can alone serve as the key to Ai.

2. THEY FAILED TO WAIT ON GOD. An accursed thing in their midst broke the link of fellowship between them and the hosts that served beneath the celestial Warrior who had appeared to Joshua. There is not the least doubt that if Joshua had been in abiding fellowship with God, the Spirit of God would have indicated the presence of evil in the host, and then Achan and his sin would have been discovered and judged before the march to Ai.

God sees the little tear in the cloth; the spot of decay in the fruit; the ulcer in the flesh, threatening to eat away its vitality. These may not be realized by us, but He knows how inevitably they must lead to defeat. Nor is He slow to warn us of them. Yet of what use is it for Him to speak to deaf ears; or to those who are self-confident in their own wisdom; or to those who pride themselves on victories that were wholly His gift?

Where God's children, like Joshua, are oblivious to the warning voices that speak in ever fainter tones as they are disregarded, God is compelled to let them take their course until some terrible disaster flings them on their faces to the ground. Ah, if Joshua had only prostrated himself amid the shoutings of victory over Jericho, there would have been no need for him to prostrate himself amid the outcry of a panic-stricken host!

Before we make some new advance, although the point of attack be but an Ai, it is our duty, as it is our best policy, to get back to Gilgal. We ought to seclude ourselves in spiritual converse with our almighty Confederate; asking Him to reveal any evil thing that He may see in us, and mustering the tribes of our heart before His scrutiny, that the Achan lurking there may be brought to light before, instead of after, the fight.

3. THEY HAD COMMITTED A TRESPASS "IN THE DEVOTED THING."

a. *Joshua was inclined to lay the charge of their failure on God.* But, in point of fact, the blame lay not with God, but wholly with themselves.

There are times in our lives when we are disposed to find fault with God. "Why have you made me this way? Why was I ever taken out of my quiet home, or country parish, or happy niche of service, to be plunged into this sea of difficulties?" When we are smarting from some defeat, caused by the overpowering might or the clever strategy of the foe, we are prone to blame God. Our Father brings us across the Jordan to give us larger experiences, to open before us vaster possibilities, to give us a better chance of acquiring His unsearchable riches. There is no task without sufficiency of grace.

The defeats we incur in the Land of Promise are not necessary. There is no reason for defeat in the Christian life; always, and everywhere we are meant to be more than conquerors. Child of God, never lay the blame of your failure on God; seek for it within!

b. *Not one of us stands alone; we cannot sin without insensibly affecting the spiritual condition of all our fellowmen.* One Israelite only had trespassed, and yet it is said, *"The children of Israel* committed a trespass in the devoted thing."

If Israel had but realized how much the safety of the whole depended on the obedience of each, every individual would have watched his brethren, as he watched himself, not for their sakes alone, but for his own; and if the members of Christian communities would understand how vast an influence for good or bad depends on the choice, the decision, the action of any, there would be a fuller and more intelligent obedience to the reiterated injunctions of the New Testament—for the strong to bear the infirmities of the weak; and for all to look not on their own things only, but also on the things of others.

Should these words be read by any person who is conscious of playing an Achan's part, take warning, and while it is called "today," confess, restore, and repent. Do this not only that you may escape an inevitable judgment, but also that you may not bring disaster and defeat on those with whom you associate, dragging the innocent down into the vortex of a common fate. The hands of Achan were stained with the blood of the thirty-six who perished in the flight to Shebarim.

c. *How careless we are of God's distinct prohibitions!* Nothing could have been more clearly promulgated than the command to leave the spoils of Jericho untouched. The city and its contents were devoted to utter destruction, only a specified number of articles being preserved for tabernacle use. But to Achan, the will of God was overborne by the lust of his eyes and the pride of life. The strong tide of passion swept over the barrier reared by the divine word.

"Israel hath sinned, and they have also transgressed my covenant which I commanded them: for they have even taken of the accursed thing. . . . Therefore . . . they cannot stand . . . before their enemies . . . neither will I be with you any more, except ye destroy the accursed from among you."

10

The Valley of Achor
Joshua 7

Was it a sudden gust of temptation that swept Achan before it when, with the rest of the host, he entered Jericho? This, at least, is clear, that in the late afternoon of the day of Jericho's capture, he had pilfered one of those robes of exquisite texture for which the plain of Shinar was famous, together with gold and silver—the latter coined, the former in a wedge—and had carried them surreptitiously away.

We can imagine him bringing them into his tent. He dug a hole in the sand and hid the spoil, which by the special order of Joshua had been devoted to Jehovah.

The whole proceeding had been conducted in such absolute secrecy, and he was so confident of the collusion of the inmates of his tent, that amid the general inquiry for the thief he braved detection and held his peace until the unerring finger of God pointed him out, as if He said, "Thou art the man!"

1. WE SHOULD GRIEVE MORE FOR SIN THAN FOR ITS RESULTS. Joshua tore his clothes and fell to the earth on his face before the ark of the Lord until evening. He was smarting from the disgrace inflicted on his people, and aghast at the results that would probably ensue as soon as the tidings had been voiced abroad. Judging simply by human standards, the worst consequences might be expected when the nations of Canaan suddenly discovered that the Israelite hosts were not invulnerable. This was Joshua's fear, that the Canaanites and all the inhabitants of the land should hear of it, and encircle them, and cut off their name from the earth.

We dread the consequences of sin, more than the sin itself; what others may say and do, more than the look of pain and sorrow on the face that looks out on us from the encircling throng of glorified spirits.

But it is not so with God. It is our sin that presses Him down, as a cart groans beneath its load. Few of us realize what sin is, because we have had no experience of a character without it, either in ourselves or in others.

It is, of course, possible to learn something of the exceeding sinfulness of sin by viewing the agony, heartbreak, and shame, of the dying Lord; by remembering its infinite cost to the love of God. And yet the true way to a proper realization of sin is to cultivate the friendship of the holy God. The more we know Him, the more completely we will enter into His thought about the subtle evil of our heart. We will find sin lurking where we least expected it. We will learn that every look, tone, gesutre, word, thought, which is not consistent with perfect love, indicates that the virus of sin has not yet been expelled from our nature; and we will come to mourn not so much for the results of sin, as for the sin itself. This is the godly sorrow that does not need to be repented of.

2. WE SHOULD SUBMIT OURSELVES TO THE JUDGMENT OF GOD. "And the LORD said unto Joshua, Get thee up; wherefore liest thou thus upon thy face?" It was as if He had said, "You grieve for the effect; grieve rather for the cause."

Whenever there is perpetual failure in our life, we may be sure that there is some secret evil lurking in heart and life. Somewhere there is a fault in the insulation of the wire through which the currents of divine power and grace come to us; and it is useless to pray that they may be renewed until we have repaired the defect. It is not a question of God's willingness or unwillingness, but of the laws of the spiritual world that make Him unable to ally Himself with consciously-permitted sin.

a. *In searching out the causes of failure, we must be willing to know the worst.* As we bare ourselves to the good Physician, let us remember that He desires to indicate the source of our sorrow only to remove it. "Be still and know." The responsibility of showing you your mistake is wholly with Him, if you have placed all in His hands. Leave it there and wait. If He has anything to say, He will say it clearly, unmistakably, and certainly. If He says nothing, it is because the set time has not come. But tomorrow, in the morning, it may be, He will speak to you and tell you all. In the meanwhile, wait and trust.

b. *When God deals with sin, He traces back its genealogy.* To deal with it thoroughly, we need to go back to its parentage. We generally deal with the wrong that flames out before the sight of our fellowmen; we should go behind to the spark as it smolders for hours, and to the carelessness that left it there. And by this insight into small beginnings, our God would forearm us against great catastrophes.

What we call sin is the outcome of sin permitted, days—perhaps weeks—before; which, during that time has been gathering strength within the heart. If we would be kept clear from great transgression, we must see to it that we are cleared from hidden faults, so subtle and microscopic that they would elude any but a conscience kept sensitive by the grace of the Holy Spirit.

c. *It is a good thing at times to muster the traits of heart and life.* We must make the principal tribes of our being pass before God—the public and private; our behavior in the business, the family, the church—until one of them is taken. Then examine that department, going through its various aspects and engagements, analyzing it in days or duties; resolving it into its various elements; and scrutinizing each.

This duty of self-examination should be pursued by those who have least relish for it, as most likely they really need it; while those who are naturally of an introspective disposition will probably apply themselves to the task without being reminded of the necessity of so doing, and should guard against its excess and abuse. Whoever undertakes it should do so in reliance on the Holy Spirit; and give ten glances to the blessed Lord for every one that is taken at the corruptions of the natural heart. It is "looking off unto Jesus" which is the real secret of soul-growth.

3. WE SHOULD HOLD NO CONFERENCE WITH DISCOVERED SIN. "And Joshua, and all Israel with him, took Achan the son of Zerah, and the silver, and the garment, and the wedge of gold, and his sons, and his daughters, and his oxen, and his asses, and his sheep, and his tent, and all that he had: and they brought them unto the valley of Achor. . . . And all Israel stoned him with stones, and burned them with fire, after they had stoned them with stones." Then Jehovah repeated the words that had preceded the capture of Jericho, "And the LORD said unto Joshua, Fear not! . . . see, I have given into thy hand the king of Ai, and his people, and his city, and his land."

Then up the long, narrow passage Joshua marched with thirty thousand men—the mighty men of valor. There was a sense in every breast of an integrity that had put away all cause of failure and defeat. The preparations were skillfully made; the appearance of flight on the part of Israel brought the men of Ai to headlong pursuit; and the city was left at the mercy of the ambush, which at the sign of Joshua's uplifted javelin arose, entered the city, and set it on fire. And in that place where Israel had met with so disastrous a defeat, the people took great spoil, especially of cattle, which they drove down in triumph to the camp at Gilgal.

So the Valley of Achor became "the Door of Hope." Ah! metaphor as true as fair! for all our inner life there is no Valley of Achor where the work of execution is faithfully performed, in which there is not a door of hope—entrance into the garden of the Lord; and a song so sweet, so joyous, so triumphant, that it would seem as if the buoyancy of youth were wed with the experience and mellowness of age.

11

Ebal and Gerizim
Joshua 8:30

This was one of the most impressive scenes that occurred during the occupation of Canaan. Jericho and Ai were heaps of blackened ruins; their kings and people utterly destroyed; their dependent villages mute with terror. And all through the land the rumor ran of the might of Israel's God. The nations of Canaan appear to have been so panic-stricken that they offered no resistance as all Israel went on a pilgrimage of thirty miles to perform a religious duty.

"It shall be," so the word stood, "on the day when ye shall pass over Jordan unto the land which the LORD thy God giveth thee, that thou shalt set thee up great stones, and plaster them with plaster: and thou shalt write upon them all the words of this law" (Deut. 11:26–32; 27:2). Joshua lost no time in obeying these minute and urgent injunctions; and within two or three days after the fall of Ai—perhaps within three weeks of the passage of the Jordan—the people were assembled in the valley of Shechem, sentinelled on the north by the sterile slopes of Ebal, and on the south by its twin-giant Gerizim.

The valley between these two is one of the most beautiful in Palestine. Jacob's Well lies at its mouth, and all its luxuriant extent is covered with the verdant beauty of gardens, and orchards, and olive groves, rolling in waves of billowy beauty up to the walls of Shechem; while the murmur of brooks flowing in all directions fills the air. There Joshua led the people that, by a solemn act, they might take possession of the land for God.

1. THE ALTAR ON EBAL. Ebal was stern and barren in its aspect. There was a congruity therefore between its appearance and the part it played in the solemn proceedings of the day. For far up its slopes gathered the dense masses of the six tribes who, with thunderous Amens, repeated twelve times, answered the voices of the band of white-robed Levites, as standing with Joshua and the elders and officers and judges in the green valley, they solemnly repeated the curses of the law.

But that was not the first proceeding in the holy ceremonial. Before the people took up their assigned places on the mountain sides, an altar was reared on the lower slopes of Ebal. Special directions as to its construction had been given in Deuteronomy 27. It was to be built of unhewn stones, on which no iron tool had been lifted. This was probably to guard against any attempt to set forth the likeness of God, and to show disapproval of the florid and lascivious ornamentations of which the surrounding heathen were so fond.

There they offered burnt offerings and sacrificed peace offerings. The *burnt offering* was what was known as a sweet savor offering. The entire victim was burned. "It was an offering made by fire, of a sweet savour unto the LORD" (Lev. 1). In this the Holy Ghost signified our duty to present ourselves without reserve to God.

The *peace offering* also belonged to the sweet savor offerings, but it was not wholly consumed; a part was eaten by the offerers, to testify that in it they had fellowship and communion with God. In the sight of Israel, therefore, Joshua and other chosen representatives partook of portions of the sacrifices, and obeyed the divine injunction, "Thou shalt eat there, and thou shalt rejoice before the LORD thy God."

As we pass into the Land of Promise we must see to it that we do not leave behind the devout and loving consideration of that precious blood by which we have been redeemed and which is our life.

Since He died, we need never stand on the mount of cursing. Because He counted not His life dear to Himself, those gaunt and forbidding slopes have become the scene of blessed communion with God. We sit and feast with Him, and from peak to peak joy chases the terrors of the curse. Because He shed His blood, there will be "dew, and rain, and fields of offerings," even on Ebal; until its terraced slopes resemble those of the opposite mount of blessing.

2. THE LAW IN CANAAN. Around the altar strong men reared great stones, and plastered them with a facing of cement, composed of lime or gypsum, on which it was easy to write all the words of the law plainly (Deut. 27:8). In that dry air, where there is no frost to split and disintegrate, such inscriptions would remain for centuries. As time could not have permitted the inscription of the whole law, it is probable that the more salient points were alone committed to the custody of those great stones, to perpetuate to generations following the conditions of the tenure on which Israel held the lease of Palestine.

But when we turn from the literal to the metaphorical, and ask for the underlying typical meaning of this inscription of the law in so prominent a position in the Land of Promise, we are at first startled. What can it mean? Is there a connection after all between law and grace? Are those who sit with Christ in heavenly places still amenable to law—"under the law," as the apostle puts it?

There is but one answer to all these questions. We are not looking to our obedience to merit the favor of God, or to win any of the blessings of the gospel. But it is also true that faith does not make the law of God of no effect.

When we yield ourselves entirely to the Spirit of life which is in Christ Jesus, and which passes freely through us, as the blood through artery and vein, He makes us very sensitive to the least commandment or desire of Him whom he has taught us to love; and so insensibly while we yield ourselves to Him, we find ourselves keeping the law after a fashion that was foreign to us when it was a mere outward observance, and we cry with the psalmist, "O how love I thy law! it is my meditation all the day" (Ps. 119:97).

3. THE CONVOCATION. When these rites were fulfilled, the third and concluding scene of this extraordinary transaction took place. In the center of the valley the ark rested, with its group of attendant priests and Levites. Nearby were Joshua and the leaders of the tribes, elders, officers, and judges. Then up the slopes of Ebal, finding seats on its terraced sides, were Reuben, Gad and Asher, and Zebulun, Dan, and Naphtali; while up the slopes of Gerizim were the larger and more important tribes of Simeon, and Levi and Judah, and Issachar, and Joseph, and Benjamin. It was as though the voice of blessing had to be louder than that of cursing—a prediction of its final prevalence and triumph.

Then Joshua read aloud "all the words of the law, the blessings and cursings, according to all that is written in the book of the law." And as he solemnly read, whether the blessing or the curse, each item was responded to by the Amens that thundered forth from thousands of throats, and rolled in reverberating echoes through the hills. Earth has seldom heard such shouts as those!

It is well worth our while to ponder the list of blessings appended to obedience in that memorable twenty-eighth chapter of Deuteronomy, that we may discover their spiritual counterparts and, having found them, claim them.

Nor can we better close our meditation than by asking that the Holy Spirit may so indwell and guide us that we may choose what He ordains, and not swerve by a hair's breadth to the right or left of the narrow path of obedience; keeping His commandments; obeying His biddings; perfectly conformed to His will. Thus will Ebal cease to frown, and Gerizim rain its blessings on us.

12

The Wiles of the Devil
Joshua 9

The whole country was in arms. Just as the Pharisees and Sadducees, who were hereditary foes, combined to destroy Christ, so did all the kings—whether Hittite or Amorite, Perizzite or Hivite—gather themselves together to fight with Israel and with Joshua, "with one accord."

Tidings of this formidable coalition found their way into the camp of Gilgal, where leader and people had recently returned from their pilgrimage to Shechem. Joshua probably heard the tidings without great dismay, but to the princes it was welcome news to learn almost simultaneously that there was the possibility of forming a league with those who were likely to stand by them at that solemn juncture. This league, however, was to cost them as much anxiety, if not more, as the sin of Achan.

Whenever we are threatened with unprecedented difficulty, we may expect to encounter just such a temptation as that which the Gibeonites presented to Israel.

1. "THEY DID WORK WILLINGLY." One day a group of strangers announced themselves, and they seemed to have come from a far country. In every article of dress, as well as in the trappings of their asses, there were the signs of a long journey. Their shoes were clouted; their garments faded; their sacks in holes; their wineskins patched; and when they turned out the remnants of their bread, the mold suggested the days that had passed since it left the oven. No one suspected for a moment that beneath the clever disguise was concealed a band of Hivites. But so it was. For the first time, within the precincts of the camp which was holy to the Lord, there stood a company of those inhabitants of Canaan whom Israel had been expressly commissioned to destroy.

Had it not been for their disguise they would not have been permitted to come within the circle of the tents. But their story was so reasonable, their references to Jehovah so reverential, their appearance so in keeping with the account they gave of themselves, that they threw Joshua, princes, and people, completely off their guard.

It is in this way that we are tempted still—more by the wiles of Satan than by his open assaults; more by the deceitfulness of sin than by its declared war. We all have to beware of those who work their way into our affections, our counsels, our homes, or our businesses; who talk glibly and falsely of the fame of God. There are plenty of Gibeonites about. "Beloved, believe not every spirit; but try the spirits whether they are of God: because many false prophets are gone out into the world" (1 John 4:1).

2. "THEY ASKED NOT COUNSEL . . . OF THE LORD." The leaders of Israel seem at first to have been a little suspicious of their visitors. "And the men of Israel said unto the Hivites, Peradventure ye dwell among us; and how shall we make a league with you?" But their suspicions were allayed as they listened to their story, and saw the apparent evidences of their long journey. Here surely was an opportunity to prove their sagacity. They had not been allowed as yet to show their bravery and might, but they could at least now give proof of their superior insight! This was altogether too obvious a matter to need to be referred to Phinehas with his Urim and Thummim! And so they took of their provisions, moldy as they were, in token of their willingness to count them allies and friends; indeed, the princes of the congregation swore to them. But they "asked not counsel at the mouth of the LORD."

What an ominous sound there is in those words! They portend disaster—and it befell. If only they had inquired of the Lord, the dimming light in the sacred stone would have betrayed the fatal secret and arrested the formation of the league.

Let us apply the moral to our heart. Never trust your own judgment. When your common sense is most sure of the rightness of a certain course of action, it will be best to make assurance doubly sure by lifting up your soul to God, that it may dim with His No, or enlighten with His Yes. If there is any doubt or hesitation left after such reference, be sure that as yet the time has not come for you to understand all of God's will. Under such circumstances—wait. And when the time for action arrives, He will have given you such unmistakable indications of His will that you will not be able to mistake them or err therein. "None of them that wait on Him shall be ashamed."

Before entering into any alliance—taking a partner in life, going into a business with another, yielding assent to any proposition that involves confederation with others—be sure to ask counsel at the mouth of the Lord.

3. "HEWERS OF WOOD AND DRAWERS OF WATER." There are some oaths better in the promise than in the observance, as would have been the case with Herod's. And if there had been certain peril that these Hivites would corrupt Israel, it would have been better for them, notwithstanding the oath of the princes, to have been cut off like the rest of the Canaanites. But all danger of this peril being fulfilled was carefully guarded against by their reduction to servitude. "Hewers of wood and drawers of water for the congregation, and for the altar of the LORD."

This is a beautiful and comforting example of the way in which God overrules our mistakes, and brings blessing out of our sins. Inadvertently, and without due consideration, some reader may have entered into alliance with a Gibeonite—whether in marriage, in business, or in some other area. Are you therefore to abandon your high privilege, and forsake your lofty ministry to the world? Must you cease to be God's portion, and the priests of men? Not necessarily. Turn to God in repentance and confession, and He will teach you how these very hindrances may become great means of help; so that you may cut the wood for the burnt offering, draw the water for the libations, and promote the prosperity and well-being of the soul.

"If any brother hath a wife that believeth not, and she is pleased to dwell with him, let him not put her away. And the woman which hath a husband that believeth not, and if he be pleased to dwell with her, let her not leave him. For the unbelieving husband is sanctified by the wife, and the unbelieving wife is sanctified by the husband: . . . for what knowest thou, O wife, whether thou shalt save thy husband? or how knowest thou, O man, whether thou shalt save thy wife?" (1 Cor. 7:12–14, 16).

It is true that the natural consequences of our sin may have to run their course. The hand of the reclaimed drunkard will still tremble. The constitution of the prodigal will never be able to throw off the effects of the fever contracted from the swine troughs. The Gibeonite will always, in this world at least, be tied to you. But these things shall not rule, but serve; shall not impede, but promote. They shall hew the wood and draw the water for the inner shrine of character, and for the promotion of the loftiest standard of Christian attainment.

13

A Memorable Day
Joshua 10:14

"There was no day like that." It stood alone in the history of the conquest, and of Joshua. Let us notice:

1. THE CONFEDERACY THAT WAS GATHERED AGAINST ISRAEL. Israel had previously dealt

with separate cities, Jericho and Ai; but now five kings of the Amorites joined together, namely the kings of Jerusalem, Hebron, Jarmuth, Lachish, and Eglon.

The traitor city of Gibeon was the object of the attack of the combined forces. This was due partly because its defection had aroused the fiercest animosity of its former allies, and partly that by its occupation they might be able to interpose one further barrier to the invasion of the Israelites. The royal city of Gibeon lay only six miles to the north of Jerusalem.

Suddenly the men of Gibeon found themselves surrounded by a vast host of infuriated warriors who, not daring to measure themselves against Joshua, were all the more eager to execute their vengeance on those who had dared to make a league with him. Relying on Joshua's fidelity to the covenant so recently formed, a message was sent in breathless haste, summoning him to their help.

2. JOSHUA'S HEROIC FAITH. There had been great days in his life before but there had never been a day in his life quite like this.

a. *It was a day of vigor.* As soon as he received the message, he saw the importance of at once vindicating the trust reposed in him. Before the sun went down, orders had passed through the camp that the men of war should be ready for a midnight march; and at dead of night he climbed the pass from Gilgal to Gibeon—fifteen difficult miles—and came on the sleeping host suddenly before they had had time to prepare themselves for fight. Inertness and indolence ill become those who are entrusted with great concerns.

b. *It was a day of fellowship.* There must have been hard fighting all morning. It was dawn when the battle began, and it would have been toward afternoon when the kings gave the signal for retreat; and the Canaanites, unable longer to sustain the successive onsets of Israel, charging to the battle cry of "Jehovah, mighty in battle," broke into flight like a flock of panic-stricken sheep. Ten miles they fled, climbing a precipitous ascent to the high ridge of Beth-horon the Upper. From that point the road drops, broken and rugged, seven hundred feet in two miles. The rock is cut into steps. Down this breakneck steep the fugitives fled to reach, if only they might, their fastness and citadels, which lay in the valley below, and longed for night to put a pause on the anguish of the pursuit. It was at this point that the storm, of which we will speak presently, burst on them with irresistible fury, as if the whole artillery of heaven had suddenly opened fire. Over the hills of Gibeon the sun was setting. It needed only an hour or two and its sudden disappearance would bring on the rapid Eastern twilight, while the moon's pale face appearing over the purple waters of the great sea was waiting to lead on the night.

It was under these circumstances that Joshua dared to ask an unprecedented gift of God—that the day might be prolonged.

There are high days in human lives when thought and purpose, which had been quietly gathering strength, suddenly leap from their leash and vent themselves in acts, or words, or prayers. In such hours we realize what Jesus meant when He said, "Whosoever shall say unto this mountain, Be thou removed and be thou cast into the sea; and shall not doubt in his heart, but shall believe that those things which he saith shall come to pass; he shall have whatsoever he saith" (Mark 11:23).

c. *It was a day of triumphant onlook.* Discomfited, weary, vanquished, the kings took shelter in the cave at Makkedah; but Joshua did not stay to send them away; he was too eager to finish what he had begun, and to prevent the Canaanites from reentering their cities. So he took measures to keep them imprisoned in the cave until his return. Presently, flushed with victory, and with (as Josephus tells us) the loss of hardly a single life, he came again. The kings were summoned from their hiding place; and as they crouched abjectly at the feet of their conquerors, Joshua called for all the men of Israel, and said to the chiefs of the men of war, "Come near, put your feet upon the necks of these kings."

3. THE EXTRAORDINARY INTERPOSITION OF JEHOVAH. The storm that broke in that late afternoon over the rugged descent to Beth-horon was no common one. Oriental hailstones are of great size: it is said that sometimes lumps of ice, of a pound or more in weight, will fall; and these would naturally kill any on whom they fell. But the remarkable thing in this case was that the storm broke in a moment when its fury could be spent on the Amorites without inflicting injury on Israel. "It came to pass, as they fled from before Israel, and were in the going down to Beth-horon, that the LORD cast down great stones from heaven upon them unto Azekah, and they died: they were more which died with hailstones than they whom the children of Israel slew with the sword."

But the stupendous miracle of the day consisted in the arrest of daylight. We place no limit to the divine power. We need not hesitate to accept any well-accredited marvel, but neither should we fail to believe that God could make the clock of the universe stop, if it were necessary that it should do so.

But it is not necessary to believe that He did this. By some process the laws of which are at present unknown to us, but of which we get glimpses, in refraction, in the afterglow of sunset, in the fantastic appearances familiar to travelers in high altitudes and among the loftiest mountains—God was able to prolong the daylight until Israel had finished slaying their foes, so that only a decimated remnant entered into the fenced cities. The *how* is not important to our present discussion. It is enough to express our belief in the fact itself. Somehow, the duration of that day's light was lengthened out until the people had avenged themselves of their enemies.

Our present purpose does not require us to follow the steps of the conquerors as they passed from city to city. All were treated with the same unsparing severity. The kings were slain, their bodies gibbeted till the evening; and all the souls smitten, so that none were left remaining, an utter destruction of all and every one by the edge of the sword.

We must remember that the Israelites were the executioners of divine justice, commissioned to give effect to the sentence which the foul impurities of Canaan called for. There is a judgment seat for nations as well as for individuals. And the almighty Judge sees to it that His sentences are carried out.

4. THE LESSON FOR OUR OWN LIFE. There are days so extraordinary for the combination of difficult circumstances, human opposition, and spiritual conflict, that they stand out in unique terror from the rest of our lives. But these days do not come, if we are living in fellowship with God, intent on doing His will, without their coming also His sweet "Fear them not; for I have delivered them into thine hands!" Our only anxiety should be that nothing divert us from His path, or intercept the communication of His grace. Like a wise commander, we must keep open the passage back to our base of operations, which is God. Careful about that, we need have no anxiety beside.

Moreover, these days may always be full of the realized presence of God. All through the conflict, Joshua's heart was in perpetual fellowship with the mighty Captain

247

of the Lord's host, who rode beside him all the day. So amid all our conflicts, our hearts and minds should there ascend, and there dwell where Christ is seated, drawing from Him grace on grace, as we need. Let us put the whole matter into the hands of God, asking Him to go before us, to fight for us, to deliver us, as He did for His people on this eventful day. In all such days we may have light that cannot be accounted for on any natural hypothesis. Only let us seek the grace of the Holy Spirit, that we may be kept in such an attitude of soul that we will miss nothing of God's gracious and timely help.

14

Claiming Victory
Joshua 11

The Merom Waters, which must have grown crimson with the blood of men on that great day, whose story we are now to tell, is described by travelers as one of the fairest scenes in Palestine.

To this sweet spot as mustering place, Jabin, king of Hazor, aroused at last to fear and action by the tidings of the day of Gibeon, summoned all the tribes of the north of Canaan. Throughout the hills of Galilee the messengers sped—to the far north beneath the shadow of Lebanon, all down the Valley of Esdraelon to Carmel, and along the shores of the Great Sea. The Jebusite heard the summons in the hill country, and the Hivite under Hermon in the land of Mizpeh; and even some remnants of the shattered southern confederacy seem to have poured their scanty contribution into the accumulated ranks of that great host.

It was no time for dalliance in the camp at Gilgal, where Joshua had led his warriors back to renew after their battles. As soon as tidings reached him, he started with his army on the five days' journey that took them from Gilgal to Merom, to the greatest battle of his life. Josephus tells us that the united forces consisted of 300,000 warriors, 100,000 horses, and 20,000 chariots. He says also that the Israelites were terrified at having to encounter the iron chariots that drove swiftly into the ranks of an opposing army, enabling the warriors to discharge their missiles with terrible effect. It may be that some word of the immense army that lay waiting for him within the circle of the hills reached Joshua when he was within a day's march of the camp, but the steadfastness of his courage knew no bounds, because simultaneously with the tidings there came the divine assurance, "Be not afraid because of them: for to-morrow about this time will I deliver them up all slain before Israel."

Joshua repeated the tactics that had been so successful before. He came against them suddenly, perhaps in the early dawn. As the Israelites fell on them, the vast host was seized with panic. The strength of the foe was broken, but for some years after this final victory Joshua carried on a campaign against the cities standing, each on its mound or hill according to the custom of the time, from which Jabin and his allies had gone forth to fight. Hazor was burned, probably to intimidate the rest, being the most prominent in the alliance against Israel. For the rest, it was deemed sufficient to destroy the inhabitants that could bear arms, to render the horses useless, and to burn the chariots.

The Anakim warriors of extraordinary height, who had been the dread of Israel, were destroyed together with their cities and the whole land passed into the hands of Israel.

1. IT WAS A DECISIVE VICTORY. Often before the Canaanites had rallied to oppose the progress of Israel, but never after this did they dare to meet them in battle.

2. THIS VICTORY NEEDED TO BE FOLLOWED UP AND APPROPRIATED. Though the victories of Israel were decisive, yet there was a sense in which they were incomplete. It is true that Joshua destroyed the cities and those whom he found in them but it would seem that many of the inhabitants had previously retired for safety to the rocky fastnesses or caves in the vicinity of their homes, so that as soon as the wave of conquest had passed over the land and subsided, they emerged from their hiding places, and reoccupied their possessions in houses and lands from which they had been temporarily dislodged.

It would have been in the highest degree inexpedient to have exterminated all the inhabitants, for the land would have gone out of cultivation; the terraces, which were so needful in that hilly country, would have become broken down; and the water-courses would have fallen hopelessly out of repair; and the wild beasts would have multiplied to an alarming and dangerous extent. How much wiser then that the displacement of the Canaanites should be by a gradual process. The victories of Joshua were decisive, but they were not final. They needed to be followed up by the various tribes. There was no more doubt as to their success in prosecuting their victories than there had been in winning them. The one was as much guaranteed by the divine promise as the other.

How rich is the spiritual lesson to be derived from the peculiarity of this gradual appropriation of Joshua's achievements! "Joshua took the whole land, according to all that the LORD said unto Moses; and Joshua gave it for an inheritance unto Israel according to their divisions by their tribes." Yet Israel had to fight over every inch of soil to drive out their conquered foes. So, as we have seen, our blessed Lord has won a decisive victory over all our foes; but we have to claim it repeatedly until, in the case of each of us, death, that last enemy, is destroyed.

The world is overcome, but we must overcome it by faith. The flesh has been nailed to the cross, and the old man has been done away, but we have by the Spirit to mortify the deeds of the body, that we may live. The devil has been vanquished once for all, but we have to hide ourselves in the only-begotten, trusting Him to keep us so that the evil one may not touch us. We are more than conquerors in all things through Him who loved us; but there never will be a day in our history when we will not need to overcome by the word of our testimony and by the blood of the Lamb.

Fear not, nor be dismayed! The Lord is with you, O mighty men of valor—mighty because one with the mighteist. Claim victory! Whenever your enemies close in on you, claim victory! Whenever heart and flesh fail, look up and claim victory! Know that it is yours, and gather spoil. Neither the Anakim nor fenced cities need daunt or surprise you. You are one of the conquering legion. *Claim your share in the Savior's victory.*

15

Rest in the Heavenlies
Joshua 11:23

The Book of Joshua naturally divides itself into two parts, the first of which deals with the conquest, the second with the partition of the Land of Promise. The junction of these two is at the close of the eleventh chapter. There the story of the conquest ends, and that of the partition begins. And just there we have the significant record, "And the land had rest from war"—a note of blessed tranquillity and peace, which is repeated in the fourteenth chapter. But even that is not all, for in the twenty-first chapter we are again told that "the LORD gave [Israel] rest round about, according to all that he sware unto their fathers."

Now, all this is in precise keeping with the spiritual analogy that we have been tracing throughout this book. He who embodied anticipations of Calvary in the sacrifices and offerings of Leviticus, embodied anticipations of the empty grave and the Ascension Mount in the conquest and apportionment of Canaan by Joshua. In the case of the glorious Anti-type, there was also a pause of blessed rest. Between the completion of His victory and the outpouring of the Holy Spirit, we are told that He sat down at the right hand of God.

The session of our Lord Jesus at the right hand of God is a graphic and beautiful metaphor, pregnant with food for holy thought. Obviously, it asserts the glorious honor of His majesty, that He is one with God in His divine nature. With equal clearness, it indicates the oneness of the Lord Jesus in the divine unity of being, although that He now wears our nature. But with similar force, it teaches us that He rests. The sitting posture naturally suggests repose. And we may reverently ask what was the nature of His rest, that we too may enjoy the Sabbath that He keeps through the ages.

1. OUR SAVIOR'S REST. It was not the rest of overweariness. The rest of the Lord Jesus, symbolized by His session at God's right hand, was not that of weakness or inactivity. What was it? Surely it meant that *He had finished* that which He rose up to do. On the cross He said, "It is finished"; from the throne He could say, "It is done." As it was said of Joshua, so it might be said of that greater Joshua, "He left nothing undone." And therefore, as the Father entered into His rest, when He had ceased from the work of creation—a rest, not of weariness or inactivity, but of a completed scheme; so did the Son enter into His rest when He ceased from laying the foundations, both of His redemptive work and of the future triumphs of His church. Not weary; not inactive; but so far satisfied. He had done all He planned to do, all that could be done, and He sat down—the attitude of completion.

When once the believer understands the meaning of the Lord's session at the right hand of God, he is not only assured of the divine majesty of Jesus, and of the Father's acceptance of His mediatorial work, but he goes further to realize that there is nothing to be added to that finished work. Since Jesus *sits* in the heavenly places, His sacrifice is sufficient and complete; His blood can avail for sins of crimson dye and for a race of sinners; His obedience unto death has satisfied the demands of law and there is now no condemnation.

But there is an *experimental* significance also in the repeated affirmation of Scripture that our Lord sits at the right hand of God. We must never fail to bear in mind that the work of Jesus, since He took our nature into union with Hmself, is as the representative man. As such He died, and rose, and reigns. And just in proportion as we are one with Him by a living faith, we also shall die, and rise, and reign.

2. IN WHAT RESPECT MAY WE SHARE CHRIST'S REST? It is a very needful question. Some of us have been men of war from our youth; we must see to it lest, like David, we should

be debarred from building the Temple of God. Only Solomons, whose names bespeak their peace, are competent for that. Our best work for God cannot be done unless we have learned to be quiet.

The restful heart lives above the storm and strife, with Christ; sensitive to human sorrow and to its own, but able to discern the purposes of divine wisdom; to await the unfolding of the divine plan; and to trust the love of the divine heart. It keeps silence for His word. It is not disturbed by emotional change. Such is its acquiescence in the divine will that it is content with whatever comes.

There is no unnatural quietism in this life—rather the most intense earnestness and activity. But in the midst of the most rapid and vehement movement there is rest—deep rest, sweet rest.

a. *There is the rest of reconciliation.* The soul no longer works up toward the cross to obtain justification. It is assured that all that needed to be done to win it had been done when Jesus said, "It is finished."

b. *There is the rest of assured victory.* Before we understand the meaning of our Lord's ascension, we oppose Satan by the armory of our own resolves and efforts at amendment. But when we realize all that Jesus has done, we come to see that Satan is a conquered foe; that his weapons cannot reach a life hidden with Christ in God; and that so long as we maintain our standing in our risen Lord, we need not dread his attacks, nor be perturbed in the affray.

c. *There is the rest of a surrendered will.* When our wills move off the pivot of self onto the pivot of God, then our lives become concentric with the life of God. Then trial and sorrow are treated as our Father's messengers, but in their winter costume. Then our very infirmities indicate the direction into which we should send our energies. Then we always have our way, because God's and ours are one. Then prayer is the discovery of God's plans, and a taking hold of His willingness.

d. *There is the rest of unbroken fellowship.* For as Jesus is one with the Father, so we become one with Him, and through Him one with the blessed Trinity. What pen can describe the blessed fellowship between the Father, the Son, and the Holy Spirit?

e. *There is the rest of perfect love.* Our affections have sorely troubled us, straying far away to forbidden things. But when we enter into the life of the ascended Jesus— which is the life of Pentecost—we find that our hearts become pervaded by the love of God. The heart has found in God all its desires more than met. It is silent in its love.

f. *There is also the rest of the holy heart.* It is not occupied with inbred lust, not tossed to and fro on seething passion, or driven by every gusty whim. The flesh is crucified, the self-principle is quelled, the empire of the Holy Savior is supreme; and all discordant elements are still.

It may be that some who read these lines are passing through great suffering. It is almost useless to bid such to rest and be still. They must learn the source of rest. Let them reverently and believingly claim this also as part of their inheritance, of which they are co-heirs with Christ.

3. HOW TO ENJOY THIS REST. But these blessed experiences are possibly only through the power of the Holy Ghost. The ascension of Jesus is mystically and inevitably connected with the descent of the Holy Spirit. If you magnify your rights in the glorified Savior, and fail to unfold the willingness of the Holy Spirit to make them your own in daily and living enjoyment, you set souls the impossible task of climbing inaccessible

heights, and they abandon hope. Teach men the meaning of Christ's session, and that they have a right to all it means of the rest of God; but tell them also that the power to claim that right is through the grace of the Holy Spirit, whom God has given to those who obey Him.

16

Land to Be Possessed
Joshua 13:1

Joshua was probably about ninety years of age when the conquest of Canaan was complete. But a very important part of his work had yet to be performed. It would not have been enough for him to have asserted Israel's supremacy over the Canaanites, unless he had taken measures to follow up his victories by settling the people in their locale. The warrior must give place to the administrator and statesman.

The first step toward the occupation of Canaan was taken in the summons of the Lord to His servant, who had so faithfully performed all His word. Though he was old and well stricken in years, he was still the confidant of Jehovah, the depository of His secrets, the executor of His plans. It was a high tribute to Joshua, that when he had overstepped the ordinary limit of human life by twenty years he was summoned to put the crown on the work of his life.

The method adopted seems to have been, first, a careful survey of the land not yet possessed; then its apportionment among the several tribes according to their size; and lastly the actual appropriation and acquisition of each portion by the efforts of the tribe to which it was assigned. It is with the first of these we will now deal. After the divine voice had summoned the veteran leader to the last great work of his life, it proceeded to enumerate the portions of land that yet remained; and some time later, when seven of the tribes were as yet unsettled, and there was urgent need for the completion of the task, twenty-one commissioners were appointed to pass through the land, and examine it, and make a report concerning it to Joshua at Shiloh.

It would be interesting, if space permitted, to examine the area designated by the divine Spirit. This at least we must notice as we pass, that it included all the region of Philistia, inhabited by some of the stoutest foes that Israel ever encountered, and who were a perpetual source of weakness and danger till the times of the kings. There were also the rich pasture lands of the south; and in addition the luxuriant plain of Phoenicia and the fertile upland valleys, cooled by the snow-capped summits and watered from the rills of Lebanon, all portions of the land on which Israel always had a very slender hold. Compare this outline sketch of the divine intentions, with the territories then actually held, and afterward possessed by Israel; and the difference between God's ideal and their real inheritance becomes striking.

The same appalling contrast appears when we recall the original promise made to Joshua at the beginning of this book. "From the wilderness and this Lebanon even unto the great river, the river Euphrates, all the land of the Hittites, and unto the great sea toward the going down of the sun, shall be your coast." Yet as a matter of fact, Israel filled up the measure of this prediction only once, and for a very short time, during its tenure of Canaan. Solomon did for a brief time realize the divine ideal; but the radiant glory of his kingdom was soon hemmed in and obscured by the clouds that drew up their dark veils over the sky. Men have sometimes used this as an argument against the divine veracity. It would rather be quoted as a melancholy confession of human frailty, and of failure to claim and appropriate the promises of God. There is no variableness in God. It is impossible even for our unbelief to make His promises of no effect.

Let us consider whether there may not be a similar contrast between that which God has intended for us and that which we have made our own. Spread out in the Bible, and set forth in the life of Jesus, there is for us, as for Joshua, a map of what God desires for His people. All is mapped out for us; and it would be wise on our part to carefully ponder it that we may be humbled as we see the slow progress we have made, and may be stirred up to apprehend all that for which we were apprehended in Christ Jesus.

1. IN THE DIRECTION OF KNOWLEDGE. We must distinguish between intellectualism and knowledge. Leisure and taste, memory and mental discipline, observation and society, will do much toward imparting that strange veneer called *culture;* but this is a very different thing from *knowledge.* A man may be utterly destitute of culture, and yet may have a direct and intuitive perception of truth, whereas a man may be quick, clever, intellectual, well-informed, and yet be utterly destitute of the true knowledge.

God meant us to know Himself even as Jesus knew Him, in His human life. Such knowledge is brought within our reach by our blessed Lord. He gives us eternal life in order that we might know the only true God. And yet how little do we know the Father! We know little about Him, and less of Him by personal intimacy and fellowship.

To take the lowest test, our knowledge *of God's Word.* The majority of professing Christians are content with a few familiar and well-trodden verses. They read and read again the same passages in the Gospels, the Psalms, or Isaiah, but they never venture into the unexplored territory beyond. And the saddest point of all is that they have no deeper perception of the words that have become so familiar to them than at the first. They are like the busy crowds that pass lightly over the graves of martyrs, obliterating the sacred inscriptions, and missing the deeper thoughts that crowd in on the historian who bends over them in reverent meditation.

There are many subjects that the bulk of Christian people, by a tacit understanding, refuse to enter. Such are, among others, the Second Advent; the restoration of Israel, and its future mission to mankind; the great question of fulfilled and unfulfilled prophecy; the mystical union of Christ with those who believe in Him. In all these respects there is much land to be possessed. Let us mend our ways, not always traverse the well-trodden paths, but seek for an acquaintance with the entire range of truth as given in God's Word.

And if we know comparatively little of the Bible, we know less of God. Some of us dwell on one trait of His character, in complete ignorance of others. We magnify His mercy at the expense of His righteousness; or His justice at the cost of His grace. Our knowledge of Him, moreover, is borrowed from hearsay evidence, and from the reports of others. We do not hear and know Him for ourselves. Oh, to know God until He break on our hearts as the morning or as the early rain! There would be a new meaning in life if we began to explore what is to many of us a terra incognita, the Being of God. There is much land here to be possessed.

2. IN THE DIRECTION OF CHRISTIAN ATTAINMENT. In us, as in Canaan of old, there are the seven nations of sin. When first we became Christians, we made a determined

onslaught on these things, and met with much success; but we have become weary of incessant watchfulness and conflict. We have no taste for the girded loin and the erect, alert soldier-attitude. Our heart is only touched here and there by Christ.

In some cases it is the business life, the factory, or the office that is not possessed by Christ; in other cases it is the social element, or the home relationships of our nature that are not brought into captivity to Him.

Consider how great God's ideal is for each of us. To be "conformed to the image of his Son"! Is that God's ideal? And does He predestinate each of us to be conformed to it? Then who of us need renounce hope? But ah, how much there is to be possessed! How little do we possess of His beauty, or strength, or tenderness, or holiness!

The soul is first possessed by Chrit, and then it begins to possess Christ. Ah, soul! why dwell in poverty and starvation? Is it not because you have withheld yourself from Jesus? Arise, and yield yourself to Him! Let Him possess you; and then claim a reciprocal possession of your Lord. Then you will begin to enter on your eternal inheritance, and begin to expend yourself on pursuits that will engage you when sun and moon are no more.

3. IN THE DIRECTION OF THE GIFTS OF THE HOLY GHOST. "To every one of us is given grace according to the measure of the gift of Christ" (Eph. 4:7). And the context clearly shows that this is not the common grace needed for daily living, but the special gifts of grace of the Pentecostal fullness of the Holy Spirit, acquired for us by the ascended Lord. If we understand the teaching of the epistles correctly, there is for each member of the mystical body of Christ a distinct share in the Pentecostal gift. There is surely something more than is ordinarily understood by regeneration, or the gift of faith, or the revelation of the living Savior. There is a power, an overflowing love, an assurance, an exuberant joy, a freedom, which are not enjoyed by all Christians, but which are as evidently their birthright as they are to be desired.

And, in addition, there are the bestowments of the Holy Spirit, by which we are especially qualified to do Christ's work in the world. Tact in leadership; wisdom to win souls; power to help believers into a fuller life; utility to administer, or to speak, or to teach; sympathy, facility in utterance, power in prayer. The whole continent of Pentecostal blessing is avoided by many believers as if it were full of swamps, of fever, of noisome pestilence. There is surely in this direction much land to be possessed.

Let us arise and conduct ourselves like men. Let us ask our heavenly Joshua to settle us in this good land; so that there may be no rill, or valley, or mountain, or tract of territory unpossessed. God has given us in Christ all things that pertain to life and godliness; let us claim the whole of our inheritance by a living faith, so that we may enter on the enjoyment of all that is possible for us on this side of heaven.

17

A Veteran Comrade
Joshua 14

It was in Gilgal that the apportionment of Canaan took place. There, where the reproach of Egypt had been rolled away, and where the main camp had stood, it was fitting that the rewards of victory should be meted out. It was a great epoch in Israelite story, as the tribes assembled around their veteran leader. Before Joshua and Eleazar stood the urns, the one containing the name of each, and the other the name of some specified portion of that fair land that lay all around.

Judah, first in war and march, was the first to draw near. It was a great people, and was destined yet to play a greater part in the history of Israel and of mankind. But an incident intercepted the casting of the lot that calls for earnest heed; stand still, then, O Christian soul, and see some counterpart of yourself in your best moments, in this demand of the gay headed warrior, this lion's whelp, for that is the underlying thought in the name "Caleb." Strong, bold, heroic, there was a great deal of the lion in him beside his name. He had been the young lion of the tribe of Judah some fifty years before, but he was as strong as he stepped out of the ranks of Judah to claim his right as he was when Moses sent him to spy out the land.

1. THE PRIME CHARACTERISTIC OF CALEB'S EARLY LIFE HAD BEEN HIS ENTIRE DEVOTION TO GOD. Repeatedly we are told both of him and Joshua that they "wholly followed the LORD." And there was some trace of this in the words of the old man as he addressed the comrade of many a hard-fought fight, of many a weary march. The rest of the spies had turned aside, dismayed by the spectacle of giants, and walled-up cities, and vast battle array. They had ceased to keep the eye steadfastly fixed on the movements of God's will, and on the might of His hand; and instead of following hard after Him, they had yielded to panic and made the hearts of the people melt.

But there had been no panic in the heart of Caleb. He had only been considering that, when God delights in men, He brings them into the land of milk and honey, and makes it theirs by deed of gift.

He followed God completely through the weary years that ensued. Amid the marchings and counter-marchings, the innumerable deaths, the murmurings and rebellions of the people, he retained a steadfast purpose to do only God's will, to please Him, to know no other leader, and to heed no other voice. Always strong, and true, and pure, and noble; a man in whose strong nature weaker men could hide.

And two things lit the path of this Greatheart, amid the gloom of the wanderings and the chaos of the conquest. There was first the consciousness that lay on his heart, like sunshine on a summer ocean, that God delighted in him; that the outgoings of God's nature toward him were full of love and joy; and that the peace of God that passes all understanding might be his inalienable possession.

There was next the thought of Hebron. Forty-five years had passed since he had seen the white buildings of that ancient and holy city nestling beneath its terebinths. Hebron, beneath whose oaks Abraham had pitched his tent; Hebron, whose soil had been trodden by the feet of the incarnate God, as with two angel attendants He visited the tent of Abraham; Hebron, where Sarah and Abraham, Isaac and Rebekah, Jacob and Leah, lay buried; each in a little niche, holding the land in trust, as the graves of the dead always hold the land for the living, until the promise of God was realized, and the seed of Abraham could return to claim its heritage.

God had read his secret, and had arranged that what his heart loved best his hand should take, and hold, and keep. Often, as he lay down to sleep beside the campfire, his last thought would be of Hebron; and amid the noontide haze, when the mirage gleamed on the horizon, it would sometimes seem to him as if the green hills of Hebron were calling to him across the waste.

We have trace of the attitude of Caleb's heart through those long years in the words he spoke at this memorable juncture, when he said: "Behold, the LORD hath kept me alive, *as he said.* . . . Now therefore give me this mountain, *whereof the LORD spake* in that day . . . as the LORD said." The promise of God was his stay and comfort and exceeding great reward. He had to wait for its fulfillment, and it seemed long; as waiting times always do, especially when man waits for God. But God was working for him while he was waiting.

2. SUCH DEVOTION AS CALEB'S HAS MARVELOUS RESULTS.

a. *It is the soil from which such a faith springs as can claim the realization of promise.* "Now therefore give me this mountain, whereof the LORD spake in that day." No common faith was needed to make so large a claim. Think of the Anakim that held it in their giant hands! But faith triumphed; and if the words, "It may be," come into his speech, words with a falter in them, the tremor, as it were, of fear, we must understand that they did not spring from any doubt of God; but of that mistrust of self which is a trait in all moral greatness. There is waiting for you an inheritance—some promised Hebron, some blessed gift of God's infinite love in Christ. It is for you to say, with the faith of a Caleb, "Give me this mountain."

b. *It leads to fellowship.* Hebron stands for friendship, fellowship, love. The old word means that, and perhaps that is why Caleb was so eager to strike out the recent giants' name of Kirjath-arba, and to bring back the word that Abraham had often had on his lips. It spoke to him of that communion with his unseen Friend whom he had enjoyed through the wanderings and vicissitudes of his long life, and which was not to end now; because in the seclusion of his estate, beneath the shadow of his own vine and fig tree, he would speak with Him as a man with his friend.

Those who follow God know Him. He turns and sees them following, and hears their inquiry to know His secret place, and bids them "Come and see."

c. *It leads to strength.* "Lo," said Caleb, "I am this day fourscore and five years old. As yet I am as strong this day as I was in the day that Moses sent me: as my strength was then, even so is my strength now, for war, both to go out, and to come in." Consecration is the source of undecaying strength. The soul must learn to take the power that God gives to the faint, and to receive the strength He increases to such as have no might.

But this strength is accessible only through obedience. God cannot and will not bestow it except where there is a thoughtful and deliberate purpose to do His will, to follow His path, and to execute His work.

d. *It gives victory.* Of all the Israelites who received their inheritance in the Land of promise, Caleb appears to have been the only one who succeeded in perfectly expelling the native occupants of the country. The Israelites generally seem to have made poor headway against their strong and mighty foes, with their chariots of iron and fenced walls. Repeatedly we encounter the sorrowful affirmation, *they were not able to drive them out.* But Caleb was a notable exception. The man who wholly followed the Lord was alone wholly victorious.

How precious and searching is the conclusion! Our failures in expelling the giants of the heart, in dealing with inbred corruption and the assaults of Satan, are almost entirely due to some failure in consecration. But when, so far as we know, we are entirely yielded to God, then no sin can stand before us, because nothing can stand before Him.

e. *It enables us to give blessings to others.* Twice we are told how Achsah got off her donkey to ask a blessing from her father's hands. "Give me also springs of water. And he gave her the upper springs, and the nether springs."

Follow the Lord fully: so will you dwell in the land; so will you be able to obtain promises, not for yourself only, but also for others. The Othniels and Achsahs of your home circle will gather around you to ask a blessing, and you will have power to open springs of spiritual blessing in the heights of the heavenly places, and in the depths of daily practical ministry, in the valley of human life.

18

Receiving and Reigning
Romans 5:17

The allotment of Canaan, which was inaugurated under the direction of Joshua and Eleazar in Gilgal, and which had been temporarily arrested by the claim of Caleb, now was carried out. To begin with, the three great tribes of Judah, Ephraim, and Manasseh, received their inheritance. Half the tribe of Manasseh had already received its lot, given by Moses, on the far side of the Jordan. Therefore the descendants of Joseph, at first, received but one lot, and cities were separated for the children of Ephraim in the midst of the inheritance of the children of Manasseh (Josh. 16:9; 17:14).

Concerning each of these tribes, the same melancholy confession is made which is heard repeatedly in this and the following book, like the monotonous note of a storm-bell rung by the wild waves on a dangerous coast: "They could not drive them out." "But the Canaanites would dwell in that land" (17:12).

Mark the strength of that word *would*. It was not an expression the Canaanites had a right to use. They were a dispossessed race. They had neither part nor lot in Canaan; and Israel made a profound mistake in allowing them to remain in the face of God's great word, "I will drive them out from before the children of Israel." Yet let us not condemn them, lest we condemn ourselves. There is not the least reason why besetting sin or fleshly lusts should hold their own, or should find any foothold in the region of the saved nature. Never allow them to say *they must* or *they will*. Even if they would be able to keep us at bay, they have no weight in the presence of that Omnipotence that vanquished them on the cross, and is pledged to destroy them completely.

The presence of the Canaanites led to an altercation between the children of Joseph and Joshua. "Why hast thou given me but one lot and one portion to inherit, seeing I am a great people?"

"If thou be a great people," Joshua replied, "there is plenty of unoccupied territory within the limits of your inheritance. Forest land perhaps! There fell trees, extract the stumps, and grow crops upon the rich and verdant soil fertilized by the leaves of many autumns." How often we ask God for wider areas of usefulness, while we fail to utilize those that lie within our reach. Do not sigh for missionary service until you have covered the whole acreage within your reach—in the home circle, or among the children of some poor district. The wood may be thick, but the axe of persevering faith will make a clearing there.

"The hill country," they persisted, "is not sufficient, and the valley is filled by Canaanites with their iron chariots; give us more."

"No," said Joshua; "you have power enough to cut down the wood, and to drive out the Canaanites—use it." For all the territory that we should win for God we have sufficient power, if we would but use it. Perhaps the best path to the speedy acquisition of spiritual power for the majority of those who will read these lines would be to claim and use the abundance of grace that is within their reach awaiting them in the living Savior.

This brings us to the text that stands at the head of this chapter, which lies in one of the most rocky and precipitous portions of the Epistle to the Romans, like a tiny lakelet on the bosom of gaunt and rugged cliffs.

In those words three things are patent:

1. THE DIFFERENCES THAT EXIST BETWEEN CHRISTIANS. Some *exist;* others *live;* others again *reign in life*. Some have life, others have it "more abundantly." To reign in life is to realize the conception of being kings and priests to God, a royal generation, a chosen people. The conception includes nobility of demeanor, such as becomes the descendant of a line of kings; generosity, as when a prince scatters his largesse among the crowd; and victory, as becomes the monarch who has placed his enemies beneath his feet, climbing to his throne.

What do you know of these? Would you say that there is anything in your days to make men think that you reign in life? Do unholy desires bite the dust in your presence? Is there nobility in your bearing? Is there a consciousness among others that your religion is not only barely sufficient for your own needs, but that the grace of God has so abounded toward you that you in turn can abound to every good work? If not, you have yet to learn what it is to reign in life.

2. THE CAUSE OF THIS DIFFERENCE. It does *not* arise, thank God, from any arbitrary allotment on his part of more or less grace. The real reason why so many fail to reign in life is to be sought, not in some arbitrary enactment on the part of God, but in the different power of receptiveness that exists among His children. Some fail to receive, either because they have not learned the art, or because they have not reached that position in Christian experience in which they can avail themselves of it.

Great saints are simply great receivers. They may be deficient in culture, education, and a thousand things that belong to others; but they have learned the happy art, denoted by that word *receive*, that is found in every part of the New Testament, and especially in connection with the Holy Spirit, which they who believe on Christ were to receive.

Do you want that royalty of bearing? *Receive* it. Do you want that generosity? You have only to *receive* it. Do you want that victory? There is no other course than to *receive* it. In a word, do you want to reign in life? Then you must *receive* it, the more royal will life become. What if the hill country is filled with wood, and the lowlands infested by Canaanites!—if you will receive and use the power within your reach, "No weapon that is formed against thee shall prosper; and every tongue that shall rise against thee in judgment thou shalt condemn" (Isa. 54:17).

3. HOW TO ACQUIRE THIS SACRED ART. The lack of joy in Christian hearts may often be traced to a failure to discern the difference between the prayer that is only supplication, and that which takes its reward from the outstretched hand of Jesus. Too often our

prayers seem like lost vessels; when, in point of fact, they have come to the docks richly freighted, but we have not been there to claim our own. Perhaps these rules may assist you to acquire this blessed art:

(a) Be sure that what you ask is according to the mind of God, offered in some promise or precept of Holy Scripture.

(b) Ask for it simply and reverently. Use the name of Jesus; that is, stand in Him, and plead for His glory.

(c) Dare to believe that God does hear and answer your prayer.

(d) Go your way and understand that God is faithful. Count on Him as bound to keep His promise.

(e) Act as you would if you had all the consciousness and enjoyment possible.

Thus you will find inevitably that the mountain will become a plain; the woods will fade into pasture lands; the Canaanites will be driven before you, as the chaff of the threshing-floor before the autumn wind; and nothing will be impossible.

19

The Conclusion of the Task
Joshua 18

The two great tribes were thus at last settled—Judah, as Dean Stanley suggests, like a lion to guard the south, and couch in the fastness of Zion; while Ephraim, like the more peaceful but not less powerful bullock, was to rove the rich vales of central Palestine, and defend the frontier of the north. And Joshua was able to turn his attention to the several items that claim a passing notice.

1. JOSHUA ERECTED THE TABERNACLE IN SHILOH. During the march through the wilderness, when the camp was pitched, the tabernacle occupied the center of the camp. Around it were grouped the tents of the priests and Levites, while the tribes occupied specified places, three to each quarter of the compass. An attentive comparison of those positions with the territories allocated to them in the Land of Promise will reveal a striking similarity. It was as though the encampment were, in its main features, repeated in their final settlement in the land. And to complete the parallel, the tabernacle was now removed from Gilgal and pitched in Shiloh, which lay as nearly as possible at the heart of Canaan.

Here, then, in the center of the land, embosomed in the keeping of the strongest tribes, on the east side of the highway that led from Bethel to Shechem, was the chosen spot where the tabernacle of God was among men; and He dwelled with them.

2. JOSHUA REBUKED THE INERTNESS OF THE PEOPLE. And Joshua said to the children of Israel, "How long are ye slack to go in to possess the land, which the LORD God of your fathers hath given you?" (18:3). At that point the twenty-one commissioners arose to walk through the land and surveyed it. They embodied the results in a book, in which the land was described by cities in seven portions. This they brought to Joshua. It may be that the account of what they had seen was the means under God of arousing the people from the apathy into which they had sunk.

259

There is the portion of Benjamin, the beloved of the Lord, a place of safety with Him, covered all the day long, and borne between His shoulders—the place where Eastern mothers cradle their babes, giving them warmth and easy carriage. There is the portion of Zebulun, to whose shores the illimitable ocean washes the treasures of the deep; in whose heart Gennesaret lies, with its fragrant memories of God manifest in the flesh. There is the portion of Issachar, which derived treasures from the sands, emblems of the precious stones, the pearls and crystals of spiritual character. There is the portion of Asher, the oil of whose wine-presses bespeaks the unction of the Holy Ghost; the strength of whose shoes speaks of that invincible might that treads down serpent and scorpion. There is the portion of Naphtali, satisfied with favor, and full of the blessing of the Lord; owning rich forests, the circle of Galilee, and the garden of Palestine. Each of these is significant of spiritual endowment, which we ought to arise to possess.

Too long have we been slack to go in to possess that fullness of the Holy Spirit that might be in us as a living spring, making us perfectly satisfied; like the fountain in the courtyard of a beleaguered castle that enables the garrison to defy the siege. There is a knowledge of Jesus, a participation in His victory, a realization of blessedness, which are as much beyond the ordinary experience of Christians as Canaan was better than the wilderness. But how sad, that of all this we know so little.

How much we miss! The nomad life could not afford those seven tribes so much lasting enjoyment as their own freehold in Canaan. But the comparison is utterly inadequate to portray the loss to which we subject ourselves in refusing to appropriate and enjoy the blessedness that is laid up for us in Jesus. Let us come to our Joshua at Shiloh, and ask Him to lead us into each of these.

3. JOSHUA RECEIVED HIS OWN INHERITANCE. "[The children of Israel] gave him the city which he asked, even Timnath-serah in mount Ephraim" (19:50). In the following book it is spoken of as Timnath-heres (Judges 2:9). It was "the portion of the sun."

The old veteran had deserved well of his people, and must have been glad to retire to his estate on which the remaining twenty years of his life were spent. And the greatness of his influence may be inferred by considering the evils that overwhelmed Israel when he was taken. His very presence among the people was a restraint. What a significant testimony to his consistency and steadfastness is furnished by the record, "The people served the LORD all the days of Joshua."

4. JOSHUA ALSO MADE PROVISION FOR THE MANSLAYER. Six cities were apportioned, three on each side of the Jordan, easily accessible. There the manslayer, who had killed any person unwittingly and unawares, might flee from the pursuit of the next of kin. Once within the city walls, all breathless with his flight, the manslayer waited at the entering of the gate of the city, until he had stated his case to the elders, who had the right of admitting him provisionally into the city. On the appearance of the avenger of blood, the cause seems to have been finally adjudicated; and if it were clearly shown that there was no animosity in the blow that caused death, the manslayer was permitted to remain there, until the death of the high priest then in office.

Take heart, O Christian soul! you have done many evil things in your ignorance or thoughtlessness. Get thee to the City of Refuge; you will not only be safe, but shall enjoy your inheritance also, for the High Priest has died, and in His death has put away your sin forever; there is therefore now no condemnation for you, because you are in Him.

The Jews killed the Prince of Life, but they did it in ignorance (Acts 3:17–18). Therefore they have lost their heritage; but they exist still as prisoners of hope, finding refuge among the cities of the priests, until such time as the Lord Jesus will inaugurate that new and glorious reign in which He will take to Himself the kingdom. Then Israel will return, each to his own house, and to the city he fled from.

5. JOSHUA APPORTIONED CITIES FOR THE LEVITES. There was an ancient curse hanging over the lots of Simeon and Levi. Brethren by birth, they had been joint perpetrators in a dark crime that had given Jacob, their father, a bad name among the inhabitants of the land, among the Canaanites and Perizzites. The dying patriarch could not forget that deed of treacherous cruelty, and as it rose before his eyes he said:

> Weapons of violence are their swords,
> Cursed be their anger, for it was fierce;
> And their wrath, for it was cruel;
> I will divide them in Jacob,
> And scatter them in Israel.

But this curse was not fulfilled in each case in the same way. With Simeon, it ran its course. Settled at the south of Canaan, between Judah and Philistia, this tribe became more and more nomadic, and finally faded out of corporate existence. In the case of Levi, it was transformed into blessing. At Sinai, when Moses called on all who were loyal to Jehovah to gather in the gate of the camp, the Levites, to a man, answered his appeal. Phinehas, also, who took such decisive action in the matter of Baalpeor, was a Levite. Therefore Jehovah entered into a covenant of life and peace with them, took them as a substitute for the firstborn sons of Israel, and pledged Himself to be their inheritance (Num. 18:20; Josh. 13:33).

At the divine command, forty-eight cities were given to the Levites, with one thousand cubits of pasture land measured outward from the city walls. There they dwelled when not required for temple service, or when they were incapacitated by age from attending to their sacred office.

As Jacob predicted, they were scattered; but the effect was salutary. They permeated the whole land with the hallowing influence of Shiloh. Moreover, the teaching of the law was a special prerogative of the Levites, who appear to have traveled through their apportioned districts.

So the work was finished. "There failed not aught of any good thing which the LORD had spoken unto the house of Israel; all came to pass" (Josh. 21:43–45).

20

Life in the Land
Joshua 22

When the seven years of fighting came to an end at last, the children of Israel settled down to the enjoyment of their land. The comparative silence of the record suggests the engrossing interest with which the people gave themselves to the culture of the land and to the occupation of large cities they had not built, of houses full of all good things they had not filled. Cisterns they had not hewn poured forth refreshing waters to vineyard, oliveyard, or garden; and they ate and were full.

1. OUR FIRST DISCOVERY IS THE MEANING OF REST. "The LORD gave them rest round about, according to all that he sware unto their fathers" (21:44). There was a very distinct measure of rest. The land rested (Josh. 11:23), and the people also. But it is equally clear that Canaan did not exhaust God's ideal. The rest of Canaan, like so much else in the Book of Joshua, could at best be only a type and shadow of that spiritual repose, that holy tranquillity, that unspeakable peace, which fill the souls of men with the rest of God Himself. Therefore, it is truly said in the Epistle to the Hebrews, "If [Joshua] had given them rest, then would he [the Spirit of inspiration by the mouth of David] not afterward have spoken of another day. There remaineth therefore a rest to the people of God" (Heb. 4:8–9).

There is rest from the first glad outburst of the new life, but it gets more intense as the years go on. The cause of this is in the ever-growing conviction that God's way is perfect, His will loveliest, His plan best. When first we enter into rest, we have to watch against distrust, to reason with ourselves that all must be well, to solace ourselves with promise and assurance. But as the days pass, each utters speech to the next, and the accumulated voice of experience gathers volume within the secret chambers of the heart.

When from some summit in life we review the past, our hearts are filled with emotions of tranquil restfulness. Such a God is yours, O my soul! be still; trust Him; He is doing all things well; be still and at rest!

And so the rest, born of trust, gets ever deeper, because the trust enlarges with growing knowledge. The more we grow in the knowledge of God, and of His Son Jesus Christ, the more absolute is our trust in His everlasting, all-pervading love; and the more unbroken is our rest.

2. OUR SECOND DISCOVERY IS THE TRUE CENTER OF UNITY. The forty-thousand warriors who had so nobly fulfilled their early promise received the public thanks of the great leader; and his last advice, "Return ye, and get you unto your tents. . . . But take diligent heed to do the commandment . . . of the LORD."

When they reached the fords of Jordan, and reflected that the stream would presently divide them from the rest of the people, a sudden fear seems to have taken them lest, in coming days, the seven and a half tribes might say to their children, "What have ye to do with the LORD the God of Israel? For the LORD hath made Jordan a border between us and you . . . ye have no part in the LORD." To obviate this, and to make clear for all coming time their identity with the rest of the people, they built an altar on the western bank of Jordan. It was a perpetual witness that its builders were loyal-hearted Israelites.

But it was a great mistake. If they had obeyed the divine instruction, that three times in the year all their males should appear before God in Shiloh, there would have been no need for this clumsy contrivance.

3. WE DISCOVER THE NEED OF PATIENCE IN DEALING WITH THE ERRING AND FALLEN. When first the tribes of Israel heard of the erection of the altar, their impulse was to go at once against their brethren to battle. Shiloh was the mustering place, for it seemed as if an offense had been perpetrated against that holy shrine.

But wiser counsels prevailed, and it seemed best to send Phinehas and ten princes, men of note, as a deputation in the name of the whole congregation of the Lord. They found the warriors in the land of Gilead on the point of dispersing to their homes, so they uttered their remonstrance; "Rebel not against the LORD, nor rebel against us."

So deeply had the spirit of love worked in their hearts, that they even proposed to share the land of western Canaan, in which the Lord's tabernacle was found, with their brothers. "If the land of your possession be unclean, then pass ye over unto the land of the possession of the Lord, and take possession among us."

There was a desire to draw back the erring, which was different from the way they had felt before. And it had its desired effect in eliciting a frank disavowal of any desire to turn away from following the Lord, accompanied by a simple explanation of the motives that had actuated them. Thus the whole episode resulted in a tightening of the bonds of brotherhood, and in glad expressions of thankfulness and praise.

21

Take Heed to Love!
Joshua 23

Probably eighteen years had passed since the events recorded in the previous chapter. The rest that God had given had not been broken in upon by any uprising of the Canaanites; and the people had been able to prosecute the toils of husbandry unhindered by the alarm of war.

Meanwhile, the years as they passed left evident traces on the bearing and energy of the great leader, who had become "old and stricken in age." Joshua, knowing that his end was drawing near, called for the leaders of the people to an audience with him; it must have been an imposing and memorable gathering, either in the vicinity of his own inheritance, or on the sacred site of Shiloh.

Standing on the vantage ground of that gathering, Joshua directed the mind of his listeners into the past, and reminded them of what God had done for them. He had brought them in and planted them in the mountain of His inheritance, in the place that He had made for Himself to dwell in; and not one thing had failed of all the good things He had spoken.

Joshua's one anxiety appears to have been about the nations that were left. Seven times he refers to the nations of the land. What God had done to them; how He was prepared to thrust them out; and especially how great a temptation would be suggested by their perpetual presence, lest the people should be tempted to cleave to them, intermarry with them, and adopt their gods.

As a preservative against these evil consequences, Joshua proposed three safeguards: the *first* of which reminds us of the admonition given to himself at the beginning of this book, that they were to be very courageous, so as to keep and do all that was written in the law of Moses. The *second* was the certainty that if they became identified with the heathen in marriage alliance or idolatrous practices, they would not be able to prevail against them in battle, but would find in them a trap, a scourge, and thorns, until they perished quickly from off the good land into which they had come.

But it is on the *third* that we would dwell particularly; "take good heed therefore unto yourselves, that ye love the LORD your God." The whole law of God, and of human life, is fulfilled in that one word, "Thou shalt love." Love God, and you will be content with nothing less than to inherit all the land, even to that great sea of His love on which the sun never goes down. Love God, and courage must possess you. Love God, and you will love His Book. Love God, and you will possess God, and be possessed by God. Love God, and you will become one with all holy beings in heaven and on earth, and throughout the universe, to whom He is the supreme Love.

The one consideration, therefore, which demands our thought is how to fulfill this command, "Take heed to love." What are the steps by which we may enter into obedience to that great law, "Thou shalt love the LORD thy God with all thy heart, and with all thy soul, and with all thy mind, and with all thy strength"?

1. REMEMBER THAT LOVE IS OF GOD. The only Being who really is, is God. There is one God, the Father, of whom are all things. He is over all, and through all, and in all. Therefore, all love, and power, and wisdom, not only reside in Him, but pass from Him into all other beings, according to the measure in which they are prepared to receive them.

It stands to reason, therefore, that those who would love purely, unselfishly, strongly, must converse deeply with God. We must get, if we would give; obtain, if we would share. Oh, for a closer walk with God!

2. BUT SUCH LOVE COMES TO US THROUGH JESUS. The love of God has been stored in the manhood of Jesus. The divine essence expresses itself in terms of human affection. And it is when we know Jesus, and are united to Him by faith, and through Him are united to God, that we begin to experience the full tide of divine love as it comes from God the Father, through the Son, to become in us a well of living water, springing up into everlasting life. Love begets love; think, then, how much He loved you, when He gave Himself for you. Talk of Him to others, until your soul begins to glow.

3. LOVE ALSO IS BY THE HOLY GHOST. The love of God has been shed abroad in our hearts by the Holy Ghost, who is given to us (Rom. 5:5). Let us lay this well to heart, that the first fruit of the Spirit is love. When we are strengthened by the Holy Spirit in the inner man, we begin to know the heights and depths, and lengths and breadths of the love of Christ.

4. THERE ARE SOME FURTHER DIRECTIONS FOR LOVING GOD. We can only enumerate them as we close.

(a) Distinguish between the emotion of love, which is variable and inconstant, and *love* itself.

(b) Remember that it is possible to love God not only with the heart, but also with the mind.

(c) The test of love is not feeling or speaking, but obeying. "He that hath my commandments, and keepeth them, he it is that loveth me."

(d) Guard against the intrusion of sense; for where any license is given to bodily appetite, instant loss is inflicted on the growth of the soul in the love of God.

(e) Climb to the love of God through the love of man. Dare to treat all men as you know you would if you *felt* to love them, and you will come to feel tenderly and pitifully toward them. Act this way always by the power of the indwelling Spirit, and you will certainly apprehend in growing measure, though never comprehend, the unsearchable love of God.

22

Evensong
Joshua 24

Once more the veteran leader, who was soldier, judge, statesman, and prophet combined, desired to see his people face to face. His meeting with their representatives was therefore followed, almost immediately, by a gathering of all the tribes of Israel to Shechem. It was here they had stood together years before in solemn convocation, while from the heights of Ebal and Gerizim had rolled the Amens of the people in answer to the blessing and the curse.

The stones on which the law had been written were still clearly in evidence, and the whole scene must have come back vividly to the memory of the majority of those assembled. But from that moment the valley would be associated especially with this touching farewell scene in which Joshua uttered his last exhortations and appeals.

1. Joshua's NARRATIVE. He told again the wonderful story of Israel's past; beginning where God began, with their fathers in their native land beyond the Euphrates, in the dim dawn of history.

Isaac, Jacob, Esau—names that made the deepest chords vibrate in his hearers' hearts—were successively recalled in the deep hush that had fallen on the vast assembly. Then the speaker reached more familiar ground, as he recalled names and events that had played a part in his own wonderful career—the mission of the two brothers; the plagues of Egypt; the cry and deliverance of the Red Sea; the wilderness; Balak, son of Zippor, and Balaam, son of Beor; the passage of the Jordan; the fall of Jericho; the overthrow of the seven nations of Canaan; the possession of their land.

But throughout the story, the entire stress is laid on the grace of God. *I* took; *I* gave; *I* sent; *I* brought; *I* destroyed; *I* gave; *I* delivered. Not a mention is made of Israel's mighty men. All is attributed to the ultimate source of nature, history, and grace—the supreme will of God.

There is nothing more beneficial than to stand on the heighth of the years in life's golden evening, and review the way by which our God has led us. The faraway home, where faces glimmer out in the daybreak of life's morning, on which we shall not look again until the veil of eternity rends; the hard bondage of early life; the many difficult situations and deliverances; the guiding cloud of the pilgrimage; the daily provision for incessant needs; the human love; the goodness and mercy that have followed all our days. Ah me! what a romance lies behind the meanest life, of sin and forgiveness, of provocation and pity, of grace and gift! Not one of us that will not hold his own history to be the most wonderful of all, when we exchange experiences in that land that we will not get by our own sword or bow, dwelling in mansions we did not build, eating of vineyards and oliveyards we did not plant.

2. JOSHUA'S APPEAL. It would appear that the people largely maintained the worship of household gods, like those Rachel stole from Laban. This practice was probably perpetuated by stealth. But the germs of evil were only awaiting favorable conditions to manifest themselves, and Joshua had every reason to dread the further development of the insidious taint. Therefore, with marked emphasis, Joshua appealed to the people to put away the gods which Terah and others of their ancestors had served beyond the river, and those which they had vainly invoked in the slave huts of Egypt. He did this first at the close of his address (v. 14), and again just before the memorable interview closed (v. 23).

3. THE PEOPLE'S FIRST REPLY. They professed that they had no desire to forsake Jehovah and serve other gods. They freely acknowledged that they owed everything to Him from the Exodus to the possession of Canaan. They also expressed their determination to serve the Lord.

4. JOSHUA'S ANSWER. Whether they uttered all these vows in thunderous unison, or by the mouth of chosen representatives, or whether the historian gathered the consensus of their feeling as it passed from lip to lip, we cannot tell. But surely Joshua detected some traces of insincerity in their voice. Perhaps he felt the unreality of their professions because they gave no sign of abandoning their strange gods. Had he hoped for a repetition of the scene that had taken place on that spot so many years before when, at the challenge of Jacob, his household gave to him all the strange gods that were in their hands, and the rings that were in their ears, and Jacob hid them beneath the oak that was by Shechem?

But there was no such response. The people contented themselves with their affirmations, but made no sacrifices. There was no holocaust, and Joshua was deeply conscious of the unreality of profession that went no deeper than words. This, he said in effect, is no way to serve the Lord. He is a holy God; He is a jealous God. He will search out these secret sins of yours; He will not be content with the service of the lip; He will not pass over transgression and sin.

5. THE PEOPLE'S SECOND REPLY. They were full of self-confidence, and vowed, come what might, that they would serve the Lord. Standing there with Joshua they forgot the many failures of the past, mocked at his fears, derided his suggestions of possible declension, and cried, "Nay; but we will serve the LORD."

What a commentary on those proud words is given by the Book of Judges! Serve the Lord! The first sentence that follows the record of Joshua's death in that book tells us that "the children of Israel did evil in the sight of the LORD, and served Baalim: And they forsook the LORD the God of their fathers" (Judg. 2:11–12). And this record recurs with melancholy monotony on nearly every page.

In point of fact, resolution, however good and however strongly expressed, is not sufficient to carry us forward into a life of obedience. Our moral nature has become so weakened by repeated failure that it is not able to resist the appeals of sense. To will is present with us, but how to perform that which is good we don't have. No one can look thoughtfully into the workings of his own nature without realizing the terrible paralysis that has befallen it. Consecration is possible only when it is conceived, prosecuted, and consummated in power not our own, and in the energy of the Holy Spirit.

6. Joshua's SECOND ANSWER. "Ye are witnesses," he said, "against yourselves, that ye have chosen you the LORD, to serve Him." In other words, he appealed to them on the ground of their own declarations, and sought to bind them to the vows they had made. Did he not intend to prove them deeper, to make them realize the solemnity of the occasion, to compel them to face the greatness of the responsibility they had assumed?

7. THE people's THIRD REPLY. "We are witnesses," they cried; as years later the people met Pilate's repeated challenge by the imprecation on themselves of the blood of Jesus. Alas, for their self-confident boast, for their headstrong pride of purpose! O my soul, be warned, that when you are challenged as to your resolves, make your boast in God. Only by your God can you leap over a wall, or run through a multitude. Ask the Holy Spirit to bind you by cords to the altar of self-surrender by the blood-red cord of Calvary; by the silver cord of hope in the Second Advent; by the golden cord of daily fellowship.

8. Joshua's RESPONSE. Further words were fruitless, and so he set up a memorial of the pledges by which the people had bound themselves. He wrote their words in the book of the law of God; and he took a great stone, and set it up there under the slab. "Behold," he said, "this stone shall be a witness unto us; for it hath heard all the words of the LORD which he spake unto us: it shall be therefore a witness unto you, lest ye deny your God." Then he dismissed the people so they could return to their homes.

There is comfort suggested to us by contrast with this solemn scene. Even in the Land of Promise, the people introduced the old Sinaitic spirit of duty and obedience as the condition of their tenure. They had said at Sinai, "All that the LORD says, we will do." And they said it again in Canaan.

Joshua did not give the people rest. Had he done so, David would not have spoken of another day. Canaan was only the *type* of the Sabbath-keeping of the people of God, but he did not exhaust it. At the best it was only a material and unsatisfying type. It afforded rest from the fatigues of the march, but not rest to the infinite capacities of the soul. The produce of cornfields, and vineyards, and oliveyards, could not appease the appetite for the infinite that must have made itself felt even in the heart of Israel, as the nation settled in its God-given land. Therefore, as the Holy Spirit tells us, there remained over and above a rest that is open by faith to the people of God of every age.

It is only when we apprehend the provisions of the New Covenant, which does mention man, but is full of the *I wills* of God, that we come into the true blessedness of rest and peace. When you confess yourself powerless to maintain the attitude of consecration, and are content to work out in the strength of His Spirit, you will experience the fullness of that rest that is deep as God's, like the azure sky that slumbers behind the bars of gold, which encase the glory of sunset.

His task ended, Joshua retired to his inheritance, but the influence of his character and life was felt as long as he lived, and afterwards. At last he died, one hundred and ten years old, and they buried him. He richly merited all the honor he received. He had none of the gifts of Moses. He may be compared to the man of two talents, while his great master was dowered with five. But he was strong and wise and true to the great trust committed to his care by the people and by God; and amid the stars that shine in the firmament of heaven, not the least bright or clear is the luster of Joshua, the son of Nun, the antetype of the risen and ascended Savior.

SAMUEL

1

An Age of Transition
1 Samuel 16:1

The story of Samuel is a divine interlude between the days of the Judges and those of David the king.

Up to now the high priesthood had been the supreme authority recognized in the Hebrew commonwealth. To Moses, its founder, there could be of course no successor; but Aaron was the first of an unbroken line of priests. No other office stood for the whole of Israel. The Mosaic era, however, was not destined to culminate in the rule of the priest who had seldom combined the sacerdotal functions with the special qualifications that constitute a great leader and ruler. The priest was to make way for the king.

A suggestion that a fresh development of the Hebrew polity was near occurs in the closing verses of the Book of Ruth, with which this book is connected by the conjunction *now*. The genealogy, which is the evident climax of that sweet pastoral story, has no connection with Aaron or his line. It expressly deals with the tribe of Judah, of which nothing was spoken concerning the priesthood. Evidently the divine purpose was moving forward—but where? From the vantage point of accomplished fact, we can see that it was slowly moving toward the establishment of the kingdom under David; and veiled from all eyes there was the yet profounder movement toward the revelation of "that Proper Man," in whose nature, fitly known as Wonderful, the priestly, the prophetic, and the royal, blend in perfect symmetry and beauty.

1. THE URGENT NEED FOR A STRONG MAN. Every age takes up the cry, "Give us men"; but if ever a strong man was needed, it was in the days of which the Book of Judges affords some startling glimpses.

Canaan had been conquered, but the ancient inhabitants were far from being subdued. In the South, the Philistines held their five cities. The mountain fortress, which was later known as Mount Zion, garrisoned by Jebusites, was proudly defiant up to the days of David. Nearly all the seacoast, and all the strongholds in the rich plain of Esdraelon, were in the hands of the Canaanites. The little kingdom of Gezer remained independent until it was conquered by the king of Egypt, and given as a dowry to Solomon's queen. On the northern frontier were the remains of those mighty nations that Joshua had overthrown in the great battle of the Waters of Merom, but which probably only gave a nominal allegiance to the Israelite suzerainty. Had it not been for the presence of these warlike tribes, we would never have heard of Gideon, of Barak, of Jephthah, of Samson, or of David.

In Israel, their incessant exposure to attack was aggravated by the absence of a strong central government. The priesthood had evidently fallen into the hands of weaklings from the days of Phinehas. Of this there is striking confirmation in the fact that Eli sprang, not from the house of Eleazar, the eldest son of Aaron, in which the succession ought to have been continued, but from the family of the younger son,

271

Ithamar. There is a strong probability that the representatives of the elder branch had proved themselves so unable to cope with the disorders of the time that they had been set aside in favor of any one who showed he was equipped enough to take the field and marshal the forces of Israel. Perhaps Eli, in his young life, had done some stirring deed of prowess that raised him to the supreme position his fellow-countrymen could give; though, when we are introduced to him, he is pitiful in his senile decrepitude and weakness (1 Chron. 6:4–15; 24:4). From time to time prophets had been raised up as a temporary expedient. "He gave them judges until Samuel the prophet." The reign of a judge was, however, a very transient gleam of light in that dark and stormy age.

Thus the nation was in danger of desolation by internal anarchy and external attack. With no principle of cohesion, no rallying point, no acknowledged leader, what was there to resist the pressure of the Canaanites from within its borders, and of the hostile nations from without? "In those days there was no king in Israel, but every man did that which was right in his own eyes"; "The children of Israel did evil in the sight of the LORD"; "The children of Israel cried unto the LORD." These three sentences, repeated frequently and emphatically, are the keynotes of the whole book. The religious ties, also, were very weak. We find, for instance, the name of Baal, a Phoenician deity, occurring three times in the names of members of the family of Saul (1 Chron. 8:30, 33, 34). The stories of Micah, of Ruth, and of the extermination of the Danites, supply graphic pictures of the disunion, independence, and wildness of the time; of wild license, and of exposure to attack.

It was necessary, therefore, to introduce a new order of things. The task demanded a preeminently strong man; and the person was superbly supplied, as we shall see, in the prophet Samuel, who conducted his people from one age to another without a revolution, and almost without the excitement that naturally accompanies so great a change.

2. HOW THE NEED WAS MET. God's greatest gifts to man come through travail. Before Samuel could be given to his people, Hannah had to be a woman of a sorrowful spirit.

Some few miles to the north of Jerusalem, on the confines of the territories of Ephraim and Benjamin, was situated the town of Ramathaim-Zophim. It was also known as Ramah, and has passed into New Testament history as Arimathea, the town from which came Joseph who begged of Pilate the body of the Lord. Ramathaim means the two Ramahs, as there were probably an upper and a lower city, to which reference is made in a later story (1 Sam. 9:13). Zophim recalls the name of an ancestor of Elkanah, named Zuph, who appears to have been a man of considerable importance (1 Chron. 6:35; 1 Sam. 9:5). In this mountain city a child was to be born who was to give the city interest and importance, not only during his lifetime, when it became the focus of the national life, but for centuries of years.

Toward the close of Samson's career in southern Judah, a family resided at Ramah consisting of Elkanah, a Levite, and his two wives, Hannah (Grace) and Peninnah (Pearl or Margaret). He had formerly lived in Ephraim, and was therefore considered to belong to that tribe (Josh. 21:20). That he had two wives was not a violation of the Levitical law, which did not forbid polygamy, but carefully regulated the marriage law.

It is supposed that Elkanah brought a second wife into his home because of Hannah's childlessness; but, whatever had been the cause, the step had been filled with misery. The house at Ramah was filled with bickering and strife, which was augmented

272

as Peninnah had child after child, while Hannah was still childless. Apart from all else, her desolate condition was an almost intolerable affliction (Gen. 30:1); but that it should be made the subject of biting sarcasm and bitter taunts was the occasion of the most poignant grief. Her soul was pierced as by the sword of the Lord, and drew near to the grave; then it was that the hunger of her soul could not be appeased even by the consciousness of Elkanah's fond affection (1 Sam. 1:5, 8; 2:5–8). But out of his soul-travail the joy of her life and the savior of her country were to be born.

2

A Woman's Anguish of Heart
1 Samuel 1:15

We may infer that Hannah's barrenness, and the provocation of her rival, were not the only reasons for Hannah's sorrow. As her noble song proves, she was saturated with the most splendid traditions and hopes of her people; her soul was thrilling with the conceptions that inspired the songs of Moses. Stricken with an agony of grief for the anarchy and confusion around her, she longed to enshrine her noblest self in a son, who should resuscitate the ebbing prosperity of the nation, and set it on a solid foundation. What if she were to be deprived of his presence and support from his earliest years, would she not be compensated a thousand times if only the Lord would accept him as His own, and use him to be the channel through which His redemptive plans might be achieved? Levites ordinarily were consecrated to the Lord's service between the ages of thirty and fifty, but her son, if only she might have one, would be given to the Lord all the days of his life, and no razor would ever touch his flowing locks.

On one occasion, while the feast was proceeding at Shiloh, it seemed as though Hannah could restrain herself no longer, and after her people had eaten and drunk—she fasting, except from tears—she rose up and returned to the outer court of the tabernacle. Most of its ancient glory had departed. "And she was in bitterness of soul, and prayed unto the LORD, and wept sore." Others went with burnt offerings, but she with the broken heart, which God will not despise.

We are told that "she prayed," and it becomes us to study her prayer and its result.

1. IT WAS HEART PRAYER. It is the custom of Orientals to pray audibly, but as she stood beside Eli's seat (v. 26) she spoke in her heart; her lips moved but her voice was not heard. This indicates that she had made many advances in the divine life, and had come to know the secret of heart fellowship with God.

2. IT WAS BASED ON A NEW NAME FOR GOD. She appealed to the Lord under a new title, "LORD of hosts." She asked Him to look down from the myriads of holy spirits who circled His throne, to her dire affliction and anguish. She vowed in words that Elkanah by his silence or consent afterward ratified (Num. 30:6–15), that she did not want this inestimable boon for herself merely, but for the glory of God; and that her son should be a Nazarite from his birth, abstaining from intoxicating drink, his locks unshorn, his body undefiled by contact with the dead.

3. IT WAS DEFINITE PRAYER. "Give unto thine handmaid a manchild." "For this child I prayed." So many of our prayers miscarry because they have no special goal. Experienced saints who are versed in the art of intercessory prayer tell us of the marvelous results that have accrued when they have set themselves to pray definitely for the salvation of individuals, or for some good and perfect gift on their behalf.

4. IT WAS PRAYER WITHOUT RESERVE. "I have poured out my soul before the LORD." Ah, how good it would be if we could more often follow Hannah's example. When the heart is breaking, when its frail machinery seems unable to sustain the weight of its anxiety, when its cords are strained to the point of snapping, then, as you remember these things, pour out your soul in you (Ps. 42:4).

5. IT WAS PERSEVERING PRAYER. "It came to pass, as she *continued* praying before the LORD." Not that either she or we can claim to be heard for our much speaking, but when the Lord lays some burden on us we cannot do other than wait before Him.

6. IT WAS PRAYER THAT RECEIVED ITS COVETED REQUEST. Eli was seated in his place at the entrance to the sanctuary, and he noticed Hannah. At first his attention was probably arrested by the signs of her excessive sorrow, and he expected that she would pour out her prayers in an audible voice, as so many other burdened souls would do. But since her lips moved, while her voice was not heard, the high priest thought she was drunk, and rather rudely and coarsely broke in on her with the rebuke, "How long wilt thou be drunken? put away thy wine from thee." Eli judged after the sight of his eyes, and clearly the mind of God had not been revealed to him. He had degenerated into the mere official, from whom the divine purposes were concealed.

Hannah answered the unjust reproach with great meekness. "No," she said, "it is not as you think. I have drunk neither wine nor strong drink, but have poured out my spirit to the LORD." She realized, even before Eli replied, that the merciful Burden bearer had heard and answered her prayer. She had entered into the spirit of the prayer, which not only asks, but takes. She anticipated those wonderful words which, more than any others, disclose the secret of prevailing supplication, "What things soever ye desire when ye pray, believe that ye receive them, and ye shall have them" (Mark 11:24). She knew that she had prevailed, and the peace of God, which passes all understanding, filled and kept her mind and heart. And she said, "Let thine handmaid find grace in thy sight. So the woman went her way, and did eat, and her countenance was no more sad."

The next day was fixed for their return home. But what a changed woman she was! How differently she had borne herself in that last brief visit to the holy shrine! And with what a glad face she entered the home that had been associated with such sorrow. Peninnah must have wondered what had happened to make so great a change; but Elkanah was the confidant of her secret, and his faith was made stronger by her unquestioning trust (v. 23).

7. THE WORKINGS OF SORROW. In this prayer we can trace the harvest sown in years of suffering. Sorrow gives an indefinable beauty to the soul. It may be that the long sharp pain, which has been your lot for these many years, the heart hunger, the disappointed hopes, the silent waiting, the holding your peace, even from good, have been necessary

to teach you how to pray, to lead you into the secret of a childlike faith, and to fit you to be the parent of some priceless gift to the world.

It fell to Hannah according to her faith. "The LORD remembered her, and . . . when the time was come about . . . that she bare a son, and she called his name Samuel, saying, Because I have asked him of the LORD."

The good Elkanah had a new joy in his heart as he went up to offer to the Lord his yearly sacrifice; but Hannah stayed at Ramah until the child was weaned, which would probably be on his completion of his third year, when Levite children were permitted to be enrolled and to enter the house of the Lord (2 Chron. 31:16).

At last the time arrived when the child should be openly presented to the Lord. The parents set out on their solemn journey with their child. The mother's heart was now as full of praise as it had formerly been of sorrow. She had learned that there was no Rock like her God. Her song, on which the mother of our Lord modeled the Magnificat, is the outburst of a soul whose cup was overflowing with the loving kindness of the Lord.

Presently the memorable journey from Ramah was finished. The sanctuary was again in sight, where she had suffered so poignantly and prayed so fervently. How it all rushed to her memory! "I am the woman that stood by thee here," she said to Eli; "For this child I prayed; and the LORD hath given me my petition."

Take heart man or woman of a sorrowful spirit! Only suffer according to the will of God, and for no wrong of sinful cause! Suffer for His church, for a lost world, for dying men! Travail in birth for souls! And if you do abide your Lord's time, He will bring you again to tread in garments of joy, where you have stood in the drapery of woe. They who go forth and weep, bearing precious seed, shall doubtless, *doubtless*, DOUBTLESS come again with rejoicing, bringing their sheaves with them.

3

The Young Levite
1 Samuel 2 and 3:1

Students of the Scriptures in every age have been arrested by the figure of this little child girded with his linen ephod, or in the little robe that his mother brought him from year to year when she came up with her husband to offer the yearly sacrifice.

With what passionate and almost irrepressible desire the mother must have anticipated that annual visit. It must have been hard to leave him at the tender age of three: but Hannah was solaced for her loss. There was the memory of those early years, when he had filled the house with his childish prattle. Other children were born to her, and as three sons and two daughters grew up at her knees, surely the thought of their older brother in his sacred office must have been a subject of lively and perennial interest! Peaceful, reverent, and loving thoughts filled the mother's heart as she embellished the robe, "woven from the top throughout and without seam," which the soldiers would not tear.

1. THE INFLUENCE OF A MOTHER. Mothers still make garments for their children—not on the loom or with their busy needles merely, but by their holy and ennobling characters displayed from day to day before young and quickly-observant eyes, by their words and conversation, and by the habits of their daily devotion.

"And the child ministered unto the LORD before Eli the priest." He slept his innocent sleep unconscious of the sins around him, attracted the growing attachment of the elderly man by his reverent affection and endearing ways, and gave many evidences that he was being prepared to become a link between God and His people, a mediator between the old and the new—between the turbulent days of Samson and the splendid peace of the reign of Solomon.

2. THE SACRILEGE AND SINS OF ELI'S SONS. "Now the sons of Eli were sons of Belial [*worthlessness*]; they knew not the LORD" (2:12). The law of Moses authorized the priest to take his portion the whole of the sin offerings, and the breast and right shoulder of the peace offerings, the fat only of the latter being burned on the altar. The remainder of the animal was handed back to the offerer to be consumed by himself, his sons and his daughters, his menservants and his maidservants, and the Levite that was within his gates (Deut. 12:12).

The first act of every peace offering was the sprinkling of blood on the altar round about; the second was the burning of the internal fat. It was never eaten, but always consumed by fire. The flame fed on it, as the food of God who, so to speak, ate with the accepted worshiper (Lev. 3:16–17). After this solemn rite was performed, the priest's portion was waved and presented to God, and the group of worshipers went after the rest, carrying away with them their portion for the joyful sacrificial feast.

Here Eli's sons stepped in with their rapacious greed. Not satisfied with their legally allotted portion, they sent their servant after the worshipers with a fleshhook of three teeth in his hand, and while the meat was boiling for the sacred meal, he thrust his hook into the cauldron and claimed as the priest's whatever was brought up.

But even this did not long satisfy them. They went on to insist that after the breast and shoulder had been handed them, but before the remainder had been boiled, they should be supplied with raw meat from the offerer's portion; nor would they burn the fat, which was the essential part of the whole sacrifice, and one for which the worshipers had to wait until their demands were satisfied. This final touch seems to have aroused the long-suffering people to exasperation. "At least," they said, "wait till the Lord's portion has been presented. Burn the fat, and afterwards take as much as you will." "Nay," was the ruthless answer of the priest, "but thou shalt give it me now: and if not, I will take it by force." "And the sin of the young men was very great before the LORD, for men abhorred the offering of the LORD."

Not content with their extortionate greed, Hophni and Phinehas perpetrated the vilest excesses of heathenism amid the woods and vineyards of Shiloh. Licentious rites had from time immemorial been associated with heathen festivals, but never before had they sullied the sacred vestures of the priests of Aaron's line. So depraved were these young men, though they had wives of their own, that they did not hesitate to lead astray the women who were appointed to perform various offices about the sanctuary.

Remonstrances were addressed to the aged priest; he heard of their evil doings from all the people (2:23), but he was content with giving only a mild rebuke. On this the divine Judge makes the terrible comment that Eli's sons made themselves vile, and he did not restrain them. And for this weak laxity he was condemned and deposed.

3. THE NEED OF FAMILY TRAINING. This suggests a serious question for those who take a prominent position in the church and before the world, but who neglect their own

families. We are held responsible for our children. Our weakness in restraining them is sin, which will be inevitably followed not only by their punishment, but also by our own. Better do less in the church and the world than allow your children to grow up a misery to themselves and a reproach to you. Remember that one essential qualification for office in the primitive church was the wise and wholesome rule of house and children. If a man could not keep his children in subjection, and rule his house well, he surely could not know how to take care of the house of God (1 Tim. 3:4, 12).

Above all, let us seek the conversion of our young children to God. As the child of godly parents, who cannot date the hour of my conversion because the love of God stole over my heart in early boyhood like the dawn of a summer sky, I put my seal to that word of God as true: "My words which I have put in thy mouth, shall not depart out of thy mouth, nor out of the mouth of thy seed, nor out of the mouth of thy seed's seed . . . from henceforth and for ever" (Isa. 59:21).

4

The Vision of God
1 Samuel 3

It is touching to notice the various references to the child Samuel as they recur during the progress of the narrative, especially those in which an evident contrast is intended between his gentle innocence and the wild license of Eli's sons—it is like a peal of sweet bells ringing amid the crash of a storm.

Hannah said, ". . . I will bring him, *that he may appear before the* LORD, *and there abide for ever.*" "And she . . . brought him unto the house of the LORD in Shiloh; *and the child was young.*" "As long as he liveth he is lent to the LORD. *And he worshipped the* LORD *there.*" "And *the child ministered unto the* LORD before Eli." "Now the sons of Eli were sons of Belial; they knew not the LORD: *But Samuel ministered before the* LORD, *being a child.*" "Now Eli was very old, and he heard all that his sons did unto all Israel. . . . *And the child Samuel grew on, and was in favour with the* LORD, *and also with men.*" "And *Samuel grew, and the* LORD *was with him, and did let none of his words fall to the ground.*"

His life seems to have been one unbroken record of blameless purity, integrity, and righteousness. One purpose ran through all his years, threading them together in an unbroken series. There were no gaps nor breaks; no lapses into sensuality or selfishness; no lawless deeds in that wild, lawless age. Toward the end of his long life he was able to appeal to the verdict of the people in memorable words, which attested his consciousness of unsullied moral virtue.

Samuel was not a prophet in the sense of foretelling the long future, but it was by his saintliness, the moral grandeur of his character, that he arrested the ruin of his people.

The noblest gift that any of us can make to our country or age is an undefiled character and a stainless life.

1. THE TRANSITION OF A YOUNG SOUL. For Samuel, however, a great change was necessary and imminent. Up to this moment he had lived largely in the energy and power of

his mother's intense, religious life. His faith had to rest, not on the assertions of another person's testimony, but on the fact that for himself he had seen, and tasted, and handled the Word of Life. It is a great hour in the history of the soul when the traditional, which has become a habit from long use, is suddenly exchanged for the open vision of God; when we say with Job, "I have heard of thee by the hearing of the ear: but now mine eye seeth thee" (Job. 42:5).

Will you believe then that God may be coming near you, and is about to reveal Himself to you in the Lord Jesus, as not to the world? He is about to transform your life and lift it to a new level.

2. THE VISION OF THE YOUNG EYES.

a. When God came near His young servant, it seemed as though *He placed His seal on his faithfulness.* Up to now only small services had been requried of him. It was right that he who had shown himself faithful in little should have a larger and wider area of responsibility assigned to him.

b. *The vision* came as night was beginning to yield to dawn; but the lamp had not yet gone out "in the temple of the LORD, where the ark of God was." Three times the boy was startled from his innocent slumbers. He heard his name called and, sure that Eli needed him, three times sped across the intervening space to report. Once, and again, and yet again, he ran to Eli, and said, "Here am I, for thou calledst me."

c. *Eli was very wise in his treatment of the young boy.* He might have posed as the sole trustee of the divine secrets, might have stood on the dignity and pride of office. But he took the boy's hand in his and led him into the divine presence. The aged man said sweetly, "Go, lie down: and it shall be, if he call thee, that thou shalt say, Speak, LORD; for thy servant heareth."

d. *The message entrusted to the boy was a terrible one.* We cannot but wonder if Samuel was afraid to show Eli the vision. With *a beautiful modesty and reticence* he set about the duties of the day, and opened, as usual, the doors of the house of the Lord. It was not for him to blurt out the full thunder that had burst on him. This was another beautiful trait in the boy's character. But he had misread Eli's character; he did not realize that men like him will resign themselves without a word of defense, determined to know the worst, and when they know it, meekly answer, "It is the LORD; let him do what seemeth him good."

5

Misfortune on Misfortune
1 Samuel 4–6

The scanty records of these chapters (4:1–7:7) bridge a considerable tract of scripture; covering, perhaps, forty years. It was an age of disunion and anarchy. After the deaths of Joshua, Caleb, and of all that generation, "there arose another generation after them, which knew not the LORD, nor yet the works which he had done for Israel" . . . (Judg. 2:10). There was no man, and no tribe, able to unite the people under one leadership, or recall them to the worship of the one Jehovah. The heart of the national life beat feebly and, in the expressive phrase that so completely represents the age of the judges, "Every man did that which was right in his own eyes."

The only common tie was afforded by the tabernacle, the ark, and the high priest-hood; but even the influence of these had become greatly reduced. "The children of Israel forsook the LORD . . . and followed other gods, of the gods of the people that were round about them, and bowed themselves unto them."

There was therefore nothing to hinder the steady encroachments of the neighboring nations. Now it was the children of Ammon on the east, then the Amelikites and Midianites from the desert, and again the Philistines on the southwest, that broke in on the Land of Promise. From time to time judges were raised up, but their authority was only temporary and limited.

Our story is especially connected with the southern and middle districts of Canaan which, notwithstanding Samson's heroic exploits—for he was contemporary with Samuel's early years—lay under the tyrannous yoke of the Philistines, who seem about this time to have been largely reinforced from the original seat of their empire in the neighboring island of Crete, and to have made the position of the Hebrews almost intolerable.

1. AN ILL-FATED ATTEMPT. "Now Israel went out against the Philistines to battle, and pitched beside Eben-ezer, and the Philistines pitched in Aphek." From these words we infer that the war was begun by Israel because the yoke of Philistia was too galling to be endured; but it is almost certain that from the first it was an ill-starred and badly-managed campaign.

Distinct directions were issued by Moses as to the way in which a campaign should be begun and conducted (Deut. 20), but none of them seems to have been put in force on this occasion. No priest was called in to ask counsel of God; not even Samuel. It was the sudden flaming out of a spirit of hatred and revenge from a race of slaves, who were stung to the depths by the taunts, the insults, and the whips of their masters.

The Israelitish hosts, hastily summoned and insufficiently armed, suffered a heavy defeat. Four thousand men lay dead on the battlefield, and a spirit of intimidation and dismay spread through the entire host. Such will always be the result when God's people leave Him out of their plans.

2. THE ARK, BUT NOT GOD, TO THE RESCUE. On the evening of that disastrous day the elders of Israel held a council of war (v. 3). It was evident that their defeat had to be attributed to some failure in their relations with the Lord. They said, "Wherefore hath *the* LORD smitten us to-day before the Philistines?" They were conscious that they had left Him out of their plans, and suddenly thought of an idea by which they might almost compel Him to take sides with them against their foes. "Let us fetch the ark of the covenant of the LORD out of Shiloh unto us, that when it cometh among us, it may save us out of the hand of our enemies."

They remembered the wonderful scenes in which that ark had played a part: Its going forth had always meant the scattering and flight of Jehovah's foes. Surely it would do the same again. They did not realize that God's very present help depended not on the presence of a material symbol, but on moral and spiritual conditions, which they should have set themselves to understand and fulfill.

The arrival of the ark, in due course, borne by the Levites, and accompanied by the sons of Eli as its custodians, was received with the exultant shouts of the entire host. Eli had evidently been unwilling to allow it to leave the sacred enclosure—"his heart trembled for the ark of God"—but he had yielded too often and too long to be able to sustain a successful protest; and probably no one else had any misgivings, for "when the ark of the covenant of the LORD came into the camp, all Israel shouted with a great shout, so that the earth rang again."

As soon as the Philistines were acquainted with the cause of this exuberant outburst, they were correspondingly depressed, for they too identified the presence of the God of Israel with the advent of the ark. It had always been associated in their minds with the hand of "these mighty gods . . . that smote the Egyptians." "Woe unto us!" they cried, "for there hath not been such a thing heretofore. Woe unto us! who shall deliver us?"

The Philistines seem to have stirred themselves to deeds of desperate valor. They advanced to the conflict with the words of their leaders ringing in their ears. "Be strong, and quit yourselves like men, O ye Philistines, that ye be not servants unto the Hebrews, as they have been to you! quit yourselves like men, and fight" (see 1 Cor. 16:13).

The issue of that terrible day was extremely disastrous. "Israel was smitten, and they fled every man into his tent: and there was a very great slaughter; for there fell of Israel thirty thousand footmen." Around the ark the ground must have been heaped with corpses, as the Hebrews fought desperately in the defense of the symbol of their faith; but in vain, for the ark of God was taken, and the two sons of Eli were slain. Samuel had foretold it, and so it happened.

That afternoon a Benjamite, with his clothes rent and dust on his head, bore the tidings to the hamlets and villages that lay along the open road to Shiloh; and a wail arose that grew in volume as he sped onwards until it reached its climax in the city of the high priest. "When the man came into the city, and told it, all the city cried out." On the still evening air arose a piercing outburst of lamentation, for what was there to hinder the immediate march of the victorious army on the city, deprived in one day of its warriors, and apparently of its God!

The old man, Eli, blind and anxious, had caused himself to be seated on his throne, facing the main thoroughfare. When the noise of the tumult arose, he anxiously inquired of the attendant priests and Levites and, perhaps, of Samuel, waiting as usual to respond to his last appeal for help, "What meaneth the noise of this tumult?" At the same moment the messenger appears to have burst into the presence of the little group, telling Eli who he was. In answer to the eager inquiry of the high priest, "How went the matter, my son?" without warning or preface, and with no care to soften the harsh words, he blurted out, with an ever-rising climax of dread awfulness: "Israel is fled before the Philistines, and there hath been also a great slaughter among the people, and thy two sons also . . . are dead, and the ark of God is taken."

The old man received the tidings in silence. The three first shots hit him severely, but not mortally; but "when he made mention of the ark of God, he fell from off the seat backward by the side of the gate, and his neck brake, and he died." With her last gasp the wife of Phinehas gathered up the horror of the situation in the single word that she uttered as the name of her child, prematurely born—Ichabod. It was sad indeed that she was a widow; sad that her father-in-law had died at the moment when he was needed so sorely; but sad most of all that the ark was taken, for with it the glory had departed. She was a true soul and was worthy to be classed with Hannah in her loyal devotion to the name and house of God!

But worse troubles befell them. In frantic haste the Israelites bore away the remnants of the sacred tent and its furniture, and concealed them. In subsequent years they were at Nob (1 Sam. 21:1). The removal of these precious relics was hardly completed before the Philistine invasion burst on the deserted city as an overflowing flood.

3. THE AWFUL NAME OF GOD. This part of the history more closely concerns the growing understanding of the surrounding nations as to the true nature of the God of Israel.

There was no other way in which the Spirit of God could inform the people of Philistia as to His holiness and power, than that which He adopted in this event. They bore the ark from the battlefield to the temple of Dagon in exuberant triumph. They would not have been impressed by the message of a prophet; but they could not resist the conclusions forced on them when, on two following mornings, they found his image prostrate before the emblem of Jehovah, and on the second occasion the head and arms were severed from the body so that the only part that was left intact was the fish's tail with which the figure ended. A terrible plague of "tumors" broke out on each successive city to which the ark was removed, and a visitation of destructive vermin on the country districts where it may have been deposited.

We must not suppose, of course, that God had no love toward these untutored souls, but there was no other way of convincing them of His real nature and prerogatives. The prostrated form of Dagon, the painful disease by which they were smitten, and the devastation of their crops, caused them to cry to heaven (v. 12), as though they realized that they were being dealt with by a greater than Dagon.

If the Philistines could have understood Epistles like those of John, they would without doubt have been written and communicated to them by some man of God; but since they could not understand such means of instruction, they were reached by the overthrow and shattering of their idol, the plagues that accompanied the progress of the ark, and the direction taken by the cows which, while crying for their little ones, bore their sacred burden along the straight road that led them from their home toward Beth-shemesh.

Similarly, the inhabitants of that frontier town had to learn by a stern lesson that God was a holy God, and that He could not permit them to manifest a wanton curiosity and irreverence in handling the sacred emblem of His presence. To pry into the ark as they did, was forbidden to the priests, and even the high priest himself; how much more to them? The swift retribution that followed on this act of irreverence extorted the reverent acknowledgment of the awesome holiness of God, as the men of Beth-shemesh said, "Who is able to stand before this holy LORD God?" When, on the other hand, the ark had been reverently borne to Kirjath-jearim, and had been carefully entrusted to the custody of Abinadab and his son Eleazar, the blessing that befell his house was an indication of the tender love and pity of the divine nature, who is willing to dwell with those who are of a humble and lowly heart, and who tremble at His word.

6

The Work of Reconstruction
1 Samuel 7:2

While the events described in the last chapter were in progress, Samuel was giving himself to the great and noble work of reconstruction. The Philistine invasion seems to have somewhat subsided from its first triumphant outburst, and to have left the occupancy of the interior portions of Israel. Samuel was therefore able to pursue his quiet and unobtrusive toils for his people, free from the zealous supervision and opposition to which, otherwise, he must have been subjected.

He seems to have taken up his abode in Ramah, so intimately associated with his earliest days. Here was his headquarters, where young men gathered to him, and were formed into the earliest of the schools of the prophets, and where also he married and became the father of two sons. Their names are suggestive of their father's piety and walk with God—the name of the one being Joel—"Jehovah is God," and of the other Abiah—"Jehovah is my Father."

Samuel knew that there were two objects that had to be realized before Israel's sad condition could be remedied or the divine ideal realized. First: the national unity had to be recovered from the anarchy in which it had been overwhelmed. It was useless to think of holding the land against the inroads of the neighboring people so long as each tribe was content with an isolated existence, repelling its own enemies for a time, but indifferent to the condition of its neighbors and of the country at large. Israel had to be one, animated by a common enthusiasm for its future independence and integrity.

This is no less desirable in our own age. The divisions of the church are her burden, and they render her impotent before her foes. It is a sad spectacle to witness the divisions between Christians in the face of a mocking world, and we will never be able to make men believe until we have learned to magnify the points of agreement, and to bear with all those who love the Lord Jesus, and are united with Him as their living Head, though their method of stating the truth may differ widely from our own.

Second: the evils that had eaten into the nation's heart had to be put away. Shrines to Baal and Ashtaroth covered the land. Foul orgies of shameless impurity were prevalent everywhere. And it was evident that only a widespread revival of religion could save the people.

This was Samuel's opportunity. "And Samuel spake unto all the house of Israel, saying, If ye do return unto the LORD with all your hearts, then put away the strange gods and Ashtaroth from among you, and prepare [or direct] your hearts unto the LORD, and serve him only."

Samuel was preeminently a man of prayer. He is known on the subsequent pages of Scripture, as he who called on the divine name (1 Sam. 9:6–9; Ps. 99:6; Jer. 15:1). In addition, he was a man of blameless reputation and life—in themselves eminent qualifications. He was also a man of practical sagacity, and by his appeals worked on the national conscience so that, as the result of his efforts, "it came to pass, while the ark abode in Kirjath-jearim, that the time was long; for it was twenty years: and all the house of Israel lamented after the LORD."

Notice those two phrases: *all* the house of Israel—there is the restoration of the lost unity; *lamented after the LORD*—there is the national repentance, which was followed by a widespread reformation: "Then the children of Israel did put away Baalim and Ashtaroth, and served the LORD only." Would that there might be a similar turning to God in our time and land!

7

The Victory of Faith
1 Samuel 7:1–14

After twenty years of quiet and unobtrusive toil, Samuel led his people to desire both to feel and manifest the old unity, and there was a distinct yearning after Jehovah. The sacred writer tells us that all the house of Israel "was drawn together" after Jehovah (v. 2, *marg.*). In being drawn to God they were drawn toward each other, as the spokes of a wheel center in the hub.

In verses 3 and 4 we probably have the substance of innumerable exhortations that Samuel delivered to all the house of Israel. From end to end he traversed the country, urging the people to return to Jehovah, to put away the false gods and Ashtaroth. On every hand idols were cast from their pedestals, and the vicious orgies were brought to an end in the groves and valleys.

1. THE CONVOCATION AT MIZPEH. The movement at last demanded a public demonstration, and Samuel summoned all Israel to Mizpeh.

The day was devoted to fasting, as the law required on the great Day of Atonement. The people confessed their sins, afflicted their souls, and humbled themselves before Jehovah. In addition, a somewhat novel rite was introduced. Water was brought from a neighboring well and solemnly poured out before the Lord, as afterward at the Feast of Tabernacles.

The pouring of water may have implied that they poured forth from their full hearts floods of penitence and tears; that they desired by the heaviness of their grief to wash their land free from the accumulated evil of the past years; or that the people realized their utter helplessness, so that they were as water spilled on the ground, which could not be gathered up. But whatever it may have signified, it must have been a very striking specatcle. It was a worthy act for his manhood's prime, and we are not surprised to learn that, as by a sudden outburst of acclamation, he was appointed judge (v. 6).

Oh, who will induce the professing church of God to put away the evil things by which her testimony is now impaired! What would not be the blessed result if the children of God would come to another Mizpeh and confess, as Israel did, "We have sinned against the LORD"!

2. THE VICTORY OF FAITH. The tidings of this great convocation reached the Philistines, who looked on it as an unmistakable sign of the returning spirit of national life, and "the lords of the Philistines went up against Israel" (v. 7). From every part the contingents of a great army were assembled, and there was every reason to fear that the terrible experiences of Aphek would be renewed. A panic of fear spread through the multitudes of Israel. There appeared but one hope: God had to arise to His people's help, or they would be trampled beneath the heel of the conqueror. "Cease not to cry unto the LORD our God for us," the people said to Samuel, "that he will save us out of the hand of the Philistines."

The power of Samuel's prayers was already known throughout the land, like those of John Knox in the days of Queen Mary. The people had come to believe in them; they felt them to be the palladium of their liberties. If only Samuel would pray, they might count on deliverance. They knew that he had prayed; they now begged that he not cease.

But Samuel did more than pray. He took a sucking lamb, and offered it as a whole burnt offering to the Lord, symbolizing thus the desire of Israel to be wholly yielded to the divine will. There must be consecration before there can be faith and deliverance. It is not enough simply to put away sin; we must also give ourselves absolutely and entirely to God. Failure in the walk always denotes failure in the heart-life. If you are perpetually overcome by the Philistines, be sure that there is a flaw in your inner consecration.

While the smoke of this offering was rising in the calm air, and the eyes of tens of thousands were fixed on the figure of Samuel, and while his piercing cries for divine help were rising to heaven, the Philistines drew near to battle against Israel. But suddenly the voice of God answered the voice of the prophet. "The LORD thundered with a great thunder [Hebrew, *the voice of God*] on that day upon the Philistines, and discomfited them." The sky was suddenly black with tempest, peal after peal rolled through the mountains. Then at a signal from Samuel, the men of Israel flung themselves on the flying foe. Josephus tells of another circumstance that added to the horrors of that irresistible onslaught. "God destroyed their ranks with an earthquake; the ground trembled under their feet, so that there was no place whereon to stand in safety. They either fell helpless to the earth, or into some of the chasms that opened beneath them."

The pursuit only stopped when the Philistines came beneath the shadow of their own fortress of Bethcar, the Well of the Vineyards, as it is now called.

This is the great message of the whole story for us. If only the church of God would put away the evils that grieve His Holy Spirit; if only we would ourselves come out and be separate, the Spirit would interpose for us too. The Lord would deliver us, fighting on our behalf against our foes, so that we would be more than conquerors through Him who loves us.

8

The Stone of Help
1 Samuel 7:12

"Then Samuel took a stone, and set it between Mizpeh and Shen, and called it Ebenezer [the stone of help], saying, Hitherto hath the LORD helped us." This was the same spot on which Israel had suffered the great defeat that led to the capture of the ark (4:1). How wonderful this was, that the story of the victory should be told on the plain that had been the scene of defeat!

From that moment Samuel's supremacy in the country was established. During his judgeship the Philistines did not return within the border of Israel. The alienated cities that the Philistines had taken from Israel were restored to Israel, from Ekron even to Gath. The Amorites, who had taken part with the Canaanites, found it to their advantage to side with Samuel and abstain from hostilities (v. 14).

It's amazing what prayer can do. It not only can open and close heaven, but will give the soul that prays an undisputed supremacy over his times, so that people will acknowledge that the savior of the city is not so much the politician, the man of intellect, or the man of affairs, but he who has learned how to walk with God.

At the foot of this stone let us linger for a little, to learn one or two more lessons, for stones have ears and voices. Joshua said that the stone he reared, at the end of his life's work, had *heard;* and our Lord said that the stones around Him might be expected to cry *out* (Josh. 24:27; Luke 19:40).

1. Its site. It stood on ground that had witnessed a terrible defeat and disaster. We are told, in the fourth chapter, that the great battle of Aphek was fought on this spot. "Israel went out against the Philistines to battle, and pitched beside Eben-ezer, and the Philistines pitched in Aphek." "Now the Philistines took the ark of God, and they brought it from Eben-ezer unto Ashdod" (4:1; 5:1).

Many who gathered around Samuel, when he raised and named this stone, must have been present twenty years before on that fatal field, the Flodden of Israel's glory. Here the fight had been fiercest, the slain thickest; in the distance the fight had raged around the ark of God as it was taken and retaken, and taken again. At this point, desperate deeds of valor ahd been done to turn back Israel from a shameful flight, but in vain. There Hophni fell, and Phinehas.

Notwithstanding all this, and though the spot was associated with the memories of disgrace and shame, yet there the stone was erected that spoke so eloquently of divine help.

What living encouragement there is in this for us! We too may be traveling at this very hour battlefields that have been sadly marked by defeat. Again and again we have met the foes of our peace in mortal conflict, only to be repulsed. We have been overthrown by our adversary, and overpowered, in spite of all our efforts, by our besetting sin. Be of good cheer! The stone of Eben-ezer will be raised on the very field of the fatal battle of Aphek.

2. Its retrospect. What a story this stone had to tell, if all were unfolded, of the wonderful dealings of God with His people. It looked back on the twenty years of patient work by which the prophet Samuel had been leading the people homeward to the God of their fathers.

It looked back on many a scene of iconoclasm as, from Dan to Beersheba, there had been a general putting away of the Baalim and Ashtaroth, the cutting down of groves and overthrow of altars. It looked back on that memorable convocation of all Israel at Mizpeh, when water was poured out before the Lord in confession of sin and humble penitence.

It looked back especially to the offering of the burnt offering, which declared Israel's resolve to be from that point on wholly devoted to God and to Samuel's piercing cry of intercession. Above all, it looked back on that memorable moment when, as the Philistines drew near to battle against Israel, "the Lord thundered with a great thunder upon the Philistines, and discomfited them, and they were smitten down before Israel."

Has anything like this taken place in your life? On your answer much will depend. If since your last failure and defeat there have been no acts of the soul, like those that took place at Mizpeh, there is no probability of there being any break in the long monotony of your reverses, unless there is the pouring out of your heart before God, the putting away of idols, and the resolve to follow Him fully.

I must bear witness to the incessant failure of my life, as long as I cherished things in my heart that were alien to God's holy will. Rules for holy living, solemn and heart-stirring conventions, helpful books and addresses, produced but small result.

There was temporary amendment, but little else. But when the scene at Mizpeh had been reflected in the inner mirror of the soul, then victory took place on the very spot marked by defeat. I would like to have you ponder this. You will never raise your stone of Ebenezer until you have stood on the watchtower of Mizpeh and put away all known sin, all complicity with what is grievous in the eyes of Christ. Then only will His keeping power avail.

You say that you cannot. Ah, that is the point where the Great Physician is willing to interpose for your rescue and deliverance! What you cannot do for yourself, He will do. The only question is, *Are you willing?* or, Are you willing to be made willing? Then tell Him that you cannot be as you would, or that you will not be as you should, and pray Him to undertake your difficult and almost desperate case. Do not doubt the result.

3. ITS INSCRIPTION. "Hitherto hath the LORD helped us." Surely if the stone had a retrospect, as we have seen, it had also a prospect. It looked forward as well as backward. It seemed to say, As God has helped, so He will continue to help.

As we go through life let us be careful to erect our Ebenezer stones, so that when new responsibilities begin to crowd on us, or fresh and unforeseen difficulties threaten, we may be emboldened to sing with Newton:

> His love in time past forbids me to think
> He'll leave me at last in trouble to sink;
> Each sweet Eben-ezer I have in review
> Confirms his good pleasure to help me quite through.

All through life, if you will only trust God, you will have occasions to raise these stones of help. The last stone that we shall erect will be on the edge of the river. As we turn our back forever on the land or our pilgrimage, and enter on the work and worship of eternity, we will set up a great stone to the glory of our God, saying once more, with a deep sigh of perfected satisfaction, "Hitherto hath the LORD helped."

9

A Great Disappointment
1 Samuel 7–8

The supreme test of character is disappointment and apparent failure. We are now to see how Samuel carried himself in the face of a great disappointment. This at least may be said of him, as of old it was said of Job, that he still held fast his integrity.

1. HOW THE DISAPPOINTMENT CAME ABOUT. During the years that followed the glorious victory of Aphek, Samuel set himself to build up in the hearts of his fellow-countrymen something of that profound belief in the reign of the divine King, which we know as the Theocracy, and which was so dear to all devout Hebrews.

His headquarters and home were at Ramah, the scene of the years of his happy childhood. From there he went on itinerating journeys. Who was he but the messenger and minister of the Lord of Hosts? With all the force of his character and eloquence of his speech he insisted that the people were the subjects of Jehovah, owing allegiance to

Him alone, and receiving from Him direction in times of perplexity, and deliverance in days of battle. They needed no king—Jehovah was King; no officials, but those who uttered His messages; no code of laws, but those that emanated from Him. It was a beautiful and inspiring concept.

a. *The same object was in his mind as he instituted the schools of the prophets.* To Samuel's wise interpretation of his times we must attribute the institution of these seats of learning. The priesthood had forfeited its right to stand between Jehovah and His people. It was clear that some other religious body must be called into existence. The times demanded an order of men who would be trained in the law of God, who would be fitted to interpret the holy oracles to the people, and from the midst of whom men would arise from time to time to proclaim on the housetops what God had whispered to their ears in secret. We find these schools flourishing in the days of Elijah and Elisha— some apparently on the same sites where they had been instituted by Samuel (10:3–5; 19:23–24; 2 Kings 2).

b. *But the failure to realize his high purpose seems to have happened because of the failure of his sons.* As Samuel became old, he was less able to administer justice; the burden of administering the government became too heavy for him, and he appointed his sons to assist him. The experiment proved however to be a disastrous failure. They "walked not in his ways, but turned aside after lucre, and took bribes, and perverted judgment."

This precipitated the catastrophe; and "all the elders of Israel" came to Samuel at Ramah. "Behold, thou art old, and thy sons walk not in thy ways; now make us a king to judge us like all the nations."

Looked at from the human standpoint, there was much to warrant the request. The Philistines were pushing their outposts into the heart of the country (13:3, 5); Nahash the Ammonite was a dangerous neighbor on the Eastern frontier (11:1); there was fear that disintegration might again separate the people on Samuel's death. But, on the other hand, the request shattered the prophet's hopes.

2. HOW SAMUEL BORE HIS DISAPPOINTMENT. "The thing displeased Samuel, when they said, Give us a king to judge us." It was not so much that they had rejected him, but that they had rejected God—that He would not be King over them. They had failed to grasp the right concept and had fallen to the level of the nations around them.

Under these bitter circumstances, he made for the one Harbor of Refuge: "Samuel prayed unto the LORD."

Then the Lord answered His servant. He always does, and will, answer. "Be careful for nothing; but in every thing by prayer and supplication with thanksgiving let your requests be made known unto God. And the peace of God, which passeth all understanding, shall guard your hearts and your minds through Christ Jesus" (Phil. 4:6).

3. THE DIVINE ANSWER AND ENCOURAGEMENT. When Samuel cried to the Lord about his deep trouble, in the divine answer it was made clear that the cherished ideal of a lifetime would have to be abandoned. The distinct impression was made on the prophet's mind that he had to renounce his high purpose, and step down to become subordinate to a king. "Now therefore" said his almighty Friend and Confidant, "hearken unto their voice."

At the same time his sorrow was greatly mitigated because he discovered that God was his Fellow-Sufferer, and that the sorrow of the divine heart was infinitely greater than his own. "They have not rejected thee, *but they have rejected me*" (v. 7). It is a great honor when a person is summoned to enter into fellowship with God in the awful pain and grief that we bring on his tender and Holy Spirit.

The suffering of God. Surely no one will count the phrase extravagant that attributes suffering to God, on account of His rejection by human hearts, and who refuse His reign and belittle the Spirit of His grace. Christ taught us that God was not impassive; but that He yearned, sorrowed, loved, as human fathers do, only with heights and depths of intensity that are indeed divine.

The prophet says that God was pressed beneath the sin and rebellion of men, as the groaning cart is pressed beneath its load.

4. SAMUEL'S NOBLE BEHAVIOR TOWARD THE PEOPLE demands our attention.

The request of the people for a king was, no doubt, in part based on Deuteronomy 17:14, which seemed to anticipate just such a crisis as had now arisen. But the present request had been sprung on Samuel prematurely. Instead of seeking to understand the mind of God, the people had made up their own mind; instead of consulting the aged prophet, they dictated the policy on which they had set their hearts.

Under these circumstances, and with the express direction of God, Samuel protested solemnly to the deputation of elders, and through them to the people, showing the manner of the king that would reign. It was impossible that a king demanded in such a spirit as characterized the people could be a man after God's own heart. They wanted one who, in his stature and bearing, in his martial prowess and deeds, would be worthy to compare with neighboring monarchs. This was much more to them than character, obedience to God, or loyalty to the Mosaic code. And as they desired, so it was done to them. Ah! how often it happens that God gives us according to our request, but sends leanness into our souls (Ps. 106:15).

Dangers that Samuel foresaw. All the Oriental extravagance and prodigality of human life, which were the familiar accompaniment of royalty in neighboring countries, were destined to reappear in the court of the kings of Israel. They would enforce the service of the young men to make their weapons, fight their battles, and minister to their royal state. They would exact unremunerated labor in the tillage of their lands. From the daughters and wives of the people they would demand confectionaries and bakemeats, and other elaborate luxuries for the royal appetite. Vineyards and oliveyards, farms and lands, would be confiscated at their desire. A system of heavy taxation would be imposed on the produce of the land, and on the flocks and herds that covered the pasture lands; while the people would have to stand still and see their hard-earned money squandered on the pleasures and self-indulgence of the palace. A brief experience of this kind would lead to a universal outcry, as the nation awoke to its grievous mistake; but the step so rashly taken would be found to be irreparable.

Samuel's protest and remonstrance were, however, alike in vain. "The people refused to hearken unto the voice of Samuel; and they said, Nay; but we will have a king over us." They trusted in man, and in the arm of flesh; their heart departed from the Lord; and in the sequel they were destined to see their king slain, their land overrun, and the national fortunes reduced as low as possible.

When Samuel saw that the people had made up their mind, he dismissed the assembly and took it upon himself to do the best he could for them. He set himself to build up an entirely new organization. In doing this he had to sacrifice his previous convictions, and do violence to his better judgment; but when once he realized that there was no alternative, he became the most devoted and efficient organizer of the new age.

10

The Voice of Circumstances
1 Samuel 9–10

It was the spring of the day. The dawn was breaking in the Eastern sky, when three men descended the steep ascent on which Ramah stood, and emerged from the city gate (19:11–12, 14, 26). The group was a remarkable one, comprising the aged seer; "a young man, and a goodly," who was the king elect, though he did not realize it; and a herdsman, Doeg, so tradition states, who later achieved an unhappy notoriety, but was at that time simply a servant in attendance on his master's son. "As they were going down at the end of the city, Samuel said to Saul, Bid thy servant pass on before us, but stand thou still a while, that I may shew thee the word of God."

1. THE CIRCUMSTANCES THAT LED UP TO THIS INCIDENT.
   a. *The asses of Kish, Saul's father, were lost.* "And Kish said to Saul, his son, Take now one of the servants with thee, and arise, go seek the asses."
   But when they left home they little realized how far their search would lead them. "And he passed through mount Ephraim, and passed through the land of Shalisha, but they found them not: then they passed through the land of Shalim, and there they were not: and he passed through the land of the Benjamites, but they found them not." Three days were consumed in this fruitless search, in stopping every traveler, asking many questions, scrutinizing every trail—but all to no avail.
   b. *By God's providence, which some call chance, the seekers found themselves in the land of Joseph,* and there the thought of his father's possible anxiety arrested the steps of the young farmer, and he said, "Come, and let us return; lest my father leave caring for the asses, and take thought for us." This remark indicated a good and commendable trait in Saul's character. On the whole, a man who cares for the feelings of those nearest to him is likeliest to be a good ruler of men.
   c. Having arranged for the offering of the piece of silver that was discovered in the bottom of the servant's pocket, as their gift to the Seer, *the two men made for the gate of the little city,* "which was set on a hill," its white houses glistening in the intense sunshine. The young women of whom they made inquiries, the fact that Samuel was in the city and on his way to a feast in the high place, the encounter with Samuel himself in the main street, and news that the asses were found—were like so many signposts that pointed them by the way they should go, until they came to the place that awaited them, the seat and portion prepared by the instruction of the prophet.
   Can we say anything that is too trivial to be a part of God's divine plan? Let it never be forgotten that straying asses, an unexpected encounter in the street, the presence of a coin in the pocket, or its absence, are all part of a divine plan, and it only awaits the quick eye, the ready ear, and the obedient heart, to detect the things that God has prepared for those that love Him.

2. THE INCIDENT OF SAUL'S FIRST ANOINTING. Saul slept at Samuel's house that night, and on the housetop. The prophet had prepared his couch there with a special purpose, which burned like a clear flame in his heart; for when the house was quiet, he went upstairs to the young man, who was pondering the strange events of the day, and "communed with Saul upon the top of the house."

With careful skill Samuel awoke the sleeping soul of the young son of the soil, who probably had lived in a narrow, circumscribed area, and who was interested in flocks and herds, in vines and crops, in the talk of the countryside, but with few thoughts of the national welfare.

He was awakened by Samuel before the breath that announced the dawn had stirred the leaves of the sleeping woods. "Samuel called Saul to the top of the house, saying, Up, that I may send thee away." Then as they reached the edge of the city the servant was sent on, and as the two stood together, Samuel took from out of his breast the vial of oil, and poured it upon the strong young head bent beneath his touch. "Is it not because the LORD hath anointed thee to be captain over his inheritance?" he said.

It was a great hour in Saul's life. No wonder that "when he had turned his back to go from Samuel," it was with *"another heart."* In a sense, though not the deepest, old things had passed away, and everything had become new.

11

As Occasion Serves
1 Samuel 10:7

Circumstances led up to Samuel's secret designation of Saul as king; and circumstances, so special and significant as to carry on their brow the divine impression, were destined to corroborate the momentous act. With unerring accuracy the old prophet anticipated them, and with unfailing precision each of them took place. "All those signs came to pass that day."

First, by Rachel's tomb, in the border of Benjamin, two men met him to say that the asses had been found, and that his father had left the care of the asses, and was taking thought for his son, saying, "What shall I do for my son?" When God has given a call, as clear and unmistakable as that which Saul received at the lips of Samuel, let the recipient wait trustfully and patiently for his hand to slacken the hold of circumstances. Before long the message will come in one form or another: "the asses are found." Any circumstance of that kind will be an unmistakable assurance that the Lord's voice has been speaking to the heart, and that His cloud is beckoning us to follow.

Next, as he went forward, filled with bewilderment and awe, near the oak, or terebinth, of Tabor (the situation of which is absolutely unknown), Saul met three men going on a sacred pilgrimage to Bethel.

These men were carrying, as Samuel said they would, their votive-offerings to the shrine—three kids, three loaves, and a bottle (or skin, *marg.*) of wine. First they saluted Saul with the invariable Eastern greeting, Peace be unto thee; and presented him with two of the loaves, as though they were obeying an inner conviction that was pressed home on them by the divine Spirit, that he whom they had encountered was no ordinary wayfarer, but one who might share their homage even with almighty God.

Finally, Saul came to "the hill of God" (Gibeah, *marg.*). Some translations note that there was a garrison of Philistines there; but other commentators, thinking it unlikely that Samuel would announce to Saul a fact that must have been so well known to him, have preferred to employ the other meaning of the word translated *garrison,* and have rendered the sentence, where the "erection, column, or monument," of the Philistines stands, probably reared by them to commemorate some famous victory.

Near this spot, and probably almost within sight of his home, Saul encountered a band of young men connected with the prophetic school that Samuel had established. They were coming down from the high place with a psaltery, a timbrel, a pipe, and a harp. The inspiration of prophetic fervor and ecstasy was on them, and as Saul beheld their holy rapture he fell under its spell. "The Spirit of God came upon him, and he prophesied among them."

This remarkable assertion need not astonish us. It is by no means uncommon to find men temporarily and spasmodically affected by strong religious impressions, who are not permanently and savingly delivered from their former worldly or selfish manner of life.

But what to Saul was only a transient and superficial influence may become, in each of us, a permanent possession. The Spirit of God may come on us to fill us, and abide, as He did with those on whom He came in the early days of the church. In successive waves of power and grace He may come on us, so that we may not only be filled suddenly and mightily for special work, but be constantly sensible of the holy infillings, as were the first converts in the highlands of Asia Minor, so that we may be permanently full, as was Stephen. (Compare Acts 4:8; 13:52; 6:5; note the change of tenses, etc.)

Whenever God calls us to special service He provides a special anointing of the Holy Spirit. This is universally true. As certainly as there is the call, there will be the equipment.

This transformation in the young farmer amazed all who knew him before, and they said one to another, "Is Saul also among the prophets?" It made as great a stir as when Saul of Tarsus joined the Christians, whom he had persecuted, or when Bunyan and Newton became ministers of the Word. One of the older people, however, understood the reason. Rumors of Saul's interview with Samuel were beginning to circulate, and he said in effect: "Has he not been with Samuel, the father of these blessed and exalted movements? What wonder, then, if he partake of his gifts!"

When the first tremor of excitement had passed, and Saul regained full mastery of himself, he went up to the high place, probably for meditation and prayer, that he might comprehend the full significance of the crowding events that had transpired recently. To whom can we turn, most holy God, in the supreme moments of life, but unto You? Only You can understand.

Before Samuel dismissed his astonished and awe-stricken guest, he urged him to act in each circumstance as occasion served (v. 7). There is always room for the exercise of sanctified common sense. The circumstances may be divinely contrived, but we must use them for good or evil, making them stepping stones or stumbling blocks. The divine guidance of our lives does not eliminate the necessity for the exercise of discretion, that looks before and after, *and upward*, in order to ascertain what the will of the Lord is.

There is always in the regimen of life an abundant need for the exercise of our judgment, through which the light of God may be shining as through a clear pane of glass. We are not dumb, driven cattle, nor the creatures of fate or chance. We are not automatons. As long as we look for guidance, it will be freely given; but when it is given we must use it, and it is useless unless we do. Only they who *receive* the abundance of grace and the gift of righteousness will reign in life.

12

Inner and Outer Conflicts
1 Samuel 11

The eleventh verse records a great victory. It was the first public act of the reign of Saul, taking place a month after his inauguration. It at once justified his selection, and silenced the voice of detraction; he stood before the eyes of his own people, and of the surrounding nations, as every inch a man and a king.

But in this chapter, if you look beneath the surface you will find the record of another fight. There was the outward fight that Saul made for Israel; there was the inner and previous fight that Saul made for himself, against himself; and it was because he had conquered in the latter, of which there was probably no symptom to the outward eye, that he carried himself erect in the fight with Nahash.

1. Saul's inward fight, conflict, and victory (v. 1).

a. *He fought the subtle temptation to pride.* Samuel, eager to constitute the new kingdom, called a great national assembly at Mizpeh, where so great a defeat and victory had been recorded earlier. In their teeming multitudes the Israelites gathered there, and proceeded to elect their king by lot, after they had appealed to God. After prayer the lot was cast, and the disposing of it was left to God. First the tribe of Benjamin was taken, then the clan of the Matrites, then the family of Kish, and ultimately the lot indicated Saul, the son of Kish; but he was not to be found. He knew from his previous conversation with Samuel that he was God's designated king; that the anointing oil had flowed over his head; that he was possessed of a kingly presence, standing head and shoulders above all ordinary men. If ever a man might have stood to the front, and allowed ambition to master him, that was the moment when Saul might have come forth and presented himself to his people as the unrivaled candidate for the crown. However, he was not to be found. They looked for him everywhere in vain. And it was only when, for the second time, they appealed to the direction of the Urim and Thummim, that he was discovered hiding among the baggage carts.

This modesty was extremely beautiful, and our admiration of the natural traits of Saul's character cannot be but greatly enhanced by his unobtrusiveness. It reminds one of Athanasius, who left the city of Alexandria that he might not be elected bishop; and of Ambrose, who more than once sought to evade the responsibility that was thrust on him at Milan.

b. *There was the strong temptation that forced him to vindictiveness.* Amid the shouts, "God save the King!" which applauded his nomination, there were the voices of detractors, men of Belial, who whispered, "How shall this man save us?" These voices must have stung the heart of Saul, but he conquered the desire for revenge, and trampled beneath his feet the smoldering embers of vindictiveness. It was not that he was timid, for we are told in this same chapter that when he heard the cry of Jabesh-gilead, "his anger was kindled greatly." He was capable of becoming angry against wrong, but in this case he held himself well in hand. "He held his peace."

The Hebrew, as suggested by the margin, is still more striking. "He was as though he had been deaf"—he pretended not to hear. He did hear; every word struck deep into his soul, but he made as though he were deaf. We exhibit great power when we can act as though we were deaf to slander, deaf to detraction, deaf to unkind and uncharitable speeches, and treat them as though they had not been spoken. We turn from man to God, leaving with God His vindication, believing that He sooner or later will give us a chance, as He most certainly gave Saul a chance of vindicating the true prowess and temper of our soul.

If Saul had listened to these men and noticed them, he might have drifted into an awkward and perplexing position, for if, on the one hand he had passed over their slander, he might have laid himself open to the imputation of cowardice; whereas if, on the other, he had noticed it, he might have been goaded to act tyrannically, and then possibly alienate a large number of his people. He could not have done better than to act as though he were deaf, and to conquer the spirit of revenge by the spirit of self-restraint.

c. *There was one more temptation which must have touched him—the temptation to ostentation.* When the assemblage was dispersed he returned from Mizpeh to Gibeah. He had been designated by Samuel, and kissed by him in token of homage. Sign after sign had indicated him to be God's choice for Israel; he had stood amid the people's clamor, the acknowledged king of the land; a number of young men, whose hearts were fired by loyal enthusiasm, had thronged about his path, and with songs of rejoicing had accompanied him to his home. He was conscious of being able to rally about him the chivalry and strength of his fatherland; and yet, when he was back again in Gibeah, he was noble enough to return to his rustic life. He took again in hand his plough, and for one whole month he drove the oxen across the fields, meditating much on the strange chance that had befallen, and wondering when God would open the door for him to step forth into the manifestation of the royalty that was already his.

These were the elements of a truly great soul. We do not forget Gilboa, and the frenzied insanity by which his career was later blasted. We remember how much more than once or twice he hurled his javelin at David; that he became moody and morose; that he betrayed the heart of a murderer and died the death of a suicide. But at this time of his life at least he remained humble; he put his foot on the spirit of revenge and left it with God to vindicate him; he put his foot on that love of ostentation that tempts us all, setting himself to do his daily work, and waiting until God summoned him to take the helm of the state. We cannot but admire this greatly.

2. THE OUTWARD CONFLICT. One evening, as Saul came back from the field, he heard that low wail of distress and panic by which the Eastern populace makes known its anguish; and as he drew near to Gibeah he asked what it meant. "What aileth the people that they weep?" Then the story was told how, across the Jordan, in the land of Gilead, the city of Jabesh-gilead was hard pressed by the Ammonites. Under Nahash, the king, they had gathered in overwhelming numbers around the beleaguered city. Its citizens had tried their best to extricate themselves, but in vain. One week of respite alone had been extracted from the contemptuous clemency of Nahash; and if at the end of that week no deliverance came, then the right eye of every man would be put out, which

undoubtedly would make every man useless for purposes of war, because the left eye was, of course, always covered by the shield.

In despair the messengers came to Gibeah, of Benjamin, because in the days of the judges Jabesh-gilead had refused to join in the war of extermination against the Benjamites, and had given four hundred of its daughters in marriage to their sons. There was therefore a blood-tie between the people of Jabesh-gilead and those of Gibeah, and in this awful hour they felt they had a claim for help—if they would not help, who would? But the people of Gibeah despaired. It seemed as if it were impossible in that short space to send effectual help. Saul was living in the midst of them, but they had no hope that he could help them. The day threatened to close in hopeless despondency.

Then the man who had conquered himself suddenly became aware of the uprising of an altogether new power in his heart. We are told that "the spirit of God came mightily upon Saul"; a little further on we learn that "the fear of the LORD fell on the people"; and still further on, "the LORD hath wrought salvation in Israel."

Saul instantly laid hold of his bullocks, slew them, cut them in pieces, and by messengers sent those pieces throughout the land. In some such way, as Sir Walter Scott tells us, the old Highland chieftains used to summon the clans for war by the mission of the fiery cross.

Similarly the entire people throughout the whole land of Israel obeyed the royal summons. They were at first but an undisciplined mob; but Saul, in the power of God, marshaled them, directing them by three different routes to fall on the Ammonites in the morning. A message was sent to Jabesh-gilead to tell the people that help was coming, and their hearts were glad. Then, as the morning broke over the quiet hills and valleys of Gilead, from three different sides Saul launched his army on the sleeping hosts. Panic-stricken, they sprang to their feet; hardly awake, they were unable to resist the onset of the men of Israel; and the rout was so complete that by noon no two men were left together. It was a wonderful victory, and an auspicious beginning for the new reign.

13

Forsaken? Never!
1 Samuel 12:22

While the entire land was ringing with the news of Saul's exploit in the deliverance of Jabesh-gilead, it appeared to Samuel to be an auspicious moment for confirming the kingdom in his hand; and therefore he summoned a great convocation of the nation at Gilgal.

On that spot Israel had encamped for the first night after crossing the Jordan, and the twelve great stones commemorating that even were still visible. There the act of circumcision had been performed, cleansing the people of the neglect of the wilderness; and there too the first Passover in the Land of Promise had been celebrated. Amid these great memorials and memories of the past the people gathered from far and near to crown Saul king. He had been designated at Mizpeh; he was to be crowned at Gilgal. It was the inauguration of his reign, its ratification and confirmation by the entire people. After this great ceremony, Saul and his people rejoiced together with peace offerings and thank offerings before God; and this was the moment that Samuel chose to lay down his office as judge—the last of the judges, and the first of the prophets.

1. SAMUEL'S RESIGNATION. Standing bare-headed before the vast audience of the men of Israel, and pointing to his white locks, Samuel said, "I am old and gray headed . . . and I have walked before you from my childhood unto this day." He was anxious to obtain from the people a vindication of the blamelessness of his career. He therefore protested: "I have not defrauded you, nor oppressed you. Whose ox have I taken? Whose ass? Can any man confront me with having taken from his hand even a sandal, as a bribe, that I should turn away my eyes from his misdoing?" And all the people, with one unanimous consent, cried: "Thou hast not defrauded us, nor oppressed us, neither hast thou taken aught of any man's hand."

But the old man was not content; he wanted to bind the people by a solemn oath, as in the very sight of God and the king; and therefore he said, lifting his hand to heaven, "I call God to witness against you this day, and his anointed king, that what you have said is true." And again, from the lips of all the people, with one unanimaous shout, there came the response, "He is witness." The old man was comforted and added, "Yes, God is witness: the very God who brought our people out of Egypt, and appointed Moses and Aaron."

2. HE DESIGNATED HIS PEOPLE'S SIN. It was a great opportunity to show them where they had done wrong; and a man whose own hands are clean is permitted to be the sincere critic of others' misdoing. In several particulars he pleaded with that dense mass of people, and dared to hold up the crimes of his nation, that they might see them as they were.

First, he showed them the difference between their former and their latter method of procedure. He carried their thoughts back to Egypt and, in effect, said: When your fathers were in bondage to the Egyptians, and under the oppression of Pharaoh, you cried to Jehovah, and in gracious answer He raised up deliverance. And when in the days of the Judges you were oppressed first by Sisera, then by the Philistines, and then by the people of Moab, you cried to God for deliverance, and it came; but now, when the threatened invasion of Nahash, the king of the Ammonites, is filling the horizon with thunderclouds, instead of holding a great convocation for prayer, you insist on my appointing a king. Why have you deteriorated? Why was prayer your natural resort three hundred years ago, and now it is neglected? Is it not because you are prayerless that you have drifted from your ancient moorings? In this is a great sin.

Second, in his dealing with the people, he put a new reading on past history. On their side, they pointed out the successive catastrophes that had befallen their country. Samuel, of course, admitted the successive afflictions that had befallen his people, but he made it clear that it was not the presence or absence of a monarchy, but the want of singleness of purpose, and devotion to Jehovah, that had been the cause and root of all their troubles.

Third, he indicated to the people that God had never failed to send them a man when a man was wanted. "See how perpetually in the dark hour, in answer to prayer, God has sent you the man who was needed. Could you not have trusted Him; and instead of being so urgent for a king, have waited for Him to do for you as He has done in the past?"

Last, he said: "My countrymen, you have greatly deteriorated; you have failed your faith; you have demanded a visible king, but have forgotten the invisible Lord. You have taken shelter under the idea of a new royalty, whereas God was your King, your true Head, the Leader and Patron of the nation. You should have rested only on Him."

It was a brave thing, a noble thing, a right thing, for Samuel to show to his people how they had drifted from the old true standing ground of faith into practical atheism and unbelief.

3. SAMUEL'S ASSURANCE. Having handed over his office to Saul, who from then on was to be the shepherd and leader of the chosen people, and having dealt with their failure and deterioration, he went on to say with inimitable sweetness, "The LORD will not forsake his people for his great name's sake." Oh, take these words to heart, and let them sink, like a refrain of music, into your soul.

The old prophet went on to say: "It hath pleased the LORD to make you his people." God hides his reasons. He loves because He will. This assurance applies to men:

a. *As individuals*. God will not forsake you. He did not choose you because of your goodness or beauty, and He will not forsake you because you have failed of your best. He has made you His child by adoption and grace, not that there was anything in you to especially attract Him, but because He would. It has pleased Him to make us His sons and daughters. We may have sinned against Him and grieved His Holy Spirit; we may have mixed ourselves with the seed of the people among whom we dwell—but God will not forsake His people. If He did, there would be a charge against His love that was not infinite, that it ceased after sin had reached to a certain height of outrage, that it could not abound over sin. His power also would be impugned, for the lost spirits in hell would boast that He had attempted more than He was able to perform—that He had not counted the cost.

There would also be an imputation on His immutability. It would be spread through the universe that He took up a sinful soul, cleansed and clothed it, loved and blessed it, and then He changed. At the news that God could be fickle, the palace of eternity would rock, the throne of heaven shake, and the mighty vault of space would reel to destruction. God dare not surrender the work that He has begun in the heart of man. That is why we may count on being saved. O soul of man, God will not forsake you.

b. *As a church*. Why could God not forsake Israel? Because the chosen people was the type of what He desired every nation to become; and therefore He had to go on building up Israel, that His type might not be broken; and He had to work through Israel to bring other nations to its level. If God had abandoned Israel, how could He have hoped to regenerate the world?

c. *As a world*. God cannot forsake this world, reeking though it be with blasphemy and impurity, with tyranny and sin. It has been saturated with the blood of His son and of myriads of His saints. It has been bedewed with the tears of the noblest souls that have ever breathed, and it is yet destined to shine amid its sister stars with an untarnished beauty; it is to be the specimen to all the universe of what God can do with a fallen world and a degraded race. God cannot forsake our earth, and some day we will see her glistening in the light that shone over Paradise, and the children of men walking in the white robes of purity, love, and truth.

14

Not Ceasing in Prayer
1 Samuel 12:16–25

In all Samuel's career there is nothing finer than the closing scene of his public action as the judge and leader of the Hebrew nation. Naturally he found it difficult to step down from his premiership, and inaugurate a régime with which he had no sympathy, since it seemed to be a setting aside of Israel's greatest glory in having God for King. But he suppressed his strong personal feelings, and did his best to start the nation on the new path it had chosen, selecting a king with the utmost care, bridging over the gulf between the old order and the new.

We cannot turn from the record of the great convocation, assembled before the Lord at Gilgal to ratify Saul's election, without noticing the repeated allusions to Samuel's power in prayer. His whole career seems to have been bathed in the spirit of supplication.

As a boy, with hands meekly clasped, as Sir Joshua Reynolds has depicted him, he asked God to speak, while his ear was quick and attentive to catch his lowest whispers. In the Psalms he is mentioned as chief among those who call on God's name, and as having been answered (99:6). Jeremiah alludes to the wonderful power he exercised in intercessory prayer when he pleaded for his people (15:1). All Israel knew the long, piercing cry of the prophet of the Lord. In their perils his intercessions had been their deliverance, and in their battles his prayers had secured them victory (1 Sam. 7:8; 8:6). There was "an open road" between God and him, so that thoughts of God's thinking were able to come into his heart; and he reflected them back again with intense and burning desire.

1. SAMUEL'S PRAYER FOR THUNDER AND RAIN. The heart of man cries out for divine authentication. If our nature realized its divine ideal, it would discern God in the ordinary and common incidents of providence. But the eyes of the soul are blinded, and men do not see the traces of the divine footprints across the world day by day.

In default of the faculty of detecting God's presence in the noiseless and ordinary providence of life, man asks for some startling phenomena to prove that God is speaking. Samuel knew this, and he perhaps longed for some divine corroboration of his words. He had surrendered his prerogatives, and introduced his successor; had confronted his people with their sins, and announced the heavy penalties that must follow on disobedience; now he desired that they should hear another voice, affirming his words, and pressing them home on conscience and on heart.

He concluded his address and appeal with the announcement, "Now therefore stand and see this great thing, which the LORD will do before your eyes. Is it not wheat harvest to-day? I will call unto the LORD, and he shall send thunder and rain; that ye may perceive and see that your wickedness is great, which ye have done in the sight of the LORD, in asking you a king."

During the wheat harvest, lasting from the middle of May to the middle of June, rain is almost unknown in Palestine, and the occurrence of a thunderstorm, coming as it did at *the call* of the aged prophet, was too startlingly unusual to be viewed as other than the divine authentication of his claims.

We cannot be too thankful for the witness of the Holy Spirit, whose voice is to the faithful servant of God all, and more, than the thunder was to Samuel. It was this that armed the primitive saints with irresistible power.

May I ask if my fellow servants realize this—that the Holy Spirit is in the church today, that He is prepared to bear His witness to every true word that is spoken in the name of Jesus, and that He will convict of sin, righteousness, and judgment; so that the faith of our hearers should not stand in the wisdom of man, but in the power of God.

This is often the fatal lack of our preaching. We speak earnestly and faithfully, but we do not sufficiently look for nor rely on the divine cowitness; we do not understand the communion and fellowship of the Comforter; and our hearers do not hear His voice thrilling their souls, as thunder in the natural world, with the conviction that the things that we speak are the truths of God. Only let the passionate longing of our heart be, "Father, glorify thy name," and voices will come as from heaven, saying, "I have both glorified it, and will glorify it again." While some that stand by may say that "it thundered," others will say, "an angel spake" (John 12:28–29).

2. SAMUEL'S UNCEASING INTERCESSIONS. Terrified by the loud thunder peals and the torrents of rain, the people were eager to secure Samuel's intercession on their behalf. "Pray for thy servants unto the LORD *thy* God," they said, "that we die not"; and the emphasis they laid on the word *thy* seemed to indicate that they felt no longer worthy of their ancient prerogative as the chosen people. Touched with their appeal, and confident that Jehovah only desired to corroborate His word, the aged seer calmed their fears, urged them never to turn aside to vain idols, which could neither profit nor deliver, assured them that the Lord would not forsake them, and ended with the striking words: "*Moreover as for me, God forbid that I should sin against the LORD in ceasing to pray for you.*"

a. *Samuel realized that prayer was action in the spiritual plane.* He could no longer exert his energies for his people, as he had done. The limitations imposed by his advancing years, and by the substitution of the kingdom for his judgeship, made it impossible that he should make his yearly rounds as before; but he was able to translate all that energy into another method of helpfulness. The prayers of God's saints were equivalent, from then on, to battalions of soldiers.

b. *Samuel viewed prayer as a divine instinct.* For him to thwart the promptings toward prayer that arose within his soul would be nothing short of sin. "God forbid," he said, "that I should sin against [Him] in ceasing to pray."

Let us recognize that, logic or no logic, men pray, and they want to pray. The instinct to do so seems to be part of ourselves. To thwart this instinct is to do violence to our noblest nature, to grieve the Holy Spirit of God, and to sin against the divine order. Prayer is the response of the soul to God, the return tide from us to Him, the sending back in vapor what we receive in showers of heavenly rain.

c. *Samuel viewed prayer as a trusteeship.* He could no longer act as judge, but he felt that the interests of the nation had been entrusted to his hands for the highest ends, and it would be treachery to fail in conserving and extending them, at least by his intercessions. The failure of Saul to realize his ideal only elicited the more strenuous appeals to God to save both king and people, and the victory we must record in our next chapter must have been due to his eager urgings.

15

The Cause of Saul's Downfall
1 Samuel 13:13-14

This chapter is the story of a great tragedy, since it contains the history of the incident that revealed Saul's unfitness to be the founder of a line of kings.

Let us gather around this story, not only because it has so much to do with the history of God's people, but because it is full of instruction for ourselves. Turning from Saul to David, Samuel said, "The LORD hath sought him a man after his own heart." It is therefore clear that in some way Saul had ceased to be "a man after God's own heart," and it becomes us to carefully inquire the reason so we may avoid the rocks on which this good ship split and foundered.

You will notice that the chapter that tells the history of this tragedy also contains the story of the unutterable distress to which the chosen people had been reduced by another invasion of the Philistines. We are told, for instance, in verse 6, that the people of Israel were in a difficult situation, that they were distressed, that they hid themselves in caves and thickets, in rocks and in pits. Indeed, some of them even crossed the Jordan, and forsook their people in the hour of their extremity; while those who were yet associated with Saul and Jonathan, as the nucleus of the royal army, followed him trembling (v. 7). A spirit of fearfulness had settled down on the entire people; the old national spirit had decayed; it seemed as though they could never again be induced to stand against the Philistines, any more than a flock of sheep against a pack of wolves.

A further proof of the hapless misery of the people is adduced in verse 19: there was no smith to be found throughout the entire land of Israel, and the Hebrews had to take their implements of agriculture down to the blacksmiths of the Philistines so that they might be sharpened for their use. Never in the history of the chosen people were there more dire calamity, more absolute hopelessness and despair, than reigned around Saul and throughout the entire country at this hour.

At this juncture Saul seems to have withdrawn his troops, such as they were, from Michmash, and to have taken up his position on the ancient site of Gilgal, where the act of circumcision was performed after Israel had crossed the Jordan under Joshua. There on the level land, and therefore exposed to the assault of the Philistine hosts at any moment, Saul seems to have pitched his camps; while his heroic son, Jonathan, kept up a post of observation in the vicinity of the Philistine hosts.

While Saul with his soldiers remained at Gilgal, every day marked the reduction of his host. This man and that stole away, either across the Jordan as a fugitive, or to hide in some hole and corner of the hills.

It may be asked why, at such a time, Saul did not make one desperate effort against the Philistines. Why did he wait there day after day, while his army evaporated before his eyes? Ah! thereby hangs a story—to understand it we must turn back a page or two in the inspired record. In 10:8, in that early morning interview when Samuel designated Saul for the crown, he told him that the crisis of his life would overtake him at Gilgal—a prophecy the fulfillment of which had now arrived. "Thou shalt go down before me to Gilgal; and, behold, I will come down unto thee, to offer burnt offerings, and to sacrifice sacrifices of peace offerings: seven days shalt thou tarry, till I come to thee, and shew thee what thou shalt do."

1. Saul's mistake. This command, uttered three years before to Saul, as he stood on the threshold of his vast opportunities, involved two things, and each of them constituted a supreme test.

First, whether or not he was prepared to act. Not as absolute monarch determining his own policy, but as God's servant, receiving the marching orders of his life through the prophet's lips; not acting as an autocrat, but as one to whom there had been a delegation of divine authority.

Second, whether he could control his impetuous nature, put the curb on his impulse, and hold himself well in hand.

It was this embargo that Samuel had laid on him that made him wait day after day. Can you imagine how his chosen advisers and warriors would come to him and urge him to do something? But he waited day after day. "He tarried seven days, according to the set time that Samuel had appointed: but Samuel came not to Gilgal; and the people were scattered from him." Then it would seem that shortly after the expiration of the allotted time he could wait no more. He thought that Samuel must have forgotten the appointment, or had been intercepted in making his way from Ramah through the Philistine lines. He had waited until within half an hour (because to offer a burnt offering and a peace offering could not take much longer), and then spoiled the whole by his inability to delay further; and he said to the priest, who still lingered by the ancient site where God had been worshiped and the tabernacle posted, "Bring hither a burnt offering to me, and peace offerings." "And it came to pass, that as soon as he had made an end of offering the burnt offering, behold, Samuel came."

The person who is after God's heart is the person who will obey God to the letter, who will wait for God to the last moment, who will stand still, until God sets him free.

We become so weary of waiting, and it seems as though God is so slow. God's mighty processes sweep around so wide an orbit. One day is as a thousand years, but His is coming as the morning, as the spring, as the millennium. "His going forth is prepared as the morning; and he shall come unto us as the rain, as the latter and former rain unto the earth" (Hos. 6:3).

2. Saul's insincere plea. Notice Saul's explanation to Samuel. He said: "Therefore said I, The Philistines will come down now upon me to Gilgal, and I have not made supplication unto the Lord: I forced myself therefore, and offered a burnt offering." That surely was insincere. He laid the blame on circumstances; he as much as said: "The circumstances of my lot forced my hand; I did not want to do it; I was most reluctant, but I could not help myself; the Philisitnes were coming."

O soul of man, you are greater than circumstances, greater than things, greater than the mob of evil counselors. You are meant to be God's crowned and enthroned king; rouse yourself, lest it should be said of you also that your kingdom will not continue.

3. Mark the alternative to this. In answer to all this Samuel, speaking in the name of God, said: "I have chosen a man after my own heart, who will perform all my will." In Jesse's home the lad was being prepared who could believe, and who would not hurry.

Wait for the Lord. Let your heart stop its feverish beating, and your pulse register no more its tumultuous waves of emotion! To act now would only disappoint the highest hopes, mar the divine purposes, and set stones rolling that will never be stopped. Wait for

God; stand still, and see His salvation. His servant is coming up the pass; His steps may not be quite so speedy as we would have them, but He will arrive to the moment—not a moment too soon, but not a moment too late. Oh, wait, my soul, wait on God; for He cannot be behind, as He will not be before, the allotted and appointed moment.

16

"Two Putting Ten Thousand to Flight"
1 Samuel 14

Just two young men, with the glow of patriotism in their hearts, and trust in God as their guiding star—imagine what they can do!

Jonathan was a true knight of God, who anticipated some of the noblest traits of Christian chivalry. We may almost say of him that he was the Hebrew Bayard, a soldier without fear and without reproach. He lived pure, spoke true, righted wrong, was faithful to the high claims of human love, and followed the Christ, though as yet he did not know Him. His character serves as a bright background on which that of his father is but a sorry contrast.

From the Jordan bank, a noble valley, twelve miles in length, leads up into the hill country of central Palestine. Two miles from the head of this narrow passage, and about eight miles due north of Jerusalem, the cliffs on either side become very precipitous, and approach each other almost to touching.

The ridge on the north was called Bozez, or "shining," because it reflects all day the full light of the Eastern sun; while that on the south, a few yards away, was known as Seneh, "the acacia," being constantly in the shade. Michmash crowned the former, and there the Philistines were encamped; while the little village of Geba lay above the latter, and there Saul had moved his army, such as it was, withdrawing from the plains of the Jordan to watch the movements of the hostile force.

How long the armies watched each other we have no means of knowing, nor can we guess what the result might have been had it not been for the heroic episode we are to recount.

1. JONATHAN ENTERED INTO THE DIVINE PURPOSE. Jonathan chafed at the inaction and the disgrace that the entire situation caused his countrymen. He was animated also by a profound faith in God, and was prompted by the divine Spirit to an act that issued in a glorious victory and deliverance.

Saul, on the other hand, had no perception of these things. Discouraged by what met his eye and ear from morning to night, he had no power to arouse himself to lay hold on the divine promise of deliverance. The sentence of deposition, which Samuel had pronounced, seemed to shut him up to despair. Happy are they who, like Jonathan, raise themselves above the depression of the moment and ally their weakness with the march of God, as He is always going forth to establish righteousness and judgment in the earth, which has been redeemed by precious blood.

2. HE YIELDED HIMSELF AS AN INSTRUMENT. God is always on the outlook for believing souls who will receive His power and grace on the one hand, and transmit them on the

other. Happy are they who are not insensible to the divine impulse, nor disobedient to the heavenly vision.

Jonathan was one of those blessed souls who are as sensitive to God as the retina of the eye to light, or the healthy muscle to the nerve; and "it came to pass upon a day, that Jonathan said unto the young man that bare his armour, Come, and let us go over to the Philistines' garrison, that is on the other side." In all probability the two slipped away silently in the gray dawn while their comrades were still wrapped in slumber. The imitation of a divine purpose thrilled the ardent spirit of the young prince, of which he gave some clue in the words, "It may be that the LORD will work for us: for there is no restraint to the LORD to save by many or by few."

Notice where Jonathan laid the emphasis. He had the smallest possible faith in himself, and the greatest faith in God. All that he aspired to was to be the humble vehicle through which the delivering grace of God might work. This is what God wants—not our strength, but our weakness, which in absolute despair turns to Him; not our armies, but two or three elect souls who expect great things and dare them.

Saul, the chosen king, had no such vision and no such faith. He was not sensitive to the divine voice speaking in his soul, but had to depend on the interposition of the priest (vv. 19, 36); he spoke and acted as though the victory depended wholly on the efforts that he and his men might put forth; and in forbidding the use of such simple refreshment as the wild honey of the woods might yield, he forfeited the full results of God's interposition. Throughout the whole day, and especially in this senseless command, which was meant to save time, but really hindered the full result, Saul showed himself oblivious of the one thought that animated the heart of his noble son—that God was working through human instruments to inflict His own judgment on the invading hosts.

3. JONATHAN TRUSTED IN GOD, AND GOD DID NOT FAIL HIM. As they ascended the steep cliff, the young men agreed on the sign that should indicate that they were indeed in the line of the divine will, and that God would not fail them. This was graciously granted in the mocking voices of the advanced outposts, which ridiculed the idea that the Hebrews were to be feared (v. 11), even though they would succeed in scaling the crags. "Behold," they said, "the Hebrews come forth out of the holes where they had hid themselves. And the men of the garrison answered Jonathan and his armour-bearer, and said, Come up to us, and we will shew you a thing [or we should like to make your acquaintance]."

This was the heaven-given sign, and conveyed the assurance that the Lord had already delivered them into the hand of Israel (v. 10).

The soul that counts on God cannot be ashamed. When the two young Benjamites reached the top they used their slings with such precision that twenty men fell dead to the ground. Because of this, a heaven-sent panic spread from them to the main army behind them, and to the bands of spoilers returning from their night raids. The Philistines could not know that the two who faced them were absolutely alone. It seemed as though they were precursors of a host of resolute and desperate men, and suddenly, in panic, each man suspected his neighbor of being in league against him; "every man's sword was against his fellow, and there was a very great discomfiture." Meanwhile, the Hebrews who had been allied to the Philistines, or silently acquiescent in their rule, even they also turned against them; and all who had hid themselves in the hill country of Ephraim, when they heard that the Philistines fled, ran after them and met them in battle.

From his outlook at Gibeah, Saul beheld the wild confusion, and how the multitude swayed to and fro, and melted away. Without delay he hurled himself with his soldiers on the fleeing foe, who fled in order to gain the Philistine frontier by the valley of Aijalon. Every town through which the fugitives passed joined the pursuit, so that the fleeing host was greatly reduced, and thousands of warriors dyed the highways of the land, which they had so grievously oppressed, with their hearts' blood. Thus did God deliver His people in answer to Jonathan's faith.

The unwise prohibition of the king against food had a terrible sequel; first, in the exhaustion of the troops, and, second, in the famished eating of the spoils of the day, without the proper separation of the blood. Still worse, when the day closed in, and Saul asked counsel of God, the divine Oracle was silent. Some sin had silenced it, and the monarch realized that some sin was crying for discovery and expiation. He did not look for that sin in his own heart, where he would have assuredly found it, but in the people who stood around him. Finally he and Jonathan stood before the people as the objects of His divine displeasure, and Saul was prepared even to sacrifice his son in his moody wrath.

But the people saved him. They cried indignantly, "Shall Jonathan die, who hath wrought this great salvation in Isarel? God forbid: as the LORD liveth, there shall not one hair of his head fall to the ground; for he hath wrought with God this day." Saul had not only missed the greatest opportunity of his life, but he was already wrapping himself in the unbelief, the jealousy, and the moroseness of temper in which his sun was to be enshrouded while it was yet day.

17

Failure Under the Supreme Test
1 Samuel 15:26

It is impossible to turn the pages of Saul's history without lamenting the fact that the bright promise of his early life was so soon overcast and that he, who stood forth in the morning of his life amid the acclaim of his people as one likely to do marvelous work for them, became one of those whom the sacred writers describe as having failed of the high purpose of his life. This chapter gives the story of his final rejection, which had indeed been threatened before, but which now became a reality.

1. THE TEST OF THE DIVINE SUMMONS AND COMMAND. "Go and smite Amalek, and utterly destroy all that they have, and spare them not; but slay both man and woman, infant and suckling, ox and sheep, camel and ass."

This command was given after several years had intervened from the incident narrated in the previous chapter; and during those years Saul had met with marvelous encouragement. The handful of men who had followed him, trembling, had increased to a great army, properly disciplined and armed, and led by his uncle Abner. He had also waged successful wars against Moab and the children of Ammon on the East, against Edom on the South, and against the kings of Zobah on the North. It is also evident that he had gathered around him important people, for we find the royal table was reserved for himself, Abner, and Jonathan; that he was surrounded by a bodyguard of runners; and that his will was law. The kingdom that had been inaugurated amid such adverse circumstances was beginning to enforce respect. It was at this time that the supreme test entered his life, as it so often comes to us in days of prosperity.

You will notice that this supreme test gave him a final chance to retrieve the past. The divine command involved the absolute extermination of the Amalekites; for the word translated "utterly destroy," would be better rendered *devote*. It is the word often used in the Book of Joshua for placing under the ban the sin-infected cities of the Canaanites. It was understood that in the case of the "devoted" city, every man, woman, child, and beast had to be destroyed, and only the precious metals were to be kept, after they were put through the fires of purification (Num. 31:21, etc.). With such absolute devastation and destruction was the name of Amalek to be wiped out from under heaven. At first it seems terrible that God demanded this act of obedience from Saul; but the Amalekites, as we are told in verse 18, were abominable sinners. We learn also from verse 33 that Agag with his sword had often made women childless. These Amalekites were a cruel and rapacious tribe of robbers, who were constantly making raids on the southern frontier of Judah. It was absolutely necessary, therefore, for the safety of the chosen people, that their power to plunder and kill should be permanently arrested.

The Amalekites had stood before the bar of God, had been weighed in His balances, and found wanting. Their sentence had been pronounced, and Saul was called on to inflict it. But Saul was only doing that which otherwise would follow in the natural process of decay; for God has so constituted us that when we sin against the laws of truth, purity, and righteousness, decay immediately sets in by an inevitable law. If Amalek had never been attacked by Saul and his hosts, the vices that were already at work in the heart of the people must have led to the utter undoing and destruction of the nation. We may infer that there was therefore mercy in this divine ordinance. It was infinitely better for Amalek, and for the surrounding peoples, which would have become infected by her slow deterioration, that by one stroke of the executioner's axe the existence of the nation be brought to an end.

2. OBEDIENCE WITH RESERVE. The story is told us in verse 9: "But Saul and the people spared Agag." When Saul raised his standard, two hundred thousand footmen from Israel, and ten thousand men of Judah, Benjamin, and Simeon, gathered around it, at Telaim, on the southern frontier; and they came to the chief city of Amalek, which probably lay a little to the south of Hebron. After lying in ambush in some dry water course, or waddy, and having given notice to the Kenites—a peaceful, friendly people—to leave, the attacking army carried the city by assault, and put to the sword men, women, and children. They pursued the fleeing remnants of the Amalekites from Havilah even to Shur, the great wall of Egypt; and with the exception of Agag, and a few who may have escaped, and the choice of the flocks and herds, the whole country was rid of its inhabitants, and was reduced to the deathlike silence of an awful solitude.

Saul returned, flushed with triumph, reared a monument of victory in the oasis of Carmel, near Hebron; and then came down to the sacred site of Gilgal that he might sacrifice to the Lord, and perhaps divide the vast plunder of sheep and goats, of oxen and camels, which had fallen into his hands, and which he and the people had not wanted to destroy.

Whether this reserve was due, so far as Saul was concerned, to greed, as appears most likely, or because as he says in verse 24, he feared to go against the people, obeying their voice rather than the voice of God, we cannot decide; but considerable light is thrown on the incident by the startling expression used by Samuel in verse 19, when he says, "Why didst thou fly upon the spoil?" employing the same expression as in 14:32, where we are told that the people, in their ravenous hunger, flew on the spoil, and ate even the blood. The same passionate vehemence seems to have characterized Saul and the men of Israel. Surely rapacity and greed were at work, and before their boiling currents all the bulwarks of principle and conscience were swept away.

There is great significance in this for us all. We are prepared to obey the divine commands up to a certain point, and there we stay. Just as soon as "the best and choicest" begin to be touched, we draw the line and refuse further compliance. There is always a tendency with the best of us to make a bargain with God, and sacrifice all to His will, if only He will permit us to spare Agag and the best of the spoil.

But an even deeper reading of this story is permissible. Throughout the Bible, Amalek stands for the flesh; having sprung from the stock of Esau who, for a morsel of meat, steaming fragrantly in the air, sold his birthright. For us, Agag must stand for that evil propensity that exists in all of us, for self-gratification; and to spare Agag is to be merciful to ourselves, to exonerate and excuse our failures, and to condone our besetting sin.

Is this your case? You are willing to give Christ the key of every cupboard in hour heart, except one; but that contains your most cherished sin, for which you find many excuses, and which you are prepared to sacrifice everything else. Thus Ananias and Sapphira kept back part of the price, and were cut off.

It is startling to learn that Saul perished, on the field of Gilboa, by the hand of an Amalekite (2 Sam. 1:1–10). What a remarkable fact! The least instructed can figure out the lesson. If we spare ourselves, and don't cut off the right hand or foot that may be causing us to offend, we will certainly perish by the hand of that which we refused to part with. The love of God, foreseeing the risk we are incurring, pleads with us to destroy without mercy the enemies of our own peace. But Agag comes to us delicately and we hold back in inflicting the divine sentence, and presently we are stricken down by the assassin. Our crown is transferred to another.

18

A Remarkable Dialogue
1 Samuel 15:12–35

An intimation of Saul's lapsed obedience was made in the secret ear of Samuel in the dead of night, when God came near him and said, "It repenteth me that I have set up Saul to be king: for he is turned back from following me, and hath not performed my commandments."

The faithful soul of Samuel was deeply moved. We are told he was *"angry"*—a righteous indignation that one who had been appointed with such solemn sanctions, and had started out so well to achieve glorious deliverances for his people, had so seriously missed his mark. "He cried unto the LORD all night."

Samuel traveled some fifteen miles to find Saul, following him from Carmel where, as we have seen, Saul set up a monument, to Gilgal, the site of the ancient shrine where, as one of the versions informs us, the king was engaged in offering sacrifices to Jehovah; and there this most remarkable dialogue took place.

1. SAUL.—It was begun by the king who, seeing the prophet coming toward him, went out to meet him with an unctuous phrase on his lips, "Blessed be thou of the LORD"; and, with great complacency in his demeanor, added, "I have performed the commandment of the LORD." Whether Saul was blinded and did not really know how far he had deteriorated, or whether he desired to gloss over his failure, and to appear as a truly obedient son so as to deceive the prophet, we cannot tell; but that "Blessed be thou of the LORD" from *his* lips, and at *such* a moment, has an ugly sound.

SAMUEL.—At that moment the sheep began to bleat and the oxen to low. A breath of wind, carrying with it the unmistakable indication of the near presence of a great multitude of flocks and herds, was wafted to the prophet's ear. It is an unfortunate occurrence when, just as a man is becoming loud in his protestations of goodness, some such untoward incident suddenly takes place, so that the lowing of the oxen and the bleating of the sheep belie his words. With sad irony the prophet said, "What meaneth then this bleating of the sheep in mine ears, and the lowing of the oxen which I hear?"

SAUL.—The king excused himself by laying emphasis on the word *they*—"*They* have brought them from the Amalekites: for *the people* spared the best of the sheep and of the oxen, to sacrifice unto the LORD thy God." Notice the subtle effort to conciliate the prophet by the emphasis laid upon the word *they*—"thy God; and the rest we have utterly destroyed." It was unroyal and contemptible to lay the blame on the people, and it was an excuse that could not be allowed.

SAMUEL.—The royal backslider would probably have gone on speaking, but Samuel interrupted him, saying, "Stay, and I will tell thee what the LORD hath said to me this night." Then the faithful old prophet went back to the past. He reminded Saul how insignificant his origin had been, and how he had shrunk from undertaking the great responsibility of the station to which God had summoned him. He reminded him how he had been raised up to the throne, and how the almighty King of Israel had delegated to him his authority, requiring that he should act as His designated vicegerent. He reminded him also that a distinct charge had been given him, and that the responsibility of determining his line of action had been transferred from himself, as the agent, to the divine Being, who had issued His mandate of destruction. In spite of all, Saul had allowed his greed to hurry him into an act of disobedience.

SAUL.—The king reiterated his poor excuse: "Yea, I have obeyed the voice of the LORD, and have gone the way which the LORD sent me, and have brought Agag the king of Amalek, and have utterly destroyed the Amalekites. But *the people* took of the spoil, sheep and oxen, the chief of the [devoted things] . . . to sacrifice unto the LORD thy God in Gilgal." It was as though he had said, "You have judged me wrongfully. If you would wait for a little while, you would see the result of my act of apparent disobedience." He may even have persuaded himself into thinking that he meant to sacrifice these spoils now that he had reached Gilgal; or he might have mentally resolved there and then to sacrifice them, and so relieve himself of the complicated position into which he found himself drifting.

SAMUEL.—In answer to this last remark, God's messenger uttered one of the greatest sentences in the earlier books of the Bible, a sentence that is the seed germ of much to the same purpose in the prophets: "Hath the LORD as great delight in burnt offerings and sacrifices, as in obeying the voice of the LORD? Behold, to obey is better than sacrifice, and to hearken than the fat of rams."

Then, tearing the veil aside, Samuel showed the enormity of the sin that had been committed by saying: "Rebellion is as the sin of witchcraft, and stubbornness is as iniquity and idolatry." These sins were universally reprobated and held up to the contempt of good men; but in God's sight there was nothing to choose between them and the sin of which the king had been guilty. Then, facing the monarch, and looking at him with his searching eyes, the prophet, in the majesty of his authority as God's representative, pronounced the final sentence of deposition, saying, "Because thou hast rejected the word of the LORD, he hath also rejected thee from being king."

SAUL.—In a moment the king realized the brink of the precipice on which he stood; and with the cry not of a penitent, but of a fugitive from justice he cringed before Samuel, saying, "I have sinned: for I have transgressed the commandment of the LORD, and thy words: because I feared the people, and obeyed their voice. Now therefore, I pray thee, pardon my sin, and turn again with me, that I may worship the LORD."

There is a great difference in the accent with which men utter those words, "I have sinned." The prodigal said them with a faltering voice—not because he feared the consequences of sin, but because he saw its heinousness in the expression of his father's face, and the tears that stood in the beloved eyes. Saul, however, feared the consequences rather than the sin; and that he might avert the sentence he said, as though Samuel had the power of the keys to open and unloose, to pardon or to refuse forgiveness, "pardon my sin."

SAMUEL.—The prophet saw through the subterfuge. He knew that Saul's penitence was not genuine, but that the king was deceiving him with his words, and he turned about to go away. Then Saul, in the extremity of his anguish, in fear that in losing him he might lose at once his best friend and the respect of the nation, seems to have sprung forward and seized the skirt of Samuel's cloak, and as he did so with a strong masterful grasp, as if to restrain and draw back to himself the retreating figure of the prophet, it tore. When Samuel felt and heard the tear, he said, "The LORD hath rent the kingdom of Israel from thee this day, and hath given it to a neighbour of thine, that is better than thou." And then he told Saul to remember that the "Strength of Israel will not lie nor repent" for His sentence is irrevocable. The word had gone out of His lips and could not be called back. There was no opportunity of changing His mind, though Saul would seek it bitterly with tears.

SAUL.—Again the king repeated the sentence, "I have sinned"; but his real meaning was disclosed in the following words: "Yet honour me now, I pray thee, before the elders of my people, and before Israel, and turn again with me, that I may worship the LORD thy God." His inner thought was still to stand well with the people, and he was prepared to make any confession of wrongdoing as a price of Samuel's apparent friendship.

Finally Samuel stayed with him, so the elders would not become disenchanted with their king, and that the people generally might have no idea of the deposition of Saul, lest the kingdom itself totter to its fall before his successor was prepared to take his place. The two knelt side by side before God; but what a contrast! *Here* was darkest night; *there* was the brightness of the day. *Here* was the rejected; *there* the chosen faithful servant.

307

At last the aged man summoned Agag, the king of the Amalekites, to his presence, and Agag came to him "cheerfully," hoping without doubt that he would be spared; and saying, as he advanced, "Surely the bitterness of death is passed—there is no reason for me to fear it." Then Samuel, strengthened with some paroxysm of righteous indignation, seized a sword that lay within his reach, and cut Agag in pieces before the Lord—a sign of the holy zeal that will give no indulgence to the flesh; and we are reminded of the words of the apostle, "Make not provision for the flesh, to fulfil the lusts thereof" (Rom. 13:14). To Amalek we must give no indulgence.

May God help us to read deeply into this tragic story. Whenever God our Father puts a supreme test into our lives, let us at any cost obey Him. Let us walk circumspectly and wisely, redeeming each opportunity, that God may make the most possible of us and that, above all, we may not become castaways.

19

"An Evil Spirit From the Lord"
1 Samuel 16:13–14

1. THE DAWN OF A FAIR PROMISE. "Samuel cried unto the LORD" for Saul, if perhaps He might arrest the terrible and imminent consequences of his sin. But he was made aware that prayer would not change His mind. The summons of the hour was therefore not to prayer, but to action. The Spirit of God urged Samuel to go to Bethlehem, and among the sons of Jesse discover and anoint the new king. Samuel was stunned by the request, and suggested that if Saul heard a whisper of such a proceeding, he would at once take measures to avenge himself by inflicting the death penalty. But the Spirit of God urged him to go, taking his long horn of oil in one hand, and leading a heifer with the other. Thus he made his way across the broken hill country of Judea, until he came to the village of Bethlehem lying along the slope of the hill, at the foot of which, not long before, Boaz had courted Ruth. The halo of the immortal story of their love was still fresh as dew.

When Samuel entered the little town the elders were filled with consternation; it was so unusual to see the great prophet visiting them without previous announcement. They asked if he had come peaceably. "Peaceably!" was the laconic reply. A sacrificial feast was at once prepared—the victim offered; but as some time must elapse between the offering of the sacrifice and the preparation of the food, Samuel adjourned to spend the interim in the house of the village chieftain, Jesse the Bethlehemite, and thus in the privacy of the home, David's career as king began.

One after another the stalwart sons of Jesse passed before the prophet, and as he looked on them in their towering stature and manly frame, he supposed that any one of them might be God's designated monarch. But his almighty Counselor told him that outward appearance was not this time to weigh in the scales of choice, but that the royal qualities of the heart alone were to determine his selection. And so son after son passed; all had come but one, and he was with the sheep. Samuel felt that probably, because he was the youngest and the least, he might be God's accepted king. He could not proceed with the holy exercises until the boy was summoned. So David was called and, coming quickly from the hills, the color mounting to his ruddy cheeks, his hair waving in the wind, his beautiful blue eyes flashing with purity and truth, he stood before the aged man, the dawn of a new age, the inauguration of a better time, the keystone of the great fabric of Hebrew monarchy—above all, the man whom God loved. As his brothers stood nearby, the aged prophet took the horn of oil, broke the capsule, poured it on the bright young locks, drenching them with the holy unction, as the boy bent beneath. As he anointed him, it seemed as though God almighty accompanied the outward sign and seal by the inward grace, for we are told that the Spirit of God came on that young life from that day forward, bathing it, permeating and filling it, so that he went in the power of the Holy Spirit to meet his great lifework, to be the sweet singer of Israel, the shepherd of God's people, and the inaugurator of Solomon's temple.

2. An overcast afternoon. We have morning with David; afternoon with Saul. Here youth; there manhood, which has passed into prime. Here the promise; and there the overcast meridian of a wrecked life.

It is affirmed that "an evil spirit from the LORD" troubled Saul. To interpret this correctly we must remember that, in the strong, terse Hebrew speech, the Almighty is sometimes said to do what He permits to be done. And surely such is the interpretation here. Therefore, when we read that an evil spirit "from the LORD" troubled Saul, we must believe that, as Saul had refused the good and gracious influences of the Holy Spirit, and definitely chosen the path of disobedience, there was nothing for it but to leave him to the working of his own evil heart.

3. The lurid gleams of an overcast sky. In 2 Samuel 21:2, we read this: "The king (that is, David) called the Gibeonites" (the Gibeonites were not of the children of Israel, but of the remnant of the Amorites. And the children of Israel had sworn to them, and Saul sought to slay them in his zeal to the children of Israel and Judah). Saul was smarting under Samuel's words, writhing under the sentence of deposition, and his soul was stirred to neutralize, if possible, the divine verdict, so as to still keep the favor of God. It was true, and Saul knew it well, that he had failed in one distinct call to obedience; he had kept the choice of the spoil for himself—but why should he not, by excessive zeal in other directions, win back his lost inheritance? Why should he not resuscitate some old command, and give it unexpected obedience?

Now there were two such commandments that seem to have occurred to him. The one said that when the children of Israel entered the Land of Promise, they had to destroy all the people of the land. The Gibeonites, however, succeeded in making sure that they should be excepted, because they had made a covenant with Joshua, and Joshua had sworn to them (Josh. 9). But in his false zeal for God, Saul seems to have laid ruthless hands on these peaceable people; and, in spite of the old covenant that bound Israel to respect their liberty and life, he exterminated them—an act that brought righteous retribution on his house years later, for you remember how, in order to offset this ruthless act, Rizpah's sons, and his own five grandsons were hanged on a tree, and left there until the rain rotted them (2 Sam. 21:8). Second, there was on the statute book a drastic law against magicians and witches, and it was commanded that these should be exterminated from the land (Exod. 22:18). Therefore Saul turned his hand against them. In his heart he still believed in them for at the end of his life he sought out one of these very women, and sought her help. However, in order to show his zeal for God, and to extort the reversal of his sentence, he began to exterminate them.

But as his edicts went forth, there was rottenness in his heart. His royal state was greatly increased; he wore from this time a gorgeous turban, like other kings, which was brought from the field to Gilboa to David. There was a great increase of luxury in his court, for he dressed the daughters of Israel in scarlet and gold (2 Sam. 1:24). A subtle admixture of Baal worship with the recognition of Jehovah appears from the naming of his sons, partly from the name of Jehovah, and partly by the name of Baal. He took to himself concubines in imitation of his neighbors. While on the one hand, therefore, there was this outburst of lurid zeal for God, his own heart was becoming more and more evil.

Let us turn from Saul for a moment to look at our own hearts. We too have disobeyed, have come short, have failed to fulfill His commands, but there is forgiveness in those flowing wounds, there is pardon in that loving heart. Seek it! Ask Him to blot out the past. Let the dead bury its dead. And may the Holy Spirit kindle on our heart altars a fire of zeal that will never be put out.

20

"Sin Bringing Forth Death"
1 Samuel 18:12

Never has there been a truer illustration of the words in which the apostle James describes the genealogy of sin and her fateful family than that furnished by the life history of Saul. No sooner are we told that he had begun to yield to the spirit of evil, than the historian hastens to tell us of the successive steps by which its early suggestions grew into a headlong passion, sending the monarch to one breach after another of the divine law.

It happened this way. About this time, while Saul was smarting under Samuel's sentence of deposition, David for the first time crossed his path. Two accounts are given of the introduction of the young shepherd to the God-forsaken and moody monarch, but they are not mutually inconsistent. The one tells of his entering the royal palace as a minstrel; the other of his prowess in war, which rendered his presence an indispensable asset to the court.

The attacks of Saul's depression and despondency become more frequent and severe; and at last it was suggested by his servants—tradition says, by Doeg the Edomite—that the effect of music should be tried on the poor diseased brain.

The king instantly fell in with the suggestion, and presently David's name was mentioned. The young shepherd was possessed of the qualities that were most captivating for the king. He was a skillful musician. He had already come to be known as a man of valor in the border skirmishes that he engaged in with robbers for the integrity of his father's flock. He was skillful in judgment, and eloquent in speech. Manly beauty characterized his countenance and bearing. It seems as though what happens in measure to all God's servants had happened to David—the unction and abiding of the Holy Spirit had brought out into fair and living prominence his natural traits.

The description of David given to him greatly pleased the king, who was always on the outlook for promising youths; and he sent a summons to Jesse to send him his son David, who was with the sheep. Such a summons could not be disregarded, and making up a present of the produce of his farm, the aged father sent his Benjamin to begin to tread the difficult and intricate paths of royal favor. "And David came to Saul, and stood before him: and he loved him greatly." And whenever Saul was overtaken by one of his fits of melancholy, David, then probably about eighteen years of age, played the harp for Saul, so that he was refreshed, and the evil spirit left him.

It is probable that the spell of music with which David sought to relieve the king's dark moods was greatly successful. Saul's fits of insanity became less and less frequent; the need for David's attendance at court was greatly relaxed; and the king may almost have ceased to think of him, amid the many suitors for his royal favor.

How long a period elapsed in this way we cannot tell, but another series of events brought Saul and David into closer and more tragic contact. The Philistines had never forgiven the Hebrews for having discarded the yoke, which for so long they had meekly borne; and at last, after a series of forays and raids on the southern borders of Canaan, the tide of invasion could no longer be restrained. It rolled across the frontiers, and poured through the valleys, until the Philistine hosts were gathered together in the valley of the Terebinth, which belonged to Judah, and pitched their camp at Ephes-dammim, "the Boundary of Blood," so called, probably from the dark and bloody encounters that had taken place there. The valley, or wady, is broad and open, and about three miles long. It is divided in the center by a remarkable ravine, or trench, formed by a mountain torrent, which is full of foaming water in the winter, though dry in summer. It was the presence of this gorge or channel, some twenty feet wide, with steep vertical sides, and with a depth of ten or twelve feet, that prolonged the issue for so long, so that the two hosts lay watching each other for forty days, neither of them daring to face the hazard involved in crossing the valley and its ravine, in the face of the other.

The full story of the combat with Goliath belongs to the life of David; we touch on it here only as it concerns the ill-fated and hapless Saul.

When the gigantic Philistine champion strode forth, and even dared to come near the lines of the Hebrew troops, and when he boldly challenged the armies of Israel to produce a man worthy to take up the gage of battle, Saul was as dismayed and panic-stricken as any of his soldiers. It is said that he was "greatly afraid" (17:11). Though he was God's chosen king, and in his earlier life had stood in the might of a simple faith, his disobedience had severed the source of his power, and he had become as weak as any other person. All that Saul could do, in the face of the braggart blasphemy of Goliath, was to hold out the most lavish promises of what he would do for the hero who would take up the challenge, and make the proud Gittite bite the dust.

When David finally was brought into his presence, avowing his determination to go alone to fight the Philistine, Saul sought to dissuade him. "Thou art not able to go against this Philistine to fight with him." The point of David's narrative of his successful conflicts with the lion and bear was entirely lost on him. Saul looked on them as the result of superior agility and sinewy strength; he did not fathom David's meaning as he spoke of the great deliverances that Jehovah had given him (17:37). Already the young psalmist was saying to himself:

> The LORD is my light and my salvation,
> Whom shall I fear?
> The LORD is the strength of my life,
> Of whom shall I be afraid?

On the ground of expediency, after his return to Gibeah, Saul set David over the men of war. The harp was exchanged, for the most part, for the sword; and as he went forth on his expeditions against the hereditary foes of Israel, he became more and more necessary to the stability of the throne, as he became increasingly the darling of the nation. "Whithersoever Saul sent him, he behaved himself wisely." Out of this popularity originated the great sin of Saul's life.

On one occasion, as Saul and David were returning from some final and decisive victory over the Philistines (v. 6), the people crowded to meet them and the troops; and the women, dressed in gay attire, danced around, singing to the music of their tambourines and three-stringed instruments. As they performed the usual sacred dance they sang responsively, "answering one another," an ode of victory, of which this was the refrain:

> Saul hath slain his thousands,
> And David his ten thousands.

The king was instantly smitten with the dart of jealousy. His soul was set on fire with the thought that it was probable that David was the neighbor of whom Samuel had spoken as being the divinely designated successor to the kingdom, which was even now passing from his hand. "And Saul was very wroth, and the saying displeased him; and he said. . . . What can he have more but the kingdom?"

"And Saul eyed David from that day forward." All the love and admiration he had entertained toward him turned to gall and bitterness. His old malady, which had been charmed away from him, came back with stronger force than before; and on the day after the incident, brooding over his fancied wrongs, it seemed as though his entire nature were suddenly thrown open to an evil spirit. Raving in a mad fit of frenzy, he caught up the spear that stood beside him as the emblem of his royal state, and hurled it at David who was sitting before him, endeavoring to charm away his malady. Not once, but twice, the murderous weapon quivered through the air; but David "avoided out of his presence twice," no doubt imputing the attempt on his life to the king's illness, and having no idea of the jealousy that was burning in his soul like fire.

21

The Sin of Jealousy
1 Samuel 18

Among the most terrible of human sins is jealousy—and of all the delineations of it none is more absolutely true to life coloring than this portrait of the first king of Israel.

1. JEALOUSY OPENS THE DOOR TO THE DEVIL. In Saul's case the interval was the briefest possible. On the next day, after the song of the women, which first aroused in his heart the feeling of jealousy toward David, we learn that "an evil spirit" came with force on the ill-fated monarch.

This evil spirit is said to have been "from God"—a phrase that can only be interpreted on the hypothesis that God permitted it to come, and that this was an obvious result of his sinful life.

2. Jealousy defeats its own good. With almost a single bound, David had leaped into the throne of universal homage and affection. "All Israel and Judah loved David" (v. 16). Not only they, but the court was enamored of him. He was set over the men of war, and his promotion was good not only "in the sight of all the people," but also "in the sight of Saul's servants"; while Jonathan loved him with a love passing the love of women; and Michal, Saul's daughter, was attracted to him. There must have been something of a spell in the influence of that pure bright soul over all who came into contact with it.

Besides this, the Lord was evidently with him. Note how constantly the sacred chronicle touches that note: "Saul was afraid of David, because the Lord was with him" (v. 12); "David behaved himself wisely in all his ways; and the Lord was with him" (v. 14); "And Saul saw and knew that the Lord was with David" (v. 28). Moreover, he behaved himself wisely, or prospered (v. 5); "wisely in all his ways" (v. 14); "very wisely," so much so that Saul stood in awe of him (v. 15); "more wisely than all the servants of Saul, so that his name was much set by" (v. 30).

Under these circumstances, how judicious it would have been for Saul to bind the son of Jesse to himself! Admitting frankly that he was his designated successor, and that he was enjoying the special favor of Jehovah, the king might have used David for the rehabilitation of his waning fortunes. It was evidently impossible to reverse the divine choice, but he might have postponed the infliction of the inevitable sentence. Nothing could have been easier, nothing more politic. But instead of this, Saul allowed his mad passion to smolder and sometimes burst into a flame, until it broke out in irresistible fury, and consumed the house of his life.

3. Jealousy is very inventive of methods of executing its purpose. Trace this in the history before us. First Saul, under the excuse of his sickness, attempts to take David's life with his own hand. He knew that the murderous deed would be charged to the deranged condition of his mind, and therefore, with impunity, twice threw the javelin at the minstrel who sought to charm away his illness.

Then he sought to throw him into positions of extreme peril, by inciting him to valiant deeds on the field of battle, and in border warfare. For a bribe he promised him his elder daughter, Merab, and to this was added the appeal of religion, and no motive could be more potent with this devout and chivalrous soul. "And Saul said to David, Behold my elder daughter Merab; her will I give thee to wife: only be thou valiant for me, and fight the Lord's battles." Then, with unsparing hand, the sacred writer draws aside the veil, and recites to us the secret thoughts that were passing in that dark and evil-haunted nature—"For Saul said, Let not mine hand be upon him, but let the hand of the Philistines be upon him."

The stratagem had failed, but it seemed too insidious, and too likely to realize the royal purpose, to be abandoned without being put to one further proof; and Michal, Saul's younger daughter, who really loved David, at this time at least, was made the prize to allure the young unsuspecting warrior to fresh encounters with the Philistines. To his servants, Saul must have seemed to be sincerely attached to David, and to desire, with genuine earnestness, to enroll him in his family. He was playing clearly a game of unusual adroitness. On the one hand, his servants really believed that the king delighted in David, and wanted the alliance; on the other, "Saul thought to make David fall by the hand of the Philistines."

It was only after the plot had failed, and it seemed as though, through the providence of God, David was possessed of a charmed life, that Saul spoke to Jonathan his son, and to all his servants, that they should slay David; again he hurled his javelin at him with such force that it stuck, quivering in the palace wall. He later pursued him, first to his own home, and finally to Samuel's home in Naioth (see chap. 19).

4. JEALOUSY OF THE INNOCENT IS UNABLE TO AVAIL AGAINST GOD. It was remarkably so with David. Saul was set on alluring him to his ruin. Through God's interposition, however, each murderous intent was foiled, and became the cause of the still greater popularity to his rival. If he is set over the men of war, he prospers wherever he is sent; if he is separated from the immediate proximity of the king, and permitted to go in and out before the people, the whole nation loves him (18:13, 15). If he is sent to fight the Philistines, he slays not one hundred but two, so that his name is "much set by" (v. 30). If Saul urges Jonathan to slay him, he drives his own son into a closer friendship, and forces him to plead the cause of the twin soul with which his own was knit. Everything that is meant for ill turns out for good.

22

"Cruel as the Grave"
1 Samuel 20:27

The home is one of the most sacred institutions of our human life. Originated by the knitting of spirit with spirit, the two become one; and from that union springs the gift of blessed children, making the race perennially young. Such a home, in David's case, was due, under God, to Saul's own arrangement. Michal, his daughter, loved David; they told Saul, and it pleased him, and he gave her to David to be his wife. Yet when David had evaded his javelin, and fled to the security of his home, saying to himself, At least my father-in-law will respect the sanctity of his daughter's love, the madly-jealous monarch sent messengers there to watch him, and to slay him the next morning.

Michal knew her father too well to trust his clemency; she warned her husband of the imminence of death, and with woman's intuition (and what will not women do for those they love!) aided him to escape, letting him down from the window with her own hands. It was due to her that the newly-formed home was not made desolate, and the light of its hearth quenched.

David hastened to tell Samuel of the turn that things were taking, and of the grave suspicion that was forcing itself on his soul, that Saul's attempts on his life were not the result of a disordered brain, but of a wicked and murderous will. For greater security Samuel led him to a cluster of booths, perhaps woven of willows (called Naioth), where a number of young men were being trained for the prophetic office.

Into this sacred assembly Saul forced three successive bands of messengers to arrest David; and finally, in hot wrath at their failure to return, came himself. Some time later it was distinctly remembered how he came to the great well, or cistern, in Sechu, and vehemently asked for Samuel and David. When he was told they were in Naioth, he went there, but was stricken down before he ever reached the place; and, divested of his royal robes for a second time in his life, lay on the ground in a kind of trance, which lasted all that day and all that night.

The very fountains of a father's love and pride dry up before the volcanic fires of jealousy. Jonathan was one of the noblest types of manhood. Whether in the court or on the battlefield, he shone as a star of the first magnitude. But these considerations had no weight with Saul, while jealousy of David laid heavy in the other scale. He might be, as his friend eloquently expressed it in his funeral elegy, "lovely and pleasant," swifter than an eagle, stronger than a lion; but Saul was prepared to sacrifice it all to the spirit of revenge.

It was on the monthly festival that this new vent of the volcano, which raged within Saul's heart, revealed itself. It was the second day, and as on the previous one, David's seat was empty. Speaking of him derisively as "the son of Jesse," as though accentuating his lowly birth, and ignoring the relationship that bound him to the royal family, the king asked Jonathan the reason for his absence. When he received the answer on which the two friends had previously agreed, he fell into a grievous rage, abused Jonathan with the vilest epithets that an Easterner can use—who today vents his scorn on the mother of the object of his hate—insisted on David's immediate arrest and execution, and ended by hurling his javelin at his noble son, who had interfered to mollify his wrath.

1. BUT JEALOUSY IS ALSO RESPONSIVE TO THE WORST POSSIBLE SUGGESTIONS. Of this there is an illustration in the following chapter (21). The fugitive fled this time to Nob, where Ahimelech the high priest presided over the relics of the ancient sanctuary. The suspicions excited in Ahimelech's mind by the unescorted and hasty advent of the king's son-in-law were removed by an evasive reply, and David was received with deference, supplied with bread, with the sword of Goliath, and such spiritual counsel as the ephod was capable of giving.

The incident was reported to Saul, some months afterward as he was encamped "on the height" above Gibeah, waiting for tidings of his hated rival, that he might at once march with his household troops, composed of trusted Benjamites, men of his own tribe, to capture and slay him.

In the heat of his spirit he vehemently complained that all his servants were in conspiracy against him, that no one cared for him, that Jonathan was at the bottom of David's conspiracy, and that each was cherishing the hope of his speedy downfall in order to receive possessions and promotions as the price of treachery from the hand of Jesse. Amid the silence that followed these undeserved reproaches, Doeg narrated what he had seen on that fateful day when he had happened to be detained at the tabernacle for some ceremonial ablution or other rite, and had witnessed Ahimelech's attentions to the king's son-in-law.

Doeg's malicious statement at once diverted the king's suspicions from his courtiers to the priests; Nob was not far from Gibeah; and a peremptory summons, after a brief interval, brought Ahimelech and all his father's house—i.e., all the males of the high priest of the house of Eli—into the presence of the king. In unmeasured terms Saul accused all of them of connivance with David for the overthrow of his throne and dynasty, and would give no heed to Ahimelech's mild expostulations. The high priest pleaded that though he had done what the king accused him of, he had done it quite innocently. He had always accounted David as one of the most faithful of Saul's servants, had looked on him as being constantly entrusted with secret commissions, and had frequently made similar inquiries of God on his behalf, believing that in this he was serving the royal will. But he might as well have tried to stem the swelling of Jordan.

The king's mind was made up before he began his defense. He said, "Thou shalt surely die, Ahimelech, thou, and all thy father's house."

The royal bodyguard shrank from executing the awful sentence; but Doeg the Edomite, a foreigner, with his herdsmen, had no such compunctions, but immediately fell on the unresisting priests, who were butchered one after another, until their mangled corpses were piled in heaps, and their white robes were saturated with their hearts' blood.

2. JEALOUSY IS, HOWEVER, SUBJECT TO STRONG REMORSE. These scourges are the remonstrances of that blessed Spirit, who allows no soul to drift unwarned to the bottomless pit. Saul was very subject to these powerful eddies in the hurrying current.

When, earlier, Jonathan reminded his father of the priceless services that David had rendered, he listened attentively, relented, and pledged his royal oath that he would not be put to death (19:1–7).

When David spared his life in the cave, near the Fountain of the Wild Goat, refusing to lift his hand against the Lord's anointed, and restraining his surprised and eager followers—touched by a generosity that was wholly unexampled in those rude days, Saul lifted up his voice and wept, and poured out the pent-up generosity that had been natural to him in earleir days, but had for long been restrained.

And, when again he came in search of David and pitched his camp on the ridge of Hachilah, on the southern hills, and again, through David's clemency, his life was spared from the fatal plunge of the spear that would not have needed a second thrust, Saul went so far as to say before all his camp: "I have sinned: return, my son David: for I will no more do thee harm. . . . I have played the fool, and have erred exceedingly" (26:21).

But, in every case his remorse was of brief duration, and failed to produce any permanent change in heart or purpose. The fire still smoldered in his soul, awaiting the least breath of air to rekindle its flames. He might exclaim, "Blessed be thou, my son David: thou shalt both do great things, and also shalt still prevail." But David, not daring to trust him, "said in his heart . . . there is nothing better for me than that I should speedily escape into the land of the Philistines" (1 Sam. 26:25; 27:1).

3. BUT THE CURE OF JEALOUSY IS CLEARLY SET FORTH IN THESE TERRIBLE CHAPTERS. Without doubt, Saul's conjectures were well known to all the members of his family, and especially to Jonathan. Before Saul had ever blurted out his threat that Jonathan's kingdom would not be established, as long as the son of Jesse lived on the ground, the heir apparent had assured his friend that he knew the time would come when the Lord would cut off the enemies of David, every one from the earth (20:14–15, 30–31). And later, while Saul was seeking David's life amid the ravines of Ziph, urged on in his madness by the treacherous Ziphites, Jonathan came to him, and strengthened his hand in God, and said: "Fear not, for the hand of Saul, my father, shall not find thee, and thou shalt be king over Israel, and I shall be next unto thee; and that also Saul my father knoweth."

Jonathan, then, was even more affected by the choice of David than his father was. It was certain that he would never succeed to the throne. Respected and loved he might be, but enthroned never. But not a cloud of jealousy ever darkened the pure heaven of his love, or cast its shadow on the crystal lake of his peace. We are told that "he loved David as his soul."

23

A Great Sunset
1 Samuel 25:1

Samuel finally came to his end, as far as this world at least was concerned; and was borne to his grave, as a shock of corn fully ripe. Though he had spent the last years in retirement, partly because of his great age, and partly because of the breach between the king and himself, he had never lost the love and respect of his people. So when the tidings sped through the country that he had fallen into that blessed sleep that God gives to His beloved, the event was felt to be a national calamity, so that from Dan in the far north to Beersheba on the southern frontier, "all the Israelites were gathered together, and lamented him, and buried him."

The impression made on his contemporaries lingered, as an afterglow, long after his death. Again and again he is referred to in the sacred record.

First Chronicles 9:22 suggests that he laid the foundations of that elaborate organization of Levites for the service of the sanctuary that was perfected by David and Solomon.

First Chronicles 26:27-28, asserts that he began to accumulate the treasures by which the house of the Lord was ultimately erected in the reign of David's mighty son.

Second Chronicles 35:18 contains a passing reference to some memorable Passover Feast, which he instituted.

Psalm 99:6, and Jeremiah 15:1, commemorate the fragrance of his perpetual intercessions.

Acts 3:24 and 13:20 indicate what a conspicuous landmark was furnished by his life and work in the history of his people.

Hebrews 11:32-33 places him in the long gallery of time. "The time would fail me to tell . . . of Samuel . . . who through faith . . . wrought righteousness. . . ."

1. THE BLESSEDNESS OF HIS LIFE. Though Samuel's career was an arduous one, it must have been filled with the elements of true blessedness.

a. *He was preeminently a man of prayer.* This was his perpetual resort; he never ceased to pray. Many a sleepless night he spent in tears and prayers for the king whom he had set up, and into whose hands he had committed the national interests as a precious charge.

All books, says an eloquent writer, are dry and tame compared to the great unwritten book prayed in the closet. The prayers of exiles! The prayers of martyrs! The prayers of missionaries! The prayers of the Waldenses! The prayers of the Covenanters! The sighs, the groans, the inarticulate cries of suffering men, whom tyrants have buried alive in dungeons, whom the world may forget, but God never! Can any epic equal those unwritten words which pour into the ear of God out of the heart's fullness? But these prayers have been deeds. In the words of James 5:16, they have availed much in their working. An energy passes from the holy soul, striving mightily in prayer, which becomes a working force in the universe, an indestructible unit of power, not apart from God, but in union with his own mighty energies.

Let us pray more, especially as life advances. "More things are wrought by prayer than this world dreams of."

b. *Samuel was also characterized by great singleness of purpose.* He could court without flinching the most searching scrutiny (1 Sam. 12:3). His had been a career of stainless and irreproachable honor. The interests of his people had been his all-absorbing concern. The troubles that had befallen his land had only led him nearer God, and bound him more tightly to his fellow countrymen; but when he discovered that they desired him to give up his position, it required all the gifts of God's grace, and all the qualities of a naturally noble nature, to sustain the shock with equanimity. But he set himself to secure the best successor the age could afford, and humbly stepped down from the supreme place of power.

Oh, to be so absorbed in a consuming passion for the glory of God in the salvation of others, that we may be oblivious of ourselves, willing to take second place.

c. *Samuel was also careful to construct.* When the whole land was disorganized, he began to lay the foundations of a new State. The time and care he expended on the schools of the prophets, his administration of justice in his itineraries, his appeals to the people in their convocations, formed a great policy that resulted in a consolidated and united people.

As first of the prophets, as the connecting link between the first days of the settlement in Palestine and the splendor of Solomon's reign, by his unblemished character, by his sympathy and strength, by his evident fellowship with the God of Israel from his boyish days to his old age, Samuel won from his people the most profound veneration; and it is not to be wondered at that one of them—who owed everything to him, though he was unable to appreciate the majesty of his personality—in the supreme hour of his desperate need, when all beside had deserted him, turned for help to the great prophet, though he had been withdrawn for a considerable time from earthly scenes, and cried, "Bring me up Samuel."

2. HIS BLESSED DEATH. Death is not a state, but a step; not a chamber, but a passage; not an abiding place, but a bridge over a gulf. We should speak of the departed as those who, for a moment, passed through the shadow of the tunnel, but are now living in the intensity of a vivid existence on the other side. "God is not the God of the dead, but of the living, for all live unto Him." None are dead, in the sense of remaining in a condition of *deadness*. Those whom we call *dead* are those who died, and passed through death into the other life.

Remember how the apostle Peter describes death. Speaking of his death, he uses the very word that had been employed in the conversation on the Mount of Transfiguration, when Moses and Elijah spoke with the Master of the decease he was to experience at Jerusalem. "After my decease" (Luke 9:31; 2 Peter 1:15). The Greek word is *exodos*. There is only one other place in which that word occurs in the whole New Testament, when reference is made to the going out of the people from Egypt (Heb. 11:22).

Death, under this conception, is a going out, not a coming in. It begins. If it ends, it ends the life of slavery and pain, and opens the way into a world where the development of the soul will be unrestrained. The Lord justly claims the title, "the resurrection and the life." He has abolished death, and brought life and immortality to light through His gospel. We are not now left to the dim light of a surmise, of supposition, or of hesitating guesswork. We *know* that there is a life beyond death, because men saw Him after He was risen.

Yes, He lives; and because He lives we shall live also. He has gone to prepare mansions for us in the Father's house. In that world we will see his face; and, in company with kindred spirits, we will do his commandments. Even now I suppose Moses and Aaron are among his priests, and Samuel among those who call on His name, "in the solemn troops, and sweet societies" of eternity.

24

Endor and Gilboa
1 Samuel 28; 1 Chronicles 13

Years had passed since David's sling had brought Goliath to the ground, and the Philistines had fled headlong at Ephes-dammim before the onset of the men of Israel. A new invasion was now planned to avenge that disgrace and reestablish the Philistine supremacy over the plain of Esdraelon, which was the necessary link between the wealthy cities of the Euphrates Valley and the vast market for their wares and produce, furnished by the cities of the Nile Valley.

Hastily gathering what forces he could collect, Saul marched northward, and pitched his camp on the slopes of Mount Gilboa, four miles distant from the invading army and on the south of the Great Plain.

The sight of the great force that was arrayed against him seems to have completely paralyzed Saul's courage. He contrasted the complete accouterments of the Philistines with the spears and slings of Israel, and "his heart trembled greatly." The heroic courage that faith might have brought him was not now possible, since the sense of God's presence was withdrawn. There was no rift in the black canopy of despair that overshadowed his terror-stricken soul. It was to this that the terrible series of tragedies, which we are now about to narrate, must be attributed. The restraining grace of God, which he had so long despised and resisted, no longer struggled with him, and he was left to follow the promptings of those evil spirits who, for mysterious purposes, are permitted to assail the sons of men. It is true that he inquired of the Lord, for probably the first time, after the lapse of many years; but there was no repentance or confession of sin, no submission of will, no patient waiting for His direction—only abject terror and frantic despair. It is hardly surprising to read that "the LORD answered him not, neither by dreams, nor by Urim, nor by prophets." "If I regard iniquity in my heart, the Lord will not hear me" (Ps. 66:18).

1. ENDOR. At some previous period, as we have seen, "Saul had put away those that had familiar spirits, and the wizards, out of the land." It became clear, however, that he had no heartfelt abhorrence of the crimes he punished, seeing that in his own dire extremity he had recourse to the very arts he had worked to abolish, and sought from the mouth of hell the help for which he had appealed to heaven in vain!

About two miles north from Shunem—in the rear, therefore, of the Philistine army—lay the little village of Endor. It was one of those spots from which Manasseh had failed to expel the old population; and among these, the descendants of the ancient Canaanites, was an old woman who professed to be able to bring up the souls of the dead.

Heavily cloaked and disguised, accompanied by two trusty companions whom tradition has identified as Abner and Amasa, Saul set forth in the early hours of the night, crossed the plain, made a detour around the eastern shoulder of Little Hermon, and arrived safely at the witch's dwelling. The door opened to admit them to the house, and amid the dark wierdness of the interior, revealed by the glimmering light of a brazier, choked with smoke, the woman was almost unable to recognize the features of the haggard man who accosted her with the request that she should bring up whomever he would name.

At first she hesitated, reminding him how perilous her profession was, and suggesting that to give him satisfaction might cost her life: "Behold, thou knowest what Saul hath done, how he hath cut off those that have familiar spirits, and the wizards, out of the land; wherefore then layest thou a snare for my life, to cause me to die?"

With an oath, which strangely implicated the God whom he was at that moment denying, and with a touch of his kingly prerogative, the king assured her that no punishment would befall her for doing what he requested.

Thus reassured, the woman asked whom she should bring up; but she must have been quite startled, when in a hoarse whisper, as of one paralyzed and awestruck by his weird surroundings, the king said, "Bring me up Samuel."

Retiring a distance from him, the wretched woman began her incantations, perhaps dropping a powder on the coals of the brazier, muttering incantations in a low voice, making passes and adjurations. But before she had completed her preparations, the Almighty seems to have interfered, sending back His faithful servant, so that the witch might not even appear to have the credit of securing so wonderful a visitation. "The woman saw Samuel."

At the same moment that she recognized Samuel, she seems to have recognized Saul also. Startled and frightened for her life, she cried with a loud voice, and spoke to Saul, saying, "Why hast thou deceived me?"

Again he reassured her, and asked her what she had seen.

"A majestic being, august and God-like," she replied, "arising as if from out of the earth."

Pressed by Saul to describe his appearance more minutely, for she was beholding a mysterious form which, though present in the same chamber as himself, was veiled from him, she said, "He resembles an old man covered with a robe." "And Saul perceived that it was Samuel, and he stooped with his face to the ground, and bowed himself."

Touching and thrilling was the conversation that followed. I am disposed to think that it was held without the medium of the witch, and that God permitted the prophet to speak with Saul, as years later Moses and Elijah spoke with our Lord of the decease to be soon accomplished at Jerusalem. It is likely that these words were actually interchanged between the king and his former friend and confidant, to whom he turned remorsefully in his awful agony. Do you not think that if, even then, Saul had turned to Jehovah with tears of confession and the simplicity of faith, he would have been answered according to the multitude of the divine compassions? Assuredly he would; but there was no sign of such a change.

Samuel did not wait to be questioned, but sadly told the awestruck king that his misdoings had filled his spirit with unrest even in the other life, so much so that he could not bear returning to speak to him once more. "Why hast thou disquieted me, to bring me up?"

Saul's answer was that of despair. "I am sore distressed; for the Philistines make war against me, and God is departed from me, and answereth me no more, neither by prophets, nor by dreams; therefore I have called thee, that thou mayest make known unto me what I shall do."

But from the lips of the prophet came no words of comfort or hope. Nothing, at this hour, could stay or avert the descending avalanche. It was therefore revealed that the Lord would deliver Israel, along with Saul, into the hand of the Philistines, and by the next day he and his sons would also have passed into the world of spirits; the Hebrew host would be annihilated, the camp sacked, and the land left to the fate that the conquered of those days knew only too well to expect.

2. GILBOA. On the next day there was some slight alteration in the disposition of the respective hosts. The Philistines moved toward Aphek, a little to the west of their camp; while the Israelites descended from the heights of Gilboa, and took up a position near the spring or fountain of Jezreel (29:1).

The battle soon began. In spite of the most desperate efforts to withstand the onset of the heavily-mailed troops that were opposed to them, the Hebrews were routed, and fled from before the Philistines. It is expressly noted by the historian that the lower slopes of Gilboa were covered by the wounded, whose hearts' blood soaked the mountain pastures (31:1).

Saul and Jonathan made the most desperate efforts to retrieve the day. But it was in vain. "The battle went sore against Saul." "The Philistines slew Jonathan, and Abinadab, and Melchishua, the sons of Saul." Then, leaving all others, the Philistines concentrated their attack on that lordly figure that towered amid the fugitives—the royal crown on his helmet, the royal bracelet flashing on his arm. "The Philistines followed hard upon Saul . . . and the archers hit him; and he was sore wounded of the archers." He knew what fate awaited him if he was captured while his life was yet in him. "Then said Saul unto his armour-bearer, Draw thy sword, and thrust me through therewith; lest these uncircumcised come and thrust me through, and abuse me."

The armor-bearer did not dare lift up his hand against the sacred person of his king; so Saul, placing his sword-hilt firmly in the earth, fell on the point, which pierced his heart.

The narrative that the Amalekite gave afterward to David suggests that the effort to take his life was not at once successful; and he seems to have asked this child of a race which he was once bidden utterly to destroy, to give him the last finishing stroke. "He said unto me again, Stand, I pray thee, upon me, and slay me: for anguish is come upon me; because my life is yet whole in me." It may be, however, that all this was a fabrication intended to win David's favor; for we are told that when the armor-bearer saw that Saul was dead, he likewise fell on his sword, and died with him.

The day of Gilboa was a veritable Chevy Chase. "Saul died, and his three sons, and his armour-bearer, and all his men, that same day together." The next day the Philistines set to work to strip the dead, and finding the bodies of Saul and his sons, they took their heads, armor, and decapitated corpses, to be carried in triumph through the streets of their principal cities, and finally to be affixed to the walls of Beth-shan. As the tidings spread, the people left the towns and villages in the neighborhood, and fled across the Jordan. Roving bands followed up the victory, and carried fire and sword into all parts of the land.

One brave deed relieved the somber hues of that terrible catastrophe. The men of

Jabesh-gilead could not forget how nobly Saul had come to their aid in the early days of his reign; and they resolved, at least, to retrieve the royal body from the ignominy to which Philistine malice had exposed it. The valiant men therefore arose, and traveling all night, took down the body of Saul, and the bodies of his sons from the temple walls, bore them reverently back to Jabesh, burned them to conceal the hideous mutilation to which they had been subjected, buried them under "the tamarisk tree in Jabesh," and lamented with genuine grief this tragic close to a reign that had once been as a morning without clouds.

25

An Epilogue
2 Samuel 1:19–27

"The Song of the Bow," for that is the title of the touchingly beautiful elegy with which David's poet mourned over the tragedy of Gilboa, is very pathetic and inspiring. It seemed as though the singer had forgotten the rough experiences that had fallen to his lot through the jealous mania of the king; and, passing over recent years, he was a minstrel-shepherd once more, celebrating the glory and powers of his King.

> *Thy glory, O Israel, is slain upon thy high places!*
> *How are the mighty fallen!*
> *Saul and Jonathan were lovely and pleasant in their lives,*
> *And in their death they were not divided.*

It makes us think of the love of God to hear David sing like that. It reminds us that God has said, "Their sins and iniquities will I remember no more." Here at least, long before the Christian era, was a love that bore all things, believed all things, hoped all things, endured all things, and never failed; which thought only of what had been noble and beautiful in them, and refused to consider anything that had been base and unworthy. This is the way that we also would think of Saul, the first king of Israel.

It is a very solemn thought! No career could begin with fairer, brighter prospects than Saul had, and none could close in a more absolute midnight of despair; and yet such a fate may befall us, unless we watch, and pray, and walk humbly with our God.

The reign of Saul would be almost too bitter to contemplate, unless under its rough covering we could detect the formation of the luscious fruit of David's kingdom, destined to sow eternal seed over the world. Similarly, we might despair of the condition to which the "trinity of evil" has reduced our world if we did not know that in the days of these kings the God of heaven will set up a kingdom that will never be destroyed, nor will the sovereignty of it be left to another people; but it will break in pieces and consume all these kingdoms, and it will stand forever (see Dan. 2:44).

"Samuel the prophet" thus practically bridges the gulf between Samson the judge and David the king: and there is deep significance in the fact that his name is identified with the two books of Scripture that describe this great transitional period, every event of which was affected by his influence.